Continuum Companion to Research Methods in
Applied Linguistics

al Rose
)1962 8

D1425449

Continuum Companions

The *Continuum Companions* series is a major series of single volume companions to key research fields in the humanities aimed at postgraduate students, scholars and libraries. Each companion offers a comprehensive reference resource giving an overview of key topics, research areas, new directions and a manageable guide to beginning or developing research in the field. A distinctive feature of the series is that each companion provides practical guidance on advanced study and research in the field, including research methods and subject-specific resources.

Linguistics titles available in the series:

Continuum Companion to Second Language Acquisition
Edited by Ernesto Macaro

Continuum Companion to Research Methods in Applied Linguistics
Edited by Brian Paltridge and Aek Phakiti

Continuum Companion to Research Methods in Applied Linguistics

Edited by

Brian Paltridge

and

Aek Phakiti

B L O O M S B U R Y
LONDON • NEW DELHI • NEW YORK • SYDNEY

Bloomsbury Academic
An imprint of Bloomsbury Publishing Plc

50 Bedford Square   175 Fifth Avenue
London   New York
WC1B 3DP   NY 10010
UK   USA

www.bloomsbury.com

First published in 2010 by the Continuum International Publishing Group Ltd
Reprinted 2011 (twice)
Reprinted by Bloomsbury Academic 2013

British Library Cataloguing-in-Publication Data
A catalogue record for this book is available from the British Library.

ISBN: HB: 978-0-8264-9924-0
PB: 978-0-8264-9925-7

Library of Congress Cataloging-in-Publication Data
A catalog record for this book is available from the Library of Congress.

Typeset by Newgen Imaging Systems Pvt Ltd, Chennai, India
Printed and bound in Great Britain

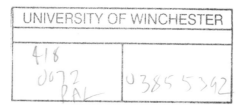

Contents

Part II Areas of Research

Notes on Contributors

David Block is Professor of Education in the Department of Learning, Curriculum and Communication, Institute of Education, University of London. He has published articles and chapters on a variety of applied linguistics topics. He is co-editor (with Deborah Cameron) of *Globalization and Language Teaching* (Routledge, 2002) and author of *The Social Turn in Second Language Acquisition* (Edinburgh University Press, 2003), *Multilingual Identities in a Global City: London Stories* (Palgrave, 2006) and *Second Language Identities* (Continuum, 2007). His main interests are the impact of globalization on language practices of all kinds, migration and the interface between identity and language learning and use.

Anne Burns is Professor of Linguistics and former Dean of Linguistics and Psychology at Macquarie University, Sydney. She is the Director of the Applied Linguistics and Language in Education (ALLE) Research Centre at Macquarie, a Member-at-Large of the Executive Board of AILA, and Chair of TESOL International's Standing Committee for Research. She has published extensively on adult migrant English programs and adult ESL curriculum development, action research, second language teacher education and the teaching of speaking from a discourse perspective. She edits *Prospect: A Journal of Australian TESOL* and serves on the Advisory Boards of several international journals including *Language Teaching*.

Christine Pearson Casanave moved to Japan in 1990, where she taught at Keio University's Shonan Fujisawa Campus until 2003. For some of those years she also taught and advised graduate TESOL students at two American university campuses in Tokyo (Teachers College Columbia University, and Temple University). She has long been interested in the connections between academic literacy practices and the disciplinary socialization and identities of graduate students and professional language educators, and in narrative and qualitative inquiry. Now based in California, she continues to work with doctoral students, to write and publish, and to review manuscripts for several journals.

Susan Gass is University Distinguished Professor at Michigan State University where she directs the English Language Center and the Ph.D. program in Second Language Studies. She has published numerous articles and books in the field of second language acquisition. In addition to her publications, she has served as President of the American Association for Applied Linguistics as well as President of the International Association of Applied Linguistics (AILA). Among other awards, she has won the Distinguished Faculty Award at Michigan State University and the Distinguished Scholarship and Service Award from the American Association for Applied Linguistics.

Lesley Harbon is Associate Professor in Languages Education and Associate Dean International in the Faculty of Education and Social Work at The University of Sydney. She works with pre-service language teachers and also teaches several postgraduate TESOL units of study. Her research is in the area of short-term international experiences for language teachers, language teacher professional development, intercultural language education and bilingual education. She is the President of the Australian Federation of Modern Language Teachers Associations, the national peak body for the teaching and learning of languages in Australian schools.

David Hirsh is a Lecturer in TESOL at the University of Sydney. He has taught on a range of postgraduate TESOL and EAP programs in Thailand, New Zealand and Australia. His research focuses on vocabulary studies, language assessment, and academic acculturation. He is currently investigating the function of scientific vocabulary in undergraduate textbooks, and undertaking research into academic pathways. Recent publications include *Teaching Academic Writing* (University of Michigan Press, Paltridge et al., 2009) and articles on scientific vocabulary in the *French Review of Applied Linguistics* and the *EA Journal*.

Adrian Holliday is Professor of Applied Linguistics at Canterbury Christ Church University. He is author of *Doing and Writing Qualitative Research* (2nd edition, Sage, 2007), *The Struggle to Teach English as an International Language* (Oxford University Press, 2005), *Intercultural Communication* (with Hyde and Kullman, Routledge, 2004), *Appropriate Methodology and Social Context* (Cambridge University Press, 1994) and *Intercultural Communication and Global Inequality* (Sage, forthcoming). He began his career as a British Council teacher in Iran in the 1970s. During the 1980s he set up the ESP Centre at Damascus University, Syria, and was a curriculum consultant at Ain Shams University, Cairo.

Rebecca Hughes is Chair of Applied Linguistics and Director of the Centre for English Language Education at the University of Nottingham. She has research interests in spoken language, academic literacy and internationalization of higher education. She is author of *English in Speech and Writing, Investigating Language and Literature* (Routledge, 1996), *Exploring Grammar in Context* (with Ronald Carter and Michael McCarthy, Cambridge University Press, 2000), *Teaching and Researching Speaking* (Longman, 2003), *Exploring Grammar in Writing* (Cambridge University Press, 2005) and editor of *TESOL, Applied Linguistics and the Spoken Language: Challenges for Theory and Practice* (Palgrave Macmillan, 2009).

Ken Hyland is Professor of Applied Linguistics and Director of the Centre for Applied English Studies at the University of Hong Kong having recently moved from the University of London. He has taught Applied Linguistics and EAP for over 30 years in Asia, Australasia and the United Kingdom and has published over 130 articles and 14 books on language education and academic writing. Most recent publications are *Academic Discourse* (Continuum, 2009), *EAP: An Advanced Resource Book* (Routledge, 2006) and *Academic Evaluation* (edited with Giuliana Diani, Palgrave, 2009). He was founding co-editor of the *Journal of English for Academic Purposes* and is now co-editor of *Applied Linguistics*.

Lourdes Ortega is an Associate Professor in the Department of Second Language Studies at the University of Hawai'i, where she teaches graduate courses in the M.A. and Ph.D. programs. Her research interests include second language acquisition, L2 writing, foreign language education and the use of research methods in applied linguistics. Recent books are *Synthesizing Research on Language Learning and Teaching* (co-edited with John Norris, John Benjamins, 2006), *The Longitudinal Study of Advanced L2 Capacities* (co-edited with Heidi Byrnes, Routledge, 2008) and *Understanding Second Language Acquisition* (Hodder Arnold, 2009).

Brian Paltridge is Professor of TESOL at the University of Sydney. He is author of *Genre, Frames and Writing in Research Settings* (John Benjamins, 1997), *Making Sense of Discourse Analysis* (AEE Publishers, 2000), *Genre and the Language Learning Classroom* (University of Michigan Press, 2001), *Discourse Analysis* (Continuum, 2006), with Sue Starfield *Thesis and Dissertation Writing in a Second Language* (Routledge, 2007) and with his TESOL colleagues at the University of Sydney, *Teaching Academic Writing* (University of Michigan Press, 2009). He has also published in *ELT Journal*, the *Journal of Pragmatics*, *Applied Linguistics*, *World Englishes*, *System*, and *English for Specific Purposes*.

Aek Phakiti is a Senior Lecturer in TESOL in the Faculty of Education and Social Work at the University of Sydney. His research interests focus on language testing and assessment, second language acquisition, aspects of strategic competence in language learning and use, second language reading and language program evaluation. He teaches courses in second language acquisition, language testing and assessment and research methods in language learning. He is author of *Strategic Competence and EFL Reading Test Performance* (Peter Lang, 2007), one of the authors of *Teaching Academic Writing* (Michigan University Press, 2009) and editor of the *University of Sydney Papers in TESOL*.

John Read is an Associate Professor in the Department of Applied Language Studies and Linguistics at the University of Auckland, New Zealand. He has taught postgraduate courses in applied linguistics at tertiary institutions in New Zealand, Singapore and the United States of America. His primary research interests are in second language vocabulary assessment and the testing of English for academic and professional purposes. He is the author of *Assessing Vocabulary* (Cambridge University Press, 2000). He was co-editor of *Language Testing* from 2002 to 2006 and is currently Vice-President of the International Language Testing Association.

Carsten Roever is a Senior Lecturer in Applied Linguistics at the University of Melbourne. He holds a first degree from the University of Duisburg (Germany), and a Ph.D. from the University of Hawai'i at Manoa. His research interests are second language pragmatics, language testing and research methods. He is the author of *Testing ESL Pragmatics* (Peter Lang, 2005), and co-author, with Tim McNamara, of *Language Testing: The Social Dimension* (Blackwell, 2006). He is the current editor of the *Australian Review of Applied Linguistics*.

Huizhong Shen is Professor and Assistant Dean (International and Engagement) in the Faculty of Education at the Queensland University of Technology. He is a widely experienced teacher at school and university level, having also taught at the University of Sydney and Fudan University in Shanghai. He has undertaken research and publications in language teacher education, teaching pedagogies, and online language teaching and learning. He has also produced language-teaching materials in print, CD-ROM, and online formats. He is regularly consulted by educational and government bodies in Australia and China on language education policy and practice, and international cooperation.

Sue Starfield is Director of *The Learning Centre* and Associate Professor in the School of Education at the University of New South Wales. She is co-author of *Thesis and Dissertation Writing in a Second Language: A Handbook for Supervisors* (Routledge, 2007). She is currently working on a team project that is examining the genre of the practice-based doctoral thesis in the visual and performing arts. She is co-editor of the journal, *English for Specific Purposes*. Her current interests include advanced academic writing, identity in academic writing and ethnographic research approaches.

Marie Stevenson is a Lecturer in TESOL at the University of Sydney where she teaches courses in the areas of literacy, grammar, discourse and language teaching methodology. Her main areas of research are second language reading and writing, and she has extensive experience in various facets of these, particularly in the measurement of second language reading and writing processes. She participated in Project NELSON, a large-scale project conducted at the University of Amsterdam that investigated the transfer of reading and writing skills and processes from L1 (Dutch) to L2 (English). She has published in journals such as *Language Learning, Journal of Educational Psychology*, and *International Journal of Bilingualism*.

Neomy Storch is a Senior Lecturer in Applied Linguistics in the School of Languages and Linguistics at the University of Melbourne. She teaches a range of ESL and Applied Linguistics courses. Her research has focused on issues related to second language pedagogy. These include the nature of pair interaction in classroom contexts and the development of academic writing skills, particularly grammatical accuracy, and the role of feedback in that development. She has published in the *Journal of Second Language Writing, System, Language Awareness, ELT Journal, Language Learning, TESOL Quarterly* and the *Canadian Modern Language Review*.

Jane Sunderland is a Senior Lecturer in the Department of Linguistics and English Language, Lancaster University, UK. Her main research area is gender and language, and she teaches gender and language to MA and doctoral students. She is also Director of Studies for the PhD in Applied Linguistics by Thesis and Coursework programme at Lancaster University. She is author of *Gendered Discourses* (2004) and *Language and Gender: An Advanced Resource Book* (2006).

Steven Talmy is an Assistant Professor in the Department of Language & Literacy Education at the University of British Columbia. His work on 'oldtimer' ESL student resistance to schooling has appeared in such journals as *Applied Linguistics, Linguistics & Education*, and *Pragmatics*, in addition to several edited anthologies. His academic interests include critical analyses of discourse, K-12 ESL, the sociology of ESL education, and qualitative research methods.

Larry Vandergrift is Professor at the Institute of Official Languages and Bilingualism at the University of Ottawa where he teaches courses in French,

English and Second Language Acquisition. His research on second/foreign language listening has been published in many journals: *Applied Linguistics, Annual Review of Applied Linguistics, Canadian Modern Language Review, Foreign Language Annals, Language Learning, Language Teaching* and *Modern Language Journal*. He has also written a number of book chapters on the teaching of listening and has served as an editor of the *Canadian Modern Language Review*.

Elvis Wagner is an Assistant Professor of TESOL in the College of Education at Temple University in Philadelphia, USA. His research interests include the teaching and testing of L2 oral proficiency, specifically focusing on how the non-verbal components of spoken language affect L2 listeners' comprehension of spoken texts, and L2 learners' attitudes towards and perceptions of the non-verbal information provided by speakers. He has also taught ESL and EFL to high-school, undergraduate, graduate and adult students.

Wei Wang is a Lecturer in Chinese Studies at the University of Sydney. His primary research interest is in the area of comparative discourse studies, especially from a genre-based perspective. He obtained his Ph.D. from the University of Sydney on a contrastive genre study of newspaper commentaries on the events of 9/11 in China and Australia. He is author of *Genre across Languages and Cultures* (VDM, 2007). He has also published in *Discourse Studies*, the *Journal of English for Academic Purposes*, the *Australian Review of Applied Linguistics* and the *University of Sydney Papers in TESOL*. His research interests also include Chinese linguistics, second language acquisition and translation studies.

Lindy Woodrow is a Senior Lecturer in TESOL at the University of Sydney. Her research interests include motivation and academic writing of ESL students, particularly among learners from China and other Confucian heritage cultures. She has developed a course in thesis and dissertation writing for the University of Sydney, written a book on the motivation of EAP learners (Woodrow, 2008) and has co-authored a book on academic writing (Paltridge et al., 2009). She has also published in *Foreign Language Annals, Modern Language Journal, Language Learning* and the *RELC Journal*.

Acknowledgements

We would like to thank the many people who have helped us with this project. Key among these are Jenny Lovell at Continuum who first took on this project and Gurdeep Mattu and Colleen Coalter who worked with us to its completion. We are also especially indebted to the students who have taken part in our research methods courses at the University of Sydney, the University of Melbourne, and the University of Waikato. Their critical questioning of what we have taught them has helped us refine our thinking in the area as well as improve our actual research practices.

There are many other people we also wish to thank who have contributed to this book. These include each of the authors of the chapters in the volume. We thank them all for agreeing so readily to write for the book, and for so patiently and promptly responding to our requests for clarification on their chapters. We also wish to thank our TESOL colleagues at the University of Sydney and Sue Starfield at the University of New South Wales for listening to what we have had to say about research and for answering difficult questions. In addition, we thank Marie Stevenson, James Purpura, Carsten Roever and Ute Knoch for the particular help they have given at various stages in the preparation of this book.

We also wish to thank the Acting Dean of the Faculty of Education and Social Work at the University of Sydney, Robyn Ewing, and the former Dean of the Faculty, Derrick Armstrong, for their support for TESOL activities in the Faculty and for creating the environment which enables us to do the kind of work that we do.

1 Introduction

Brian Paltridge and Aek Phakiti

Chapter Overview	
Part I: Research Methods and Approaches	1
Part II: Areas of Research	2
Resources for Further Reading	3

This book is aimed at beginning researchers in the area of applied linguistics, whether they be advanced undergraduate students, Masters students, or Ph.D. students doing courses in research methods prior to starting on their doctoral work. The book is in two parts. The first is on methods and approaches and the other on areas of research; that is, areas in which students are often interested in carrying out research. In each chapter the authors have included a sample study which illustrates the points they are making in their discussion. Topics that the authors have addressed include assumptions which underlie the particular method or approach, issues of validity or trustworthiness and research techniques and instruments appropriate to the goal and method of research. The authors have also identified resources for further reading on the particular method or issue under discussion.

Part I: Research Methods and Approaches

In the chapter on Experimental Research, Susan Gass describes a study that investigates feedback and the role it plays in the development of second language knowledge. This study, importantly, combines both quantitative and qualitative data as a way of getting at an answer to its research question. Elvis Wagner, in his chapter on Survey Research, describes a study which examines how strategy use affects second language test performance. This chapter has an extensive discussion on sampling, an issue that is relevant to many other research approaches as well. Aek Phakiti's chapter on Analysing Quantitative

Data uses a study on strategy use and its relationship to students' performance on a reading test to illustrate the points he is making. There is a detailed discussion in this chapter of statistical procedures and how they are used, and understood, in quantitative studies.

Sue Starfield draws on her experience as a qualitative researcher for her chapter on Ethnographies. Her sample study is an ethnography of academic writing that she carried out at a university in South Africa. Christine Casanave's chapter on Case Studies describes a Chinese doctoral student's attempts to fulfil his university's publication requirement for graduation as a way of illustrating the many important points that she makes. Anne Burns draws on her wide experience with Action Research for her chapter. Her sample study describes a teacher who wishes to introduce adult immigrant learners to conversational skills and cultural norms of the local variety of English of the country in which they are studying. In his chapter on Analysing Qualitative Data, Adrian Holliday describes the very many issues involved in this method of research. His sample study is a project which examines the descriptions of national cultures, using email interviews, reconstructions of intercultural events and the research and training literature on intercultural communication. The chapter by Lourdes Ortega on Research Synthesis details an approach which, while relatively common in some areas of study, has only recently been introduced in applied linguistics research. She lists article-length syntheses that have been published in applied linguistics research, then describes a research synthesis which investigated the effectiveness of different types of second language instruction. In the final chapter of this section of the book, Steven Talmy discusses Critical Research in Applied Linguistics, drawing on a study he conducted in a high school ESL program in Hawai'i in order to illustrate the points he makes.

Part II: Areas of Research

The chapter by Rebecca Hughes on Researching Speaking describes a range of ways of looking at speaking in applied linguistics research. The study she then presents examines differences in turn-taking behaviour in face-to-face interaction and interactions on the telephone. In his chapter on Researching Listening, Larry Vandergrift describes a mixed-methods study on teaching students how to listen, using a pedagogical cycle grounded in metacognitive theory. Marie Stevenson's chapter on Researching Reading includes a study that uses verbal protocol analysis as a data collection technique to illustrate methodological issues involved in collecting and analysing data on reading. Ken Hyland, in his chapter on Researching Writing, describes a study he carried out of Hong Kong undergraduates' writing, looking at preferred choices of pronoun use in the students' writing then interviewing them about their choices. In her chapter on

Researching Grammar, Neomy Storch describes a study which investigated the efficacy of different forms of written feedback on second language students' grammatical development. David Hirsh's chapter on Researching Vocabulary includes a study carried out by one of his students which investigated vocabulary learning in a foreign-language high school in China. In his chapter on Researching Pragmatics, Carsten Roever describes a study which investigated knowledge of Korean requests by native-English speaking Korean as a foreign language learners in the United States of America. The chapter on Researching Discourse by Brian Paltridge and Wei Wang discusses a study which examined newspaper commentaries in Chinese and English on the events of September 11 from a discourse perspective.

In their chapter on Researching Language Classrooms, Lesley Harbon and Huizhong Shen present a study that examined the teaching in a school in China, where the language curriculum was becoming increasingly oriented towards the use of Information Communication Technologies. The chapter on Researching Language Testing and Assessment by John Read describes a study that examines the form of input in listening test design. Lindy Woodrow's chapter on Researching Motivation focuses on her work on adaptive language learning in English for academic purposes settings. Jane Sunderland's chapter on Researching Language and Gender examines electronically circulated jokes about women, and how these jokes are dealt with by feminist readers. The final chapter in the book on Researching Language and Identity by David Block examines how teachers from Germany dealt with being positioned as different or foreign by the students with whom they came in contact as they did their teaching practice during their studies in Britain.

As can be seen, each of the chapters of this book has been written by an expert in the particular topic being discussed. They have each provided a wealth of detail in their chapters and given many practical suggestions and much useful advice for people who are new to carrying out applied linguistics research. We thank these authors for having agreed to contribute to this volume, and for sharing their expertise and experience with the wider applied linguistics community in this way.

Resources for Further Reading

Each of the chapters of this book lists resources for further reading on the particular topic being discussed. Here we list some more general books on research methods in applied linguistics that readers will find useful as well.

Allison, D. (2002), *Approaching English Language Research*. Singapore: Singapore University Press.

This book is about the process of carrying out research. It discusses practical problems in undertaking research, reading and reporting on research, data analysis and the interpretation of findings. There is a chapter on writing a research proposal as well as a section on problems that students often meet in carrying out research.

Brown, J. D. and Rodgers, T. S. (2002), *Doing Second Language Research*. Oxford: Oxford University Press.

Brown and Rodgers's book discusses both qualitative and quantitative research. Specific topics include case-study research, introspective methods, classroom-based research, the use of statistics, and language programme evaluation. There are many self-study exercises in this book.

Dörnyei, Z. (2007), *Research Methods in Applied Linguistics*. Oxford: Oxford University Press.

In this book Dörnyei provides an extensive discussion of quantitative, qualitative and mixed-method research. There are also chapters on data analysis and reporting on research.

Gass, S. and Mackey, A. (2007), *Data Elicitation for Second and Foreign Language Research*. Mahwah, NJ: Lawrence Erlbaum.

Gass and Mackey's book provides a detailed discussion of data elicitation techniques for second and foreign language research. This includes a discussion of psycholinguistics-based research, research which examines cognitive processes, survey research, pragmatics-based research and classroom-based research.

Mackey, A. and Gass, S. (2005), *Second Language Research: Methodology and Design*. Mahwah, NJ: Lawrence Erlbaum.

In this book Mackey and Gass discuss issues in data gathering, common data collection techniques and the coding of data. They also discuss qualitative and quantitative research, classroom-based research and issues in the reporting of research.

McKay, S. L. (2006), *Researching Second Language Classrooms*. Mahwah, NJ: Lawrence Erlbaum.

This book provides a very good overview of methods that can be used for researching second language classrooms. It contains chapters on different types of research, ways of researching classroom discourse, and gives guidance for writing research reports. Particular attention is given to action research, survey research, introspective research, case studies, and ethnographic studies.

Part I:
Research Methods and Approaches

2 Experimental Research

Susan Gass

Experimental research is a way of determining the effect of something on something else. In other words, a researcher begins with an idea of why something happens and manipulates at least one variable, controls others, to determine the effect on some other variable. To take a simple example from every day life, let's suppose that an individual has developed a rash, but the source of the rash is not known. There are a number of possibilities: (1) something eaten, (2) a medication taken, (3) touching an object that causes an allergic reaction. We might eliminate one factor at a time, let's say, something eaten to see if the rash disappears. If it does not, then one eliminates a medication taken. This continues until the culprit is discovered. There is, of course, a fallacy in this reasoning because the rash could disappear on its own, given the many unknown workings of the human body. Nonetheless, experimental research is a way of determining to the extent possible, what the source of the rash is.

We turn to an example from language. Let's assume that we want to know whether focusing a learner's attention on some aspect of language increases that individual's learning of that aspect of language. One way to do this is to find two groups of learners which are matched on their pre-experiment knowledge of this aspect of language. There would then be a treatment session in which the experimental group would receive focused attention on the particular part of language under investigation while the control group would receive exposure to the same part of language, but their attention would not be focused. A post-test would measure improvement from the pre-test. In sum, experimental research involves the manipulation of at least one variable, known as an independent variable, while keeping other relevant variables constant, and observing the effect of the manipulation on some other variable (known as a dependent variable), for example, a test score.

Underlying Assumptions of the Methodology

Even though a discussion of the philosophy of science is beyond the scope of this chapter, it is important to at least acknowledge some of the philosophical underpinnings when considering what experimental research is and why some individuals are 'married' to this approach and others do not see its value. In the history of Second Language Acquisition (SLA) research, there are those who tend to be what might be called rationalists in their approach to research and others who are considered relativists in their approach (see Jordan 2005 for a disentanglement of these and other related terms). In the former approach, one finds a strong role for experimental research. The latter group sees the value of multiple realities; in other words, there is no objective reality – only our perceptions of reality.[1]

Larsen-Freeman and Long (1991) discuss two approaches to research that are differentiated by whether they might be considered inductive or deductive. Conducting research and then coming up with a theory (research-then-theory) is inductive whereas a theory-then-research approach is deductive. Experimental research with its rationalist underpinnings falls into this latter category.

Specifics of Experimental Research

With experimental research, there are a number of components that researchers include. First, there is a specific and precise research question. This research question follows from some theoretical vantage point and is generally based on something that remains unanswered from previous research. Second is a set of explicitly stated variables, that is, what is being varied and what is being measured. These must reflect the construct under investigation. Third is a randomly selected group of participants who are randomly assigned to various treatment conditions and/or control groups. Additionally, in reporting research results, the treatment must be described explicitly and must relate in a direct way to the research question. Interpretation of the results, that is, of the effects of the treatment is generally done through statistical means. Finally, to ensure that the interpretation of the treatment effects is accurate, there must be controls and there must be appropriate counterbalancing. In the following section, we elaborate on each of these parts.

Research questions must be stated explicitly and must have some basis in previous literature. For example, consider the following two examples:

1. Does focused attention on noun-adjective agreement in Italian promote learning to a greater extent than focused attention on *wh*-movement in Italian for beginning learners of Italian?

Prior research (Gass, Svetics and Lemelin 2003) argued that focused attention promoted learning in some parts of the grammar and not in others and differentially affected learners at different proficiency levels.

2. Should language classes be introduced early in a school's curriculum?

The first question is explicitly stated, although as we will see below, there are variables that are in need of further elaboration and greater explicitness. The second question, while interesting and one which school districts are constantly debating, is not researchable given the vagueness as well as the word *should* which implies some sort of right or wrong and which, as a result, cannot be empirically evaluated.

In sum, in experimental research, there need to be answerable questions. There are a number of characteristics that one can think of when determining whether a question is answerable or researchable. Given the limited resources (time and money) of most researchers, questions must be feasible in relation to the time and budget of the problem. This often entails scaling back on the level of complexity of the research question. As is implied from the discussion above, the question needs to be significant in relation to current research in the field of inquiry. And, of course, ethics must play a role in the questions that are asked. This topic is dealt with in greater detail below. Question 2 above fails in that it would probably not be feasible given the never-ending number of variables involved even though it is significant in that it is an important question for all school districts.

In experimental research, there are not only research questions, but also hypotheses. Hypotheses are predictions based on the research question. For example, in research question 1 above, the following hypothesis might obtain.

1. Focused attention on noun-adjective agreement in Italian will promote learning to a greater extent than focused attention on *wh*-movement in Italian for beginning learners of Italian.

9

Alternatively, if there is no reason to expect anything other than a difference, the hypothesis might be phrased as follows:

2. Focused attention on noun-adjective agreement in Italian will promote learning to a different degree than focused attention on *wh*-questions in Italian for beginning learners of Italian.

Often, these are expressed as *null* hypotheses which state that there are no differences between/among groups. The research goal is to reject the null hypothesis.

Variables are characteristics of a class of objects that vary, as in the variable of eye colour or height or weight for humans. In experimental research, variables need to be made explicit. This is actually one of the most difficult parts of a research project. To take research question 1 above, there are a few variables about which decisions need to be made to render those variables sufficiently explicit so that a researcher can conduct his/her research. For example, how will focused attention be operationalized (by colouring instances of noun-adjective agreement in a written text? By providing an explicit grammatical description? by frequency – that is by introducing numerous instances of noun-adjective agreement in a passage)? When conducting and reporting experimental research, researchers must be clear on how they are defining their terms.

A second variable in the research question under consideration is the notion of learning. In the history of SLA, different definitions have been used and here too numerous decisions have to be made. Is learning measured by a paper/pencil (or computer) test or by spontaneous use? If the former, what kind of test? If the latter, how does one elicit spontaneous use? And, what does it mean if a form is not used? The learner does not know it or does not think she or he needs to use it? If the latter, then learning may have taken place as a result of the treatment, but there may be extraneous reasons for it not being used. Further, if spontaneous use is the criterion for learning, how many instances of the structure/sound/lexical item are being investigated? Mackey (1999) for example, required 'the presence of at least two examples of structures in *two* different posttests' (p. 567). Is learning being operationalized only through a test given immediately following the treatment? One week later? A month later? Another variable that has to be considered, although this one is notably easier than the others, is noun-adjective agreement. Are only feminine nouns to be included, only masculine nouns, a combination? Nouns that end in –*a* or –*o* because those indicate almost invariably what the gender of the noun is? Or, will nouns that do not obviously indicate gender (e.g., *ponte*, m. bridge) be included? Similarly, for questions (*wh*-movement), one will have to determine which questions to include; does one include questions that include prepositions (e.g., *for whom, with what*).

In sum, variables are characteristics that vary. In experimental research, there are essentially two primary variables of concern: independent variables and dependent variables. Independent variables are the object of investigation. They are those variables that the researcher is investigating in order to determine their effect on something else. In the above example, focused attention on the two grammatical structures is the independent variable. Dependent variables are those variables that the independent variable is having an effect on. Thus, learning is the dependent variable in the above example. In addition to these variables are extraneous variables; these variables are independent variables that the researcher has not controlled for. In essence, they can seriously interfere with the results of a study. In the above example of focused attention, let's assume that a researcher has operationalized focused attention by colouring red all instances of noun-adjective agreement in a reading passage. Let's also assume that the researcher did not test for possible colour-blindness of the participants. Then, colour-blindness is an uncontrolled variable that could have interfered with the interpretation of the results.

A third hallmark of experimental research is the *random assignment* of participants to one group or another. Random assignment of individuals means that each individual has an equal chance of being assigned to any of the conditions of the study (experimental or control). That is, the process of assignment is random. In reality with educational research, this is often not feasible given that entire classes are the population under investigation. Randominization of this sort is intended to eliminate the possibility that extraneous variables will creep into the research design. To take the above example, had there been randominization, there would have been an equal chance of having colourblind individuals in both the adjective-noun group and the *wh*-question group.

In general, in educational settings, we cannot always have random assignment of individuals and we are more often dependent on the contexts that already exist (e.g., intact classes) for our research. This is known as quasi-experimental research (as opposed to true experimental research) because not all variables can be completely controlled; in particular, we are dependent on assignment of participants based on class placement rather than on random assignment. But, in such instances, there should be random assignment of the group/class to one condition or another.

Interpretation of results is done as a first step through statistical analyses. A discussion of different kinds of statistics and designs is beyond the scope of this chapter, but there are numerous books that deal with these topics (see Dörnyei 2007; Mackey and Gass 2005 for recent publications). In general, for most research in the field of second language acquisition or applied linguistics more generally, the significance level (α level) is generally set at .05. This means that when we look at statistical results, there is a 95 per cent chance that our results are due to the experimental treatment and only 5 per cent chance that the results are due to chance alone. In many studies, researchers will talk about the results *approaching significance* when the statistical analysis is slightly about .05 (e.g., .06–.09). In disciplines where the consequences of a chance finding are greater (e.g., life-altering medical treatment), different α levels are required. In other words, the α level is a generally accepted guide that is used by researchers in a discipline. When we are accepting or rejecting hypotheses, we want to avoid any errors in interpretation. There are two noteworthy error types, known as Type I (also known as an α error) and Type II (also known as a β error). The former refers to the rejection of a (null) hypothesis when it should not be rejected and the latter refers to the acceptance of a (null) hypothesis when it should be rejected. Both of these errors are minimized through rigorous and appropriate use of statistics.

As part of the interpretation process, one has to be able to eliminate with a reasonable degree of confidence that other factors did not enter into the picture. There are ways to minimize the possibility that other variables are at play. One, we have already discussed and that is randomization. Another was hinted at with the colour-blindness example and that is by testing for that variable and eliminating those participants who have that characteristic. One could also include that variable into the design by including it as a variable and then testing for its influence. And, a variation of the latter is to match participants so that one has a particular characteristic and another does not. This latter is perhaps better understood if one took the variable of gender. Let's assume that in the focused-attention experiment we have reason to believe that males might behave differently than females, we then would want to balance males and females in all groups.

Validity/Trustworthiness/Reliability

With all research, we need to be able to be confident in our results; our results need to be trustworthy and valid. Validity encompasses many of the concepts already discussed in this chapter. In the following section, we refer to a concept that is often discussed together with validity and that is reliability. Validity refers to the correctness and appropriateness of the interpretations that a researcher makes of his/her study. Reliability refers to score consistency across administrations of one's instrument. For both concepts, accurate and appropriate instruments are at the core. Thus, if our hypothesis involves learning, we need to have an accurate and appropriate instrument to measure learning. For example, if we are looking at knowledge representation, we need to have a measure that appropriately reflects that and not something that just measures an ability to use the language. In many instances (see discussions in Gass and Mackey 2007; Gass and Selinker 2008), part of the theoretical discussions in the literature involve how best to represent particular constructs.

Often variables cannot be measured directly. In these instances, we come up with a working definition that allows us to identify the variable in question with something that is understandable and measurable. This is known as an operationalization. Thus, in our example presented earlier of focused attention, we cannot directly measure this construct but we can come up with a reasonable surrogate (e.g., colouring or highlighting in some way). Once we have operationalized a variable, we can more easily work with it.

The last thing that a researcher wants is to spend time, effort and money on a project and then realize that the study itself did not reflect what we had thought it would and might only apply to the population of the study and not to the broader community at large. Validity comes in many different colours; in this section we discuss the most common types of validity: content, face, construct, criterion-related and predictive validity. Following that brief introduction, we turn to a discussion of internal and external validity.

Content validity refers to the representativeness of our measurement regarding the phenomena that we want information about. If, for example, we want information about noun-adjective agreement in Italian, we cannot generalize these findings to say that we have fully investigated all types of agreement (article-noun, singular-plural, regular-irregular, nouns that end in *–a-o* and those that are not morphologically marked as masculine/feminine). In other words, if we want to claim that we have investigated agreement, we need to ensure that our instruments include a representative range of what constitutes agreement.

Face validity is closely related to the notion of content validity and takes us into the realm of the consumers of research. Is our instrument readily recognizable as measuring what we claim it measures? For example, the construct of intelligence can be measured in various ways, but there are certain instruments that are well-accepted as measuring this construct, even if it is a somewhat elusive construct. Thus, face validity refers to the familiarity of our instrument and how easy it is to convince others that there is content validity to it. If a school district wants to measure intelligence with a newly developed instrument, there may be a perception by the community (e.g., parents) that this instrument is not valid (unless of course their child receives a high score!). If the participants do not perceive a connection between the research activities and other educational or second language activities, they may be less likely to take the experiment seriously.

Construct validity refers to the extent to which the research adequately captures the concept in question. In second language and applied linguistic research, construct validity is of great concern because a great deal of what we investigate is not easily quantifiable and not directly measurable. Some variables, such as height, weight, shoe size are easily measureable and there is little controversy over what they reflect. Thus, a height of 5'5" is clear to everyone who uses this scale, but in second language research, we are dealing with such constructs as proficiency. What precisely does this mean? How can we measure it so that we can compare individuals on a common scale? Because these constructs are not directly measurable, their validity can be called into question. One way to enhance construct validity is to have multiple measures. Thus, if we were to measure proficiency, we might have measures that reflect oral use, written use, extent of vocabulary knowledge and so forth. If we were to use these measures as an aggregate, we could have greater confidence in our ability to differentiate individuals along a scale of proficiency.

Criterion-related validity refers to the relationship that a given measure has with some other well-established measure. For example, if a researcher develops an overall measure of language proficiency, it will have criterion-related validity if it measures language students in much the same way as another well-established test. To be more specific, if we are doing a study using first, second and third year English learners of Spanish and we developed a test that measures oral proficiency, criterion-related validity would be increased if we could show that on our test, third-year students did better than second-year students who did better than first-year students. Our test, then, would correspond to some other reasonably accepted measure, that of class placement.

Predictive validity deals with how well the measure we are using predicts performance on some other measure. In other words, if we have a test that measures working memory capacity, it has predictive validity if it predicts performance in class performance in a language class.

In addition to these five types of validity, there are two other types of validity that are noteworthy: internal validity and external validity. Each of these is important when conducting experimental research.

To what extent are the results of a study truly reflective of what we believe they reflect? This is known as internal validity. In other words, are our dependent and independent variables related in the way we think they are? A researcher must control for (i.e., rule out) all other possible factors that could potentially account for the results. This was discussed in the example above in relation to colour blindness. In that study, had we not controlled for colour-blindness, we would be left with the unfortunate conclusion that the study had little internal validity. Before conducting any research study, we need to think carefully through the design to ensure that we eliminate or minimize threats to internal validity (see Mackey and Gass 2005 for a more thorough treatment of this topic and for ways to minimize threats to internal validity).

External validity refers to the potential generalizability[2] of a study. We can make conclusions about the behaviour of the participants in a study, but this is not particularly interesting unless the results have broader implications and are relevant to a wider range of language learners and language learning contexts.

Thus, if we conduct a study with English-speaking learners of Italian studying at University ABC, we are interested not just in those specific learners, but also the extent to which the results are applicable to learners of other languages possibly in different contexts. This is the case because we are interested in general principles of learning and not just a particular group of learners.

External validity can be increased with appropriate sampling procedures, as mentioned above. In particular, it is important that our sample be selected randomly which, in essence, means that each member of the population to be studied has an equal and independent chance of being selected. This is the ideal situation, but one which, in reality, is not always practical. Rather, in second language research, nonrandom sampling is frequently used. Researchers often seek volunteers to participate in a study, as is required by most university ethics review boards. Even when intact classes are used, students can opt out of participation according to university ethical requirements. Sufficiently large sample sizes are always a goal as a way to increase the likelihood of true differences between groups (e.g., experimental and control). Small sample sizes leave the researcher with the uncertainty of understanding the results. Are the differences between groups true or just coincidental? Many statistical tests help researchers avoid drawing unwarranted conclusions.

Because true random sampling is not always likely in second language research, it is important for researchers to fully and accurately describe the population studied as well as provide details about the materials, methods and procedures. In this way, a particular study can be replicated by others which, in a way, broadens the population base of the original study (see Polio and Gass 1997 for a fuller description of replication and reporting). Mackey and Gass (2005) provide additional discussion on issues of external validity and outline ways of minimizing threats to external validity.

Reliability refers to consistency and is a way of ensuring that our constructs are being measured appropriately. In applied linguistics research, it is frequently used when raters are making judgements about data. This is referred to as interrater reliability (when more than one rater is involved) and intrarater reliability (when only one researcher's evaluations are used). In the former instance (e.g., judging oral speech samples on a scale of 1–10), consistency across raters indicates that raters are measuring the same construct in the same way. In the latter case, one might rate the same speech sample at two different points in time to ensure consistency.

Both validity and reliability are ways of ensuring quality in research. As noted, experimental research is a way of finding answers to questions in a disciplined way. These results may have far-reaching impact (including decisions relating to educational practices), and it is incumbent on the research community to ensure that research (experimental and other) is carried out in as careful a way as possible, ensuring quality at each step of the way.

Techniques and Instruments

There are as many techniques and instruments as there are research projects. A description of even a few would go beyond the scope and appropriate length of this chapter. Two recent books (Ellis and Barkhuizen 2005; Gass and Mackey 2007) deal with data elicitation methods and methods of analysis respectively and can serve as useful sources of information.

Ethical Considerations

As with all research, numerous ethical considerations abound. The most obvious concerns the protection of human subjects and will not be dealt with here (see Mackey and Gass 2005, Chapter 2) as they are elaborated on by each institution's ethical review board. In brief, in most educational settings, one must obtain permission from a human research committee before conducting any research or before recruiting volunteers for a research project (see https://www.citiprogram.org/rcrpage.asp?affiliation=100 for information on responsible conduct of research – accessed 11 October 2009). The overriding concern is that no harm comes to participants with the ideal being that there be benefits.

As researchers design studies, there is often a control group against which to measure the effects of a particular treatment. But, here too, there is an ethical question. If we have reason to believe that our treatment is beneficial, then we have recruited volunteers who will not receive the treatment. One possibility is to provide the treatment to the control group after all data have been collected. Polio and Gass (2007) designed a study in just this way, although even in this study, there were limitations of equal treatment. The main research question was: Can a brief intervention study in which pre-service teachers are instructed on how to interact with learners promote learning in a subsequent interaction? The design involved an experimental and a control group. The experimental group received a 15–20 minute session with a researcher who went over ways to increase student output (e.g., asking open-ended questions rather than yes/no questions). This was followed by an interactive session with an ESL learner in which they were asked to put into practice what they had learned. So as not to disadvantage the control group and maintain the integrity of the study, the training session with the control group was conducted following the interactive session. Thus, all pre-service teachers had the benefit of a training session which had been hypothesized to be beneficial in the promotion of learning. Yet, the control group's training was conducted after the experiment so as not to influence the research results. This, of course, does not take into account the benefits that the ESL students in the experimental group had over those in the control group. Unfortunately, the complete balancing of benefits would have required the control group of ESL students to return for a second round and this was not logistically possible. In general, it is important to strictly follow the guidelines established by one's institution regarding all aspects of a study, including modes of recruiting, actual treatment and assessment details and the reporting of information in such a way as to respect privacy and anonymity issues. In addition to local review boards, the American Psychological Association (2010) has important guidelines for many aspects of the research process.

A final point to be made which has ethical ramifications has to do with honesty in reporting, and in particular with the elimination of participants. Elimination of some participants has to be done judiciously and with justification. For example, in studies which measure reaction time, it may be the case that a participant is not focused on the task. This may be determined by inordinately fast reaction times which make it clear that she or he is just pushing a response button without processing the required material. Often in such studies, a cut-off point will be determined, such as 2 standard deviations[3] above or below the mean, with individuals falling on the outside limits of this cut-off point being eliminated from analysis. It is important that detailed and principled justification be provided to avoid any question of impropriety.

A Sample Study

The study that I have chosen to highlight is a study by Alison Mackey, Susan Gass and Kim McDonough, 'How do learners perceive interactional feedback' published in 2000 in *Studies in Second Language Acquisition*. This study was selected because it is an empirical quantitative study, bolstered with qualitative data. The study illustrates the problem of a possible uncontrolled variable cropping up in the study which in this case led to a further study. Thus, it illustrates the cycle of conducting a study, analysing the results (including a post hoc analysis – an analysis that did not result from the research questions that guided the study), postulating an uncontrolled variable that led to a further quantitative study (Gass and Lewis 2007).

Description and research questions: As stated in Mackey et al. (2000, p. 477)

> The focus of the current study is an exploration of the claim that, through negotiated interaction, learners' attention may be directed toward particular aspects of language. In order to explore whether interactional feedback and the allocation of focal attention to feedback play a role in the development of L2 knowledge, it is important to first investigate the extent to which that feedback is in fact perceived as such by learners and whether their perceptions about the target of the feedback are correct.

17

The specific research question was: how do learners perceive the feedback they receive in the course of interaction?

Method and participants: There were 17 ESL learners and 11 Italian as a foreign language (IFL) learners in this study.

Task: Each learner carried out an interactive task with a speaker of the language they were learning (English or Italian). When there were errors, the researcher provided corrective feedback to the learner. Following the interaction (which had been videotaped), the video was replayed to the learner who, using a Stimulated Recall procedure (see Gass and Mackey 2000), was asked to comment on what they were thinking during the moments of feedback. These tapes were coded by two raters with the rating being based on the feedback given and the perception of that feedback. Interrater reliability was calculated and reported. There were four (excluding those that were unclassifiable or had no classifiable content) categories of feedback: (1) phonological, (2) morphosyntactic, (3) lexical or (4) semantic. The responses were then paired according to whether the intent of the feedback corresponded with the perception of the feedback. In other words, was phonological feedback perceived as phonological feedback?

The study did not have a control group-experimental group design; rather, it dealt with static perception, that is, perception of an event. Results were presented in terms of percentages (no statistics in the main study) of feedback of phonology, of morphosyntax and of lexis (semantics had too few responses to comment on).

There are times when the data from a study reveal possibilities of interpretation that had not been planned for from the outset. In this study, there were two post hoc analyses that were conducted as well as a suggestion that led to a further study.

The post-hoc analyses first analysed the type of feedback (recast, negotiation or a combination) in relation to the error tape. This analysis was necessary (but not planned) because the interactions had not been scripted and the feedback was naturally occurring. The second post-hoc analysis related learners' perceptions about feedback and their immediate uptake.

Results: The results of this study showed that learners perceive different error types differentially, that there was a different distribution of feedback type depending on error type and that uptake was different depending on error type. Interestingly, there were differences between the ESL group and the IFL group. It was speculated that the difference might relate to the heritage population[4] that had been included in the IFL group.

Further research: Much research leaves as much unanswered as answered. This research was no exception and, in fact, spawned a different study (Gass and Lewis 2007) which dealt with the variable that 'snuck' into the study (also known as an intervening variable), and which may have influenced the results, that of heritage versus non-heritage learners.

Notes

1. Other terms that are used are constructvist/interpretivists who primarily use qualitative research methods and positivists or empiricists who rely primarily on quantitative methods. In reality, research today crosses both camps and it is not uncommon – yours truly included – to find researchers using both quantitative (experimental) and qualitative methods in their quest to answer research questions.
2. There are instances where generalizability may not be a goal of a study. This might be the case within a particular instructional context in which curricular changes are being debated. In such instances there is a need to determine the extent to which a proposed curricular change (e.g., inserting a technological component into the curriculum) results in increased learning, although in the case of a technological component, the goal might be 'no decrease in learning' because the purpose behind a technological component in a curriculum might be financial.
3. A standard deviation is a measure of dispersion. It is a numerical value that indicates how the scores in a sample are spread out in relation to the mean and therefore indicates the homogeneity or lack thereof of a sample.
4. Heritage learners are those who come to the learning situation with some degree of exposure to the language being learned through their family background. There is a wide range of learner profiles within this category, ranging from the target language being spoken exclusively as a home language to only infrequent use of that language, as for example, visiting relatives abroad during summer visits.

Resources for Further Reading

Brown, J. D. and Rodgers, T. (2002), *Doing Second Language Research*. Oxford: Oxford University Press.
This book covers a range of research topics including qualitative (case studies, introspective data, classroom data), and quantitative research. In the latter category, there is a discussion of descriptive statistics, correlational research and quasi-experimental research. Within these categories is information about compiling and analyzing data as well as guidelines for designing and interpreting data.
Dörnyei, Z. (2007), *Research Methods in Applied Linguistics*. Oxford: Oxford University Press.
This text covers a range of research types (quantitative, qualitative, longitudinal). Included are discussions of theoretical and philosophical underpinnings of research types. Basic issues such as data collection and analysis are discussed, as are guidelines for reporting research.

Gass, S. and Mackey, A. (2007), *Data Elicitation for Second and Foreign Language Research*. Mahwah, NJ: Lawrence Erlbaum Associates.
This book is an extension of Mackey and Gass' (2005) book on research methods (see below). The book focuses extensively on ways of collecting second language data. Chapters, organized around research approaches (e.g., psycholinguistics, formal approaches, interaction) include a discussion of research questions and historical underpinnings of some of the techniques. Each research approach is exemplified with data elicitation techniques including naturalistic language, prompted linguistic production, and non linguistic experimental responses.

Mackey, A. and Gass, S. (2005), *Second Language Research: Methodology and Design*. Mahwah, NJ: Lawrence Erlbaum Associates
This book, targeted towards students of second language acquisition, addresses basic issues related to research design, providing step-by-step instructions for how to carry out studies. Topics include identifying research problems and questions; selecting elicitation measures; dealing with ethical issues related to data gathering; validity and reliability in research; research in classroom contexts; qualitative research, data description and coding; and data analysis. Also included is a chapter on writing research reports with suggestions about preparing research results for publication.

Porte, G. (2002), *Appraising Research in Second Language Learning: A Practical Approach to Critical Analysis of Quantitative Research*. Amsterdam: John Benjamins.
Porte's book focuses on understanding and interpreting research reports. The goal of the book is to produce critical readers of research. The book is organized around research reports, namely, the abstract, introduction, review of literature, participants, materials, procedures, results, discussion and conclusion. Questions are peppered throughout each of the sections leading the reader to a critical understanding of appropriate content for a sound research article.

References

American Psychological Association (2010), *Publication Manual of the American Psychological Association* (6th edition). Washington, D.C.: American Psychological Association.

Dörnyei, Z. (2007), *Research Methods in Applied Linguistics*. Oxford: Oxford University Press.

Ellis, R. and Barkhuizen, G. (2005), *Analyzing Learner Language*. Oxford: Oxford University Press.

Gass, S. and Lewis, K. (2007), 'Perceptions of interactional feedback: Differences between heritage language learners and non-heritage language learners', in A. Mackey (ed.), *Conversational Interaction in Second Language Acquisition: A Series of Empirical Studies*. Oxford: Oxford University Press, pp. 173–196.

Gass, S. and Mackey, A. (2000), *Stimulated Recall Methodology in Second Language Research*. Mahwah, NJ: Lawrence Erlbaum Associates.

—(2007), *Data Elicitation for Second and Foreign Language Research*. Mahwah, NJ: Lawrence Erlbaum Associates.

Gass, S. and Selinker, L. (2008), *Second Language Acquisition: An Introductory Course* (third edition). London: Taylor and Francis.

Gass, S., Svetics, I. and Lemelin, S. (2003). Differential effects of attention. *Language Learning*, 53(3), 497–545.

Jordan, G. (2005), *Theory Construction in Second Language Acquisition*. Amsterdam: John Benjamins.

Larsen-Freeman, D. and Long, M. (1991), *An Introduction to Second Language Acquisition Research*. London: Longman.

Mackey, A. (1999), 'Input, interaction and second language development'. *Studies in Second Language Acquisition*, 21, 557–587.

Mackey, A. and Gass, S. (2005), *Second Language Research: Methodology and Design*. Mahwah, NJ: Lawrence Erlbaum Associates.

Mackey, A., Gass, S. and McDonough, K. (2000), 'Learners' perceptions about feedback'. *Studies in Second Language Acquisition*, 22, 471–497.

Polio, C. and Gass, S. (1997), 'Replication and reporting: A commentary'. *Studies in Second Language Acquisition*, 19, 499–508.

—(2007), The conflict between language learning and task completion: The case of preservice teachers and communicative tasks. (Paper under review)

3 Survey Research

Elvis Wagner

Virtually everyone is familiar with survey research. People are constantly surveyed about their buying habits, political views, personal beliefs and just about everything else, and the results of this type of research are published and consumed constantly in newspapers, magazines and television. Survey research is a very powerful tool that is used extensively by governments, businesses, educational institutions and by individual researchers, and it has long had an important role in the field of applied linguistics. Researchers have used survey research to investigate the characteristics, attitudes and opinions of language learners. Perhaps most prominently, applied linguistics survey research has provided valuable insights in the areas of learner beliefs (e.g., Horwitz 1988), learning strategies (e.g., Chamot and Kupper 1989; Purpura 1999), learner motivation (e.g., Gardner 1985; Dornyei 2001) and language learning anxiety (MacIntyre and Gardner 1991), among others. As Brown (2001) describes, these notions (i.e., beliefs, strategies, motivation, anxiety) are psychological constructs, abstract notions that are assumed to exist, although they cannot be observed directly. Therefore, survey research instruments allow researchers to operationalize (and consequently, measure) these constructs.

Underlying Assumptions and Methodology

Survey research differs from experimental research in that the researcher does not manipulate the setting or environment in order to investigate how this affects particular variables, or the relationship between variables (see Gass this volume; Nunan 1992). Instead, the goal of survey research is to get information about learners' characteristics, beliefs, or attitudes; information that is usually not available from production data, such as performance or observational data (Mackey and Gass 2005). Brown (2001) describes survey research as primary research distinct from both qualitative and statistical research, although survey research will often have both qualitative and quantitative components.

Steps in Doing Survey Research

Because survey research is so prevalent in the social sciences, virtually everyone is familiar with the methodology. In many ways this presents advantages to the beginning applied linguistics researcher who wants to conduct survey research. The methodology is familiar, and the experience of taking surveys can be useful in creating survey instruments. However, this familiarity can also present unique challenges. Because people are familiar with the methodology, they sometimes gloss over or skip entirely some of the important steps in planning and creating viable research projects. Therefore, a framework for the steps a researcher should follow might be useful. In reality, these steps are not very different from research projects utilizing other methodologies:

- Planning the project
- Designing the survey
- Administering the survey
- Analysing the data

It is very important to note, however, that while these are useful steps to follow when conducting survey research, it is vital that the researcher consider all of these steps during the 'planning the project' phase. That is, unless the researcher has considered how she will administer the survey and analyse the data *before* designing the survey, the research project is almost certainly destined for failure.

Planning the Project

When doing the initial planning of the project, the researcher must consider *what* she wants to investigate (reviewing the literature and formulating the research questions), *why* she wants to investigate this topic (identifying the gap in the literature) and *who* she wants to investigate (the population, and the sampling techniques that will be used). Based on this planning and research, the researcher then must decide *how* she is going to investigate this topic (the methodology that will be used; the instruments that will be used for the data collection; whether the data will be qualitative, quantitative or both; and how the data will be analysed).

One of the fundamental underlying assumptions to consider when planning survey research is the issue of sampling. Survey research involves trying to find out information about a particular population (e.g., all ESL learners in Great Britain; all university EFL learners in Malaysia; all of the EFL learners in a particular language programme in Korea). Rarely is an entire population surveyed (an obvious exception is a national census, where a government seeks to obtain information from every member of the population). Because of the huge amount of resources needed to actually complete a census, most research utilizes surveys, in which information is obtained from a sample of the population. While it might be possible for a government to attempt to survey all L2 language users in a country, it is much more feasible (and often useful) to sample from this population. The notion of sampling is a very important consideration in survey research, because the quality and representativeness of the sampling determines the extent of the generalizability of the results of the research of the sample to the larger population (Vogt 2007). Unfortunately, sampling is a consideration that is often overlooked or neglected by educational researchers (including applied linguistics researchers). Because of its importance in a sound research design, a quick overview of the two basic sampling procedures, probability and nonprobability sampling, is provided here.

Probability sampling techniques (i.e., random, stratified random, systematic and cluster) are used to select a small group (the sample) from a larger group (the population), in order to create samples that are representative of the population. These techniques can be utilized according to the needs, resources, size of the population and quest for generalizability of the individual research projects. *Random sampling* is a variety of sampling in which the researcher seeks to include a truly representative sample of the population in the study. The goal is to assure that every member of the population has an equal chance of being included in the sample. Unfortunately, it is actually quite difficult to obtain a truly random sample, and the representativeness of the sample will always be affected by sampling error. A *stratified random sample* is a version of random sampling in which subgroups are selected from within a particular population, and samples are then generated for each of these subgroups. *Systematic sampling*, a more widely used technique, is a sampling technique in which every *n*th person is selected. Finally, *cluster sampling* is a technique in which natural subgroups (clusters) within a population can be identified, and then random samples are generated for each of the clusters.

An example might serve to make the notion of sampling clearer. Say that a researcher is hoping to explore why students at a particular university are studying English as a foreign language. If a list of all the EFL students existed, the researcher could survey each of these learners (in essence, conduct a census) about their motivation for learning English. However, this list might include 1,000 learners, and surveying 1,000 participants would require huge amounts of resources, so the researcher instead chooses to survey a random sampling of these learners. She could have a computer randomly choose 100 participants from the list. If the researcher were interested in comparing particular groups within this population of EFL learners (e.g., to compare the motivation of English majors with non-English majors), she might choose instead to perform stratified random sampling by having a computer randomly choose 50 English majors with 50 non-English majors). She could also perform systematic sampling by generating a list of the 1,000 EFL learners in alphabetical order, randomly choosing one of the first 10 names on the list, and then selecting every 10th learner to survey.

Random sampling, stratified random sampling and systematic sampling all assume that a 'list' of all the learners in the population exists (in this example, all of the EFL students in this particular university). In reality, however, for many researchers, no such list of all the individuals in a chosen population exists, or else the researcher does not have access to this list. If this is the case, then cluster sampling is an option. Again, using the example of our university EFL students, it is possible or even probable that a list of all the current EFL students does not exist (or is out of date, or the researcher does not have access to the list). But the researcher does know that there are eight different levels of EFL classes offered at the university. The researcher might then choose to sample eight different classes of students, randomly choosing one class from each of the eight different levels. She could also randomly choose 12 students within each class to survey.

Using appropriate probability sampling helps support the generalizability of the results of survey research. Nevertheless, much of the survey research conducted in applied linguistics utilizes nonprobability sampling – convenience samples. As its name implies, *convenience sampling* involves surveying individuals who are readily available and that the researcher has access to. The use of convenience samples can be informative, and can yield very interesting and useful results. However, the drawback is that it is not possible to generalize the results to a larger population. Returning to our EFL university student example, if a researcher surveyed the students in her own two classes (a convenience sample) about their motivation for learning English, she might find useful information about the students in these classes, but she could not generalize her results to the rest of the population (all of the university EFL students).

The survey researcher must also be concerned with other sampling issues, including *nonresponse bias, sampling error, self-selection* and *sampling with replacement* (see Fowler 1993; Fink 1995; Perry 2005; Vogt 2007).

Designing the Survey Instruments

After the initial planning stage, the researcher needs to design the survey instruments that will be used in the data collection. The design process includes selecting the instruments to be used (see the section below for the different types of survey instruments), creating the instruments (or adapting instruments used by other researchers), piloting the instruments and revising the instruments based on the piloting process.

There are two different types of survey data collection instruments: questionnaires and interviews. Questionnaires and interviews are differentiated by the mode in which they are administered and the type of information that each are designed to elicit. Typically, questionnaires are given in written form, and are used in order to get information from or about a large number of individuals, while interviews are administered orally, and are used to get more in-depth information from a smaller sample of individuals. A questionnaire is a written instrument in which respondents read questions or statements and respond to these questions by selecting a choice offered or writing their own response. Interviews are conducted orally by a researcher in order to elicit oral responses from a participant. An interview schedule refers to the list of questions that the interviewer will ask the participant, and serves to ensure that all participants will be asked all of the same questions, in the same order.

In many ways, questionnaires and interviews reflect the larger quantitative versus qualitative data analysis dichotomy. Questionnaires are designed for efficiency; they can be administered to a large number of participants easily, they can be objectively scored, and the data can analysed quantitatively. The shortcomings of questionnaires, however, are also readily apparent. The data derived from questionnaires often provide only a superficial assessment of sometimes very complex constructs. Conversely, the data derived from interviews can be quite rich, and in-depth. However, this richness comes at a cost of efficiency, in that the researcher (usually) has to meet individually with the participant to administer the interview. The data elicited must then be transcribed, and then analysed qualitatively. Questionnaires and interviews are not mutually exclusive – many survey research projects will employ both instrument types in order to get richer interview data that complement the broader questionnaire data. The purpose of the study and the research questions investigated will dictate the type of data collection instruments used. Because of space constraints, the focus here will be on the design of questionnaires.

Questionnaires can be either closed or open-ended. Closed-ended questionnaires have a stimulus (these can be questions or statements, although I will refer to these from this point on as questions) that the participants read, and then choose the most appropriate response from a list of possible responses. These possible responses can be in a variety of formats. They can be dichotomous choices (e.g., *yes/no, true/false, agree/disagree*); they can be in multiple choice format where all of the possible answers are listed; or they can be Likert scale items, in which the respondents have a number of possible responses to choose from. Open-ended questionnaires require the participant to write an answer to in response to the stimulus question. The responses elicited with open-ended questionnaires can vary from one word (in response to 'What is your native language?'), to extensive written texts (e.g., in response to 'What is your motivation for learning English?').

Questionnaires (closed and open-ended) can be designed to elicit objective data – information about the characteristics of the participants such as age, length of residence in an English speaking country, years of English study, etc., and they can elicit subjective data – information about the beliefs, attitudes and values of the participants. Often, a particular survey will elicit both types of information, such as the background characteristics of the participants, as well as their attitudes about learning English.

One of the most commonly used items in survey research is the Likert scale item. This type of item usually includes a statement, and then generally has four or five response options, typically including *strongly agree, agree, don't know* (or *no opinion*, or *neutral*), *disagree*, and *strongly disagree*, or some variation of these. These response options are then assigned a number by the researcher (typically 5 for *strongly agree* and 1 for *strongly disagree*), which can be used for quantitative analysis. Some researchers prefer to use more than five categories, with response options such as *somewhat* agree, *slightly* agree, *somewhat* disagree, etc. Including a larger range of response options can serve to improve the psychometric properties of the questionnaire, but can also serve to make it more difficult for participants to respond in that they might have difficulty differentiating between the different degrees of agreement or disagreement. There is no consensus among researchers about the use of the *no opinion* or *don't know* response. Some researchers suggest not giving the survey takers this option, because participants who do not have strong feelings about the material in the survey tend to select this category, and if many of the participants choose this category, the results of the overall survey often will not reach statistical significance. Thus, not giving the participants this option can lead to more interpretable results. However, Vogt (2007) argues that respondents choose this neutral response because it most accurately describes their response to the statement, and that it is inappropriate to not offer this response simply because it is inconvenient for the researcher.

One of the reasons that these Likert scale items are particularly useful is that a number of items can be used to try and assess the same construct. So, to return to our motivation example, the researcher might want to investigate a particular population's motivation for learning English. Based on her personal experience and the review of the literature conducted in planning the project, she might want to investigate a number of possible external motivators (e.g., *needed for a good job, desire to communicate with English speakers, desire to live or travel in an English speaking country*). The researcher can then create a number of Likert scale items to assess the participants' attitudes for each of these different components of the motivation construct. Then, the items measuring a particular component can be summed or averaged to form a composite scale, although the idea of Likert scale items being treated as composite variables is not universally accepted by statisticians. Likert scales are not really interval scales, in that the intervals between the different responses are probably not equal intervals, and thus they are more accurately seen as ordinal data. Nevertheless, many, if not most, applied linguists do treat Likert scale items as interval data.

Generally speaking, the more items that are used to measure a particular concept, the more reliable and accurate is the overall scale. Often, items that are measuring the same construct will include *reverse-coded* items. So, for example, one item in the 'job' motivation scale might state, 'Speaking English is necessary for my job,' while the reverse coded item would be something like, 'Learning English is not important for my occupation.'

After the individual items have been created, the questionnaire is then compiled and formatted. The importance of the formatting cannot be under-estimated. Brown (2001) and Dornyei (2003) stress the importance of creating a questionnaire that looks professional, with no typographical errors or formatting inconsistencies. The respondents will automatically make a number of assumptions about a questionnaire based on its appearance. If the questionnaire looks professional, participants are more likely to respond to it seriously. For more formatting issues, the reader is urged to consult Brown (2001) and Dornyei (2003).

For reliability purposes, the goal for the researcher is to standardize the questionnaire so that every one of the respondents gets the exact same items, in the same order. Brown (2001) suggests that questions should be ordered from shortest and easiest to answer to longest and most difficult to answer. He also suggests keeping together all questions of a single type, of a single function, of a single response format and question form and all questions on a given topic.

After the initial questionnaire has been created, it is important to pilot the questionnaire to see how it performs. Ideally the questionnaire can be piloted on participants that are members of the target population, and then analysed statistically (see the 'analysis' section below). Based on this analysis of which items seem to be working well and which items are problematic, the developer can delete or revise certain items, and add different items if necessary. Then the researcher can do another pilot administration of the questionnaire, analyse the results and revise as needed.

Unfortunately, this extensive piloting and revision process is not always feasible. Nevertheless, it is imperative that some sort of piloting is performed. Resources spent piloting the instrument at this phase of the project are generally resources well spent. It is vital that someone other than the questionnaire developer actually take the questionnaire. At the very least, the researcher can trial the questionnaire on friends or colleagues, and get their feedback about the questionnaire. Even if these respondents are not part of the population for which the questionnaire is intended, they can give the researcher valuable information that will assist in the revision process. Often the developer is too close to the questionnaire – he or she cannot see the problems or issues that might be obvious to someone who has not spent many hours researching and developing this survey instrument.

Administering the Survey

Only after the instrument has been piloted and revised should it be administered to actual participants. With interviews, the researcher should make sure to schedule enough time to complete the interview. The piloting process should help make clear how much time is needed, but in my experience interviews often take longer than anticipated, and the data from a rushed interview is suspect. The researcher should always strive to be professional, and the interview space should be clean, quiet and unobtrusive. Part of being professional is to be familiar with the interview schedule, and rehearsing the questions to be asked. For reliability purposes, it is important that the interviewer follow the interview question wording exactly (Brown 2001). The interviewer should strive to make the interviewee comfortable, welcoming the interviewee at the beginning of the session, thoroughly explaining the research purposes and interview procedure, and answering any questions the participant may have. If audio- or video-recording equipment is used to record the interview, it should be as unobtrusive as possible, and tested beforehand to make sure it is recording properly.

For questionnaire administration, which often includes larger groups of participants, if at all possible the researcher should attend the administration in person. While it might be possible for the classroom teacher to administer the questionnaires to his or her class of students, the classroom teacher will

29

invariably not be as invested in the research as the primary researcher, nor will he or she be as knowledgeable about the research, and able to answer all the questions participants might have. Administering the questionnaire in person, in a polite and professional manner, generally leads to a higher response rate and better results.

It is very important that the researcher anticipate issues that might arise during the administration. Again, the process of piloting the questionnaire should help the researcher anticipate possible problems. A useful suggestion is, as much as possible, to prepare the participants for the questionnaire *before* they appear for the large-scale administration. This can be accomplished by providing participants in advance with information about the study and its purpose (email is often useful for this) and about the questionnaire procedure itself. The researcher should check out the space where the administration will occur, making sure that there is adequate and comfortable space for the respondents. While it may seem obvious to mention that the researcher should double-check that she has enough copies of the questionnaire, and that these copies are collated and in the appropriate order, numerous questionnaire administrations have been scuttled by photocopying problems. As with interviews, when the participants arrive for the administration, the researcher should welcome them, and make them feel as comfortable as possible, explain the purpose of the research, the instructions for responding to the questionnaire and answer any questions respondents might have. Again, this might seem obvious, but large-scale administrations can be quite stressful, and if not adequately prepared, the researcher can forget to make the respondents as comfortable as possible. The goal, of course, is to make participants want to respond to the interview or questionnaire as fully and truthfully as possible. Respondents who feel unwanted or unwelcome are much less likely to devote their time and attention to the survey, and the results will be of dubious value. After the administration is completed, the researcher should thank the respondents for their participation.

Sampling issues were described in the 'Planning the Project' section, but sampling is also an administration issue. Appropriate sampling procedures necessitate that the researcher try to get everyone that was targeted in the sampling procedure to actually perform the interview or complete the questionnaire. Even the most conscientious sampler can end up with an unrepresentative sample if not everyone in the targeted sample completes the survey. This is called *nonresponse bias*. For example, if a researcher is exploring students' motivation for learning English, and uses a sampling procedure that randomly chooses four classes in a language programme to be surveyed, it is important that every student in those four classes be surveyed. If the researcher administers the questionnaire in the four classes in which 75 of the 80 students are present, it is very important that the researcher follow-up and try to get the remaining five students who were not present in their classes that day to complete the questionnaire.

This might sound trivial, but these missing five students could represent serious nonresponse bias. Perhaps these five students often skip class because they are not motivated to learn English. By not getting these students' input, the results of the study are of questionable value.

Questionnaires do not have to be administered in person, of course. Often, questionnaires are sent through the mail to possible respondents, so that the respondent can complete the questionnaire and return it to the researcher. This presents special problems related to response rate, and is beyond the purview of this chapter (see Vogt 2007 for further information about postal surveys and questionnaires).

Surveys and questionnaires can also be conducted on the internet, or via email. This type of survey research has a number of advantages, the most obvious being the lower costs involved. Rather than having to create and administer physical questionnaires (either in person or via postal mail), the questionnaires can be presented on a website, or emailed to potential participants, allowing the participants to respond to the questionnaires when it is convenient for them. The other major advantage is that much of the data entry can be done automatically. When using a web-based survey service, the participants usually complete the questionnaires online, and the data is entered automatically, and the results are immediately available for the researcher. Web-based surveys do pose special research problems that have to be addressed, however. Like all other surveys, it is important that adequate sampling procedures be followed, and that the researcher endeavour to follow-up with potential participants who did not respond. Web-based surveys might be especially prone to bias issues like self-selection bias. Another issue is the need to make online surveys password protected. When participants are solicited for participation in the survey, they should be given a special password that is only able to be used once, or else participants might skew the results of the survey by responding multiple times. Web-based surveys also present security issues, and special care should be taken to ensure that secure connections be used so that anonymity can be ensured, especially if the survey is of a sensitive nature.

Analysing the Data

After the interviews or questionnaires have been administered, it is necessary to analyse the data. For interviews, the data needs to be transcribed and then coded and analysed qualitatively (see Holliday, this volume, for more information about analysing qualitative data). Questionnaire data, however, usually entails larger sample sizes, and generally necessitate inputting the data into a spreadsheet such as Excel, or a statistical programme such as SPSS, so that the data can be analysed statistically. One of the most important things to consider is the issue of reverse coded items. Although it might seem obvious, it is imperative that the researcher remember to reverse code these items when inputting the data. That is, if a Likert scale was used with 5 for *strongly agree* and 1 for *strongly disagree*, when inputting the values for the reverse coded items, it is necessary to input 1 for *strongly agree*, 2 for *agree*, etc.

After the data are inputted, descriptive statistics (mean, standard deviations, skewness and kurtosis) can be computed. If statistical procedures that require a normal distribution are going to be used in the analysis, these descriptive statistics can be consulted to check that the assumptions regarding normality are met (see Phakiti this volume).

It is also important to examine (and report) the reliability of the questionnaire. Usually, the internal consistency reliability will be estimated using Cronbach's alpha. Internal consistency reliability is used to estimate the extent to which scores on the different items correlate with each other, and Cronbach's alpha is a coefficient (ranging from 0 to 1) that indicates the extent to which the items are measuring a single (unidimensional) construct. The closer this coefficient is to 1, the more consistently the items are measuring the same thing. Depending on what the questionnaire is intended to assess, the reliability can be estimated for the overall questionnaire, for each subsection of the questionnaire, or for the individual scales. If the questionnaire is narrow in scope, composed of ten items that are all intended to assess the unidimensional construct 'Learners' motivation in their English classroom', for example, then the reliability should be assessed for the overall questionnaire. If the questionnaire is broader in scope, with three subsections, all designed to measure different components of motivation for learning English (for example, 'English in the classroom', 'English on the job' and 'English for tourism'), then it would be appropriate to estimate reliability for each of the distinct subsections. If the questionnaire is very broad in scope, with numerous scales all designed to measure different components of motivation, then it would be most appropriate to estimate reliability for each scale. Internal consistency reliability is an estimate of the degree to which the different items are consistently measuring a single construct (see Phakiti 2003). If the questionnaire is designed to measure different things (multiple constructs), then one would expect that the individual items indeed are not measuring consistently.

One of the difficulties with estimating internal consistency reliability for a composite scale (that might be measured by only three or four items) is that often the reliability estimate will be quite low, because Cronbach's alpha is affected by the number of items in the scale. While it is impossible to give a predetermined cut-off on how high the alpha should be for a questionnaire, Dornyei (2003) suggests that even short scales composed of only three or four items should have a reliability coefficient alpha of at least .70 (i.e., 70 per cent of the items are reliable in terms of measuring the construct), and he suggests that an alpha that is less than .60 is problematic. Similarly, Perry (2005) advises that while questionnaires tend to have lower reliability coefficients than test instruments, a reliability coefficient below .60 is considered low. Vogt (2007) is even more stringent, stating that an alpha of .70 is the minimum acceptable. A reliability coefficient much below .70 indicates that the items are not consistently measuring the same unidimensional construct, but may in fact be measuring a number of different things.

If the questionnaire has a large number of items and a large number of scales, and if the questionnaire has been given to a large group of respondents, it is more appropriate to use factor analysis in addition to internal consistency reliability to investigate the extent to which the different items designed to measure a specific component of the construct are indeed measuring the same thing. Factor analysis is a more sophisticated statistical technique than reliability analyses, and can give the researcher more information about what the different items in the questionnaire are actually measuring (see Vogt 2007 for more information about factor analysis).

Validity/Trustworthiness

There are a number of issues that the survey researcher must be aware of and address in order to make the results of survey research as trustworthy and valid as possible. Perhaps the most important consideration involves the issue of sampling. This has been addressed above, but it is worth stressing the notion that unless adequate sampling procedures have been instituted, the research is of little use outside the immediate context of the research, and generalizing to a larger population is inappropriate.

Another difficulty inherent in much survey research is related to the nature of what is being investigated. As noted, much survey research in applied linguistics is aimed at exploring abstract constructs like motivation, strategy use, attitudes and the anxiety of language learners. Dornyei, perhaps the pre-eminent researcher of L2 motivation, and who uses questionnaires extensively in his research, describes how motivation is an abstract term for a construct that is unobservable, multidimensional and inconstant (Dornyei 2001). Needless to say, it is no easy task to measure an unobservable, multidimensional and inconstant construct using only a number of statements or questions that a participant has to respond to. To complicate matters even further, many of the constructs being investigated in survey research include behaviours that are unconscious – automatized behaviours that the language learner may do without even being consciously aware of doing so. There is disagreement about whether unconscious behaviours can actually be accessed by conscious recollection, thus calling into doubt the validity of the results of this type of

survey research. In addition, questionnaires using Likert scale items to measure these abstract constructs compound the difficulty in that they require respondents to note the strength of choice (e.g., the extent that they *strongly agree* versus just *agree* with the statement). As argued by Vogt (2007), one participant's conception of *agree* might be very different from another participant's conception of *agree*. Even *yes* or *no* answers are problematic in that for many statements, they provide a false dichotomy. For example, a participant asked to respond *Yes* or *No* to a statement 'I listen to the radio to learn English' might become frustrated if she used to listen to the radio in English, but does not anymore, or if she has listened only once or twice. What is the correct answer? While the researcher needs to try and anticipate these types of issues, often they will only become apparent in the trialing and piloting phase.

Again, investigating these abstract constructs is difficult under the best of conditions, but the applied linguistics survey researcher also has to address language and literacy issues. By definition, language learners have an imperfect control of language. If the interviews or questionnaires are presented to the participants in the target language, it is imperative that the language used in eliciting the data be at a level comprehensible to the respondents. This is, of course, much easier said than done. One way around this issue is to elicit the data in the native language of the participants, but this is not always feasible, and also introduces translation issues.

Another issue that can affect the validity and trustworthiness of survey research is the issue of fatigue. As a general rule of thumb, the more items on a data collection instrument (e.g., a test, questionnaire or interview), the more reliable that instrument will be. That is, the Cronbach's alpha for a questionnaire that has 20 items will tend to be higher than for a questionnaire that has 10 items. There is a point, however, where additional items will lead to diminishing returns. Anyone who has ever completed a questionnaire that was too long can attest to this phenomenon. Respondents can read and answer the questionnaire items for only so long before they become fatigued and lose concentration. At this point, the responses provided by the participant become suspect, the reliability of the responses suffers, and the validity of the research is questionable. With respondents who are reading and responding in a second language, it is likely that fatigue will set in even sooner. Obviously, the point at which fatigue sets in will vary by the individual respondent, but Dornyei (2003) suggests that no survey or questionnaires require more than 30 minutes to complete.

Another issue that the applied linguistics survey researcher has to acknowledge and try to address is the issue of respondents who are unmotivated or unreliable. Often, a survey researcher will contact a teacher, or a language programme administrator, and get permission to administer her survey or questionnaire to a classroom of students. These students are a captive audience for the researcher, and while they might complete the questionnaire as instructed, if they are unmotivated to concentrate on the questionnaire and answer truthfully, the reliability and validity of the results are questionable. At the same time, survey research is prone to many different forms of bias. That is, the respondents will often respond (consciously or unconsciously) to the survey prompts by giving answers that will enhance their own standing (*prestige bias*), or their responses will reflect how they would like to think of themselves as acting, rather than how they really act (*self-deception bias*). Some respondents are also prone to responding to the interview or questionnaire according to how they think the researcher wants them to respond (*acquiescence bias*).

The point here is thus twofold. It is vital that the researcher pilot and validate the instruments used in survey research (see Brown 2001 for further information about validating survey instruments). In addition, while survey research can be quite informative, the inherent limitations in this type of research must always be remembered and acknowledged by the researcher.

A Sample Study

Purpura (1999) employed questionnaires to investigate low-ability and high-ability learners' cognitive and metacognitive strategy use, and how strategy use affected second language test performance. Drawing on a review of the literature of previous strategy use studies, Purpura created cognitive strategy and metacognitive strategy use questionnaires based on a model of human information processing. The cognitive strategy use questionnaire contained 40 questionnaire items designed to measure 12 different cognitive strategy types (e.g., *analysing contrastively, linking with prior knowledge, practising naturalistically*). Each cognitive strategy type was measured by at least two different questionnaire items, although some strategy types were measured by up to five items. The items that were measuring the same cognitive strategy type were averaged to create a composite scale of that variable. Similarly, the metacognitive strategy use questionnaire contained 40 questionnaire items designed to measure five different metacognitive strategy types (e.g., *setting goals, assessing the situation, formulating a plan*). Each metacognitive strategy type was measured by at least three items, and one strategy type was measured by 10 questionnaire items. Again, the items that were measuring the same metacognitive strategy type were averaged to create a composite scale of that variable.

These strategy questionnaires were then administered to 1,382 English language learners. The participants also took the First Certificate of English Anchor Test, so that the strategy use of the learners could be investigated in conjunction with second language test performance.

Purpura used a number of statistical procedures to analyse the questionnaire data. He first calculated descriptive statistics (including the means, standard deviations, skewness and kurtosis). Calculating these statistics allowed him to check that the assumptions regarding normality for each variable were met, and that statistical procedures requiring a normal distribution would be appropriate for these data. He then performed a series of reliability analyses using Cronbach's alpha for the strategy use questionnaires, estimating the reliability coefficient for both the cognitive questionnaire (alpha = .84) and metacognitive questionnaires (alpha = .89), as well as the reliability coefficient for each of the scale variables (the 12 different cognitive strategy types, and the five different metacognitive strategy types). These reliability analyses allowed Purpura to investigate the extent to which the different items within each scale were actually measuring the same underlying trait, in the hopes of validating the questionnaire. In other words, if three items were designed to measure the strategy *analysing contrastively*, then it would be expected that these three items would have a very high internal consistency. And indeed, a number of the scale reliability coefficients were relatively high (above .70), suggesting that the items in these scales were measuring the same construct. However, a number of the composite scale variables were much lower, suggesting that while the items measuring these strategies were designed to measure the same trait, they might in fact have been measuring different traits.

Purpura then used exploratory factor analysis to examine the underlying factorial structure of the two questionnaires. These factor analyses suggested that the cognitive strategy questionnaire was measuring 11 different factors, rather than the 12 different factors (hypothesized cognitive strategies) that Purpura had expected, and that the metacognitive strategy questionnaire appeared to be measuring four different factors, rather than the five different factors (hypothesized metacognitive strategies) that he had originally expected.

Based on the results of these exploratory factor analyses, substantive rationale and a rethinking of the original theoretical models, Purpura then used confirmatory factor analysis to test a number of competing models of cognitive strategy use and metacognitive strategy use. In other words, he used these reliability and factor analyses in order to 'generate empirically-based, composite variables, which could then be used to posit a model of strategy use' (Purpura 1999, p. 67), which could be related to a model of second language test performance.

Resources for Further Reading

Brown, J. D. (2001), *Using Surveys in Language Programs*. Cambridge: Cambridge University Press.

This book, by a leading authority on statistics and research in applied linguistics, is aimed at teachers and researchers in language programmes that are interested in conducting survey research. It provides in-depth coverage of issues related to survey research. The book is organized according to the steps involved in conducting survey research (*planning, designing the instrument, gathering data, analysing data statistically, analysing data qualitatively,* and *reporting*). The chapter devoted to statistical analysis is especially thorough and useful for researchers interested in using survey methodology.

Dornyei, Z. (2003). *Questionnaires in Second Language Research: Construction, Adminis-tration, and Processing.* New York: Erlbaum.

A very practical guide to the construction and administration of questionnaires in L2 research, from a researcher who has used questionnaires extensively in his research, especially pertaining to the cognitive components of language learning. Perhaps the book's greatest strength is its practical nature – the author gives specific instructions and suggestions for creating reliable, valid and useful questionnaires.

Some useful websites for hosting online surveys

www.surveymonkey.com

www.questionpro.com

www.KeySurvey.com

www.polldaddy.com

http://freeonlinesurveys.com

There are numerous websites and software packages devoted to the creation and administration of surveys and questionnaires. Most of these websites allow users to try out the service for free.

http://nces.ed.gov/statprog/2002/stdtoc.asp

Part of the United States Department of Education, The National Center for Edu-cational Statistics runs this website that provides and sets standards for survey data sampling and collection. The Center provides these standards in order to ensure the quality of statistical surveys, and their analyses.

References

Brown, J. D. (2001), *Using Surveys in Language Programs.* Cambridge: Cambridge University Press.

Chamot, A. and Küpper, L. (1989), 'Learning strategies in foreign language instruc-tion'. *Foreign Language Annals,* 22, 13–24.

Dornyei, Z. (2001), *Teaching and Researching Motivation.* Harlow, UK: Longman.

—(2003), *Questionnaires in Second Language Research: Construction, Administration, and Processing.* New York: Erlbaum.

Fink, A. (1995), *How to Sample in Surveys.* Thousand Oaks, CA: Sage.

Fowler, F., Jr. (1993), *Survey Research Methods* (2nd edn). Newbury Park, CA: Sage.

Gardner, R. (1985), *Social Psychology and Second Language Learning: The Role of Atti-tudes and Motivation.* London: Edward Arnold.

Horwitz, E. (1988), 'The beliefs about language learning of beginning university foreign language students'. *Modern Language Journal,* 72, 283–94.

MacIntyre, P. and Gardner, R. (1991), 'Language anxiety: Its relation to other anxieties and to processing in native and second languages'. *Language Learning*, 41, 513–34.

Mackey, A. and Gass, S. (2005), *Second Language Research: Methodology and Design*. Mahwah, NJ: Erlbaum.

Nunan, D. (1992), *Research Methods in Language Learning*. Cambridge: Cambridge University Press.

Perry, F. (2005), *Researching Applied Linguistics: Becoming a Discerning Consumer*. Mahwah, NJ: Erlbaum.

Phakiti, A. (2003), 'A closer look at the relationship of cognitive and metacognitive strategy use to EFL reading comprehension test performance.' *Language Testing*, 20, 26–56.

Purpura, J. (1999), *Learner Strategy Use and Performance on Language Tests: A Structural Equation Modeling Approach*. Cambridge: Cambridge University Press.

Vogt, W. (2007), *Quantitative Research Methods for Professionals*. Boston, MA: Pearson.

4 Analysing Quantitative Data

Aek Phakiti

A good deal of research in applied linguistics involves quantifying aspects of language learning or factors which influence language learning or use such as knowledge about language, motivation, self-regulation and anxiety (see Lazaraton 2005). This chapter discusses issues involved in the preparation of quantitative data for analysis. It will discuss two types of statistical analyses (descriptive and inferential statistics) that are used in quantitative research. The chapter then discusses a sample study, paying particular attention to quantitative data analysis. In this chapter, data preparation and analysis will focus, particularly, on the use of SPSS (Statistical Package for the Social Sciences), a program which can help with the statistical analysis of quantitative data.

Quantitative Data Preparation

There is a wide range of quantitative data that can be used in applied linguistics research. Quantitative data can derive from measurement instruments that quantify variables and factors, such as language tests or responses on Likert-scale questionnaires. They can also derive from qualitative data collection techniques such as think-aloud protocols, retrospective interviews, diaries and written, visual, audio or spoken texts (Gass and Mackey 2005). There are a number of stages researchers typically move through in the preparation of quantitative data for analysis. In working with and preparing quantitative data for analysis, researchers move back and forth to earlier stages. The first of these stages is the *checking and organizing data phase*. That is, the data need to be checked to see whether each study participant has fully completed all sections or items in the data collection procedure. Interview data, for example, need to be transcribed and organized prior to quantification processes (such as tally and frequency counts). Once all data (quantitative or qualitative) have been double-checked, participant identification (ID) codes need to be assigned, so that the data can be referred to again later if necessary for checking accuracy after the data have been inputted into SPSS or at some other later stages in the research.

The second stage is the *data coding phase*. The aim of data coding is to classify or group the data sets in order to make sense of them, thereby reducing the complexity of the data set. Coding allows us to quantify and represent the area under investigation using numbers. To achieve validity in the data coding, we need to code the data in a systematic and principled way.

Coding quantitative data depends on the nature of scales used to measure the variables. There are three basic types of quantitative data we deal with in our research, *nominal data, ordinal data* and *interval data* (Dörnyei 2007). The distinctions between these are important when selecting appropriate statistical techniques with which to analyse the data. *Nominal data* (also referred to as categorical data) are used for classification and group comparison purposes. We may, for example, ask participants to report whether they are native or non-native speakers of English. Here, for statistical analysis (e.g., frequency counts or percentages), we can code this data by assigning 1 to native speakers of English and 2 to non-native speakers of English. Nominal data do not have a mathematical property. For example, we cannot say that people assigned 2 have higher scores than people with 1. *Ordinal data* (meaning 'ordering' the data) are known as rank-ordered data. Examples of this include academic grades, Likert-scale data, rank of class achievement and ranking on personality or psychological traits. For example, we can code academic grades as follows: A (coded 5), B (coded 4), C (coded 3), D (coded 2) and F (coded 1). Ordinal data can tell us that an individual is greater or less than others in a characteristic or aspect being measured, but they do not tell us how much greater or lesser in terms of equal intervals. For example, in an agreement scale ranging from 1 (strongly disagree) to 5 (strongly agree), we can see that one is greater or less than another in terms of level of agreement, but we cannot say that the distance between the scores of 4 (agree) and 5 (strongly agree) is the same as the distance between the scores of 1 (strongly disagree) and 2 (disagree). Whether ordinal data can be seen as interval data (as discussed next) has been an ongoing debate among statisticians and quantitative researchers. *Interval data* imply that different values have equal distance between them in regard to the characteristic being measured. Examples of interval data include language test scores, a number of years and age. Interval data are suitable for inferential statistics (discussed below) because they have continuous values.

Coding qualitative data such as think-aloud, written, oral or interview data for quantitative data analysis is not as straightforward as coding quantitative data and can be more time-consuming than coding quantitative data. The approach to coding qualitative data is different from that in other qualitative research (see Holliday, this volume), as here we are focusing on quantification of the qualitative data. To achieve this, researchers need coding systems to help them quantify the variables of interest. Much of this process is subjective in the sense that each coder/rater may interpret the meaning or content in the qualitative data differently. Hence, we need to be mindful of coding consistency for each individual coder/rater (intracoder/rater reliability) and between two or more coders/raters (intercoder/rater reliability; see Mackey and Gass 2005). Data coding training and moderation of coding need to be incorporated carefully into this kind of coding. There are some inter-coder reliability estimates that can be used such as: (1) simple percentage agreement (the ratio of all coding agreement over the total number of coding made by two or more coders), and (2) Cohen's Kappa (a statistic indicating the average rate of agreements for an entire set of data, taking into account both agreement and disagreement between coders).

The third phase is the *data entry stage*. Once the data have been coded and numerical values have been assigned, the data can be keyed into a statistical software program such as SPSS. It should be noted that quantitative data files can also be imported from Excel to SPSS. Issues relevant to data entry include naming data files, defining variables for data recording and entering data into a designated file. Data entry can be very time-consuming and labour-intensive, particularly when there are a large number of participants with a large number of variables and instruments per participant. Having someone take turns in doing this can ease this demand and increase accuracy in the data entry (Dörnyei 2007). While doing this task, we may need to deal with issues of missing data as well as potential outliers (e.g., extreme cases which can distort statistical results). It is in this phase that we can get to understand the nature of the quantitative data.

The fourth phase is the *data screening and cleaning stage*. This phase concerns data entry accuracy and a decision-making process of how to deal with missing data and incorrect data entry. One strategy to deal with this is to compute a minimum and maximum value of each variable and frequencies of occurrences. If, for example, the maximum value of an item is 5, but SPSS reports 55 as a maximum value, it means that there is a data entry error for this item. We then need to check where the mistake has occurred in the data file and correct it.

Another strategy to perform data screening is through the use of diagrams such as histograms or charts. Through a visual inspection of the diagrams looking for admissible values, we can observe impossible values in the data set. Data screening allows us to identify and correct data entry problems as well as cleaning extreme cases (or outliers) in our data set (see Mackey and Gass 2005, pp. 257–258 for further discussion of outliers).

The fifth phase is the *reliability analysis stage*. Quantitative researchers need to make sure that their data are derived from reliable instruments/measures. Reliability is a necessary, yet insufficient condition for validity because a study cannot be valid if its instrument is not reliable. The reliability of an instrument is related to its consistency in capturing the focus of the investigation across points in time and to discriminate well among participants who posses different levels in terms of the focus of the research (e.g., writing ability, motivation levels). Research participants should respond similarly to the same question or item under the same condition at different times. The validity of an instrument refers to the fact that the instrument actually measures what it claims to measure (see Gass this volume). To achieve this, items or questions in the instrument need to be representative, inclusive and comprehensive of the aspects of research under investigation.

In quantitative research, reliability of the data is often determined by reliability coefficients or internal consistency. In language test/assessment data, researchers usually report KR-20 (Kuder-Richardson 20) as a reliability estimate (Brown 1996). In rating-scale or Likert-scale questionnaires, researchers report a Cronbach Alpha coefficient (Dörnyei 2007). Generally speaking, a reliability estimate ranges from 0 (0 per cent reliable) to 1 (100 per cent reliable). A reliability coefficient of 0.90 onwards is desirable, although a coefficient of 1 is rare. In some contexts, a reliability coefficient of 0.70 can be acceptable for research (Dörnyei 2007).

The sixth phase is the *data reduction stage*. It is often the case that we have a large number of variables in the same data file for analysis (e.g., test score variables, strategy use items, motivation items). Without reducing the number of variables, we will experience difficulty in managing and analysing the data. If we do a correlational analysis (discussed in the Sample study), there can be hundreds of correlation coefficients to interpret, report and discuss. Hence, we need some theoretical rationale to help us reduce the number of variables for quantitative data analysis to answer our research questions. Many psychological and cognitive constructs, such as language proficiency, metacognition, motivation and anxiety, can be inferred through observations of various behaviours or thoughts. Hence, we use multiple items to assess one construct. For example, we may be able to understand metacognitive strategy use by devising questionnaire items measuring planning, monitoring and evaluating strategy use. Within each of these subscales, there are a number of items which can be combined to form a single score (or a *composite*). This is to ensure that the construct of interest is not under-represented by our measurements. By aggregating items, we gain richer information about the construct under examination.

There are different statistical techniques that can minimize the chance of aggregating irrelevant or problematic items with reliable ones. First, *correlation coefficients* (discussed below) can inform us as to whether the items measure the same construct. Here, we should expect a strong correlation among them. Secondly, reliability analysis in SPSS can help us decide whether some items are suitable for inclusion. In *Cronbach alpha analysis*, SPSS allows us to check whether the reliability of each subscale will increase or decrease if we exclude a particular item in the subscale. This information can help us decide whether we should include a particular item to form a composite. Thirdly, we can employ *exploratory factor analysis* to help us reduce the number of items for inferential statistics. This statistical method allows us to eliminate items which poorly or redundantly measure the behaviours of interest (see Diekhoff 1992 for procedures for carrying out a factor analysis, Woodrow this volume for a discussion of exploratory factor analysis).

Basics of Statistical Concepts

Much of what we do in quantitative data analysis involves *statistics* because we cannot always have all the information we need from the entire population of interest. If the data are from all members of the population, we deal with *parameters*. However, in most circumstances such as in a classroom context, we only have access to a sample of the target population. In order to estimate the parameters of the population from the sample, we use statistics. Sometimes in our research, we only need basic statistics such as frequency counts, percentages or means (average scores) to answer our research questions. Here we most likely deal with *descriptive statistics* (i.e., statistics for describing, summarizing and explaining the distribution of a data set). At other times we need to go through detailed statistical procedures to answer our research questions because of the complex nature of the issue we are researching and the nature of the research. Here, we work with *inferential statistics* (i.e., statistics for making inferences about population parameters).

Descriptive Statistics

An average score is an example of the use of a descriptive statistic to describe a data set. Instead of using raw test data to show how students performed in an exit test, we can show an average score which shows in general how well all the students did in the test. Descriptive statistics can be divided into the measures of frequency, central tendency and dispersion.

Measures of frequency are mostly used with nominal data. Frequencies can be represented using a histogram, a pie chart or a bar chart. Frequencies can also be represented in a table with an accumulated percentage. *Measures of central tendency* provide an overall picture of our data. The three common measures of central tendency are the mean, the median and the mode. The *mean* is the most common indicator of central tendency. It can be calculated by summing up all scores of a variable in the data set and dividing the sum by the number of scores. For example, the mean of the data set 1, 2, 3, 4, 5 is 3 (i.e., 15 ÷ 5). The *median* is the value that divides the data set exactly in the middle. In the data set for the above mean, the median is also 3. The median can be useful as a descriptor if the mean is distorted by an extreme case or outlier. In 6, 7, 8, 9, 11, 76, the mean is 19.5 while the median is 8.5. The *mode* is the value that occurs most frequently in the data set. In 12, 13, 14, 14, 14, 16, 18, the mode is 14. *Measures of dispersion* describe *variability* of the numeral data away from the central tendency. Measures of central tendency do not however necessarily tell the entire story of the data. For example, a mean of 24.66 could be achieved in a *homogenous* data set such as 24, 24, 24, 25, 25, 26 or by a *heterogeneous* data set such as 2, 7, 15, 28, 46, 50. The mean also depends on the sample size and hence we cannot always compare the means of two different learner groups due to extreme different sample sizes. Hence, we need other measures of descriptive statistics called measures of dispersion. The *standard deviation* is a method to describe the variability of the data. The standard deviation is the average point from the mean which indicates on average how much the individual scores spread around the mean.

Inferential Statistics

Inferential statistics are used to help us look beyond raw data and descriptive statistics. They help us make inferences about population parameters (e.g., a relationship between two variables or group differences in a variable of interest). To perform inferential statistics, however, we need to understand some prerequisites such as normal distribution, probability and parametric and non-parametric tests (see Brown 1991, 1992 for an accessible discussion of these terms).

Normal distribution: The normal distribution of a data set is related to the spread of the data around the mean. This is related to the standard deviation discussed above. The normal distribution has a bell-shaped figure. In perfect normal distribution, the mean, median and mode have equal values. A variable affecting normal distribution includes a sample size and range of scores. Hatch and Lazaraton (1991) suggest a minimum of 30 participants for quantitative data analysis as the size may yield a distribution of a range of scores. However, the more seems to be the better as this leads to stability of the data distribution. A range of scores is also important. This is perhaps why interval data are desirable for statistical analysis. A dichotomous variable such as yes (coded 1) or no answer (coded 2) cannot lead to a normal distribution regardless of a large sample size. Some ordinal scores which appear continuous with a large sample size may have a normal distribution.

SPSS can produce a histogram flagging a normal distribution curve. Perfect distribution is however scarce in applied linguistics data, so we need some criteria to help us determine if the distribution is considered acceptably normally distributed. There are two statistical measures which SPSS can produce to help us determine whether the data are normally distributed. The first is the *skewness statistic*, which tells us the extent to which a score distribution deviates from perfect symmetry (i.e., mode = median = mean). A negative skewed value suggests that the distribution is skewed toward the left (i.e., mode > median > mean) while a positive value suggests that the distribution is skewed to the right (i.e., mode < median < mean). The *kurtosis statistic* is related to the peaked-ness of a distribution (e.g., flat or sharp). A kurtosis value of 0 suggests that the dataset is normally distributed. A negative kurtosis statistic suggests that the distribution tends to be flat, whereas a positive kurtosis statistic suggests that the distribution is peaked. Conservatively, values of skewness and kurtosis statistics within *plus and minus 1* suggest that the data set is normally distributed (see Carr 2008 for an accessible discussion of this through the use of Microsoft Excel).

Probability: Probability is related to the degree to which the statistical finding occurs by chance (i.e., random variation). This is related to *statistical validity*, which asks whether or not the statistical finding is true or incidental (i.e., found by chance). The p-value (p = probability) is the likelihood that we will be wrong in the statistical inferences that we make from the data. $p < 0.05$ (i.e., there are 5 in 100 chances of being wrong) is commonly used in applied linguistics research.

Parametric or non-parametric tests: There are two types of inferential statistics. These are parametric and non-parametric. The distinction between the two is the set of statistical assumptions (i.e., preconditions essential for accurate applications of a statistical test) that must be met before the statistical analysis is applied. These assumptions are not optional and if they are not met, there is a heightened risk of making a false inference. The main assumptions for parametric tests are (1) normal distribution, (2) interval or continuous data and (3) independence of data scores across measures. A non-parametric test (or distribution-free test) is suitable for frequency data (as discussed earlier) or when a normal distribution assumption cannot be met. A non-parametric test can analyse discrete variables, frequencies or ranked-order data. Although parametric tests are more preferable in quantitative research, non-parametric tests are important for applied linguistics research because some data are not always strongly interval or continuous. Furthermore, in some cases where the nature of the data is categorical or dichotomous (e.g., pass or fail scores), we cannot employ parametric tests because we would violate the normal distribution assumption. For example, we may want to see if gender, with male learners (coded 1) and female learners (coded 0), is relevant to passing (coded 1) or failing (coded 0) an English test. With this kind of data, there can be a true connection between two different dichotomous variables.

A Sample Study

I have chosen Phakiti (2003) as an example of quantitative data analysis. This study investigated the nature of cognitive and metacognitive strategy use and its relationship to English as a foreign language (EFL) reading test performance. Three hundred and eighty-four Thai university students participated in the study. The study employed an 85-item, multiple-choice reading test to assess the students' English reading achievement in a course in which they were enrolled and a 35-item, 5-point Likert-scale strategy use questionnaire to measure their cognitive and metacognitive strategy use (e.g., 0 = never to 5 = always). The participants first took a 3-hour reading test followed by the questionnaire. For the purpose of data matching, the questionnaire was put together with the test answer sheet. The first part of the questionnaire asked the participants to provide demographic information such as gender, age and number of years learning English. The second part asked them to report on their degree of strategy use during the test completion.

Data preparation: In order to key the test score data and strategy use data into SPSS, I assigned each participant an ID code, so that I could recheck the data at later stages. This helped to keep the data set in order. With regard to the questionnaire data, I coded them according to different types of data as discussed above. For example, for the demographic data, I coded males as 1 and females as 2. All this data were then keyed into SPSS. Here I had a colleague take turns in keying in the data as I had a large set of data to enter. On average it took about two and a half minutes to key one questionnaire into SPSS. I double-checked for accuracy in the data entry at the end by scanning the data file, as well as randomly checking the data against the actual questionnaires.

After I completed the data entry, I used descriptive statistics to identify the mean, median, mode, maximum, minimum and skewness and kurtosis statistics of the reading test and questionnaire data. This helped me to see if there were missing data or any outliers in the data. I also checked whether the data were normally distributed. Because it was important to see if the data in the reading test and questionnaire were reliable, I performed a reliability analysis. The reliability estimate of the overall test (like KR-20) was 0.88. The Cronbach alpha coefficients (as discussed earlier) for the cognitive strategy and metacognitive strategy variables were 0.75 and 0.85, respectively.

Data analysis and results: In this study, I asked three research questions. However, for the purpose of this chapter, only research question 2 will be discussed. This research question was 'what is the relationship of cognitive and metacognitive strategies to EFL reading comprehension test performance?' Here I will only focus on the relationship between cognitive strategy use and the reading comprehension performance. I employed the Pearson Product Moment correlation, which is a parametric test. A fundamental principle for the Pearson Product Moment correlation test is an expression of a correlation on a scale from 0 to 1. If two variables are strongly correlated, this means that an increase or decrease in one variable will be accompanied by an increase or decrease in the other variable. If two variables are uncorrelated (i.e., 0), there is no systematic relationship between them. A positive (+) correlation scale suggests a positive association between two variables (i.e., the two variables are associated and move in the same direction in a systematic way). A negative (–) correlation scale suggests a negative relationship (i.e., the two variables are associated and move systematically in opposite directions). In this study, a correlation coefficient was used to test whether a relationship between cognitive strategy use and the reading test performance was equal to 0 (which means that there was no relationship). If it was not equal to 0, I then asked how strong the relationship was. I set a p-value to be less than 0.05.

To achieve this correlational analysis, I needed to check for the data distribution (e.g., by examining descriptive statistics and graphical displays because there could be two modes in the data distribution affecting the r coefficient). I used a *scatterplot* (which matched the score of one variable with the score of the other variable for all participants in a plot) to check whether the two variables (i.e., cognitive strategy use and test performance) could be related. Based on the examination of the scatterplots, I observed that the relationships were linear and positive. Based on the Pearson correlations, I found a positive relationship between cognitive strategies and the test performance. The correlation coefficient between cognitive strategy use and the test performance was 0.39. In reporting a correlation, we do not usually put a plus sign (+) in front of the positive correlation, but we put a minus sign (–) if it is a negative correlation. As discussed above, a positive or negative sign does not suggest the strength of the correlation. In Pearson correlations, we multiply the value of r with itself to interpret the strength of the relationship between two variables. r^2 (i.e., r × r) is known as shared variance or co-variance in statistics. This indicates the degree of an overlap between the sets of observations (i.e., strength of the relationship).

The values of r^2 here suggest how much the two variables overlapped in percentage. In this study, the shared variance (r^2) between cognitive strategy use and the reading comprehension performance was 0.15 (0.39×0.39) or 15 per cent shared variance. In this study, I argued that this degree was reasonable because there were other factors influencing language test performance at the same time, for example, communicative language ability, test-taker characteristics, test-method facets and random error as outlined by Bachman and Palmer (1996). I also argued that although this correlation coefficient appeared to be weak, it was important in the context of the study because if cognitive use could contribute to 15 per cent of the language test performance, we knew that people who successfully used this strategy would be at an advantage. In summary, Pearson's correlation allowed me to examine the relationship between the two variables by analysing quantitative data. It helped me evaluate how much variance they shared and whether the detected relationship was meaningful and reasonable.

Resources for Further Reading

Bachman, L. (2004), *Statistical Analyses for Language Assessment*. Cambridge: Cambridge University Press.
  This book presents both conceptual and statistical procedures useful for general applied linguistics research. It discusses the basics of quantitative data analyses and kinds of statistical tests.
Dörnyei, Z. (2007), *Research Methods in Applied Linguistics: Quantitative, Qualitative, and Mixed Methodologies*. Oxford: Oxford University Press.
  This book treats quantitative research comprehensively from the design stage through to the analysis and reporting stages. Chapter 9 provides a thorough overview of quantitative data analysis.
Hatch, E. and Lazaraton, A. (1991), *The Research Manual: Design and Statistics for Applied Linguistics*. Rowley, MA: Newbury House.
  This book covers a large number of conceptual and statistical topics that are essential for good quantitative research. It also provides a number of examples of studies in the literature as part of the explanations and applications.
Lomax, R. G. (2007), *An Introduction to Statistical Concepts (2nd edn)*. Mahwah, NJ: Lawrence Erlbaum Associates.
  This book is a comprehensive, reader-friendly, introduction to statistics. The prerequisites to inferential statistics as well as statistical tests are discussed. It relates statistical analyses with SPSS and has a data CD for practice.
Mackey, A. and Gass, S (2005), *Second Language Research*. Mahwah, NJ: Lawrence Erlbaum Associates.
  This book provides an accessible account of the procedures of quantitative data analysis. Chapter 9 provide a discussion of issues involved in quantitative data analysis and procedures for carrying out statistical analysis.
Urdan, T. C. (2005), *Statistics in Plain English* (2nd edn). Mahwah, NJ: Lawrence Erlbaum Associates.

This book discussed many conceptual and methodological concepts for social science research using accessible language. Quantitative data analysis considerations are discussed with examples. This book includes a CD-ROM with sample data files for analysis.

Online Resources

The following websites discuss the statistical concepts necessary for quantitative data analysis introduced in this chapter. Basic assumptions of most statistical methods for research are explained.

Education Commission of the States: (http://www.ecs.org/html/educationIssues/ Research/primer/understandingtutorial.asp , accessed 11 August 2009);

Robertniles.com: (http://www.robertniles.com/stats/, accessed 11 August 2009);

StatSoft: (http://www.statsoft.com/textbook/stathome.html, accessed 11 August 2009)

References

Bachman, L. F. and Palmer, A. S. (1996), *Language Testing in Practice*. Oxford: Oxford University Press.

Brown, J. D. (1991), 'Statistics as a foreign language – Part1: What to look for in reading statistical language studies'. *TESOL Quarterly*, 25, 569–586.

— (1992), 'Statistics as a foreign language – Part2: More things to consider in reading statistical language studies'. *TESOL Quarterly*, 26, 629–664.

— (1996), *Testing in Language Programs*. Upper Saddle River, NJ: Prentice Hall.

Carr, N. (2008), 'Using Microsoft Excel to calculate descriptive statistics and create graphs'. *Language Assessment Quarterly*, 5, 43–62.

Diekhoff, G. (1992), *Statistics for the Social and Behavioral Sciences: Univariate, Bivariate, Multivariate*. Dubuque, IN: Wm. C. Brown Publishers.

Dörnyei, Z. (2007), *Research Methods in Applied Linguistics: Quantitative, Qualitative, and Mixed Methodologies*. Oxford: Oxford University Press.

Gass, S. M. and Mackey, A. (2007), *Data Elicitation for Second and Foreign Language Research*. Mahwah, NJ: Lawrence Erlbaum Associates.

Hatch, E. and Lazaraton, A. (1991), *The Research Manual: Design and Statistics for Applied Linguistics*. Boston, MA: Heinle and Heinle.

Lazaraton, A. (2005), 'Quantitative research methods', in E. Hinkel (ed.), *Handbook of Research in Second Language Teaching and Learning*. Mahwah, NJ: Lawrence Erlbaum Associates, pp. 209–224.

Mackey, A. and Gass, S (2005), *Second Language Research*. Mahwah, NJ: Lawrence Erlbaum Associates.

Phakiti, A. (2003), 'A closer look at the relationship of cognitive and metacognitive strategy use to EFL reading achievement test performance'. *Language Testing*, 20, 26–56.

5 Ethnographies

Sue Starfield

Chapter Overview

Why adopt an ethnographic approach to research in applied linguistics? The broad research questions you have in mind as well as your understanding of language, learning and communication shape your choice of methodology. If you see writing, reading, speaking and listening and language learning as primarily shaped by the social contexts in which they occur and you are interested in uncovering the meanings that participants in these processes bring to the communicative events in which they engage, then ethnography may be an appropriate methodology for your research project. As ethnography privileges the direct observation of human behaviour within particular 'cultures' and settings and seeks to understand a social reality from the perspectives of those involved in the observed interactions, it also has implications for the role of the researcher which will be discussed further below. If, moreover, you see your role as researcher as encouraging social change in the community within which you are carrying out your research, you may be more interested in what is known as *critical* ethnography.

Ethnographic work, as Hesse-Biber and Leavy (2006) point out, is labour-intensive and requires time, energy and resources. However, the rewards of prolonged engagement within a specific community and the richness of data generated via 'fieldwork' make it a methodology worthy of serious consideration by those seeking to engage in qualitative research. According to Harklau (2005), ethnography is currently one of the major approaches to research on second language learning and teaching. Moreover, ethnography is seen as distinct from other qualitative approaches; for example, one of the leading journals in the field, *TESOL Quarterly*, now provides separate sets of substantial guidelines to authors on conversation analysis; case studies and (critical) – their parentheses – ethnography (see Resources for Further Reading).

In this chapter, I consider the different strands or traditions and methodological assumptions that inform contemporary ethnographic approaches to applied linguistics research, including critical ethnography, and discuss various methods that are typically used. This leads to a discussion of ethical issues particularly pertinent to ethnographic research. As the writing of ethnographic texts and the key role of the researcher have been topics of much discussion over the last two decades, I also provide explicit consideration of these two areas. The chapter concludes with an account of an ethnographic study of academic writing that I carried out at a South African university.

Underlying Assumptions and Methodology

Ethnography's home is within qualitative research as 'qualitative researchers study things in their natural settings, attempting to make sense of, or interpret, phenomena in terms of the meanings people bring to them' (Denzin and Lincoln 2005, p. 3). However, as Watson-Gegeo (1988) pointed out 20 years ago, ethnography is not synonymous with qualitative research. Impressionistic accounts, fixed category observations, brief engagement or a study based on a few in-depth, semi-structured interviews should neither be considered ethnography nor ethnographic[1] (Lazaraton 2003).

According to Hammersley (1990, pp. 2–3), the key features of a broadly defined ethnographic method include studying people's behaviour in everyday rather than experimental contexts; gathering data from a range of sources chiefly by 'observation and/or relatively informal conversation' and collecting data that are not based on pre-set categories or explicit hypotheses but that arise out of a general interest in an issue or problem. Ethnographic research is typically small in scale and focused on a single setting or group. Prolonged engagement by the researcher in the research setting is also a defining feature of ethnography.

Whereas positivist researchers who use questionnaires and surveys assume that they already know what is important, participant observation, in contrast, makes no such assumptions. Researchers are encouraged to immerse themselves in the everyday activities of the group of people whose meaning-making (also known as 'emic' or insider perspectives) practices they are attempting to understand. Rather than testing preformed ideas or theories (as in deductive research), ideas are developed inductively from the observations. This is not to suggest that ethnography is atheoretical; rather it is seen as hypothesis generating, with theory being *emergent*,[2] leading to the development of theorization and possible generalization (also called 'etic' or outsider perspectives) as the research progresses. Participant observation therefore allows for the possibility of 'surprise' – that is the emergence of knowledge that is not predetermined by the original research position or paradigm (Willis 1980). For example, through Grimshaw's (2007) extended observation of Chinese students in a Chinese university setting, he was able to develop a set of arguments that draw on postcolonial theory to challenge commonly-held views in much Western literature of 'the Chinese learner' as passive, uncritical and lacking in autonomy.

While these methods can be identified as 'core' characteristics of ethnographic approaches, the meanings attached to the status of the data collected vary according to different epistemologies and theoretical frameworks adopted by the researchers. It is therefore important that those embarking on ethnographic research have an understanding of the differing histories of ethnography that inform current approaches. In the section that follows I provide an outline of this history and its implications as I understand them.

The Origins of Ethnography

Ethnography as a research methodology has its roots in the cultural and linguistic anthropology of the early twentieth century and certain branches of sociology and has, more recently, been adopted by educational researchers concerned about school failure of certain groups (Lazaraton 2003; Harklau 2005). While western anthropology's object of study was distant, 'foreign' cultures, the sociologists who practised ethnography in the West from the early twentieth century on, adapted anthropology's approach to understanding culture 'from the inside' to intensive observations of everyday urban environments, often studying 'subcultures' in economically and socially disadvantaged communities. From the 1960s, under the influence of Hymes' call for an ethnography of communication (Hymes 1972; Saville-Troike 1982) and the development of the broad field of sociolinguistics, ethnographic approaches have been embraced by some in the newer field of applied linguistics. Work that draws on the ethnography of communication has looked at teacher-learner classroom interactions and differences between home and school literacies (e.g., Cazden et al. 1972; Heath 1983) and, more recently, Duff (2002).

The use of ethnographic approaches has been encouraged by what has been called the 'social turn' in language study which has led to the desire to develop in-depth understandings of language learning and teaching events in the specific (and frequently unequal) social contexts within which they are taking place. The combination of long-term observation and the collection of diverse forms of data provide understandings of participants' perspectives and mean-ing-making practices within the complex sociocultural worlds they inhabit that more traditional methodologies may not have succeeded in capturing.

Applied linguists typically use ethnographic approaches to study language practices within communities and institutions that are familiar to the researcher rather than exotic and strange as in traditional ethnography. Applied linguistics is almost by definition interdisciplinary and a number of applied linguists are now working collaboratively with colleagues in fields such as health, the work-place, organizations, the justice system and education broadly defined, carry-ing out ethnographic work on the communication practices at these sites (see, for example, Sarangi and Roberts 1999). While acknowledging the diversity of perspectives and traditions that inform ethnography as well as the variety of sites that applied linguists may be asked to investigate, Rampton (2007) and colleagues in the UK have developed what they call 'Linguistic Ethnography' – an interdisciplinary approach influenced by *inter alia* critical discourse analysis; the new literacy studies and interactional sociolinguistics (see *Linguistic Ethnography Forum* in Further Reading and Resources below).

While some stress the need for those embarking on ethnographic research to locate themselves within a 'tradition' (Harklau 2005; *TESOL Quarterly Guidelines* in Further Reading and Resources Below), others argue that the 'traditions' or 'perspectives' have always been characterized by their 'own cultural diversity' (Atkinson et al. 2001, p. 3) and encourage researchers to be aware of and open to this richness. Whatever alignments and identifications are ultimately chosen, Ramanathan and Atkinson's (1999, p. 48) claim in their study of ethnographic approaches and methods in L2 writing research that few ethnographically ori-ented L2 writing studies 'make their theoretical bases explicit' should be at the forefront of the researcher's thinking and writing (see also Peirce 1995).[3]

The Impact of Postmodernism – The Researcher's Role and Authority

Postmodernism and post-structuralism (see Clifford and Marcus 1986; Harklau 2005), sometimes called the 'linguistic' or 'textual' turn in ethnography, have had a profound effect on the production of ethnographic texts, particularly with regard to undermining 'realist' accounts and focusing on the subjectivity of the ethnographer as the writer/producer of an ethnographic text (see van Maanen 1988). By realist accounts, I am referring to the belief that ethnography can provide 'holistic, richly detailed descriptions' (Watson-Gegeo 1988, p. 588) that 'present' an observed 'reality' or 'culture'. Watson-Gegeo's very useful account of ethnography in ESL does not problematize the role of the researcher in the construction of the ethnographic account – a central preoccupation of post-structural approaches in which issues of identity, subjectivity and the production of multivoiced accounts come to the fore.

The original meaning of the term 'ethnography' is 'writing culture', highlighting the significance of both the textual nature of the ethnographic account and its construction by a researcher who is also a writer. The applied linguistics researcher who adopts an ethnographic approach needs to be aware that an extensive literature has discussed both representation and authority in ethnographic writing (see Van Maanen 1988). As Clifford (1986, p. 23) argued in his introduction to *Writing Cultures*: 'the grounds from which persons and groups securely represent each other' have been dislodged. This has led to what has been called the 'reflexive turn' in ethnographic writing. Reflexivity refers to the researcher/writer's ability to reflect on their own positioning and subjectivity in the research and provide an explicit, situated account of their own role in the project and its influences over the findings. Reflexivity is a counter to the positivist construct of the dispassionate, objective researcher who is absent from the account produced (see Foley 2002). Cameron et al. (1992) stress that textual representation is power as the writer/researcher is a member of a powerful social group who selects and mediates the talk and identities of the research participants in the act of writing.

The *TESOL Quarterly Qualitative Research: (Critical) Ethnography Guidelines* encourage writers of ethnographic studies to 'develop a mode of textual representation that suits your research experience, objectives, beliefs about the nature of ethnographic knowledge, and preferences' (see Resources for Further Reading). I would urge readers who have a desire to explore alternative forms of representation to examine recent issues of *TESOL Quarterly* and other relevant journals to assess for themselves the extent to which practice is following espoused theory in this instance. This said, Richardson's (2000) criteria for evaluating ethnographic research (see Resources for Further Reading) clearly indicate that it is not a case of 'anything goes'.

Critical Ethnography

When Tara Goldstein (1997) sought to understand the meanings that particular language practices had for immigrant workers in a Canadian factory and how these related to their experiences of living in an ethnically stratified society, she chose a research approach that was not only ethnographic in the traditional sense of carrying out observation and describing the meanings language usage had for the workers but that would also take into account the influence of class, gender and power relations in a post-industrial capitalist society, both at work and outside the workplace. Her critical ethnography helps us understand why it is that many immigrant workers in Canada do not take up the English language courses on offer.

Critical ethnographic researchers therefore consider the social location of the group they are studying through 'examining their access to economic, political and cultural resources' (Carspecken 1996, p. 204) and consciously employ macro-perspectives such as sociological theory to examine 'micro' ethnographic data gathered by the researcher. In turn, the macro-theories may be challenged, refined and altered. For example, the detailed microethnographic analyses of classroom discourse carried out by Bloome et al. (2005) locate classroom language and literacy events within broader social and historical contexts. As in Goldstein's study, critical ethnographic research accounts acknowledge the complex relationships between social structures and human agency (Anderson 1989). For Brodkey (1987, p. 67) 'the goal of critical ethnography is always the same: to help create the possibility of transforming such institutions as schools.'

Motha's (2006) year-long critical feminist ethnography embodies these meanings of the term 'critical' in 'critical ethnography' and is located within a post-structural theoretical framework that draws on critiques of multiculturalism, Whiteness studies, identity theory and the intersection of native speaker status, race and colonialism. She studied the racial meanings that student and teacher identities and language acquire in a North American school context. Race, whiteness and the status of native speaker teachers of English in linguistically and racially diverse classrooms are sensitive and complex issues that have been underexplored in applied linguistics. Her data were collected in a range of contexts and included classroom observation, interviews and regular 'afternoon teas' with the four novice teachers who participated in her research. She provided the teachers with drafts of all her writing, discussed her interpretations and representations of events with them and has also co-presented at conferences with them. Her work moves through the description of classroom interactions to interpretation and analysis to suggest implications both for pedagogies that seek to confront racism in the ESOL classroom and for the TESOL profession more broadly.

Validity/Trustworthiness in Ethnographic Research

In *Critical Ethnography in Educational Research*, Carspecken (1996, pp. 87–89) lists six techniques to support validity claims if qualitative researchers are to produce reports in which the findings can be considered sufficiently trustworthy for colleagues to rely on them in their own research. These are: using multiple recordings devices and multiple observers, using a flexible observations schedule, practising prolonged engagement, using a vocabulary in the fieldnotes that is not overly coloured by the writer's interpretations, using peer-debriefing and using member checking. Most of these techniques are self-explanatory I believe and should be part of the methods of those engaging in ethnographic research, however critical. Member checking refers to sharing your fieldnotes and interpretations with the people one is studying. In what they called 'collaborative ethnography', Barton and Hamilton (1998) shared their interview transcripts and thematic analyses of participants' literacy practices with them, partly to check the validity of their own analyses. To the extent, however, that participants' involvement in the research process altered their self-understandings and empowered them to explore new literacy practices, the study can be seen to have achieved 'catalytic validity' (Lather 1991): a type of validity that many critical researchers would argue is an important outcome of the research process.

It could however be argued (and other chapters in this volume do so) that validity is a concern inasmuch as researchers still seek to justify their work in relation to the positivist paradigm. Rather than use the term 'validity', ethnographic research as with much qualitative research, prefers to talk of 'truswothiness'. Multiple methods of data collection are seen to contribute to the trustworthiness of the research (Maykut and Morehouse 1994). Triangulation or the collation of data from a range of sources and/or gathered through a range of research methods such as participant observation, informal and formal interviewing and document collection strengthens the validity (or credibility) of the analyses and interpretations (see Watson-Gegeo 1988). Triangulation is further used to ascertain participant perspectives on their own meaning-making practices. These emic perspectives also contribute to the trustworthiness of the findings.

Clifford Geertz (1975) saw ethnography as being 'thick description': description that goes beyond simple description to include interpretation. Thick description can also be seen as providing greater trustworthiness and may also allow for 'transferability' of findings to different contexts. At the same time, generalizability as conceived of in quantitative research is not necessarily the aim of ethnographic research but rather to 'understand deeply, through a thorough, systematic, iterative analysis' (Duff 2007, p. 983).

Techniques and Instruments Used in Ethnographic Research

Ethnographic research methods of data collection include the techniques of observation through fieldwork, with participant observation (observation that entails interaction with those being studied) being commonly used, the keeping of fieldnotes, formal and informal interviewing of informants/participants, typically using either audio- or videotaping and the collection of relevant documents available at the site or archivally. These multiple methods help the researcher provide the thick description considered essential for ethnographic research and enable triangulation. As indicated earlier, one of the distinguishing features of ethnographic research is that the researcher is the primary instrument of data collection. The awareness that the researcher gains through 'being present' in the setting brings a great richness of understanding. Goldstein (1997) writes that her role as an English teacher in the factory enhanced her access to the Production Departments as many of the workers were her students. This view would obviously run counter to views of the researcher as detached and objective. In the following section, I discuss participant observation and ethnographic interviewing in more detail as they can be seen to form the cornerstone of the ethnographic approach.

Participant Observation/Fieldwork in Ethnographic Research

Participant observation is carried out through prolonged engagement by the researcher in a setting or field, hence the use of the term 'fieldwork'. Fieldwork aims to provide a description and interpretive explanatory account of what people do in a particular setting and what meaning their interactions have for them. Goldstein (1997) for example observed bilingual workers' interactions on the production line, at the t-shirt printing machines, in the warehouse, in the offices, in language classes, at breaks and at lunch over a two-year period. Her observation included details of the language choices made by the workers in these different contexts. She would stand next to the production line and note down the communication patterns in use, building up an extensive set of field-notes in the different settings. Her fieldnotes were both audio-recorded and hand written, particularly on the noisy production lines. They also included sketches of where participants were standing at the time and a description of the activity being done.

These rich observational data in combination with data from 39 audio-recorded ethnographic interviews enabled her to generate broad hypotheses about language choices on the shopfloor which she was able to check with workers and employers. Goldstein's critical framework and commitment to transformation enabled her to understand why it was that many factory workers were resistant to English language classes when it would have seemed obvious that learning English would improve their life chances.

Ethnographic Interviews

While numerous approaches to research utilize interviewing, ethnographic interviews can be distinguished by their duration, frequency of contact and, with the infuence of post-structuralism and feminism, an awareness that the interview is itself a site of meaning construction and that the inteview 'produces' a text for interpretation (Heyl 2001). According to Heyl (2001, p. 370), the core components of ethnographic interviews are listening well and with respect; developing an ethical enagement with the participants at all stages; acquiring self-awareness of one's role in the co-construction of meaning; being aware of ways the ongoing relationship and broader social context affect participants, processes and outcomes; and acknowledging that 'dialogue is discovery' and that only partial knowledge is possible. More critical approaches recognize that many interview situations involve unequal power relations and are sites of identity negotiation. In multilingual contexts a decision may need to be made as to whether to use an interpreter. In applied linguistics research, language is not only the medium of communication but frequently the topic of study as well, requiring perhaps an even greater level of reflexivity on the part of the researcher.

Ethical Considerations

As Murphy and Dingwall (2001) point out, ethnographic researchers share the same minimal responsibility to protect participants from harm that all research with human participants requires with particular regard to anonymity, identification and informed consent that emergent research design may complexify. For example, it may not be possible to specify in advance who will be interviewed or what sorts of information or documentation will be sought as issues that emerge in the course of the research mean that fully informed consent was not possible at the outset (Fox et al. 2006).

While it should be evident that ethnographic research requires approval from a University ethics committee and that permission to conduct observation and interviews, particularly in classrooms, must be sought, Duff (2007, p. 977) points out that gaining permission may be difficult to obtain because of the 'perceived invasiveness' of such practices. Ironically, perhaps, newer technologies such as video recording may increase the perception of invasiveness in groups that may feel vulnerable. Furthermore, it is considered by many ethics committees that seeking informed consent from one's current students in order to carry out classroom-based inquiry is coercive (Duff 2007) as they are in what is termed a 'dependent' relationship with the researcher.

At all times, informed consent must be sought and most universities provide guidelines in this regard. Those new to the field should study the comprehensive and clear *TESOL Quarterly* Informed Consent Policy Statement and Release (http://www.tesol.org/s_tesol/sec_document.asp?CID=198&DID=1014, accessed 4 December 2007). Have you, for example, considered whether the participants in your study speak English well enough to understand the informed consent form? Would you consider making the form available in the participants' first language or perhaps using an interpreter?. If the participants are not literate in any language, could you obtain oral consent?

A Sample Study

In this section, I discuss a year-long ethnographic study of students' writing development within a disciplinary context that I carried out at a South African university in the final years of official apartheid. My attempts to better understand why it was that black students who spoke English as an additional language and who were learning to write in a course called Sociology One were much less successful than their white peers led me to adopt a critical ethnographic perspective. As the research evolved, I became more aware of how broader socio-economic and political inequalities shaped the possibilities available to students to negotiate successful identities for themselves.

In my professional academic life I was working in the field of student academic support and was concerned that generic academic writing skills were not helping the students sufficiently. I wanted to find out more about the lived experience of students learning to write within a specific discipline and knew that the Department of Sociology was concerned about the inequitable pass rates of black and white students.

As is common in ethnographic research, my initial question was broadly based. Drawing on Saville-Troike (1982, p. 2) it asked: 'What does a writer need to know to communicate appropriately within a particular discourse community and how does he or she learn?'. As the research progressed, several more focused questions emerged, again fairly typical of ethnographic research:

- What is the nature of the written genres which students in Sociology One are expected to produce?;
- How do students from apartheid schools learn and teachers teach these genres?;
- What are the processes whereby students are initiated into the new discourse community?;
- What are considered to be successful texts and what are the processes whereby students do or do not 'succeed'?

Eleven students participated in my year-long study. Nine of the students were African, three were women and two were white, one male and one female. They were all new to Sociology One. All of the African students were from socio-economically disadvantaged apartheid schooling backgrounds. There is more information on the students' backgrounds and the context of apartheid education in Starfield (1999).

To ensure trustworthiness, I used a combination of observation – along the full continuum from non-participant to participant – within as many teaching and learning contexts as possible, in-depth semi-structured interviews and document collection, including copies of students' written texts. I triangulated by checking my evolving understandings of their reality with the different participants as I built my thick description of the students' experiences of learning to write in Sociology One.

I collected data in multiple sites that included lecture halls, tutorials of different kinds, markers' meetings, weekly tutor briefings, one of the tutor's offices and corridor conversations. I took extensive fieldnotes.

In some respects I was like a student. I attended all four weekly lectures in a hall with several hundred students, and one weekly tutorial of about 30 students. I read the materials included in the *Course Reader* which enabled me to trace different student interpretations (or misinterpretations) of the readings and develop the concept of what I called (after Bourdieu) 'textual capital' (see Starfield 2002).

Each student took part in a semi-structured interview of about one and a half hours which included discussion of their essays and tests. Eight of the students took part in a second interview and some were interviewed a year later. In addition, I had numerous less formal conversations with the students in the course of the year. I collected copies of all eleven students' essays, tests and exams.

I conducted an in-depth semi-structured interview with all academic staff who taught on the first-year course of at least one hour. Some were later approached to review students' essays and exams that they had marked and to discuss criteria employed and feedback as part of the process of triangulation (Starfield 2002, 2004). I audio-taped and transcribed all interviews including the two markers' meetings that I observed.

I also collected relevant documents such as the student newspaper and political pamphlets distributed by the various student organizations on campus. I use some of this data in support of my analysis of the ways in which a student whom I called Ben negotiates his textual identity in his successful essay (Starfield 2004). I draw on arguments in favour of the anonymous marking of student essays to reduce perceived bias in the assessment of black students that appeared in the student newspaper.

I used critical discourse analysis (Fairclough 1992) combined with systemic functional linguistics (Halliday 1994) as my main analytic tool for textual analysis. I examined the linguistic and discursive resources students drew on as they wrote their assignments in order to create identities in written texts that were more or less successful. A critical discourse analysis of the *Student Handbook* enabled me to see how the department positioned and constructed students from disadvantaged backgrounds vis-à-vis students from 'mainstream' backgrounds. Thematic analysis of interview data provided insights into student perceptions of their experiences of success and failure which complemented the textual data. I was able to argue that successful texts were the outcome of complex identity negotiations (see Ivanič 1998) and that key academic genres were not 'fixed' or easily identifiable.

Data collected at one of the markers' meeting and analysed using the work of Bourdieu (1982) helped me develop a critique of the concept of discourse community as used in English for Academic Purposes – challenging my initial conceptualizations. I came to view academic discourse communities as being themselves sites of power and contestation; a view not reflected in much of the literature on the teaching of writing (Starfield 2001). While I had titled my project 'Making and sharing meaning', by the end of my year in Sociology One I was to conclude that the effects of apartheid were such that meaning could not be shared equally by all.

Future Developments in Ethnographic Research

It is likely that the attention currently being paid to multimodal literacies and the ever increasing impact of technology in schools, workplaces and other sites of communication will give rise to applied linguistic ethnographic studies of the multimodal communicative practices of their inhabitants (see, for example, Scollon et al. 1999). Relatedly, the development of virtual communities facilitated by technology and the impact of globalization have the potential to produce ethnographic studies that call into question the notion of community as based in a single setting (see Slembrouck 2005).

Autoethnography – a blend of autobiography and ethnography – has become a popular approach in a number of fields including education (see Foley 2002). Will such studies begin to emerge in applied linguistics or will they struggle to be published? We may begin to see more attempts at different reporting formats (see Lee and Simon-Maeda 2006). Goldstein's (2003) ethnographic playwriting is a rare example of such an attempt. *Hong Kong, Canada*, a play that is included in an appendix to her book length critical ethnography of a multilingual Toronto high school, invites readers to perform/read the play which creatively raises many of the issues examined in the research itself.

Of course, challenging the dominant genres in any academic field is potentially risky but I would encourage readers of this chapter contemplating ethnographic work to read widely and consider how best to represent their work and the voices of those who participate.

Notes

1. The term 'ethnography' is contested. Educational researchers have been urged by many to not use the term unless studying a culture 'holistically' and critical researchers have problematized the notion of culture, cultural description and the impossibility of 'holistic' accounts. 'Ethnographic' is often a preferred alternative.
2. The theoretical perspectives derived from this data are sometimes known as grounded theory.
3. The sustained engagement in a 'field' that ethnographic work requires makes it a suitable methodology for a doctoral study. Journal articles that describe ethnographic work (often the outcome of such a study) are however typically constrained by length requirements to limit details of the methodological framework and methods adopted. It is therefore worth reading the dissertation in its entirety to obtain an understanding of the researcher's engagement in the field.

Resources for Further Reading

The Centre for Urban Ethnography, Graduate School of Education, University of Pennsylvania, convenes the Ethnography in Education Research Forum, an annual meeting of qualitative researchers in education. See http://www.gse.upenn.edu/cue/.

The Ethnograph is a software package that allows you to store, code, search data, write and store analytic memos. More information is available at http://www.qualisresearch.com/

Ethnography and Education is a new international, peer-reviewed journal published by *Routledge*. More information can be found at http://www.informaworld.com/smpp/title~content=t716100709. The *Ethnography and Education* website http://ethnographyandeducation.org/index.htm is run by the group that started the journal and who host an annual *Oxford Ethnography and Education Conference*.

The Linguistic Ethnography Forum http://www.ling-ethnog.org.uk/ (Accessed 1 December 2007).
This website hosts the *UK Linguistic Ethnography Forum*, a Special Interest Group of the British Association for Applied Linguistics (BAAL). There is information about participants; past and planned events and discussion papers they have produced.

Richardson, L. (2000), 'Evaluating ethnography'. *Qualitative Inquiry*, 6(2) 253–255.
Richardson, who describes herself as a 'poststructural ethnographer', shares five of the criteria she uses when reviewing papers or monographs. These are: substantive merit, aesthetic merit, reflexivity, impact and expressing a reality. The criteria are described in more detail in the article.

Tesol Quarterly Qualitative Research: (Critical) Ethnography Guidelines (http://www.tesol.org/s_tesol/sec_document.asp?CID=476&DID=2157 accessed 30 November 2007).
These extensive guidelines are essential reading for anyone beginning ethnographic research within the broad fields of language and education. They also offer an open-minded perspective on what they call the 'critical ethnography

report', suggesting that the traditional Introduction-Method-Results-Discussion format of the research article embodies a positivist attitude to research that may not be appropriate for ethnographic writing when the researcher was not a detached 'objective' observer but an active participant.

References

Anderson, G. L. (1989), 'Critical ethnography in education: Origins, current status and new directions'. *Review of Educational Research*, 59(3), 249–270.

Atkinson, P., Coffey, A., Delamount, S., Lofland, J. and Lofland, L. (2001), 'Editorial introduction', in P. Atkinson, A. Coffey, S Delamount, J. Lofland and L. Lofland (eds), *Handbook of Ethnography*. London: Sage, pp. 1–7.

Barton, D. and Hamilton, M. (1998), *Local Literacies*. London: Routledge.

Bloome, D., Carter, S. P., Christian, B. M, Otto, S. and Shuart-Faris, N. (2005), *Discourse Analysis and the Study of Classroom Language and Literacy Events: A Microethnographic Perspective*. Mahwah, NJ: Lawrence Erlbaum.

Bourdieu, P. (1982), *Ce Que Parler Veut Dire*. Paris: Fayard.

Brodkey, L. (1987), 'Writing critical ethnographic narratives'. *Anthropology and Education Quarterly*, 18, 67–76.

Cameron, D., Frazer, E., Harvey, P., Rampton, M. B. H. and Richardson, K. (1992), *Researching Language: Issues of Power and Method*. London: Routledge.

Carspecken, P. F. (1996), *Critical Ethnography in Educational Research*. New York: Routledge.

Cazden, C., John, V. and Hymes, D. (1972), *Functions of Language in the Classroom*. Prospect Hills, IL: Waveland Press.

Clifford, J. (1986), 'Introduction: Partial Truths', in J. Clifford and G. Marcus (eds), *Writing Culture*. Berkeley: University of California Press, pp. 1–26.

Clifford, J. and Marcus, G. (eds), (1986), *Writing Culture*. Berkeley: University of California Press.

Denzin N. and Lincoln, Y. (2005), 'Introduction: The Discipline and Practice of Qualitative Research', in N. Denzin and Y. Lincoln (eds), *The Sage Handbook of Qualitative Research* (3rd edn). Thousand Oaks, CA: Sage, pp. 1–32.

Duff, P. A. (2002), 'The discursive co-construction of knowledge, identity, and difference: An ethnography of communication in the high school mainstream'. *Applied Linguistics*, 23(3), 289–322.

—(2007), 'Qualitative approaches to classroom research with English language learners', in J. Cummins and C. Davison (eds), *International Handbook of English Language Teaching*. New York: Springer, pp. 973–986.

Fairclough, N. (1992), *Discourse and Social Change*. Cambridge: Polity Press.

Foley, D. (2002), 'Critical ethnography: The reflexive turn'. *Qualitative Studies in Education*, 15(5), 469–490.

Fox, J., Artemeva, N., Darville, R. and Woods, D. (2006), 'Juggling through hoops: Implementing ethics policies in applied linguistic studies'. *Journal of Applied Ethics*, 4, 77–79.

Geertz, C. (1975), *The Interpretation of Cultures*. London: Hutchinson.

Goldstein, T. (1997), *Two Languages at Work: Bilingual Life on the Production Floor*. Berlin: Mouton de Gruyter.

—(2003), *Teaching and Learning in a Multilingual School: Choices, Risks and Dilemmas*. Mahwah, NJ: Lawrence Erlbaum.

Grimshaw, T. (2007), 'Problematizing the construct of "the Chinese learner": Insights from ethnographic research'. *Educational Studies*, 33(3), 299–311.

Halliday, M. A. K. (1994), *An Introduction to Functional Grammar*, 2nd Edition. London: Edward Arnold.

Hammersley, M. (1990), *Reading Ethnographic Research: A Critical Guide*. London: Longman.

Harklau, L. (2005), 'Ethnography and ethnographic research on second language teaching and learning', in E. Hinkel (ed.), *Handbook of Research in Second Language Teaching and Learning*, Mahwah, NJ: Lawrence Erlbaum, pp. 179–194.

Heath, S. B. (1983), *Ways with Words*. New York: Cambridge University Press.

Heyl, B. S. (2001), 'Ethnographic interviewing' in P Atkinson, A. Coffey, S Delamount, J. Lofland and L. Lofland (eds), *Handbook of Ethnography*. London: Sage, pp. 368–383.

Hesse-Biber, S. N. and Leavy, P. (2006), *The Practice of Qualitative Research*. Thousand Oaks: Sage.

Hymes, D. (1972). 'Toward ethnographies of communication', in P. P. Giglioli (ed.), *Language and Social Context*. Harmondsworth: Penguin, pp. 21–44.

Ivanič, R. (1998), *Writing and Identity: The Discoursal Construction of Identity in Academic Writing*. Amsterdam: John Benjamins.

Lazaraton, A. (2003), 'Evaluative criteria for qualitative research in applied linguistics: Whose criteria and whose research?' *The Modern Language Journal*, 87, 1–12.

Lather, P. (1991), *Getting Smart: Feminist Research and Pedagogy with/in the Postmodern*. New York: Routledge.

Lee, E. and Simon Maeda, A. (2006), 'Racialized research identities in ESL/EFL research'. *TESOL Quarterly*, 40(3), 573–594.

Maykut, P. and Morehouse, R. (1994), *Beginning Qualitative Research: A Philosophical and Practical Guide*. London: Falmer Press.

Motha, S. (2006), 'Racializing ESOL teacher identities in U.S. K-12 public schools', *TESOL Quarterly*, 40(3), 495–517.

Murphy, E. and Dingwall, R. (2001), 'The ethics of ethnography' in P. Atkinson, A. Coffey, S. Delamount, J. Lofland and L. Lofland (eds), *Handbook of Ethnography*. London: Sage, pp. 339–351.

Peirce, B. N. (1995), 'The theory of methodology in qualitative research'. *TESOL Quarterly*, 29(3), 569–576.

Ramanathan, V. and Atkinson, D. (1999), 'Ethnographic approaches and methods in L2 writing research: A critical guide and review'. *Applied Linguistics*, 20(1), 44–70.

Rampton, B. (2007), 'Neo-hymesian linguistic ethnography in the United Kingdom'. *Journal of Sociolinguistics*, 11(5), 584–607.

Richardson, L. (2000), 'Evaluating ethnography'. *Qualitative Inquiry*, 6(2) 253–255.

Sarangi, S. and Roberts, C. (eds) (1999), *Talk, Work and Institutional Order: Discourse in Medical, Mediation and Management Settings*. Berlin: Mouton de Gruyter.

Saville-Troike, M. (1982), *The Ethnography of Communication*. Oxford: Basil Blackwell.

Scollon, R., Bhatia, V., Li. D. and Yung, V. (1999), 'Blurred genres and fuzzy identities in Hong Kong public discourse: Foundational ethnographic issues in the study of reading'. *Applied Linguistics*, 20(1), 23–43.

Slembrouck, S. (2005), 'Discourse, critique and ethnography: Class-oriented coding in accounts of child protection'. *Language Sciences*, 27, 619–650.

Starfield, S. (1999), 'Making and sharing meaning: the academic writing of first-year students in the department of sociology who speak English as an additional language'. Unpublished Ph.D. thesis, University of the Witwatersrand, Johannesburg.

— '"I'll go with the group": Rethinking discourse community in EAP', in J. Flowerdew and M. Peacock (eds), *Handbook of Research on English for Academic Purposes*. Cambridge: Cambridge University Press, pp. 132–147.

— (2002), '"I'm a second-language English speaker": Negotiating writer identity and authority in Sociology One'. *Language, Identity, and Education*, 1(2), 121–140.

— (2004), 'Wordpower: Negotiating success in a first-year sociology essay', in L. J. Ravelli and R. A. Ellis (eds), *Analysing Academic Writing*. London: Continuum, pp. 66–83.

Van Maanen, J. (1988), *Tales of the Field: On Writing Ethnography*. Chicago: University Chicago Press.

Watson-Gegeo, K. A. (1988), 'Ethnography in ESL: Defining the essentials'. *TESOL Quarterly*, 22(4), 575–592.

Willis, P. (1980), 'On method', in S. Hall, D. Hobson, A. Lowe and P. Willis. *Culture, Media, Language: Working Papers in Cultural Studies, 1972–79*, London: Routledge, pp. 88–95.

6 Case Studies

Christine Pearson Casanave

Chapter Overview	

In this chapter, I describe some characteristics of case studies, discuss some methods that are commonly used in case study research, point out some issues in ethics, validity and generalizability, and give an example of case study work in the applied linguistics field.

Characteristics and Assumptions of Case Study Research

Let me say that in spite of the fact that this chapter has found its home in a section on methods, 'case study' does not refer to a method of doing research. Many methods may be used in conducting a case study, both quantitative and qualitative (Yin 2003a, 2003b). Rather, a case study more accurately refers to a research *tradition* (Cresswell 2007) or an approach in which the object of inquiry is unique (in the sense of singular) and bounded and in which the researcher's interest is in the particular rather than the general. By 'bounded' we mean that the phenomenon we are investigating is delimited – we are pretty sure we know what is and is not the case, and the context in which the case is situated is also particular and delineated. Without attention to context, we do not have a case

(Yin 2003b). So the research can be called a case study if it investigates one person, one group, one institution or one community (Stake 1995, 2005; Merriam 1998). A multiple case study investigates several particular groups, institutions, or case studies of individuals. The purpose of most case studies is to enhance our understanding of a person, process or group, not to compare, experiment and generalize to other populations. The term 'case study' refers both to the process of doing such a study and to the final report that it generates.

Perhaps the primary feature of case studies that distinguishes them from other types of research is that they explore (describe, analyse) particular bounded phenomena. We assume that there is something unique about the case we choose to investigate, and are interested in the particulars of what makes the case special, not necessarily what makes it representative of larger processes or groups of people (Stake 2005). If we speak of generalization at all, it is to theoretical propositions (Yin 2003b) or to the kind of vicarious experience in readers that Stake (2005) calls naturalistic generalization. However, by choosing to investigate a case, we presume to be able to identify what makes the case particular and bounded, and therefore what is not a case. But identifying boundaries may not always be straightforward (Cresswell 2007). Researchers often fudge here and there, and draw some artificial lines around a case. This is a normal part of case study research.

Second, by choosing a case study tradition, we demonstrate an interest in in-depth portrayals of particular people or sites, rather than in a broader, more superficial sampling of the phenomena we are investigating. This choice usually requires a commitment of time and a mix of data types. For instance, in applied linguistics, people who are interested in the L2 language acquisition of just one person can conduct a longitudinal study of the language learner (see a discussion of some of these studies in Duff 2008 and Van Lier 2005); and people who are interested in L2 writers (for example) can follow one or more individual writers over time as they learn how to write in particular settings for particular purposes (e.g., Berkenkotter et al. 1988; Blakeslee 1997; Casanave 1998; Prior 1998; Li 2005, 2007; Leki 2007). The point is that depth and detail are essential in a good case study.

A third characteristic of case studies, whatever methods are employed, is that the case is clearly situated or embedded in a particular context (which may be physical, historical, temporal). Without a thorough understanding of context, we will not be able to interpret what the particulars of the case mean.

Types of Case Studies

Many types of case studies can be imagined, but I find Stake's (1995, 2005) discussion especially useful. He distinguishes between intrinsic and instrumental case studies. Intrinsic case studies hold our interest because the case itself is interesting. It can be difficult to convince dissertation committees and journal reviewers that we are doing a study solely because the case fascinates us and because we want to gain deep understanding of it for its own sake. We typically need to produce a rationale that argues why a study will benefit others or contribute to larger bodies of research. But Stake (2005, p. 445) tells us that an intrinsic case study

> is not undertaken primarily because the case represents other cases or because it illustrates a particular trait or problem, but instead because, in all its particularity *and* ordinariness, this case itself is of interest.

He insists that intrinsic case studies contribute to knowledge even if they do not follow typical 'rules' of scientific research.

> With an instrumental case study, on the other hand, something external to the case itself holds our interest, and the case study is conducted in order to further our understanding of the external interest. The case itself may or may not be typical, but is chosen 'to advance understanding of that other interest' (Stake 2005, p. 445).

Procedures in Case Study Research

Because there is so much variability in how case study research can be conducted, I can give only the briefest of overviews of procedures here. I urge readers who are attracted to the case study tradition to read more widely. Useful examples and procedures for applied linguistics research, for instance, are described in Duff (2008). In this section I consider how L2 researchers might choose a case, collect and analyse data, and write up a case study report. The section concludes with some comments on researcher roles and responsibilities.

Choosing a Case

As is advised for all research, case study research begins with questions and curiosities that the applied linguistics scholar has, rather than with the tradition or method. Perhaps the most pervasive mistake of novice researchers is to start with pronouncements such as: 'I plan to do a mixed-method study,' or 'I will do a case study.' As attractive as one approach or the other may look, this is putting the cart before the horse.

So: Start with questions, puzzles and curiosities. These will lead to an appropriate choice of approach and method, and if case study is called for, to choosing a case or cases.

For instance, when I was looking for a dissertation topic in graduate school, I was attracted to issues in academic literacy (both first and second language) but was not sure why. With some reading and thinking, mainly about myself and my struggles to read and write in graduate school, I realized that I was not interested in ESL writing as much as I was in the role that writing was playing in disciplinary socialization. I was struck that when people entered graduate school, they often did not have clear identities as particular kinds of scholars who fit within disciplinary communities or communities of practice. Then, some years into their programs, they had taken on previously unfamiliar ways of thinking, using language, writing and researching. The one activity that they seemed to be doing all the time was reading and writing. Moreover, we were all evaluated in graduate school on our writing rather than on tests. Writing and interacting with written texts must hold the key to this miraculous transformation of identity in graduate school.

My curiosity was about the individual's experience of the role of writing in this transformation, not in general processes of the acquisition of academic literacy or in text analysis of academic writing. I wanted to know what specific people were experiencing. In those days we did not talk about studying ourselves (doing autoethnographies, for example), so I had to find some people to follow around for a while, at least a year – long enough to begin to see some transformations. A case study approach was thus well-suited to my curiosities. I requested permission in writing from the head of the sociology department nearby and from some of his students and ended up studying a first year doctoral cohort (cf. Prior 1998, for a comparable study of disciplinary socialization).

But of course this is not the only way to choose a case, nor are individual people the only examples of what a good case might be. A researcher might have a strong instrumental purpose for doing research, and want to select case study participants and sites or programmes much more systematically and purposefully. An applied linguistics researcher, for example, may wish to learn how a beginning L2 learner, or an especially successful learner, strategizes learning over time. (Note: In case study research, comparisons are not needed; we could focus on a successful or unsuccessful learner only.) Another researcher may be interested in how a particular language programme functions. The researcher also needs to make decisions about a case based on many practical factors: How much time will participants have to spend with you without their feeling pressed or resentful? Where are participants and programmes located – close to or far from home? Will you and the participants share a language or will one of you be using an L2? Is the particular programme you are curious about one that you are affiliated with or are you an outsider? Will administrators or teachers whom you wish to learn from consider you a spy or an ally? These are just a few of the practical questions to consider in choosing a case.

The main point is to start with strong curiosities about particular people, processes and programmes, beginning with yourself.

Collecting and Analysing Data

Unlike some other research approaches, almost any data can be used in case study research. However, particularly in qualitative inquiry, case study data are typically collected over time, in some depth, and from a limited number of people and settings. If the study is of one or more individuals, then interview data, recorded and transcribed (and possibly translated), will be central, as will be other sources of information from the participants (email, journals, casual conversation, documents) (see Yi 2007 for a nice description of multiple data sources that she used in her study of a Korean high-school student's out-of-class composing). Interviews with key people who interact with the participant(s) may also play a part. Depending on the topic, data may also include multiple observations of classroom learning or teaching or other group settings (e.g., meetings) in which the participant is involved. Depending on circumstances, these observations may or may not be videotaped. The researcher's own reflections, in the form of research memos and write-ups of early responses to participants and their experiences, also become data. In a case study, the researcher can be seen as one of the participants.

If the case study is of a programme or a school rather than of one individual, the researcher needs to gain access to key people in the organization (this can be tricky). Data may consist of interviews or even a survey of people in the organization, documents of many types and a great deal of observation recorded as field notes and research memos. The researcher may also collect visual data in the form of photographs or videos. The point in a case study is to come to know the case well, thoroughly, and from different perspectives. Any data that contribute to this effort are included.

Analyses of many types can be used in case study research. Quantitative analyses can be done of surveys, content analyses of documents and linguistic and content analyses of interview transcripts, classroom transcripts, and writing samples. Observations, interviews, and documents can also be analysed by means of prose descriptions of themes and narrative analyses of stories in which themes and impressions become the main focus.

Finally, a good analysis proceeds from concepts at a higher level of abstraction – a conceptual framework – that helps readers see the connections between the individual study of one person or place and others that may be similar. The analysis may also be used to help build or modify theoretical concepts.

Writing a Case Study Report

A case study needs to be written in a detailed and accessible way so that readers can be in some sense transported into the world(s) of the case. As I mentioned earlier, Stake (1995) calls this kind of connection with readers 'naturalistic generalization,' in the absence of the kind of the type of generalization we find in statistical studies:

> Naturalistic generalizations are conclusions arrived at through personal engagement in life's affairs or by vicarious experience so well constructed that the person feels as if it happened to themselves (Stake 1995, p. 85).

As Stake (p. 85) says, even if we can't generalize to a larger population, 'people can learn much that is general from single cases.'

Therefore, the standard technical report style is usually not appropriate for a case study report because it will lack the kinds of details needed, even though comparable sections are usually present in a case study (e.g., an introduction, description of context and methods, examples and interpretations of data, and discussion, regardless of what headings the writer uses). The case study report includes the writer's reasons for doing the study and his or her roles in the interaction with the participants, class or programme are made clear. Descriptions abound, and may include visuals – readers need to vicariously see and experience contexts, people and events. Case studies may include quite a bit of narrative – what happened in the research process and what happened in the participants' lives. There may also be photographs or drawings in the report, or in a website established by the researcher. The website can also include full transcripts and sound recordings, assuming that participants have given permission for their data to be used in this way and that their confidentiality is protected. In the report, alternative interpretations may be offered, and conclusions about a person or programme tend to be tentative. In all write-ups, the case report needs to be presented with enough convincing detail so that readers can judge for themselves whether the insights and observations of this particular object of investigation pertain to their own situations.

Some people believe that a good case report, in the naturalistic or qualitative tradition, requires better writing skills than does a technical report. Lincoln and Guba (1985) mention this, and certainly their criteria for evaluating a case study report (see below) focus primarily on qualities of writing. After all, a case report must persuade readers of its credibility. Persuasiveness will happen not only as a result of the quality of the research, but also through the writing (Ely et al. 1997). But novice scholars or L2 speakers should not despair: Most of us are not inherently good writers. We learn to write better as we practice; we get feedback from others; and if our research questions lead us to a naturalistic case study project, we will be required to write. (See Belcher and Hirvela 2005, who found that some of the L2 doctoral students they worked with were obligated by their research interests to write qualitative dissertations. They succeeded admirably.)

Researcher Roles and Responsibilities

In conducting all research, researchers need to be alert to how their investigation might possibly harm participants. Qualitative inquiry in particular often depends on close contact with and descriptions of particular people and places and thus needs to pay attention to qualities of 'honesty, justice, and respect for persons' (Soltis 1991, p. 247). Case study research that adopts qualitative methods places the researcher in an even more sensitive position: The case study is by definition an in-depth study of a particular person, group or programme. As the study becomes more and more particularized, it becomes difficult to protect participants' identities and to separate private issues from those that can be written about without risk. A written agreement with case study participants (*informed consent*) that alerts them to possible risks, that assures them of anonymity, that informs them that all data are confidential and that gives them the right to withdraw from the study at any time should be made early in the research process. It is also a good idea, whenever possible, to share transcripts, descriptions and drafts with participants and to check with them regularly about whether they want any material excluded in the interest of privacy and confidentiality. (But note that interpretations, as opposed to descriptions and transcripts, usually remain the prerogative of the researcher, even when they are negotiated with participants.)

It behooves researchers as well to consider not only the risks to their participants, but the possible benefits. Researchers who only take, and do not give something back, are deservedly looked at sceptically by those they research. For example, L2 students in a case study project might benefit by receiving special long-term attention from researchers, and if the study is done even partially in the L2, they will benefit from extra language practice. In one of my case study projects, I requested quite a bit of interview time from one of my Japanese participants, a busy professor (Casanave 1998). She benefited by being able to use me to check the English in some of her professional papers.

Researchers themselves develop complex and sometimes personal relationships with case study participants and sites, and thus need to reflect constantly (e.g., in research memos) on the roles they are playing in their own study. For example, to what extent are researchers viewed as insiders or outsiders to the community they are involved in (Richards 2003)? Power, gender and status differences need to be attended to carefully. L2 students, young or old, may feel especially vulnerable to the requests by and interactions with an interviewer, even if the interactions take place in the students' L1. Students may not be able to express their discomfort or resistance. An open discussion of the investigators' roles and relationships in the project will wisely take place with participants, and become part of the case study report as well.

Issues of Validation

A standard question about the need for validation in all research asks what Maxwell (2004) has asked: How might you be wrong? Why should we believe what you have said about your case? Responses to these questions have been debated for decades, and range from traditional criteria adapted from the sciences to radical rejection in certain kinds of qualitative inquiry of any criteria that look too *realist* or too scientific.

Whether readers are planning a quantitatively or qualitatively based case study, one of the ways they can address issues of validity is from a modernist or realist position. This is the traditional position that claims there is a real world out there, that our job is to represent it as accurately and objectively as we can, knowing that there is no pure Truth to be known or found, and yet that there are ways to check on the accuracy of our interpretations and representations. Maxwell (2004) acknowledges that he is a realist, not a postmodernist, and as such he uses a very commonsense definition of validity, which, as realists, we could adopt for a case study:

> [. . .] I use validity in a fairly straightforward, commonsense way to refer to the correctness or credibility of a description, conclusion, explanation, interpretation, or other sort of account. (Maxwell 2004, p. 106)

He then points out that we do not need to believe in *objective truth* to hold this commonsense view, and that most researchers are not seeking such truth. Rather, most of them want 'some grounds for distinguishing accounts that are credible from those that are not' (p. 106; see also Phillips and Burbules 2000; Cresswell 2007). This view recognizes that we cannot eliminate researcher bias, or the influence of researchers on participants and settings, but that we can openly acknowledge that bias in our interpretations and writing. Some or all of the items in his validity checklist can be applied to case study research if we see ourselves as realists-modernists: long-term involvement in the field, detailed and varied data; participants' feedback on our interview transcripts and interpretations (*member checking*), informal intervention by the researcher (and recognizing that our presence is always an intervention), searching actively for discrepant cases, triangulating (primarily by collecting data from multiple sources), using numbers (tables, etc.) where appropriate ('quasi-statistics – a term coined by Howard Becker many years ago to refer to 'the use of simple numerical results that can be readily derived from the data' [Maxwell 2004, p. 113]) and comparing one case with others (Maxwell 2004, pp. 110–113). This perspective on validity in qualitative case study projects will not usually raise eyebrows with dissertation committee members or with journal editors. It is quite widely accepted.

However, Denzin's (1997) take on the validation issue may raise both eyebrows and hackles. Given that some of the changes and flux that are being experienced in qualitative inquiry are influencing research in applied linguistics and second language education, I believe that we need to listen to arguments for viewing evaluation criteria in new ways. Denzin uses the term 'legitimation' rather than validity. From his critical post-structural perspective, he sees the 'crisis of legitimation' in qualitative inquiry (with ethnography as his example) as one in which we can no longer rely on traditional scientific claims of authority and empirical credibility in the texts we write from our research. Rather, post-structural legitimation must be seen as subjective, emotional, moral and political performances (including drama and poetry) of words and texts that draw audiences in and move them in some way (emotionally, to take action). The text or performance will be endlessly contested. The researcher's goal, in other words, is to present multiple versions of 'reality' and to deal openly with contested views.

I conclude this section by presenting the ideas of Lincoln and Guba (1985, 2002), on judging the processes and products of qualitative inquiry, and case studies in particular. In their 1985 book, Lincoln and Guba recommended the criteria of trustworthiness to evaluate the research *process* for all naturalistic inquiry. These criteria concern the ways data are collected and treated. They offer the criteria of credibility, transferability, dependability and confirmability as replacement criteria for the traditional criteria for evaluating scientific and technical projects (e.g., reliability, validity, generalizability). Like Maxwell, they assert that to know a particular case well, researchers need to spend a great deal of time getting to know the case, observing contexts and events and triangulating data by looking at the case from multiple perspectives (diverse data, methods and investigators). They also suggest that we share ideas in interim reports with peers and with participants themselves, and create some kind of archive (tapes, videos, documents) against which we can check findings. Their point is that, even though we can never prove anything, we need to find ways to help make case study findings believable, applicable to readers and dependable and confirmable to the extent possible by our system of record keeping. Because case study research, focusing as it does on a particular and bounded case such as an individual or a programme, is even more susceptible to criticism by traditional researchers than other naturalistic inquiry, these techniques for legitimating the research process take on special importance.

In a later publication, Lincoln and Guba (2002) ask how to judge the *products* of naturalistic inquiry, case reports in particular, at a time when innovations and alternatives in approaches to research are proliferating. They comment on four qualities of the product (the case report itself) that can be used to evaluate it (see my comments above on the importance of writing).

First, they state that resonance criteria should be used to assess the fit between the written report and the belief system, or philosophical assumptions that underlie the report. A naturalistic case study would reflect multiple realities, for instance, including reflection by the researcher on his or her role, whereas a more traditional study would seek more unified and distanced explanations and representations. Second, rhetorical criteria would be applied to the report that reflects qualities of good writing: unity, organization, simplicity and clarity, craftsmanship (elegance and creativity of the writing, involvement of the writer). Third, empowerment criteria are used to judge whether the report moves readers to undertake some action, even if it is just consciousness-raising. Finally, applicability criteria ask whether the case study can be applied to readers' own contexts. This is the only way that case study research can in any sense be *generalized*.

In all three of these views of evaluation criteria, researchers no longer presume that interview transcripts or observation field notes represent uncontested or unmitigated facts, truth or unbiased perspectives of participants and observation sites. All case studies result in texts, not accurate representations of reality, and all are constructed by researchers in the act of doing research and writing, and must be judged in this light. As texts, they can always be contested and reinterpreted. The good news here is that we exist in an era of methodological, representational, and evaluative diversity. All approaches require rigorous attention to both research procedures and to writing. The researcher's task is therefore one of knowing what is out there and making reasoned choices and clear explanations of those choices.

A Sample Study

In this section, I summarize one case study to exemplify some of the characteristics of one kind of case study research – the case study of one individual. This is the study of a Chinese doctoral student of physics who was attempting to fulfil his university's publication requirement for graduation (Li 2005; see also another case study by Li 2007). The author chose this topic because she herself was also learning to write for publication in English as an L2 graduate student and so was interested in how others learned to do this. Her project, in other words, was driven by her own experiences and curiosities. She met her case study participant, Fei (pseudonym), in a required English class for graduate students that she was teaching. She wondered, with his limited English, how he would fare having to write publishable papers in English. Her report, a naturalistic case study, is organized in a very traditional way (introduction and framework, participant and setting, data collection, findings, discussion, conclusion).

In her case study report, Li first frames her study within Lave and Wenger's (1991) community of practice framework, using the concept of legitimate peripheral participation to help her interpret what Fei was going through during the two and a half years that she worked with him. She then describes Fei, giving his background and situating the study in the particular university department. Her data consist of much more than interviews with Fei, although these were central. She also collected all the email correspondence with him, the drafts of his main manuscripts, his correspondence with journal editors and reviewers, and had several interviews with his supervisors and fellow students. Li recorded the interviews when possible, took notes otherwise and wrote up summaries of the interviews immediately after they took place.

In long-term in-depth case studies like these, the researcher is always faced with more data than can possibly be used even in a dissertation, let alone in a short journal article. Li therefore had to decide what to use for this particular report, what to put aside, and what issues to focus on. She decided to present her findings in three themes, all of which concerned Fei's successful learning, within the legitimate peripheral participation concept. These themes were: learning from texts, learning from his main supervisor and learning from his research community. We trust her findings for a number of reasons: how long she worked with Fei; the varied sources of her data, both textual and interview; her choice of a suitable framework from which to interpret her findings, the applicability of the core issues to readers who have gone through similar experiences themselves or who are working with students who are struggling with similar issues; and the careful attention to the quality of her writing. In short, although this is a study of just one person, the questions and issues apply more broadly.

Strengths and Limitations of Case Study Research

If researchers want to understand deeply a particular person or a site (a class, a programme), with the goal of understanding and interpreting rather than of comparing, experimenting, hypothesis testing or generalizing to other populations, then a case study is an appropriate choice of approach. Moreover, the case study approach benefits by being able to accommodate many different methods, mainly qualitative but also quantitative, including detailed linguistic analyses of L2 development (Duff 2008). In applied linguistics, a case study is able to look closely at contexts, people and change over time (Van Lier 2005, p. 195). For researchers who enjoy uncovering the particulars of a person or phenomenon and spending time doing so, case studies will suit them.

On the other hand, case studies often involve more time than some researchers have, and require social skills that they may not be comfortable with. Moreover, if researchers really want to say something about a population of people, rather than about an individual, then a case study may not be the best choice. The case study report itself requires good writing skills in order that rich and varied details can be presented in a convincing way. Readers need such details to be able to apply the case study findings to their own lives and settings. Anyone can polish their writing skills, however, so this should not deter researchers unless they truly hate to write. Additionally, qualitative case studies are still finding their way into the applied linguistics repertoire of valued research approaches in dissertations, journals and books. Therefore, researchers who feel they need to please gatekeepers should assess the political scene before committing to a qualitative case study project.

Speaking for myself, I find nothing quite so engaging as a case study when I am curious about an aspect of another person's life. Moreover, we look closely at ourselves in this kind of research, and can include personal reflections as part of the case study report. Both self and others become characters in the stories we tell.

Resources for Further Reading

Duff, P. A. (2008), *Case Study Research in Applied Linguistics*. Lawrence Erlbaum Associates, Taylor and Francis Group.
  This readable book provides a good introduction to case study research in applied linguistics. It includes many examples from well-known case studies from the 1970s and 1980s as well as more recent examples, and how-to chapters on doing and writing up case study research. Most of the discussion presumes that researchers will be investigating language acquisition, but Duff also refers to research on topics such as identity and socialization.
Leki, I. (2007), *Undergraduates in a Second Language*: *Challenges and Complexities of Academic Literacy Development*. New York: Lawrence Erlbaum Associates/Taylor and Francis Group.
  Leki's case studies look at how individual L2 undergraduates in a US university find their way into the literacy practices of their subject matter areas. Even for

those not interested in L2 literacy, the case studies provide models of how to conduct and write up one kind of case study research.

Merriam, S. B. (1998), *Qualitative Research and Case Study Applications in Education.* San Francisco, CA: Jossey-Bass Publishers.

This book covers issues in qualitative inquiry in educational fields, with special attention to case studies. It is a readable but fairly conservative treatment and does not draw on any work in applied linguistics. Still, all the issues apply to case study work in second language education and applied linguistics research.

Prior, P. A. (1998), *Writing/Disciplinarity: A Sociohistoric Account of Literate Activity in the Academy.* Mahwah, NJ: Lawrence Erlbaum Associates.

Although Prior's book can be quite densely theoretical in places, his case studies of second language writers provide good models for one kind of case study research that includes analysis of L2 writers' texts and the many social and personal factors that help shape those texts.

Stake, R. E. (1995), *The Art of Case Study.* Thousand Oaks, CA: Sage Publications.

Stake's work on case study is perhaps the most frequently cited in the education, sociology, and applied linguistics literature. It is rather prescriptive, but those who are new to case study research will appreciate its guidelines.

Yin, R. K. (2003), *Case Study Research: Design and Methods* (3rd edn). Thousand Oaks, CA: Sage Publications.

This often cited book gives readers in a variety of disciplines a systematic introduction, with examples, to designs and methods that can be used in case studies. Notable is Yin's point that case studies do not inherently call for qualitative methods, but can utilize many quantitative and computer-associated methods. Exercises are included at the end of each chapter.

References

Belcher, D. and Hirvela, A. (2005), 'Writing the qualitative dissertation: What motivates and sustains commitment to a fuzzy genre?'. *Journal of English for Academic Purposes,* 4, 187–205.

Berkenkotter, C., Huckin, T. N. and Ackerman, J. (1988), 'Conventions, conversations, and the writer: Case study of a student in a rhetoric Ph.D. program'. *Research in the Teaching of English,* 22, 9–45.

Blakeslee, A. M. (1997), 'Activity, context, interaction, and authority: Learning to write scientific papers in situ'. *Journal of Business and Technical Communication,* 11(2), 125–169.

Casanave, C. P. (1998), 'Transitions: The balancing act of bilingual academics'. *Journal of Second Language Writing,* 7, 175–203.

Cresswell, J. W. (2007), *Qualitative Inquiry and Research Design: Choosing among Five Traditions* (2nd edn). Thousand Oaks, CA: Sage Publications.

Denzin, N. K. (1997), *Interpretive Ethnography: Ethnographic Practices for the 21ˢᵗ Century.* Thousand Oaks, CA: Sage Publications.

Duff, P. A. (2008), *Case Study Research in Applied Linguistics.* New York: Lawrence Erlbaum.

Ely, M., Vinz, R., Downing, M. and Anzul, M. (1997), *On Writing Qualititative Research: Living by Words*. New York: Routledge Falmer.

Lave, J. and Wenger, E. (1991), *Situated Learning: Legitimate Peripheral Participation*. Cambridge, UK: Cambridge University Press.

Leki, I. (2007), *Undergraduates in a Second Language: Challenges and Complexities of Academic Literacy Development*. New York: Lawrence Erlbaum Associates/Taylor and Francis Group.

Li, Y. (2005). 'Multidimensional enculturation: The case study of an EFL Chinese doctoral student'. *Journal of Asian Pacific Communication*, 15(1), 153–170.

—(2007), 'Apprentice scholarly writing in a community of practice: An intraview of an NNES graduate student writing a research article'. *TESOL Quarterly*, 41(1), 55–79.

Lincoln, Y. S. and Guba, E. G. (1985), *Naturalistic Inquiry*. Beverly Hills, CA: Sage Publications.

—(2002), 'Judging the quality of case study reports', in A. M. Huberman and M. B. Miles (eds), *The Qualitative Researcher's Companion*. Thousand Oaks, CA: Sage Publications, pp. 205–215.

Maxwell, J. A. (2004), *Qualitative Research Design: An Interactive Approach* (2nd edn). Thousand Oaks, CA: Sage Publications.

Merriam, S. B. (1998), *Qualitative Research and Case Study Applications in Education*. San Francisco, CA: Jossey-Bass Publishers.

Phillips, D. C. and Burbules, N. C. (2000). *Postpositivism and Educational Research*. Lanham, MD: Rowman & Littlefield Publishers.

Prior, P. A. (1998), *Writing/Disciplinarity: A Sociohistoric Account of Literate Activity in the Academy*. Mahwah, NJ: Lawrence Erlbaum Associates.

Richards, K. (2003), *Qualitative Inquiry in TESOL*. New York: Palgrave MacMillan.

Soltis, J. F. (1991), 'The ethics of qualitative research', in E. W. Eisner and A. Peshkin (eds), *Qualitative Inquiry in Education: The Continuing Debate*. New York: Teachers College Press, pp. 247–257.

Stake, R. E. (1995), *The Art of Case Study*. Thousand Oaks, CA: Sage Publications.

—(2005), 'Qualitative case studies', in N. K. Denzin and Y. S. Lincoln (eds), *The Sage Handbook of Qualitative Research* (3rd edn). Thousand Oaks, CA: Sage Publications, pp. 443–446.

Van Lier, L. (2005), 'Case study', in E. Hinkel (ed), *Handbook of Research in Second Language Teaching and Learning*. Mahwah, NJ: Lawrence Erlbaum Associates, pp. 195–208.

Yi, Y. (2007), ''Engaging literacy: A bilterate student's composing practices beyond school'. *Journal of Second Language Writing*, 16(1), 23–39.

Yin, R. K. (2003a), *Applications of Case Study Research* (2nd edn). Thousand Oaks, CA: Sage Publications.

—(2003b), *Case Study Research: Design and Methods* (3rd edn). Thousand Oaks, CA: Sage Publications.

7 Action Research

Anne Burns

Chapter Overview	

Action research (AR) is gaining acceptance in applied linguistics studies as an empirical approach adaptable to higher degree and other research, as well as to engagement of practitioners in their personal professional growth through reflective practice and local practical enquiry. I describe the major philosophical and paradigmatic assumptions of AR, its origins and essential processes. Issues of validity and value, which remain contentious in AR, are then raised. I also outline briefly the main research techniques and tools, after which key ethical considerations are briefly discussed. Following the pattern of other contributions to this volume, the chapter ends with an illustrative example.

Underlying Assumptions and Methodology

What is Action Research?

AR is the superordinate term for a set of approaches to research which, at the same time, systematically investigate a given social situation and promote democratic change and collaborative participation. *Participatory action research* (PAR), *critical action research* (CAR), *action learning, participant enquiry, practitioner enquiry* and *cooperative enquiry* are all terms broadly underpinned by the assumptions and approaches embodied in AR. The common features they share are to: (a) undertake research to bring about positive change and improvement in the participants' social situation; (b) generate theoretical as well as practical knowledge about the situation; (c) enhance collegiality, collaboration and involvement of participants who are actors in the situation and most likely to be affected by changes; (d) establish an attitudinal stance of continual change, self-development and growth. Those engaged in AR experience self-reflection on their behaviour, actions and interactions with others; deliberate interventions to question and enhance current practices; adaptation of research processes and methods to address directly issues that emerge; unpredictability and openness to changes in research goals and questions as knowledge of the social situation expands and deepens. By way of summary:

> Action research involves a self-reflective, systematic and critical approach to enquiry by participants who are at the same time members of the research community. The aim is to identify problematic situations or issues considered by the participants to be worthy of investigation in order to bring about critically informed changes in practice (Burns, cited in Cornwell 1999, p. 5).

Typically, the situations that participants wish to investigate are those they perceive to be 'problematic'. Rather than suggesting that the participants or their behaviours are the 'problems', the term *problematic* reflects a desire on the part of participants to 'problematize', that is question, clarify, understand and give meaning to the current situation. The impetus for the research is a perceived gap between what actually exists and what participants desire to see exist. In this sense, action researchers are change agents aiming 'to take a stand for a preferred future' (Atiti 2008) and interested in resolving, reformulating or refining dilemmas, predicaments or puzzles in their daily lives through systematic planning, data gathering, reflection and further informed action.

In its historical applications within educational contexts, action research is typically depicted as three broad movements over the past 60 years (see Burns 2005, 2007 for detailed discussion): *technical-scientific* (a technically motivated, step-wise activity seeking basic improvements to practice), *practical-deliberative* (a solution-oriented approach to morally problematic situations) and *critical-emancipatory* (an empowering approach embedded in critical theory and addressing broader socially constituted educational structures at the local level). Crookes (1993) argues that in language education contexts critical-emancipatory approaches are still uncommon.

Processes in Action Research

In contrast to research approaches which follow more predictable, well-established procedures, AR is characterized by dynamic movement, flexibility, interchangeability and reiteration. Broad research phases are, however, discernible. Despite the large number of (contested) models in educational AR (Zuber-Skerritt 1990 calculates that there are at least 30), typical representations show spirals or cycles of (i) planning, (ii) action, (iii) observation and (iv) reflection (cf. Kemmis and McTaggart 1988). The spirals are interwoven, fluid and repeated throughout the investigation; thus, a researcher conducting AR should be prepared for unanticipated variations and reiterations in the process. For example, Burns (1999, p. 35) and the Australian practitioners she collaborated with experienced a 'series of interrelated experiences' involving numerous dynamic phases (Table 7.1).

One challenge for novice action researchers is to distinguish how AR differs from everyday educational practice. Everyday *action* and investigative processes of *research* are brought together in AR; the researcher must plan, act, observe and reflect 'more carefully, more systematically and more rigorously than one usually does in everyday life; and [to] use the relationships between these moments in the process as a source of both improvement and knowledge' (Kemmis and McTaggart 1988, p. 10).

In AR the action in and on the social situation is deliberately interventionist; researchers are simultaneously critical participants *in* the action and researchers *of* the action. AR is essentially an exploratory and decision-generating process invoking key questions, actions and challenges. Table 7.2 presents the major phases and processes, and suggests the kinds of actions and challenges that can arise.

Table 7.1 Interrelated experiences in action research phases (based on Burns 1999: 35)

Phase	Focus of phase
Exploring	Identifying generalized areas for investigation
Identifying	Undertaking fact-finding to refine ideas
Planning	Developing a viable plan of action
Collecting data	Selecting and enacting initial data-gathering techniques
Analysing/reflecting	Simultaneously scrutinizing and reflecting on emerging data
'Hypothesising'/speculating	Developing initial predictions/explanations based on data
Intervening	Deliberately changing practices in response to predictions
Observing	Observing and evaluating outcomes of interventions
Reporting	Articulating processes formatively or summatively to others
Writing	Summarizing and disseminating written research accounts
Presenting	Summarizing and disseminating oral research accounts

Table 7.2 Typology of phases and processes in action research

Broad phases of AR	Key questions	Key actions	Key challenges
Plan	• What problematic areas for investigation and change can be identified in this social situation? • What changes to current practice are anticipated? • What outcomes are desired? • Who is involved in this situation? • What resources are needed?	• Develop statements /reflections/ questions • Identify, collaborate and dialogue with co-participants (colleagues, administrators, parents, students) • Outline initial action and research designs and processes • Identify scope, timing, resources	• Articulating implicit and explicit cultural and professional assumptions about status quo • Interrogating relationship of professional experience to research issues • Scanning political, social and educational constraints
Act	• What strategies and actions should be put in place? • What is distinctive in this action/ how will it lead to change? • What ethical issues are involved? • What evidence is emerging for renewed action?	• Initiate actions over critically selected time period • Observe deliberately, consciously and non-judgmentally • Collaborate with co-participants • Adjust actions on basis of emerging observations	• Avoiding personal bias and interrogating preferred actions • Questioning preconceptions about outcomes • Maintaining openness to unpredictable or unwelcome outcomes
Observe	• What evidence about actions is required? • What types of data-gathering techniques should be used? • What additional forms of data are needed? • What kinds of interim analyses are possible?	• Evaluate the nature of evidence required to document actions systematically • Identify/adapt/develop relevant data collection tools and techniques • Clarify range of perspectives required for adequate coverage • Identify roles of co-participants in data-gathering	• Connecting data sources to research purpose and action • Selecting/reselecting data collection tools • Ensuring triangulation of data techniques • Locating resources/materials required for data collection • Reviewing/readjusting actions on basis of evidence • Maintaining rigour and thoroughness of procedures

(Continued)

Table 7.2 Cont'd

Broad phases of AR	Key questions	Key actions	Key challenges
Reflect	• What evidence is emerging and/or re-merging from systematic observation? • What intended and unintended outcomes are identifiable as a consequence of the intervention? • What reformulations of the problem are required? • What ethical issues are arising from the research? • What balances in judgement need to be achieved?	• Adopt a formative approach to the emergence of findings • Maintain openness to possible revisions, redirections and new problems /questions • Interrogate personal and professional preconceptions/ assumptions • Ensure equitable and just consequences for all participants	• Rechecking and cross-checking evidence • Revising focus and aims of intervention and observation based on emerging evidence • Identifying and challenging pre-conceptions/assumptions • Informing research participants about progress and purpose • Involving participants in cross-checking judgements about evidence • Analysing evidence impartially • Maintaining awareness of the intersubjective nature of personal involvement

Validity/Trustworthiness

Validity is a contested notion in AR. Criticisms about quality and validity have long been levelled against educational AR in relation to: its lack of scientific rigour, replicability and generalizability; the tentativeness and unpredictability of the initial design and therefore its inability to set out validity measures in advance; the localized and therefore unreplicable nature of AR; the capacity of practitioners to design and conduct rigorous research (e.g., Jarvis 1983); the level of rigour in research design (Brumfit and Mitchell 1989) and data analysis (Winter 1987).

However, proponents argue that these criticisms misconstrue the nature and purpose of AR. Like the process of AR itself, validity in AR is highly dynamic and subject to variation, determined by the ongoing and changing aims of the research. Because of the complexity and contentions surrounding the term 'validity', as well as its strong associations with positivist and quantitative-experimental paradigms, AR commentators tend to avoid using it, instead preferring terms such as 'trustworthiness'(Zeichner and Noffke 2001), 'worthwhileness' (Bradbury and Reason 2001) or 'credibility' (Greenwood and Levin 2007). Trustworthiness refers to whether the data analyses, reports and interpretations constitute honest and authentic reconstruction of the research and of the knowledge that emerged in the social environment, while the value accruing to participants in undertaking the research contributes to its worthwhileness. Credibility relates to 'the arguments and the processes necessary for having someone trust research results' (Greenwood and Levin 2007, p. 67); internal credibility means that knowledge created is meaningful to the participants generating it, while external credibility is to do with convincing those uninvolved in the research that the outcomes are believable.

Fundamental to reconceptualizing validity in AR is the challenge of how to make judgements about the quality of the research. Altrichter et al. (1993, pp. 74–81) argue that four key questions should be considered when formulating criteria to evaluate AR quality:

Have the understandings gained from research been cross-checked against the perspectives of all those concerned and/or against other researchers?

Have the understandings gained from research been tested through practical action?

Are the research aims compatible with both educational aims and democratic human values?

Are the research design and data collection methods compatible with the demands of teaching?

Taking these questions in turn, the following measures can enhance trustworthiness in AR (see Altrichter et al. 1993, pp. 74–81 and Burns 1999, pp. 163–166).

Cross-Checking Perspectives

In line with qualitative research procedures more generally, this criterion concerns repetition and comparison of data in order to uncover discrepancies or alternative perspectives, typically sourced through:

Triangulation, a term derived from navigation where different bearings are taken to give accurate positioning on an object. In AR, triangulation means using more than one data collection method (e.g., observations, followed by interviews, or surveys complemented by observations and focus groups), or making comparisons across different types of data (e.g., quantitative analyses compared with qualitative survey responses). Other procedures include investigator (using different researchers), theory (using multiple theoretical approaches) and environmental (using different locations) triangulation. By using different perspective sources, confidence that findings are not simply the result of using a particular method is increased.

Member-checks which involve taking the data to various participants and/or stakeholders for verification of the accuracy of the findings. The researcher's interpretations are cross-checked by those who supplied the data or by other 'members' of the social context in a position to provide views (e.g., principals, administrators, close colleagues). In some cases, *peer comparison,* using the perspectives of those relatively uninvolved are also sought to test out the extent of the account's credibility (e.g., colleagues or administrators in other educational contexts, or parents).

Perspectives comparison which involves testing findings against research in comparable situations. Sources come from the literature, other action research accounts, presentations at professional workshops and conferences, or the researcher's deepening reflections. Failure to find rival explanations that show alternative data explanations, or *negative cases,* that confirm that patterns and trends identified in the data are accurate, increases confidence in interpretations.

Cyclical iteration where the trustworthiness of findings and interpretations are compared with and tested against previous iterations of the AR cycle in order to build on previous evidence, expand the scope, purpose and central questions of the study, further triangulate the data and guard against researcher bias.

Testing through Practical Application

AR involves not just practical application but the development of empirical and theoretical insights about the social situation under investigation. Given the dynamic interaction between action and reflection, the strength of the theories that emerge rests on their ability to generate improvement in practice. Theory-testing is related to how the researcher demonstrates practical application for improvement, and critical reflection on the capacity of the intervention strategies to bring about changes and developments. This does not imply that intervention strategies will show immediate and clear-cut improvements in practice; but it does mean that the purpose and forward movement of the AR process is consistently focused on enhancing practical conditions within the social situation The knowledge generated is based, not on received wisdom or 'grand theory', but on 'experiential knowing' (Heron 1996).

Compatibility with Educational Aims and Democratic Values

This criterion relates to ethical considerations (see below). As mentioned, AR is deliberatively interventionist, aimed at disturbing and unsettling the status quo. Consequently, participants may find themselves confronting surprising or even unpalatable realities or changing things in unanticipated ways. Despite disturbances to accepted practice, it is important that essential *educational* aims in the context are kept in mind. Also, methods should be compatible with research aims; if, for example, the aim is to work with novice teacher colleagues to understand and improve early teaching experiences, interviewing experienced colleagues about 'problems' in supporting novices is counterproductive to fostering good collegial relationships. Similarly, sharing these data with novices and asking for perspectives on their colleagues' views is only likely to increase feelings of alienation. AR strives to enhance cooperate participant relationships, and so showing how this aspect was treated within the research is relevant. Indicating explicitly how ethical principles were achieved and how participants' roles and relationships were (re)negotiated through different research cycles is essential to ensuring research quality.

Compatibility with Teaching Demands

AR practitioners must be simultaneously researchers and actors in the social situation. Thus, the scope and aims of the research need to be realistic and justifiable within the constraints of the teaching context. The research should show how it builds upon, rather than detracts from, practitioners' major responsibilities for teaching. It should also show how it links to the notion of enhanced professionalism for educators and the personal and professional development of the participants. These criteria are closely tied to the notion of compatibility with educational aims and the concepts of reflexivity and praxis, in which theory and practice become mutually informing (e.g., Freire 1970).

Notwithstanding these considerations for enhancing the quality and rigour of AR, debates about what constitute underpinning validity criteria are very much at an evolutionary and contested point. And as Greenwood and Levin note, in attempting to defend AR as a valid research approach, it would be unfortunate to assume 'transcendentally high standards' (2007, p. 113) that deter the very practitioners most likely to want to participate. Rather, 'The key in good AR practice is to design and sustain a process in which important reflections can emerge through communication and some good practical problem-solving can be done in as inclusive and fair a way as possible' (p. 113). If action researchers approach research in the spirit of providing fair and honest disclosure, and reflections on the contexts, the research issues, the cyclical phases and processes, the methods, the presentation and interpretation of the data, convincing 'validation' of the research (Heron 1996) is likely to ensue.

Techniques and Instruments

Generally action researchers employ qualitative techniques common in naturalistic exploratory research. There are essentially two main sources for data gathering: observing and recording what people do; and asking people for their views and opinions. As in other forms of research, techniques should be closely aligned to the central questions or focus – it is pointless to try to understand what participants think about aspects of language learning by observing them undertake a particular task, for example. The techniques highlighted here do not imply, however, that AR data cannot be quantified through percentages, rankings, ratings and so on. However, using statistical calculations typical of quantitative approaches (see Phakiti this volume) is uncommon in AR. Burns (1999, Chapters 4 and 5) describes observational and non-observational techniques in detail.

Observing What Participants Do

Modes of observation include *other-observation* (researcher observations of other participants); *self-observation* (one's own behaviours, thoughts, actions, interactions) and *peer-observation* (observation by and with research colleagues, acting as mentors, influencers, critical friends, supervisors). Participant observation (where the researcher is part of the setting rather than a detached observer) is inevitable in AR; thus, peer-observation is a useful source of data triangulation to verify one's own observations. In some cases (more likely in formalized AR studies submitted as dissertations), *a priori* observational schemes developed for language acquisition research, such as FOCUS (Fanselow

1987) or Communicative Orientation to Language Teaching (COLT) (Spada and Fröhlich 1995) might be used; but more commonly AR observations focus on specific issues under investigation. Richards (2003) suggests four main areas for focusing observations: (i) the *setting* (e.g., context, spaces, locations); (ii) the *systems* (e.g., typical routines and procedures); (iii) the *people* (e.g., roles, relationships, responses); (iv) the *behaviours* (e.g., timing, activities, events).

Observation is accompanied by techniques for capturing the phenomena observed so that the researcher can revisit the situation objectively. Classically, anthropological ethnographic observation uses field-notes made during (obtrusive to other participants) or immediately afterwards (unobtrusive to others) observation, that record in an objective and factual style. Increasingly field-notes include reflective commentary, questions for further consideration, evaluations or self-observations, all relevant to the dynamic and evolving nature of AR. Another 'classic' of AR observation is the researcher journal or diary (see Perkins 2001 for an example), a self-reflective tool written for various purposes. Personal journals, are often used to 'let off steam', ruminate on passing thoughts or insights, record hopes, anxieties or even confessions. Other kinds of journals are 'memoirs', more objective and factual reflections on events or people, or even 'logs', running records of what contacts and transactions occur during the day. In a variation on free-form journals, some AR practitioners use grids or tables with relevant headings, for instance dates/times, issues arising, actions taken, changes made, reflections, comments, reactions, literature references. Journals sometimes include drawings, sketches, diagrams, maps, illustrations of student work or mindmaps. With the advent of technology, field notes and journals can be shared creatively among researchers or set up as blogs (Weblogs, such as Blackboard) or vlogs (visual Weblogs, like Flikr) for running commentary between participants.

Audio or video-recordings have the advantage of capturing observational data verbatim and are accurate and reliable sources of data. Audio-recording is less intrusive, while video, although more intrusive includes non-verbal behaviour. Accustoming participants to the presence of the recording device is likely to result in more authentic records of typical interaction. A challenge in AR observation is that the researcher is also an actor in the context. Thus, if peer observation is not readily available other recording mechanisms are needed. Typical techniques include: handheld recorders for short, rapid commentary; post-it notes for passing insights or reminders; 'jottings' on lesson-plans or class handouts; electronic whiteboard copies; focused observations by students acting as co-researchers; photographs by teacher or students using disposable, digital or mobile phone cameras; maps and diagrams; mindmaps linking key observations and insights; spoken and/or written debriefings with peer-observers immediately after observations. Undertaking and documenting observations are limited only by participants' creativity; the key consideration is making them focused, flexible, convenient and adaptable to preferences and circumstances.

Asking Participants for Views and Opinions

Non-observational and introspective techniques involve seeking views, beliefs and opinions about issues under investigation. They also include collecting artefacts from the research site, such as documents (policies, curricula, lesson plans, student work, test results) providing a track record or paper trail that reflect people's activities. Two mainstays of non-observational data collection are interviews and surveys or questionnaires. Structured (pre-planned sets of questions posed in fixed order), semi-structured (sets of questions used flexibly) or unstructured (open-ended conversational interactions) interviews offer various ways to tailor this technique to a specific focus and purpose, as do different combinations of participants (individualized, paired, focus group oriented). Interviews can easily double as classroom learning activities. A variation on formal interviews, well adapted to AR for example, is a class or group discussion angled toward the research topic. For greater reliability, interviews are frequently recorded, audio-recording usually being sufficient to capture participants' introspections for later analysis.

Surveys or questionnaires eliciting written data through closed and/or open-ended questions are also well adapted to classroom activities. Closed questions involve selecting specified responses and lead to tabulation and quantification (percentages, averages, frequency), while open-ended questions elicit fill-in or short answers and offer qualitative data from which the researcher derives themes, patterns and trends. Questions focus typically on factual, behavioural or attitudinal information (Dörnyei 2003). A major challenge lies in question preparation so as to avoid lack of clarity, ambiguity, bias and 'leading-the-witness', and for this reason piloting the questions is recommended. Decisions also need to be made about the language and literacy levels required and whether responses should be completed in the mother tongue or alternative language.

One problem that inevitably arises in using these techniques is teacher-student power-relationships. McKay (2006, p. 55) suggests minimising this threat to authenticity by: (i) explaining the purpose of the interview, what will be done with the information, and the benefits to participants; (ii) being sensitive to students' responses and any awkwardness or nervousness that might arise; (iii) providing feedback and reinforcement during the interview through thanks, praise and support. This advice applies equally to the preparation and distribution of questionnaires. Linked to the power-relation issue is the problem that 'self-report' data is notoriously unreliable; responses may be simplistic, aimed to please, impress or cover up actual opinions for fear of reprisal. Consequently, action researchers should critically evaluate data obtained in this way against other sources.

Finally, as in other research, AR data are 'traces' or representations of events that provide evidence for the researcher's findings and interpretations. Inevitably what is highlighted from the data is selective, subject to researcher interpretation, and ultimately represents dynamic situations statically. In AR, as perhaps in no other approach to research, to impact on practice the evidence from the data must be supplemented and supported by what can be learned from and made meaningful about the practical social situation through deep reflection and experiential application.

Ethical Considerations

As already noted, ethical considerations are tied up with the quality, value and democratic worth of the AR in changing and enhancing social situations for the participants. Thus, a fundamental ethical question is how the design of the research works towards educational improvement, more effective outcomes for students and the empowerment of teachers, professionally, educationally and politically. Underpinning AR goals are at least three important ethical issues:

Whose Permission or Consent is Needed for the Research?

It is vital to consider two types of permission. First, permission may need to be sought from the researcher's university, school board, district or school. Second, the researcher needs to obtain informed consent from other participants, such as colleagues and students. Even when written consent is not required, all stakeholders and participants have a right to information about the purpose, procedures, possible effects and how the research will be used, as well as assurances of anonymity, voluntary participation and withdrawal from the research without penalty. This is particularly important in an approach where researchers could be accused of 'experimenting' on their students and 'threatening' their educational achievement.

Who Will be Affected by the Research?

Action researchers need to maintain vigilance about the possible consequences of the research on participants. No harm, risk or disadvantage should ensue, and again explanation and communication about the purpose of the research should be foregrounded. In AR it is particularly important to be aware of the power differences inherent in the educational situation and how they might affect participants' behaviours and reactions.

Who Should be Told About the Research When it is Completed?

Participants need to know that the outcomes of the research will be fed back to them for their input. Not only does the researcher do them the courtesy of sharing what comes out of the research but researcher interpretations are (re) affirmed. Information about how the research will be used and to whom it will be disseminated on completion also meets good ethical standards.

Conducting AR ethically involves confronting continual decisions, challenges and choices, which are not always self-evident because of the dynamic and shifting nature of the processes. Nevertheless, an ethical orientation is fundamental to the reflective and democratic spirit of AR and plays a central role in focusing and strengthening its quality, trustworthiness and credibility.

A Sample Study

The focus of Heather Denny's (2008) action research, conducted in a New Zealand (NZ) university over three semesters, was how to introduce her adult immigrant English as an additional language (EAL) learners to conversational skills and cultural norms of the local variety of English, as rapidly and efficiently as possible. The institutional curriculum required students to achieve criterion-based competencies in various spoken genres (e.g., *Is able to manage a conversation and keep it going for 6 minutes: opening, small talk, turn taking, responding to questions, remarks, etc., transitions, closing*). Perceiving that conversational models from available textbooks were inauthentic and non-reflective of local situations, she drew on work by Burns (2001), Butterworth (2000), Carter and McCarthy (1995), de Silva Joyce and Slade (2000) and Eggins and Slade (1997) to develop more realistic semi-scripted role play dialogues. The approach involved 'giving native speakers a scenario based in real-life interactions . . . and asking them to role-play an exchange' which was recorded and transcribed (Denny 2008, p. 44). To facilitate and understand the development of her teaching practice using this approach, she undertook three cycles of AR with three different classes of mixed-age students at a level equivalent to 4.5 General on the International English Language Testing System (IELTS).

In the initial cycle, she used unscripted or semi-scripted conversations from published Australian materials (e.g., Delaruelle 2001), also experimenting by developing semi-scripted recordings and activities involving NZ native-speaker colleagues. Activities focused particularly on weaknesses identified in pre-tests; using formulaic expressions for conversational initiation and introducing discourse markers (*so, well, anyway*) to maintain interaction. Students conducted role-plays rated by peers using the institutional assessment criteria mentioned above.

The second cycle took the investigations further by focusing on the staging of conversational transitions from initiation, to requesting and giving advice and concluding the interaction. Three transitional strategies, identified from semi-scripted recordings and published material, provided data for class activities, including student demonstrations, discussion of strategies used and role-play of complete conversations, during which students self-assessed, using yes/no/sometimes responses against given criteria (e.g., Start a conversation; Speak fluently in conversation using discourse markers (e.g., well, anyway, so, listen, look, now); Find the right question to get information from my partner).

The final cycle extended skills by introducing more complex conversational negotiations, including strategies for gaining attention, introducing a situational problem such as with an employer, teacher, real-estate agent, and insisting. Students listened to models, which were from authentic or simulated sources compiled by Denny, and responded to questions about vocabulary, linguistic features, staging of the conversational genre, getting attention and stating the problem in general and in detail, and using discourse strategies such as introducing softeners, suggesting compromises and checking outcomes. Discussions about conversational models focused on context, participants, power relations, situations and politeness. Other activities involved paired practice, identification of relevant discourse transitions, strategies and markers, demonstration role-plays, peer-coaching and peer assessment.

During all three cycles data were collected through teacher-created pre-tests and institutional post-tests, initial and final written self-assessments, a student survey and a reflective researcher journal. Pre- and post-tests consisted of role plays observed and evaluated by Denny according to criteria. For pre-tests, Denny created her own set of criteria (e.g., Uses appropriate language to manage transition to discussion topic) designed to diagnose each students learning needs. Post-tests utilized the institutional requirements mentioned earlier. After each teaching period students completed self-assessment checklists evaluating discourse competencies. In cycle three, self-assessment occurred before teacher assessment so that responses were not influenced by results. Surveys were completed at the same time as post-teaching self-assessments and students were asked to identify various activities they found most effective: (i) direct activities using models; (ii) more indirect activities such as practising with partners; (iii) most indirect activities such as practising outside class. Denny's reflective journal recorded classroom activities, events and perceptions about effectiveness of activities, student progress and her own practices.

By comparing test results she found that all students improved their weakest skills, but improvement across competencies was uneven. However, the self-assessments showed lower perceptions of individual improvement, particularly for activities in cycle two where students rated themselves higher on the pre-test. Surveys on preferred activities indicated that students found teacher information, practice in class, listening to tapes and studying transcripts the most useful across all cycles. Denny concluded that authentically oriented materials combined with classroom practice did contribute to student improvement. In relation to personal insights and skills development, she claimed that her professional learning about materials development as well as her knowledge about naturalistic data analysis increased: 'I have learned to trust the data in them and have progressively worked more directly with the tapes and transcripts, becoming gradually less worried that learners would find them too complex' (p. 55).

One area identified for future cycles was to investigate ways to enhance sociocultural knowledge of the discoursal features of naturalistic interaction. She also refined her research knowledge and skills realizing, particularly by the third cycle, the importance of recording student interaction for greater reliability in assessment and analysis, and wording surveys clearly and unambiguously. For further cycles, she saw follow-up student interviews as a way of triangulating data and increasing trustworthiness. She concluded: 'In all cycles I learned again that careful and trustworthy research takes more time than anticipated. However, I am convinced that the gathering of data facilitated more focused and rapid development of my teaching' (p. 56). Denny's research is a good example of a practitioner deepening her confidence in addressing a locally contextualized teaching issue and engendering self-reflective empirically based insights.

Resources for Further Reading

Altrichter, H., Posch, P. and Somekh, B. (1993), *Teachers Investigate their Work. An Introduction to the Methods of Action Research*. London: Routledge.
While not focused on language teaching, this book is a classic for teachers, teacher educators and administrators wanting to understand and begin using action research alone or with professional colleagues. Organized as a handbook, it provides numerous practical methods and strategies.

Burnaford, G. Fischer, J. and Hobson, D. (eds), (2001), *Teachers Doing Research. The Power of Action Through Inquiry* (2nd edn). Mahwah, NJ: Lawrence Erlbaum Associates.
Using numerous examples from mainstream teacher action research projects in US schools and colleges, this book describes the processes of doing action research, discusses how technology can be integrated into methodology and

explores the relationships between teacher research and the broader field of educational research.

Burns, A. (2010), *Doing Action Research in English Language Teaching. A Guide for Practitioners*. New York: Routledge.

This volume is a hands-on, practical guide for practitioners wishing to get started in action research. It introduces the main concepts and offers a step-by-step guide to the action research process. It includes numerous examples from language teacher action researchers internationally.

Edge, J. (ed.) (2001), *Action Research*. Case Studies in TESOL Practice Series (Jill Burton, Series Editor). Alexandria, VA: TESOL.

This was one of the first books to provide chapter length examples of action research carried out in the field of language teaching internationally. The opening chapter offers an interesting synopsis of the history of action research, its developments within mainstream educational and applied linguistics/TESOL contexts and its relevance to teacher research and professional development.

Farrell, T. (Series editor) *Language Teacher Research in . . .* Series. Alexandria, VA: TESOL.

This series of edited books is valuable in providing chapter length examples of research, including AR, carried out by language teachers in different international contexts – *Asia* (Farrell, 2006), *Europe* (Borg 2006), *the Americas* (McGarrell (2007), *the Middle East* (Coombe and Barlow 2007), *Australia and New Zealand* (Burns and Burton 2008), *Africa* (Makalela and Kurgatbut 2009).

References

Altrichter, H., Posch, P. and Somekh, B. (1993), *Teachers Investigate their Work. An Introduction to the Methods of Action Research*. London: Routledge.

Atiti, A. (2008), 'A Critical Action Research on Organisational Learning and Change for Sustainability in Kenya'. Unpublished Ph.D. thesis, Macquarie University, Sydney.

Bradbury, H. and Reason, P. (2001), 'Conclusion: Broadening the bandwidth of validity: Issues and choice-point for improving the quality of action research', in P. Reason and H. Bradbury (eds), *Handbook of Action Research*. London: Sage, pp. 447–455.

Brumfit, C. and Mitchell, R. (1989), 'The language classroom as a focus for research', in C. Brumfit and R. Mitchell (eds), *Research in the Language Classroom* (ELT Documents 133). London: Modern English Publications and The British Council, pp. 3–15.

Burns, A. (1999), *Collaborative Action Research for Language Teachers*. Cambridge: Cambridge University Press.

—(2001), 'Analysing spoken discourse: Implications for TESOL', in A. Burns and C. Coffin (eds), *Analysing English in a Global Context*. London: Routledge, pp. 123–148.

—(2005), 'Action research', in E. Hinkel (ed.), *Handbook of Research in Second Language Teaching and Learning*. Mahwah, NJ: Lawrence Erlbaum Associates, pp. 241–256.

—(2007), 'Action research: Contributions and further directions in ELT', in J. Cummins and C. Davison (eds), *International Handbook of English Language Teaching*. New York: Springer, pp. 987–1002.

Butterworth, A. (2000), 'Casual conversation texts in listening to Australia', in H. de Silva Joyce (ed.), *Teachers' Voices 6: Teaching Casual Conversation*. Sydney: National Centre for English Language Teaching and Research, Macquarie University, pp. 3–10.

Carter, R. and McCarthy, M. (1995), 'Grammar and the spoken language', *Applied Linguistics*, 16(2), 141–158.

Cornwell, S. (1999), 'Interview with Anne Burns and Graham Crookes'. *The Language Teacher*, 23(12), 5–10.

Crookes, G. (1993), 'Action research for second language teachers: Going beyond teacher research', *Applied Linguistics*, 14(2), 130–144.

de Silva Joyce, H. and Slade, D. (2000), 'The nature of casual conversation: Implications for teaching, in H. de Silva Joyce (ed.), *Teachers' Voices 6: Teaching Casual Conversation*. Sydney: National Centre for English Language Teaching and Research, Macquarie University, pp. viii–xv.

Delaruelle, S. (2001), *Beach Street* 2. Sydney: New South Wales Adult Migrant English Service.

Denny, H. (2008), 'Teaching conversation and negotiation skills using teacher-made, semiscripted conversation models', in A. Burns and J. Burton (eds), Language Teacher Research in Australia and New Zealand. Alexandria, VA: TESOL, pp. 43–60.

Dörnyei, Z. (2003), *Questionnaires in Second Language Research: Construction, Administration and Processing*. Mahwah, NJ: Lawrence Erlbaum Associates.

Eggins, S. and Slade, D. (1997), *Analysing Casual Conversation*. London: Cassell.

Fanselow, J. (1987), *Breaking Rules: Generating and Exploring Alternatives in Language Education*. New York: Longman.

Freire, P. (1970), *The Pedagogy of the Oppressed*. New York: Herder & Herder.

Greenwood, D. J. and Levin, M. (2007), *Introduction to Action Research. Social Research for Social Change* (2nd edn). Thousand Oaks: Sage Publications.

Heron, J. (1996), *Co-operative Inquiry: Research into the Human Condition*. London: Sage.

Jarvis, G. (1983), 'Action research versus needed research for the 1980s', in D. L. Lange (ed.), *Proceedings of the National Conference on Professional Priorities*. Hastings-on-Hudson, NY: ACTFL Materials Center, pp. 59–63.

Kemmis, R. and McTaggart, R. (1988), *The Action Research Planner* (3rd edn). Geelong: Deakin University Press.

McKay, S. (2006), *Researching Second Language Classrooms*. Mahwah, NJ: Lawrence Erlbaum Associates.

Perkins, A. (2001), 'Here it is rough though it may be: Basic computer for ESL', in J. Edge (ed.), *Action Research*. Alexandria, VA: TESOL.

Richards, K. (2003), *Qualitative Inquiry in TESOL*. London: Palgrave.

Spada, N. and Fröhlich, M. (1995), *Communicative Orientation of Language Teaching Observation Scheme: Coding Conventions and Applications*. Sydney: National Centre for English Language Teaching and Research, Macquarie University.

Winter, R. (1987), *Action-Research and the Nature of Social Inquiry*. Aldershot: Gower Publishing.

Zeichner, K. M. and Noffke. S. E. (2001), 'Practitioner research', in V. Richardson (ed.), *Handbook of Research on Teaching* (4th edn). Washington, DC: American Educational Research Association, pp. 298–330.

Zuber-Skerritt, O. (1990), *Action Research in Higher Education. Examples and Reflections*. London: Kogan Page.

8 Analysing Qualitative Data

Adrian Holliday

In this chapter I will first set out some of the basic premises of qualitative research as a mainstream research approach which is used by applied linguists as they develop their interests in wider social and political issues connected with language and language education. It is important to begin in this way because analysing qualitative data is very much integrated with other stages of the research approach. The central section on techniques and instruments of analysis will demonstrate this; and the extended example in the final section will show how the basic issues connected with the approach come back again and again during analysis.

Underlying Assumptions and Methodology

There are a wide range of approaches to qualitative data analysis. The field is however moving increasingly towards a postmodern acknowledgement of the inevitability of qualitative research being subjective (Walford 1991, p. 1). While in quantitative research the emphasis is on controlling variables to the extent that the influence of the researcher is minimized, in qualitative research the aim is to search for the richest possible data. It is recognized that the ideas and presence of the researcher will be influential in what the data looks like and the way in which it is interpreted. Postmodernism acknowledges that 'truth' is mediated by ideology. Therefore, the outcomes of the research will always be influenced by the researcher's beliefs. There are also strong indications that quantitative research is itself increasingly recognizing these influences and becoming less naïve in its attitudes towards data.

The basic aim of qualitative research is to get to the bottom of what is going on in all aspects of social behaviour. It tends to do this within specific social settings such as schools, factories, hospital wards and so on, which are treated as cultures of activity, and pose basic ethnographic questions to do with power structures, tacit behavioural rules and modes of organization. Its roots are therefore closely associated with social and cultural anthropology and with the sister discipline of ethnography (see Starfield this volume), which is more precisely concerned with describing human communities, but from which it borrows much of its method. Within applied linguistics, qualitative research has been more traditionally applied to the linguistic aspects of communication, and as such has been quite limited; but it is now being applied to a wide range of scenarios from the politics of language teaching to the non-linguistic environment of language behaviour (e.g., Holliday 2006, 2005).

The types of data that can be collected are very varied; and it could be said that the data comprises whatever can be seen or heard which helps the researcher to get to the bottom of the issues implicit in the research questions. Such types of data are listed in Table 8.1. It needs to be noted here that interviews, observations, diaries and so on, as listed in the third column, are not really types of data, but means of collecting it.

As the data is collected it begins to indicate a picture of what is going on. Each piece of data, in itself a single instance of behaviour, contributes to this emerging, picture. The outcome needs to be a *thick description*, which is a narrative of what has been found that shows the full complexity and depth of what is going on. For example, a thick description of the roles and aspirations of a school head teacher was created by juxtaposing a description of her dealing with a pupil, a description of what happens when she enters a class, a description of her role in the school, a description of her office and its artefacts, her own account of her mission in the school, a pupil's account of her effect on timekeeping and a clause on the role of headmistresses in a ministry document (Holliday 2007, p. 74).

Central to the process of data collection and analysis is gradual focusing. Ideally, decisions about what sort of data should be collected will not be made until the researcher has entered the field, the place where the research will be carried out. An initial broad observation of what is going on will enable the researcher to establish what sorts of data will be relevant. More focused data collection then begins; but there should still be room for further refinement of focus and data collection choices.

Table 8.1 Types of data

Type	Characteristics	How collected
Description of behaviour	What people are seen or heard doing or saying	Observation notes, research diary etc.
Description of event	Piece of behaviour, defined either by the people in the setting (e.g., wedding, meeting) or by the researcher (e.g., bus journey, argument)	Observation notes, research diary etc.
Description of institution	The way the setting operates in terms of regulations, tacit rules, rituals	Observation notes, research diary etc.
Description of appearance	What the setting or people in it look like (e.g. space, buildings, clothing, arrangement of people or objects, artefacts)	Observation notes, research diary, drawings, diagrams
Description of research event	What people say or do in interview, focus group etc.	Observation notes, research diary etc.
Personal narrative	Reconstruction of experience that aids understanding	Narrative, research diary etc.
Account	What people say or write to the researcher – actual words	Interview, audio recording, questionnaire, participant's diary, transcription, verbatim notes
Talk	What people are heard saying – actual words	Audio recording, transcription, verbatim notes
Visual record	What is actually seen	Film, video recording
Document	Piece of writing belonging or pertaining to the setting	Photocopy, scan

Validity/Trustworthiness

Because of the inevitability of subjectivity, the validity and trustworthiness of the research will depend on how this subjectivity is managed. Good research therefore depends on three principles. First, *transparency* of method, which requires a description of how the research was carried out, from decisions regarding data collection and analysis, to how the beliefs and influence of the researcher were excavated and addressed.

Second, *submission*, which requires that, while being aware that she or he is the designer of the process, the researcher must submit to the data in such a way that the unexpected is allowed to emerge and perhaps change the direction of the research. A good piece of research will have built into the research design something which will enable the research to take on a life of its own. There is therefore an inherent weakness in qualitative research which tries to imitate quantitative research by starting with research questions, asking these questions in interviews and then reporting the answers. In such a design the researcher will only be able to get answers to questions she has thought of, and which have led the interviewees' responses. An important discipline is for the researcher to put aside professional preoccupations. For example, while carrying out classroom research, the researcher must try as hard as possible to stop thinking like a teacher or a teacher trainer, and try and see the classroom from a stranger's point of view. Another connected discipline is that of *making the familiar strange* in which the researcher tries as hard as possible to take on the role of a stranger in order to experience what it is like to approach a situation for the first time and to be acutely aware of how it operates as a culture.

Two methods for allowing the research to take on a life of its own are through a holistic thematic analysis (see below), and through attending to detail. This can best be illustrated in descriptive data. The following description of classroom behaviour, while clearly being subjective in what the researcher has chosen to describe, contains detail which travels beyond his initial questions and leads him to look further:

> The teacher walks around at the back monitoring while the students work.
> Those writing seek comment from their peers. . . . A student near the
> camera leans back to speak to friend. One girl student is arranging her hair.
> Several students talk to peers while the teacher explains. This does not
> seem to be a problem. The student who has been 'talking' is also clearly
> getting on with her work (Holliday 2005, p. 90).

The research question which drove this description was 'what are the students' role and behaviour in the classroom?' By noticing certain types of informal behaviour and being prepared to think laterally about it, the researcher was driven to consider that communicative activity took place outside and sometimes in conflict with the teacher's plan. I shall return to the issue of detail in methods of analysis below.

The third principle is that of *making appropriate claims*. Qualitative research looks at instances of behaviour rather than broad tendencies in that it cannot prove, for example, that certain percentages of people believe certain things. An appropriate claim would therefore be that in a particular location at a particular time, certain things *seem* to be the case. This shows that the purpose of qualitative research is not to prove anything, but to generate ideas which are sufficient to make us think again about what is going on in the world. It is not therefore possible to use qualitative studies to prove or disprove other studies by means of replication. Three different researchers looking at the same set of qualitative data may easily arrive at three very different interpretations; and it may well be the case that the data can only be made sense of by a researcher who has taken part in the total experience of collecting it.

Techniques and Instruments

The process of analysing qualitative data is not always separate from collecting data. Indeed, an ongoing dialogue between collecting data, writing and analysis should be encouraged. A research diary should be kept throughout the whole process, in which comments made at the time of data collection are kept. An example of these is in the right hand column of Table 8.2. Even though it must be acknowledged that the data is already itself a product of the researcher's interpretation, it is important that the researcher should learn to separate this from what can be said about it.

The classic method for analysing qualitative data is to begin by taking the following steps:

1. Coding: convert the comments on each piece of data to key words or phrases – e.g., 'informal behaviour', 'gender division', 'teacher control'. There may be more than one such code for each piece of data; but basically this is a method for seeing how each code is distributed throughout the data.
2. Determining themes: The codes which occur with significant frequency are then grouped within themes.
3. Constructing an argument: The themes are then used as the headings and subheadings for constructing an argument about what can be learnt from

Table 8.2 Data and comment (adapted from Holliday 2007: 107)

Data: what can be seen or heard	Comment: what this seems to mean at the time of data collection
The women tended to sit down the right of the room while the men tended to sit down the left of the room. Down the centre of the room there were many instances where the division was not precise, as men and women sit shoulder to shoulder and talk to each other.	This might connect with gender segregation seen in other parts of the society – for example, on buses. But the men and women sitting together in the centre seem comfortable. Other factors might therefore easily override the segregation principle. This connects with observation of men and women working together in small groups.

the data. Under each thematic heading, extracts from the data which exemplify the theme are collected and used as evidence for the points made in the argument.

4. Going back to the data: Collecting extracts to support the argument will involve going back to the data, reassessing the codes and refining or possibly changing the themes. The process of drafting and redrafting the argument will also add to this process of refinement.

There is a parallel here with writing a literature review, where the literature as a whole is like the data, and where extracts from the data are used in the same way as quotations from the literature, to provide evidence for what is being said about it. Note that I refer to data throughout as an uncountable noun – 'data is' rather than 'data are' – because in qualitative research it is not a sequence of items, but collectively a single body of experience. For this reason, for the purpose of analysis, it is better not to divide the data into parts (e.g. according to stages or types), but to deal with it holistically.

There is a range of computer software for analysing qualitative data. This can be very helpful in and collating codes and determining themes. However, I would not personally recommend using software as it cannot replace the intuition of the researcher who was there when the data was collected. The entire meaning may not be confined to the data, as the research diary is also an important source of interpretation. Also some data is so complex that it defies coding, and the narrative needs to be written in a more creative manner directly from the data and the research diary.

The following extract from a dissertation (Duan 2007, pp. 156–157) shows the resulting interaction between (a) an extract of data (indented), (b) comment made specifically about the extract and (c) the broader argument about what the data means (underlined). *Teachers* is the thematic heading for this part of the analysis. The three dots indicate that material is missing.

Teachers

. . .

> The reasons for Teacher Liang passing the letter to us were, I thought, to teach us something from the letter, to offer us encouragement, and hard-working spirit. I felt that Teacher Liang was a good teacher.
> The reasons for her to hit us or scold us were to nurture and educate us – to enable us to become useful, successful people. She did everything for our own good! (Diary, Wang Yang, 7 March 2002)

This Teacher Liang is the same one that scolded Wang Yang in the first extract. It seemed that he had already changed his view regarding this teacher. In the incident above, Wang Yang seemed to dislike the teacher.

But in this extract, it seems that he tries to find some justification for his teacher's ill treatment of him, even defending his teacher for what she had done to him, showing his understanding for her scolding him. This does not necessarily mean that he has changed his view. It may indicate consistently ambivalent feelings towards her. On the one hand, he hated his teacher for scolding him in public. On the other hand, he showed consent in witnessing his teacher's recital of the discourse. <u>This may suggest that there is evidence of the dominant discourse within the students' discourse</u>. The following extract shows just such a feeling:

> I know that Teacher Liang is a good teacher, that she always wants the best for us and that she has been doing all these things for our own good. But I could still not forget that she had scolded me in front of the other students, that she scolded me for 'grinning cheekily', saying that I did not study hard. Thinking of these events, I felt heavy and painful. It was difficult for me to forget these things. When she did these things, I really hated her because I thought she should not have scolded me in public, she could do it privately in her office instead of in public. That really hurt my self-esteem. It made me lose face.

It also seemed that teachers have contradictory feelings towards students. As Teacher Xiao comments:

> Student life is really hard. They have too much homework to do every day. All their subject teachers compete with each other regarding the amount of the homework they assign to the students. They want the students to spend most of their time after school on the subject *they* teach. As a result, the students have to suffer from over-assigned homework. Take my daughter, for instance. She is only in Year One in N1MS. But she has to work until the middle of each night to try to finish her homework, sometimes even until 1:00 o'clock in the following morning. I feel sorry for them, these poor students. (Individual Interview, Teacher Xiao, 1 August 2004)

Teacher Xiao seems here to show her empathy for the students in their suffering. This may be because she has an interested daughter. But it seemed that she even complained on the students' behalf about this homework issue. <u>And this may suggest that there is indeed a student's discourse within the teachers' dominant discourse.</u>

It is important to note how the data extracts are carefully referenced so that they can be traced back to the larger corpus of data. Also, the extracts are cross-referred to other extracts to show how meaning is built through their interconnection within the thick description; and the researcher goes into considerable detail in explaining what each extract means, while showing due caution through the use of phrases like 'not necessarily' and 'seem'. It may well be the case that there are other interpretations. In this discussion Duan first of all exercises restraint from jumping too quickly into an interpretation. He sets the extract from the diary against another 'incident above' and uses this juxtaposition to move gradually from one possible interpretation to another.

Qualitative researchers need to be excellent writers. It may be the case that small extracts of data are not sufficiently effective in expressing the richness and complexity of what the researcher experienced. Researchers may decide to present longer extracts of data, or reconstructions, or even fictionalized representations. There is no restriction on what can be done as long it is explained and justified in the text, and as long it is made clear in what way faithfulness to the data is maintained, and what sense is being made of the data. Many novice qualitative researchers make the mistake of thinking that presenting raw data will speak for itself. What is important to understand is that because the reader was not there, the data left alone will never be sufficient to communicate what was going on.

Ethical Considerations

There are clearly considerable ethical issues in qualitative research. At the most basic level the integrity and privacy of the people taking part in the research must be preserved at all costs. It is not however always a matter getting permission. The following points need to be considered: (a) People will very likely have far more important things to do and think about than taking part in your research project. Involving them in extended procedures for getting permission, collaborating or checking interpretations may in itself be an unfair imposition. (b) It may be unfair to expect that the people in the research setting should understand or be interested in the research project. (c) Different cultural settings will require different forms of consent, with different degrees of formality, informality and understanding. (d) What people are prepared to say, or how they are prepared to appear in front of a researcher may have as much to do with their perceptions of the researcher as with the questions the researcher is asking. They may be researching you as much as you are researching them – if they care to take the time. Researchers are usually far more unusual than the people they are researching. (e) It may be unfair to develop relationships within a research setting which cannot be sustained in their own terms. (f) Whatever claims you may have to being an insider, these will always be contaminated by the fact that you are a researcher.

A Sample Study

The study I have chosen for this section is still ongoing and involves my own investigation into the politics of established descriptions of national cultures.

My driving suspicion is that these descriptions are not as neutral as they purport to be; and I am led into this by previous work on the way dominant English teaching methodology employs negative stereotypes of 'other cultures'. The purpose of the research is thus to question an established belief. My data comprises (a) email interviews with 30 informants from a range of countries, (b) reconstructions of intercultural events from a range of ethnographic sources and (c) research and training literature on intercultural communication as examples of academic or professional ideology. Here I will focus on my initial analysis of the interview data, while being aware that eventually it will need to be looked at holistically along with the rest of the data. I am happy with email as a means for interviewing because it allows my informants the space to take their time, solves the issue of distance, has the (so far unused) potential for group discussion and produces written responses which do not need to be transcribed. It also means that the social setting does not have to be a physical one, but could be a community of people. I am open about the fact that my informants are friends, colleagues and students who are hand-picked for having encountered cultural difference, and I must keep this in mind when I begin to make claims at the end of my research.

I have so far asked each person the same three questions: (1) 'What are the major features of your cultural identity?' (2) 'What role does nation play in this?' (3) 'Are you comfortable with how others define your cultural identity?' These are purposefully very broad to allow maximum richness; and I have invited each person to use them simply as starting points, with the possibility that I will get back to them later with further questions which may grow out of their responses. My aim as a qualitative researcher is not to attempt to control variability, but to invite complexity.

The data I have received, now about 22,000 words, has begun to defy classic thematic analysis. I began by following the procedure described above, by first marking the interview text directly with a number of codes, as exemplified in Table 8.3.

It needs to be noted here that this was not a linguistic analysis of the interview responses, but an analysis of opinion. The total list of 25 codes which emerged from this initial exercise were as follows, some of which I have glossed in brackets: (1) Ancestry, (2) Gender/sexuality, (3) Geography (other than nation), (4) Language, (5) Layered (different realities at the same time), (6) Moral (judgements about the world), (7) Multicultured, (8) Multi-loyal (to more than one 'culture'), (9) Nation first (the most important category), (10) Nation complex (too complex to be an easy category), (11) Nation insufficient (too simple to be an easy category), (12) Nation limiting (too stereotypical to be realistic), (13) National imagery, (14) Nation repressive (repressive ideologies), (15) Nation critical (critical of what it means), (16) Non-exclusive (others can join and can

Table 8.3 Example of coding

Sample of data from question 1	Codes
First of all, what is my cultural identity? . . . I suppose it is defined according to a set of identifiable features that I share with others who belong to the world I most frequently inhabit. These features can only be described in terms that I am familiar with and that I consider important because of where I come from culturally. This sounds a rather circular approach: I define my cultural identity according to factors which are recognized as important for the group I see myself as part of.	Relative to group
Defining factors seem to be language, education, ancestry, religion, profession (I left language till last but it seems to have emerged as number one and although there is more to be said about everything else, I'll leave it for now!)	Small culture Religion ancestry
Most people can claim a first language and it helps us to establish ourselves within a particular discourse community but I'm not sure how to explain the role of an English native speaker as part of my cultural identity. If I think about cultural identity as a set of features I share with others, language is too broad, or maybe it's that English is too widely spoken to indicate a particular culture.	Language

join others), (17) Othered (negatively stereotyped), (18) Reflexive (defined in response to, others), (19) Relative to audience, (20) Religion, (21) Politics, (22) Small cultures (family, work, class, group etc), (23) Shifting, (24) History (personal), (25) Uncertain. The large number concerning nation (9–15) resulted from their being a specific question about it – for the reason that I was concerned with how far national culture is problematic.

I then began to rationalize these codes into a smaller and more manageable group of subthemes, each of which could be grouped under a smaller number of themes, as shown in Table 8.4. At this point it became very clear that this approach to coding and deriving themes was *very unsatisfactory*. The problem was that: (a) every time I looked back at the data, I found something different, *because* what people were saying was so complex; (b) this totally invalidated my attempt, in the final column of Table 8.4, to try and validate themes on the basis of the percentage of times they were indicated; (c) and as a result, trying to be too systematic in the analysis was actually taking me progressively further away from what the informants were actually saying, which in itself was far from clear.

There was something else, which initially seemed problematic, but then took me in a direction I had not expected – which was the truly validating element of the research, as I have referred to above. I had chosen informants partly because

Table 8.4 Deriving themes

Themes	Subthemes	Codes subsumed	Percentage of informants mentioned by (%)
The significance and ambivalence of nation	Nation as the most important category	(9)	50
	Nation as complex, insufficient and only a part of one's identity	(10–11)	50
	Nation as limiting, confining, repressive or morally distasteful	(12–15)	50
Other locational categories	Language as a means of distinguishing group boundaries	(4)	50
	Ancestry and personal and family history	(1, 24)	30
	Small or large entities other than nation	(3, 22)	25
	Religion	(20)	25
Complexity	The shifting and multiple nature of cultural identity and its ability to be different things at the same time	(5, 8, 23, 25)	75
	Reflexivity and relativity to changing circumstances and other groups	(18, 19)	50
	Loyalties and memberships transcending group boundaries	(7, 8)	25
Struggling with otherness	Being reduced by majority and inaccurate imaginations of who one really is	(17)	50

of their range of nationalities, which was in turn led by my interest in the way in which the West negatively stereotypes the rest of the world. However, ethically I could not declare their nationality unless they gave me permission. I therefore had to ask them in my next question –

> To help me to preserve privacy, would you like to be referred to either as yourself or with a pseudonym? Can you then provide a phrase about who you are – something like 'Adrian – a British academic living in Britain'.

This prompt was purposefully tentative because I was aware of my agenda and of the dangers of pushing it. The responses I got back gave names or pseudonyms, followed by phrases, several of which avoided clear reference nationality:

> ' . . . a young academic from Oaxaca, Mexico'
> '. . . an English teacher living in France'
> '. . . an Iranian-Australian Academic'
> '. . . who currently lives and teaches in the UAE'
> '. . . an ESL academic working in Saudi Arabia'

There was also one which explicitly raised the question of how far it was important to refer to 'profession, nationality, residence, etc'.

Other questions which arose as a result of this initial analysis were to do with the type of informants who had been approached. Were they too special *because* of being at 'cultural interfaces', of having travelled, of being good at expressing their complex ideas in writing, of being middle class, academics or students – or were they just particular examples of what many of us, everywhere, are like? This in turn led to thoughts about whether or not to interview other types of people. I also decided to leave behind the coding approach to analysis and derive themes directly from reading the interview text. However, the most significant outcome was a stronger appreciation of the moral imperative embedded in how we should deal with data – taking disciplined care to refrain from imposing meaning, not only on data, but also on the people who it represents.

The purpose of this example has been to illustrate that qualitative data analysis is far from a straightforward process. Rather than bringing the research to neat closure, it can raise as many questions as it seeks to answer, and is always unfinished. On the one hand there is comfort in its extreme open-endedness. Other the other hand, immense caution has to be applied.

Resources for Further Reading

All the texts listed below deal with mainstream qualitative research methodology and provide a holistic picture within which data analysis is part. None of them are specific to applied linguistics because I feel the mainstream is where the best roots for the research approach can be obtained.

Denzin, N.K. and Lincoln, Y. S. (eds) (2005), *Handbook of Qualitative Research* (3rd edn). Thousand Oaks, CA: Sage.
   Though expensive, this is an essential body of work for any serious qualitative researcher. Fairly short chapters between them cover the whole range

of qualitative research activity, from an overview of approaches through such methods as action research, grounded theory, narrative enquiry and so on.

Geertz, C. (1993), *The Interpretation of Cultures: Selected Essays*. London: Fontana.

This is a classic text for those who wish to get into the intricacies of thick description.

Hammersley, M. and Atkinson, P. (1995), *Ethnography: Principles in Practice*. London: Routledge.

This is an excellent description of the scope and use of qualitative research methodology. While the title refers to ethnography, this is treated liberally; and it becomes clear that ethnography, grounded theory, phenomenology and so on are different sides of a common approach.

Holliday, A. R. (2007), *Doing and Writing Qualitative Research* (2nd edn). London: Sage.

This is the text from which most of this chapter is taken. It is a practical introduction while also dealing with theoretical issues, and based on an analysis, with interviews and examples of how a number of researchers, from undergraduate to doctoral students, have carried out their studies. Though these studies are taken from a range of disciplines, a significant number are within applied linguistics.

Spradley, J. P. (1980), *Participant Observation*. New York: Holt, Rinehart and Winston.

Though now old, this is an excellent manual for classic qualitative research methodology. It works gradually through the basic steps from broad to gradual narrowing of focus.

References

Denzin, N. K. and Lincoln, Y. S. (eds) (2005), *Handbook of Qualitative Research* (3rd edn). Thousand Oaks, CA: Sage.

Duan, Y. P. (2007), 'The influence of the Chinese university entrance exam (English)'. Unpublished Ph.D. thesis, Department of Language Studies, Canterbury Christ Church University.

Hammersley, M. and Atkinson, P. (1995), *Ethnography: Principles in Practice*. London: Routledge

Holliday, A. R. (2005), *The Struggle to Teach English as an International Language*. Oxford: Oxford University Press.

—(2006), 'The value of reconstruction in revealing hidden or counter cultures'. *Journal of Applied Linguistics*, 1(3), 275–294.

—(2007), *Doing and Writing Qualitative Research* (2nd edn). London: Sage.

Walford, G. (1991). 'Reflexive accounts of doing educational research', in G. Walford, (ed.), *Doing Educational Research*. London: Routledge, pp. 1–17.

9 Research Synthesis

Lourdes Ortega

Chapter Overview

Research synthesis refers to a continuum of techniques and research procedures that have been developed by social scientists with the aim of reviewing past literature systematically. Simply put, the methodology produces contemporary literature reviews that differ from traditional literature reviews in taking an empirical perspective on the task of reviewing. Syntheses (also known as *systematic reviews* in some fields) investigate and evaluate past findings in a systematic fashion, always explicating the methodology followed in the review so as to enable replication by other reviewers. The approach began in the late 1970s in the fields of psychology, education and medicine and its use has been widespread across the social sciences since the late 1980s. In applied linguistics, the methodology has only recently been introduced. Table 9.1 lists 18 article-length syntheses published in the first 15 years of application of this method in our field.

Meta-analysis is probably the best-known technique for systematically synthesizing quantitative research. However, synthesists can engage in meta-analysis only when the body of research to be synthesized is clearly quantitative, that is, experimental, quasi-experimental, or correlational. In addition, the methodology of meta-analysis is driven by questions about the magnitude of an effect or causal relationship and involves mathematical ways of summarizing past findings that demand the availability of a large number of studies.

111

Table 9.1 Article-length systematic research syntheses published in *Applied Linguistics* (1994–2008)

Study

1. Thomas (1994)*	How have SLA researchers measured proficiency for research purposes in their studies?
2. Ross (1998)**	How well does L2 self-assessment work?
3. Norris and Ortega (2000)**	How effective is L2 grammar instruction, and does type of instruction matter?
4. Goldschneider and DeKeyser (2001)**	How much of the L2 English morpheme accuracy order can be attributed to frequency and salience?
5. Masgoret and Gardner (2003)**	How well does amount of motivation predict L2 achievement in Gardner's Attitude/Motivation Test Battery?
6. Ortega (2003)*	What is the relationship between syntactic complexity and L2 writing proficiency?
7. Dinsmore (2006)**	How different are native and non-native speaking performances in Universal Grammar studies?
8. Keck et al. (2006)**	How effective is task-based interaction in fostering L2 grammar and vocabulary gains?
9. Russell and Spada (2006)**	Is oral and written corrective feedback effective?
10. Jeon and Kaya (2006)**	How effective is L2 pragmatics instruction, and does type of instruction matter?
11. Taylor et al. (2006)**	How effective is explicit reading strategy instruction in improving L2 reading comprehension?
12. Téllez and Waxman (2006)†	What are best teaching practices to teach English Language Learners in k-12 schools in the US?
13. Thomas (2006)*	How do SLA researchers measure proficiency for research purposes in their studies, 12 years after Thomas (1994)?
14. Indefrey (2006)**	Are L1 and L2 processed differently, according to hemodynamic research evidence?
15. Mackey and Goo (2007)**	How effective is task-based interaction in fostering L2 grammar and vocabulary gains?
16. Truscott (2007)**	Is written corrective feedback effective for improving L2 writers' accuracy in new writing?
17. Lee and Huang (2008)**	How effective is typographical input enhancement as an L2 grammar implicit teaching technique?
18. Spada and Tomita (2008)**	Are L2 instructional gains moderated by whether structures are simple or complex?

Note: * Systematic quantitative synthesis. ** Meta-analysis. †Systematic qualitative synthesis. Studies are listed in chronological order. Full citations are given in the references.

Other bodies of literature, however, offer descriptive, qualitative or mixed-methods data that cannot be appraised exclusively by notions of effect or causality, or they are too small for meta-analytic quantification. In such cases, synthesists employ a number of empirically oriented methods in order to systematically review the literature, but they do not necessarily engage in all the formal quantitative procedures of meta-analysis. It is for this reason that we say that all meta-analyses are also syntheses, but not all syntheses are meta-analyses. It can be seen in Table 9.1 that in applied linguistics a good range of topics have been submitted to synthesis, but mostly in the form of meta-analysis.

Underlying Assumptions of the Methodology

For a review to be considered a research synthesis, it must go beyond the collating and summarizing of individual study findings. Thus, none of the following summative techniques, in and of themselves, make a literature review into a synthesis: (a) presenting an authoritative narrative recount of past research activity in a given area, (b) summarizing many studies together in tabular form or (c) taking a count of how many studies yielded statistically significant findings in support of a given hypothesis. These are only traditional practices of good, traditional literature reviews. Research synthesists, on the other hand, must transcend such practices if they are to produce synthetic findings that are more than the sum of the parts and go beyond the individual results contained in any of the primary investigations synthesized (Norris and Ortega 2007).

Another trademark of many syntheses and meta-analyses (although not all) is a critical stance towards statistical significance. Many synthesists believe that while *probability* is an important dimension of quantitative research, *magnitude* is a distinct piece of information that is as important as probability and must be interpreted in conjunction with it (Kramer and Rosenthal 1999; Thompson 2006). When we pose questions about probability or statistical significance, we ask ourselves whether our observations are spurious (i.e., non-significant) or trustworthy (i.e., significant). This would only tell us whether the findings observed in a given study are likely to hold true if we carried out the same study again with a different sample drawn from the same population. Naturally, the issue of trustworthiness is very important in quantitative research paradigms, since it goes to the heart of generalizability. However, in the end, the questions of interest to experts – as well as to the public – are about magnitude. In applied linguistics, for example, an important question about the size of an effect would be: *How large or important* is the difference between providing instruction on an L2 grammar form or leaving it up to simple exposure to that form? And a central question about the strength of a relationship would be: If someone has below-average working memory capacity, *how severe or disadvantageous* can the consequences be for his or her potential to learn an L2 fast and well? By putting the emphasis on magnitude rather than probability, or at least by always extracting and interpreting information about both probability and magnitude together, synthesists and meta-analysts seek to redress the many misuses and abuses of statistical significance that have been documented in all the social sciences (Harlow et al. 1997; Ziliak and McCloskey 2008), including applied linguistics (Lazaraton 2000).

Finally, and as can be surmised from the discussion thus far, research synthesis typically has a positivist and quantitative orientation. This orientation is expected, given that the approach arose out of the desire to make sense of quantitative findings (Glass 1976). Nevertheless, some synthesists have recognized the need to explore appropriate methods for the systematic review of accumulated *qualitative* literatures. For example, over twenty years ago educational sociologists George Noblit and Dwight Hare developed an approach for synthesizing ethnographic research that they called meta-ethnography (Noblit and Hare 1988) and more recently a research team in medical sociology led by Mary Dixon-Woods at Leicester University has explored new principles for conducting critical interpretive syntheses of research (see Dixon-Woods et al. 2007). In applied linguistics, as indicated in Table 9.1, only one systematic synthesis of qualitative research exists (Téllez and Waxman 2006). In the future, and mirroring the evolution of research synthesis in the wider landscape of the social sciences, interest in qualitative forms of systematic reviewing may grow in our field (Norris and Ortega 2007).

Validity and Trustworthiness in Research Synthesis

Several key issues impinge on the validity and trustworthiness of a research synthesis. Reliability and validity can be weakened or strengthened at the point in the research process when effect sizes need to be calculated, aggregated and reported, as you will see when you read about *Techniques and instruments for research syntheses* in a later section. In this section, I discuss important validity considerations that arise during the sampling of the primary studies to be included in the review.

Apples and Oranges, or the Problem of Relevance

From the beginning of the research process, the synthesist faces two basic questions of relevance that can affect the validity of the review findings: How closely related to a given research question must a study be in order to be included in the synthesis?; and How similar to each other must studies be in order for their findings to be combined meaningfully in the same synthesis? These questions can only be answered by carefully considering the purposes and research questions that guide a given synthesis. If we want to understand apples, it would be unwise to mix them with oranges in the same review. On the other hand, if we want to understand the two most popular fruits consumed daily in western countries, then we may need to include precisely apples and oranges. If we want to understand fruit as a full category, moreover, we would want not only to mix apples and oranges, but to include a wide palette of other types of fruit as well.

The apples and oranges question must be well justified in any synthesis and can only be satisfactorily answered if the synthesist has strong expert knowledge about the topic in question. In the end, therefore, substantive expertise in the research domain is as important as methodological expertise in the practice of research synthesis, and both are necessary to enhance the validity of the review. Coupled with the importance afforded to issues of coding, reliability and replicability, this is perhaps one of the reasons why research syntheses are often carried by teams rather than individuals (cf. Norris and Ortega 2006a).

Publication Bias or the File-Drawer Problem

The problem of publication bias is little understood in the field of applied linguistics but well documented in all forms of quantitative research in the social sciences (Rothstein et al. 2005). First, studies that do not report at least some statistically significant result are likely to be rejected by journal referees. Secondly, authors are also inclined to give up on trying to publish a study which yielded no statistically significant outcomes, probably because they are well aware of the unspoken rejection bias of journals. In either case, the result is the same: Studies that report statistically non-significant results are likely to be filed away in researchers' drawers and rarely make it into the public light. This means, in turn, that findings associated with a given research question are over-inflated if we only consider the universe of published studies, because statistically significant results are overrepresented (and statistically non-significant results underrepresented) in published literatures.

Therefore, good syntheses must always address the issue of publication bias. Among synthesists and meta-analysts, the preferred solution is to include unpublished or so-called fugitive literature in the synthesis. However, when including fugitive literature one must be doubly systematic and exhaustive in the sampling efforts. Particular care must be taken not to over-rely on word-of-mouth knowledge of fugitive literature offered by immediate and far-away colleagues and their mentees and students. This knowledge, albeit valuable, is inevitably partial and most likely biased geographically and substantively. An arbitrary and incomplete sampling of unpublished studies can threaten the validity of the synthesis as much as an arbitrary and incomplete sampling of published studies would.

Whenever only published studies are included in a synthesis – unfortunately, the default case in applied linguistics thus far – the synthesist should assess the gravity of the publication bias at work. A wide range of sensitivity analyses has been developed specifically for this purpose (Rothstein et al. 2005). For example, Ross (1998) applied a mathematical estimation called the *fail-safe formula* and Norris and Ortega (2000) employed a visual technique called the *funnel plot*. If both published and fugitive literatures are included in a synthesis, it is also informative to compare the main findings to the findings that obtain if published and fugitive studies are aggregated separately, something that both Taylor et al. (2006) and Lee and Huang (2008) did in our field.

Garbage in, Garbage out or the Problem of Research Quality

Ultimately, the quality of a synthesis is largely dependent on the quality of the primary evidence on which it is built. Some research synthesists follow the advice of educational psychologist Robert E. Slavin (1986) who advocated the *best evidence* approach to synthesizing. He proposed that only studies that meet the highest standards of methodological quality should be included in a synthesis. He was careful to warn that in the best evidence approach the task of determining what methodological rigour means must be explicitly rationalized anew by the synthesist for each research domain. It must also be justified for each study included in the synthesis, published or unpublished. A good illustration of these two points is offered in a meta-analysis by Slavin and Cheung (2005) that compared the effects of bilingual and English-only reading programs offered in elementary schools. Most synthesists, however, follow the broadly inclusive approach proposed by Gene Glass, the founder of meta-analysis (Glass 1976). As long as a study meets the set of inclusion criteria established at the onset of the synthesis, it will be included, so as to later perform sensitivity analyses that will help ascertain empirically whether, and in what ways, differences in research quality may have impacted the results of the review.

Norris and Ortega (2006b) argue, in agreement with most synthesists, that the inclusive approach serves well the field of applied linguistics. If the synthesist excludes certain studies a priori on grounds of poor research quality, this decision may always be contested, as methodological rigour is often in the eye of the beholder. Consider, for example, whether when carrying out a synthesis on effects of L2 instruction, intact classroom studies should be excluded because of their low internal validity due to lack of experimental control, or whether laboratory studies should be excluded for their low ecological validity, despite their high internal validity. Either decision would always dissatisfy one or another sector of the research domain. On the other hand, if the reviewer is as inclusive as it is reasonable at the initial stage of study sampling, the accumulated evidence can be made sense of more fully in the synthesis, and any possible biases introduced by the varying research quality of the individual designs can be more closely inspected and appraised.

Techniques and Instruments for Research Synthesis

A research synthesis will typically entail several steps, which derive from the empirical perspective on reviewing it embraces:

- *Problem specification*: As a first step, the research problem or question to be synthesized must be specified carefully and precisely; this is analogous to the step, necessary in any primary study, of formulating well thought-out research questions.
- *Literature search and study eligibility criteria*: These two steps entail explicating how the primary studies will be located and which ones will be included or excluded in the synthesis and why; this parallels the need in any empirical study, quantitative or qualitative, to carefully plan the selection of participants and justify sampling procedures.
- *Coding book development*: At this step, a systematic coding scheme must be devised by which all variables under study in the synthesis will be extracted from each primary report; this is analogous to the design of an instrument (e.g., a test) or a procedure (e.g., an interview or an observation protocol) that will elicit the relevant evidence from each participant in as consistent and well-motivated a fashion as possible.
- *Coding of studies*: This step documents how the study coding was done and how the reliability of the coding process was safeguarded.
- *Data analysis and display*: This step is parallel to the processes involved in analysing and displaying results in primary research. The evidence reported in study after study must be extracted first by application of the coding scheme and then it must be processed and made sense of; and subsequently, the findings must be organized in numerical, visual and narrative displays.
- *Interpretation and dissemination*: As with all research activities, synthesizing ultimately is a process that demands interpretive and dialogic efforts within a disciplinary community; the results must be interpreted in a historical and disciplinary context and the findings disseminated in reports that others can read, judge, replicate and use for their own purposes.

Many research syntheses, and all meta-analyses, involve the calculation of what is known as *effect sizes*. An effect size is an index that captures numerically, and in a standardized form, the strength of a relationship or the magnitude of a difference. Effect sizes must be demystified. We all know r, or the correlation coefficient, and have learned to interpret it. This is, in fact, an effect size. It expresses the strength of a relationship between two variables represented by two sets of scores. The closer r is to positive 1 or negative 1, the stronger the relationship between the two variables is known to be (and this observed relationship may or may not be trustworthy, depending on the output we obtain for the probability value or p associated with each r; see Phakiti this volume). Correlations are always interpretable in this same way (from 0 to plus or minus 1), regardless of the variety of tests, instruments and methods by which the scores submitted to correlations are obtained. There are also many instances when researchers report their findings in natural units, such as words produced, hours studied or cigarettes smoked. Proportions and percentages are also effect sizes that everyone understands and uses in daily matters. When this is the case, the results do not need to be translated into a mathematical unit of some other kind, but can be most meaningfully expressed in natural units and in proportions and percentages. For example, according to the famous report released by the US Department of Health, Education, and Welfare in 1967, cigarette smoking has been proven to increase mortality rates at different bands of magnitude: When compared to no smoking at all, smoking up to half a pack a day (or less than 10 cigarettes) increases the chance of mortality by 40 per cent, and if we raise the consumption of cigarettes by four times, to two packs or more a day, the risk rate increases by three times (120 per cent). These are effect sizes that everyone understands.

But when a researcher reports mean performances of groups and subsequently compares mean group differences, the scores reported are specific to that study's instruments (e.g., a 42-point difference on the TOEFL in one study, a 3.68 difference on a 15-point test in another study, and so on). In order to compare mean results across many studies, therefore, each of the individual study results must first be converted into a common index, or an effect size, which can then be aggregated together in a total mean effect size. This effect size is typically d (Cohen 1988), which simply expresses the difference between two group means in standard deviation units. For example, a d of 1.45 indicates that the experimental group scored 1.45 deviation units above the control group on the post-test, or that the advantage conferred by the treatment can be gauged to have had a magnitude of roughly one and a half deviation units in that study. Once we convert the results from each study into a d, we can average them and we will have the overall mean magnitude of a given treatment, based on however many studies we were able to combine. For example, a mean d of 1.45 indicates that, after inspecting study after study in our synthesis, we found that experimental groups had an average advantage over control groups of 1.45 deviation units in their favour.

It is important to emphasize that research synthesis, given its empirical take on the task of reviewing, adheres to the foundations of quantitative research in general. In order to enhance the reliability of the evidence and the validity of interpretations in primary quantitative research, it is important to consider the following issues against the context of the research questions and the design chosen: (a) sample size, (b) reliability of the instruments, (c) score distributions and (d) trustworthiness of the results. The same issues must also be considered by the synthesist, who will do well in thinking of each study as a 'participant' or 'informant' in the review. Thus, the synthesist must consider whether the number of accumulated studies is sufficient to carry out a full-blown meta-analysis, or whether a synthesis using less powerful quantitative techniques is more appropriate in light of a small sample size. Furthermore, as with any elicitation instrument, the coding system employed to extract the same information consistently across all studies must be carefully developed and its reliable use enhanced and evaluated in the synthesis. In addition, if effect sizes are calculated, the synthesist should always make interpretations not only about the overall grand mean or average effect size but also about how spread out the results across individual studies are. Specifically, it is important to address the question: How representative of individual study results can a given average effect size be said to be? This can be achieved by reporting and inspecting the standard deviation associated with each mean effect size. Finally, whenever mean effect sizes are reported, confidence intervals that express the amount of error around the observed mean should also be calculated and reported. This information helps us determine how trustworthy the average findings really are, as it is equivalent to carrying out a statistical significance test.

Ethical Considerations in Research Synthesis

Because synthesists only work with existing studies and previously reported results, they need not be concerned with norms for ethical conduct towards human participants. However, there are other ethical considerations worth mentioning. As with most quantitatively oriented research, syntheses and meta-analyses can be dangerously attractive and persuasive in their claim to take stock of accumulated evidence and in their aspiration to provide so-called final answers to important but elusive questions in a given domain of study. A related danger is what well-known meta-analyst Robert Rosenthal has called high-tech statistication (Rosenthal and DiMatteo 2001), which occurs when technical virtuosity in quantitative synthetic techniques is achieved at the expense of substantive quality and depth.

Being cognizant of these traps and knowing the limits of research syntheses is important (Norris and Ortega 2006b, 2007). No single synthesis can give a definitive answer to a research problem, because research is a human enterprise that is contingent on the time and space in which it is produced. Like all research, syntheses may be able to answer questions of now and here, but these questions will evolve. All knowledge will always be reevaluated and recalibrated, as human history and consciousness change. In addition, no dose of statistical or technical expertise can make up for lack of substantive expertise. Finally, research syntheses are always purely descriptive and correlational and cannot completely dispel debates surrounding causality, because the synthesist has no choice over the studies that make it into the review or over how individual researchers operationalized their variables and designed their investigations. In sum, syntheses can only produce evidence that is firmly rooted in the contexts in which the primary research has been carried out.

In the end, an ethical approach to practising research synthesis may come from 'a research ethic to think and act synthetically', and from 'a commitment to intelligible and respectful communication: between past and present studies, across theory and research and practice divides, between research contexts or camps, and among members of each research community' (Norris and Ortega 2006b, p. 36).

A Sample Study

I conclude this chapter with a quick tour of a meta-analysis that my colleague John Norris and I carried out (Norris and Ortega 2000), and which illustrates the methodology and its main concepts and procedures.

Problem specification: We set out to investigate the effectiveness of different types of L2 instruction. After examining the concepts most often discussed in this research domain, we decided against trying to gauge the effects of particular pedagogical techniques (e.g., recasts, grammar translation, input processing and so on) because there were insufficient numbers of studies accumulated for any such technique. On the other hand, we adopted the theoretical notions of focus on form versus forms (Long 1991) and explicit versus implicit grammar teaching (DeKeyser 1995), because we reasoned they were workable characterizations of type of instruction that could be found in all specific techniques. We also decided to include as moderating variables the type of outcome measure (e.g., grammaticality judgement or free production task), the length of instruction (e.g., half an hour or 50 hours) and the durability of effects (i.e., whether any gains were maintained on delayed post-tests). The rationale was that these variables had been discussed in previous literature as important concerns when evaluating the effectiveness of L2 instruction and that information for at least the first two moderating variables could be extracted from each study (we expected that delayed post-tests would be present in only a subset of the studies).

Literature search and study eligibility criteria: Although we initially identified over 250 studies that were potentially relevant via electronic and manual searches, subsequently only 77 study reports met the inclusion criteria for the synthesis that we had previously developed based on our knowledge of the research domain. Furthermore, we were able to include only a subset of these (specifically, 49 unique sample studies) in the meta-analysis part of the synthesis, because the remainder studies did not contain sufficient information to calculate effect sizes. The studies had been published between 1980 and 1998 and therefore represented the research domain as was practised in the 1980s and 1990s. The designs varied widely but all were (quasi-) experimental and involved instruction of a specific L2 form as the independent variable and measurement of performance on the same specific form as the dependent variable(s). After long deliberations, we decided to include only published studies and to inspect publication bias by means of a funnel plot. While we found no direct evidence of publication bias, we cautioned that this was most likely due to the fact that most individual researchers used complex multiple-treatment designs and therefore were able to report both statistically significant and non-significant results for different treatments within the same study. We also decided not to use methodological quality as a criterion for excluding studies and instead to adopt a broadly inclusive approach. That is, we decided to investigate research quality as an empirical matter, inspecting and synthesizing in full detail the research practices found across all 77 studies.

Coding book development: An important and time-consuming step was to develop the coding book, which had to include a large number of categories in order to address each research question. For example, we decided that each study would be coded for methodological and background features such as learner characteristics, study design, sample size, length of treatment, timing of tests and statistical information reported. We also coded each study (and for multiple-treatment designs, each treatment group within each study) for substantive features, including: type of instruction (with five values: focus on form, focus on forms, focus on meaning, explicit and implicit), type of outcome measure (with four values: meta-linguistic judgement, selected response, constrained constructed response and free constructed response) and length of instruction (with four values: brief, short, medium and long; these categories were defined bottom-up, according to the range of observed instructional lengths in the 77 studies).

Coding of studies: Both of us were involved as coders in the process of study coding. For most methodological, low-inference categories each coded a different half of the studies. Because we knew type of instruction and type of outcome measure would involve high-inference coding decisions, we decided to calculate and report reliability for these two categories only. Therefore, we set apart 20 per cent of the sample of studies and independently coded them for these substantive features. The reliability of the codings was satisfactory with values above 0.90 for both simple per cent agreement and *Cohen's kappa* (see Phakiti this volume).

Data analysis and display: We tallied all values for the coded methodological study features, aggregated them and presented them in tabular form (these results can be found in Tables 1 to 6 and Figures 1 and 2 in the original 2000 report). In order to answer the main research questions, we extracted effect sizes from the 49 unique sample studies for which sufficient information for this calculation was available. It is important to note that we calculated two distinct types of effect sizes, which we then aggregated and reported separately (as it should always be done, if both types of effect sizes are used in the same meta-analysis): (a) standardized mean difference *d*s, which compared post-test performances of treatment versus control groups and (b) standardized mean gain *d*s, also called within-group pre-post contrasts, which expressed pre-to-post-test change for each group, including control or baseline groups. For each of the two effect size types, aggregations resulted in average effect sizes. We presented the information in the form of means, standard deviations and confidence intervals (which can be found in Tables 7 to 12 and Figures 3 to 8 in the original 2000 report).

Interpretation and dissemination: We found that L2 instruction overall was superior to simple L2 exposure or meaning-driven communication by nearly a full standard deviation unit on average ($d = 0.96$ based on 49 studies) and that explicit treatments were clearly superior to implicit treatments, in terms of both magnitude ($d = 1.13$ versus $d = 0.54$, based on 69 and 29 contrasts, respectively) and probability (the confidence intervals around these two means did not overlap, which amounts to saying that the two means were statistically significantly different from each other). On the other hand, the difference between focus on form and focus on forms treatments was small ($d = 1.00$ versus 0.93) and statistically not significant, indicating that both qualities of instruction were effective and neither one was superior to the other in the evidence examined (43 and 55 contrasts, respectively). We could offer no conclusive answers with regard to the influence of type of outcome measure or the varying lengths of instruction, due to insufficient sample size across categories for both variables. However, to our surprise, we found that the 22 studies which featured delayed post-tests yielded an average effect size of 1.02, and that the lower boundary of the associated confidence interval was 0.78, and from this we concluded that the effects of instruction were indeed durable for the participants involved in these 22 studies. Finally, we documented empirically a number of endemic methodological weaknesses typical of this domain, based on the full sample size of 77 studies. We discussed these problems in detail and proposed some solutions.

It is important to stress that the main findings of this synthesis, as much as any other one, are contingent upon and grounded in the available accumulated evidence (Norris and Ortega 2006b). As authors of the synthesis, we have always felt readers of this study should not think of these results as directly generalizable to the abstract concept of 'L2 instruction.' This is simply because the real-world of L2 instruction goes well beyond the world captured in those 77 (or 49) studies and offers a much richer kaleidoscope of contexts for the instruction of additional languages and much more varied approaches to the teaching of grammar than was possibly investigated in the particular investigations synthesized. Moreover, the many methodological weaknesses uncovered and carefully documented also call for caution when extrapolating the findings beyond the concrete body of evidence synthesized. More modestly, we find value in the results of this meta-analysis because we hope they offer 'a useful empirical context within which future single-study findings from L2 type-of-instruction research can be more meaningfully interpreted' (Norris and Ortega 2000, pp. 499–500).

Resources for Further Reading

Cooper, H., Hedges, L. V. and Valentine, J. C. (eds). (2009), *The Handbook of Research Synthesis and Meta-analysis (2nd edn)*. New York: Russell Sage Foundation.
    This edited collection constitutes the most comprehensive and encyclopedic treatment of meta-analysis to date. The utility (and difficulty) of chapters varies, but all have been written by international experts in specialized sub-areas of meta-analysis.
Hunt, M. (1997), *How Science Takes Stock: The Story of Meta-Analysis*. New York: Russell Sage Foundation.
    This book offers a lively and accessible chronicle of the history of meta-analysis. Readers can learn a great deal of technical concepts in an intuitive fashion thanks to the variety of concrete examples offered from the fields of psychology, education and medicine.
Light, R. and Pillemer, D. (1984), *Summing Up: The Science of Reviewing Research*. Cambridge, MA: Harvard University Press.
    This book is an unsurpassed classic treatise about research synthesis. It goes well beyond meta-analysis and offers many visual and descriptive techniques for synthesizing quantitative findings. For this reason, it is an invaluable tool to learn about the many options available in the methodology of synthesis.
Lipsey, M. W. and Wilson, D. B. (2001), *Practical Meta-Analysis*. Thousand Oaks, CA: Sage.
    There are several textbook-like manuals about meta-analysis, but this one is particularly accessible and complete. It answers most technical questions that beginning meta-analysts will have about formulas for the calculation of different types of effect sizes, strategies for keeping track of study codings and so on.
Norris, J. M. and Ortega, L. (eds) (2006a), *Synthesizing Research on Language Learning and Teaching*. Amsterdam: John Benjamins.
    This is the only collection that exemplifies the methodology of research synthesis in applied linguistics. It includes applications of the methodology to universal grammar, interaction, negative feedback, pragmatics, reading strategies, the measurement of proficiency and best practices for English language learners in US schools. The variety of topics sampled in the empirical studies will help readers understand how synthesis can be applied to very diverse areas of research

within applied linguistics. In the first chapter, the co-editors offer a critical, extensive overview of the principles and uses of synthesis.

References

Cohen, J. (1988), *Statistical Power Analysis for the Behavioral Sciences* (2nd edn). Hillsdale, NJ: Lawrence Erlbaum.

DeKeyser, R. (1995), 'Learning second language grammar rules: An experiment with a miniature linguistic system'. *Studies in Second Language Acquisition*, 17, 379–410.

Dinsmore, T. H. (2006), 'Principles, parameters, and SLA: A retrospective meta-analytic investigation into adult L2 learners' access to universal grammar', in J. M. Norris and L. Ortega (eds), *Synthesizing Research on Language Learning and Teaching*. Amsterdam: John Benjamins, pp. 53–90.

Dixon-Woods, M., Booth, A. and Sutton, A. J. (2007), 'Synthesising qualitative research: A review of published reports'. *Qualitative Research*, 7, 375–422.

Goldschneider, J. and DeKeyser, R. M. (2001), 'Explaining the "natural order of L2 morpheme acquisition" in English: A meta-analysis of multiple determinants'. *Language Learning*, 51, 1–50.

Glass, G. V. (1976), 'Primary, secondary, and meta-analysis of research'. *Educational Researcher*, 5(10), 3–8.

Harlow, L., Mulaik, S. and Steiger, J. (eds) (1997), *What if There Were No Significant Tests?* Mahwah, NJ: Lawrence Erlbaum.

Indefrey, P. (2006), 'A meta-analysis of hemodynamic studies on first and second language processing: Which suggested differences can we trust and what do they mean?', in M. Gullberg and P. Indefrey (eds), *The Cognitive Neuroscience of Second Language Acquisition* (*Language Learning* 56 Supplement 1). Malden, MA: Wiley/Blackwell.

Jeon, E. H. and Kaya, T. (2006), 'Effects of L2 instruction on interlanguage pragmatic development: A meta-analysis', in J. M. Norris and L. Ortega (eds), *Synthesizing Research on Language Learning and Teaching*. Amsterdam: John Benjamins, pp. 165–211.

Keck, C. M., Iberri-Shea, G., Tracy-Ventura, N. and Wa-Mbaleka, S. (2006), 'Investigating the empirical link between task-based interaction and acquisition: A meta-analysis', in J. M. Norris and L. Ortega (eds), *Synthesizing Research on Language Learning and Teaching*. Amsterdam: John Benjamins, pp. 91–131.

Kramer, S. H. and Rosenthal, R. (1999), 'Effect sizes and significance levels in small-sample research', in R. H. Hoyle (ed.), *Statistical Strategies for Small Sample Research*. Thousand Oaks, CA: Sage, pp. 59–79.

Lazaraton, A. (2000), 'Current trends in research methodology and statistics in applied linguistics'. *TESOL Quarterly*, 34, 175–181.

Lee, S.-K. and Huang, H. T. (2008), 'Visual input enhancement and grammar learning: A meta-analytic review'. *Studies in Second Language Acquisition*, 30, 307–331.

Long, M. H. (1991), 'Focus on form: A design feature in language teaching methodology', in K. D. Bot, R. Ginsberg and C. Kramsch (eds), *Foreign Language Research in Cross-Cultural Perspective*. Amsterdam: John Benjamins, pp. 39–52.

Mackey, A. and Goo, J. M. (2007), 'Interaction research in SLA: A meta-analysis and research synthesis', in A. Mackey (ed.), *Conversational Interaction in Second Language Acquisition*. New York: Oxford University Press, pp. 379–452.

Masgoret, A.-M. and Gardner, R. C. (2003), 'Attitudes, motivation, and second language learning: A meta-analysis of studies conducted by Gardner and associates'. *Language Learning*, 53, 123–163.

Noblit, G. W. and Hare, R. D. (1988), *Meta-Ethnography: Synthesizing Qualitative Studies*. Newbury Park: Sage.

Norris, J. M. and Ortega, L. (2000), 'Effectiveness of L2 instruction: A research synthesis and quantitative meta-analysis'. *Language Learning*, 50, 417–528.

Norris, J. M. and Ortega, L. (eds) (2006a), *Synthesizing Research on Language Learning and Teaching*. Amsterdam: John Benjamins.

—(2006b), 'The value and practice of research synthesis for language learning and teaching', in J. M. Norris and L. Ortega (eds), *Synthesizing Research on Language Learning and Teaching*. Amsterdam: John Benjamins, pp. 3–50.

—(2007), 'The future of research synthesis in applied linguistics: Beyond art or science'. *TESOL Quarterly*, 41, 805–815.

Ortega, L. (2003), 'Syntactic complexity measures and their relationship to L2 proficiency: A research synthesis of college-level L2 writing'. *Applied Linguistics*, 24, 492–518.

Rosenthal, R. and DiMatteo, M. R. (2001), 'Meta-analysis: Recent developments in quantitative methods for literature reviews'. *Annual Review of Psychology*, 52, 59–82.

Ross, S. (1998), 'Self-assessment in second language testing: A meta-analysis and analysis of experiential factors'. *Language Testing*, 15, 1–20.

Rothstein, H. R., Sutton, A. J. and Borenstein, M. (eds) (2005), *Publication Bias in Meta-Analysis: Prevention, Assessment and Adjustments*. Chichester, UK: Wiley.

Russell, J. and Spada, N. (2006), 'The effectiveness of corrective feedback for the acquisition of L2 grammar: A meta-analysis of the research', in J. M. Norris and L. Ortega (eds), *Synthesizing Research on Language Learning and Teaching*. Amsterdam: John Benjamins, pp. 133–164.

Slavin, R. E. (1986), 'Best evidence synthesis: An alternative to meta-analytic and traditional reviews'. *Educational Researcher*, 15(9), 5–11.

Slavin, R. E. and Cheung, A. (2005), 'A synthesis of research on language of reading instruction for English Language Learners'. *Review of Educational Research*, 75, 247–284.

Spada, N. and Tomita, Y. (2008), 'The complexities of selecting complex (and simple) forms in instructed SLA research', in A. Housen and F. Kuiken (eds), *Proceedings of the Complexity, Accuracy and Fluency (CAF) Conference*. Belgium: University of Brussels, pp. 227–254.

Taylor, A., Stevens, J. R. and Asher, J. W. (2006), 'The effects of explicit reading strategy training on L2 reading comprehension: A meta-analysis', in J. M. Norris and L. Ortega (eds), *Synthesizing Research on Language Learning and Teaching*. Amsterdam: John Benjamins, pp. 213–244.

Téllez, K. and Waxman, H. C. (2006), 'A meta-synthesis of qualitative research on effective teaching practices for English Language Learners', in J. M. Norris and L. Ortega (eds), *Synthesizing Research on Language Learning and Teaching*. Amsterdam: John Benjamins, pp. 245–277.

Thomas, M. (1994), 'Assessment of L2 proficiency in second language acquisition research'. *Language Learning,* 44, 307–336.

—(2006), 'Research synthesis and historiography: The case of assessment of second language proficiency', in J. M. Norris and L. Ortega (eds), *Synthesizing Research on Language Learning and Teaching.* Amsterdam: John Benjamins, pp. 279–298.

Thompson, B. (2006), *Foundations of Behavioral Statistics: An Insight-Based Approach.* New York: Guilford.

Truscott, J. (2007), 'The effect of error correction on learners' ability to write accurately'. *Journal of Second Language Writing,* 16, 255–272.

U.S. Department of Health, Education, and Welfare (1967), *The Health Consequences of Smoking: A Public Health Service Review.* Washington, DC: Public Health Service Publication No. 1696.

Ziliak, S. T. and McCloskey, D. N. (2008), *The Cult of Statistical Significance: How the Standard Error Costs us Jobs, Justice, and Lives.* Ann Arbor, MI: The University of Michigan Press.

10 Critical Research in Applied Linguistics

Steven Talmy

Chapter Overview

Critical research in applied linguistics has become an increasingly productive area of empirical inquiry in recent years, generating studies on a range of topics and themes, in an array of settings and employing a variety of research methods. What unites this diverse stream of research is a general effort on the part of critical applied linguistics researchers to identify linkages, broadly construed, between local occasions of language learning and use to broader social processes, formations and discourses, that is, '[to draw] connections between classrooms, conversations, textbooks, tests, or translations and issues of gender, class, sexuality, race, ethnicity, culture, identity, politics' (Pennycook 2008, p. 169).

In this chapter, I provide a methodologically oriented overview of critical applied linguistics empirical inquiry. I begin with a brief discussion of certain assumptions and principles motivating the 'project' (Simon and Dippo 1986) of critical research. Afterward, I describe some methodological options open to critical applied linguistics researchers, with particular emphasis on critical ethnography and critical discourse analysis. My purpose in selecting these two methods is not only because they are commonly employed for empirical second language (L2) research, but because of the benefits that accrue when using both 'complementarily' (Miller and Fox 2004), particularly in terms of analytic accountability (how defensible or warranted an analysis is) and demonstrability of research claims (how warrants for research claims are demonstrated). I then spend the remainder of the chapter elaborating the discussion by describing a critical ethnography I conducted in a high school ESL programme in Hawai'i.

Assumptions and Principles of Critical Research in Applied Linguistics

The task of defining 'critical' is difficult, as there is a plurality of critical theories, based on the diverse work of a range of scholars, including Marx, the Frankfurt School, Volosinov, Gramsci, Freire, Althusser, Bernstein, Foucault and Bourdieu, among others. Just as critical theories are not monolithic, neither are they static, as they change and shift due to ongoing, 'synergistic' relationships among themselves, and with cultural studies, post-structuralism, postmodernism, and postcolonialism (Kincheloe and McLaren 2000). To arrive at a settled-upon definition would be to deny a productive dissensus among critical researchers, who would prefer 'to avoid the production of blueprints of sociopolitical and epistemological beliefs' (Kincheloe and McLaren 2000, p. 281), since such a perspective would 'assume an epistemological stance in which the social world can be precisely defined—a position that is not very critical' (Quantz 1992, p. 448).

While there is no single agreed-upon definition of 'critical,' there are certain principles and objectives shared in the critical 'project.' At the risk of producing the sort of 'blueprint' that Kincheloe and McLaren (2000) advocate against, these include a conception of *society* as stratified and marked by inequality, with differential structural access to material and symbolic resources, power, opportunity, mobility and education. Accordingly, society is characterized by asymmetries in *power* arrangements. Because '[p]ower operates not just on people but through them,' (Simon and Dippo 1986, p. 197) there is a reciprocal, mutually constitutive relationship between social structures and human *agency*. That is, social structures shape or mediate social practices, but do not determine them (Giddens 1979; also see Ahearn 2001). This means that *social reproduction* (i.e., the reproduction of unjust social relations) is never 'guaranteed' since power is not uni-directional or top/down. One consequence of this is a conception of *culture* as an 'ongoing political struggle around the meanings given to actions of people located within unbounded asymmetrical power relations'

(Quantz 1992, p. 483). Further, society, power, agency and culture do not exist atemporally; they are *sociohistorically situated*. Historicization in critical research 'show[s] the conditions of possibility of a definite set of social forms and thus simultaneously establish[es] the historical limits of their existence' (Simon and Dippo 1986, p. 198). Relatedly, critical researchers are not content to simply 'describe' what they see; they attempt to promote change of inequality through sustained critique and direct action, or *praxis*. This 'emancipatory impulse' has garnered considerable criticism (see, for example, Ellsworth, 1989), resulting in recent conceptions of praxis as more circumspect, situated, collaborative and *reflexive*. Finally, critical researchers dispute the contention that there is 'value-free' research, instead embracing their 'openly ideological' *values* (Lather, 1986). It is ironic that because critical researchers are explicit about their values, they are susceptible to reproach regarding the so-called 'imposition' of them.

These general principles and objectives are shared and extended in critical research in applied linguistics, as evident in its increasingly diverse literature. Indeed, in many ways, the focus in critical applied linguistics on the conditions of language learning and use in everyday life uniquely positions researchers to examine in detail the role of language in producing, sustaining, challenging and transforming power asymmetries, discrimination, inequality, social injustice and hegemony as they pertain to race, ethnicity, class, gender, sexuality and more.

Research Methods

The research methods most often employed in critical research in applied linguistics are qualitative, ranging from diary and/or interview studies (e.g., Norton 2000; Motha 2006;), to critical pedagogical classroom research (e.g., Morgan 1997; Crookes and Lehner 1998; Benesch 2001), some form of critical discourse analysis (e.g., Fairclough 1992; Van Dijk 2001; Blommaert 2005), and critical ethnography (Toohey 2000; Talmy 2005, 2008). In this review, I confine my remarks to the latter two methods, particularly in terms of how the former can work to ground and elaborate findings generated in critical ethnography.

Critical ethnography developed as a response to more 'conventional' forms of ethnography (Masemann 1982; Anderson 1989). Canagarajah (1993), one of the first to have published a 'politically motivated ethnography' in applied linguistics, maintains that critical ethnography is 'an ideologically sensitive orientation to the study of culture that can penetrate the noncommittal objectivity and scientism [of] descriptive ethnography' (p. 605). May (1997) notes that this approach 'reject[s] the abrogation of a theoretical perspective for the "open-ended" collection of data' that is advanced in conventional ethnography; that it explicitly acknowledges its critical theoretical orientation and how it shapes interpretation; that 'reality' is conceived 'for what it is – a social and cultural *construction*, linked to wider power relations, which privileges some, and disadvantages other[s]' and that critical ethnography 'attempts to move beyond the accounts of participants . . . to examine the ideological premises and hegemonic practices which shape and constrain these accounts' (May 1997, pp. 198–199; also see Anderson 1989; Foley and Valenzuela 2005).

Methodologically, critical ethnography maintains the conventional ethnographic requirements for persistent, prolonged engagement in the field, recurrent and iterative data analysis, and an emergent, recursive relationship between (critical) theory, data, research questions and interpretation (see Starfield this volume). A key distinction, however, is the above-mentioned commitment to the critical project. A critically located ethnographic methodology highlights the interplay between social structure, material relations and agency; addresses the ways that social structure is (or is not) instantiated, accommodated, resisted and/or transformed in the micropolitics of everyday life; contends with issues of ideology, hegemony and culture; critically addresses its own historically-, materially- and culturally specific interpretations; works toward change and does so with the collaboration of research participants (see, for example, Thomas 1993; Carspecken 1996).

Rigour and Care in Critical Discourse Analysis and Critical Ethnography

What distinguishes critical ethnography from other forms of ethnography also presents it with one of its more enduring challenges: 'trustworthiness.' Verschueren (2001, p. 60) casts the challenge in particularly stark terms, arguing that

> [i]f critical approaches to language use in the context of social practices
> fail to be convincing as a result of a lack of theoretical and methodological
> rigour . . . they destroy their own *raison d'être* and make the task all the
> more difficult for anyone who does observe the basic rules of
> documentation, argumentation and explicit presentation.

Lather (1986) has characterized the issue of rigour and care in critical ethnography as being 'between a rock and a soft place,' where the rock is 'the unquestionable need for trustworthiness' and the soft place 'is the positivist claim to neutrality and objectivity' (p. 65). She advocates adopting measures from conventional ethnography to ensure rigour and care, including triangulation, member checks and systematized reflexivity, in addition to what she calls 'catalytic validity,' that is, the extent to which the research promotes social change.

Another approach that can be enlisted in the pursuit of rigour and care in critical ethnography is critical discourse analysis, which can work to generate, warrant and elaborate (critical) claims in demonstrable and data-near terms. There has been a significant upsurge in critical discourse research in recent years, much of which has been based in the quasi systemic functional framework proposed by Fairclough (1992, *inter alia*; see Blommaert 2005). Despite the significance of Faircloughian 'CDA' (Critical Discourse Analysis) in critical research in applied linguistics, scholars have made several substantive critiques of it, ranging from its theoretical and methodological ambiguity, to a tendency to undertheorize context, to a problematic lack of reflexivity (see, for example, Slembrouck 2001; Verschueren 2001; also see Pennycook 2001, 2003). Further, Blommaert (2005, p. 24) notes a propensity within Faircloughian CDA to 'identify itself as a "school"'. This 'create[s] an impression of closure and exclusiveness with respect to critique,' and 'result[s] in suggestive divisions within discourse analysis – "critical" versus "non-critical" – that are [in fact] hard to sustain in reality.' Indeed, there are many different analytic methodologies that can be (and have been) used in critical discourse research, including interactional sociolinguistics, applied conversation analysis, membership categorization analysis and language socialization; it is these various approaches in general to which I refer below with the lower-case 'critical discourse analysis.'

Although discourse analysis has been used in conventional ethnographic research in applied linguistics for some time, critical discourse analysis has been notably underutilized in critical ethnography. Anderson (1989), for one, has lamented the tendency toward 'macro' cultural and social analysis in critical ethnography, arguing that it is imperative to include examination of what he calls 'microsocial interaction.' By neglecting analysis of social interaction, he maintains, critical ethnographers overlook the potential of critical discourse analysis 'to systematically explore how relations of domination' are produced, reproduced, contested and transformed in everyday conduct (Anderson 1989, pp. 262–263). Widdicombe (1995, p. 111) makes a similar point, stating that 'it is precisely in the mundane contexts of interaction that institutional power is exercised, social inequalities are experienced, and resistance [is] accomplished' (also see, e.g., Blommaert 2005; Wilkinson and Kitzinger 2008).

Techniques and Instruments for Critical Research in Applied Linguistics

The techniques and instruments for empirical inquiry in critical applied linguistics depend on the particular method adopted, but generally tend not to be much distinct from their 'descriptive' counterparts (Thomas 1993; Carspecken 1996). In critical ethnography, for example, fieldwork techniques generally include participant-observation, fieldnotes, interviews, audio- or video-recordings of interaction and artefact analysis, while instruments can range from notebooks, research journals, interview protocols and survey questionnaires. Data analytic procedures can include thematic analysis, various coding schemes, memo-writing and graphic data-displays in addition to the use of computer-assisted qualitative data analysis software, a primary distinction being the theoretical framework motivating critical ethnography. Similarly, while critical discourse analysis is distinguished by its base(s) in critical theories, its techniques and instruments will similarly depend on the particular analytic approach(es) adopted, with objects of study ranging from textbooks, newspapers, magazines, site documents and pop-culture artefacts, to transcripts of recorded interactions, for example interviews, classroom talk or computer-mediated-communication (Van Dijk 2001).

A Sample Study

To elaborate the discussion above, I turn now to discuss briefly a 2.5 year-long critical ethnography that combined critical discourse analysis, which I conducted in the ESL programme of Tradewinds High, a public high school in Hawai'i (Talmy 2005, 2008, 2009, in press). Generally, the Tradewinds High study concerned the production of ESL as a stigmatized identity category at the high school, particularly among long-term or 'oldtimer' 'Local ESL' students in the ESL programme, and the central role that linguicism (Phillipson 1988), or linguistic prejudice, played in this. As several applied linguistics studies of ESL in North American public schools attest, ESL in these settings is often considered a 'dummy program' (McKay and Wong 1996, p. 586), with ESL students cast in various ways as 'candidate[s] for cognitive overhaul and rescue' (p. 590). In the Tradewinds study, I observed the same sorts of stigma associated with ESL, and in contrast, positive attributes associated with the 'mainstream.' I characterized this as a pervasive 'mainstream/ESL' hierarchy that was in evidence throughout the wider Tradewinds context, with mainstream in the 'unmarked' superordinate position, and ESL in the 'marked' subordinate (cf. Bucholtz and Hall 2004). This hierarchy was constituted by and constitutive of normalized language ideologies and linguicism concerning immigrants, bi- and multilingualism and assimilationism in North America (see Figure 10.1). I used critical discourse analysis, particularly of oldtimer Local ESL student interaction, to elaborate how these discriminatory language ideologies played out in everyday ESL classroom life.

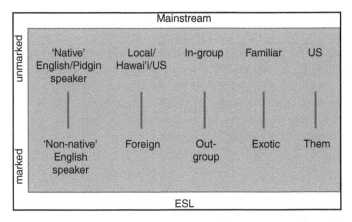

Figure 10.1 Representing the 'mainstream/ESL' hierarchy at Tradewinds High

Local ESL

'Local' is an identity category in wide circulation in Hawai'i, and generally sig-nifies someone (usually Asian/Pacific Islanders) who has been born and raised in the islands. 'Local ESL' is an 'etic' (see Starfield this volume) category that refers to students who were institutionally identified as ESL by Tradewinds, yet who displayed cultural knowledge of and affiliation with Local culture, cultural forms, and social practices (including speaking Pidgin, or Hawai'i Creole, the Local language of Hawai'i)[1]; difference from newcomer or low-L2-proficient classmates, who many Local ESL students characterized as 'FOBs' (fresh off the boat); and the L2 expertise and interactional competence neces-sary to participate in these practices.

Local ESL Cultural Productions of the ESL Student

A primary argument from the Tradewinds study was that the knowledge, ori-entations and social practices of an 'institutionally disapproved interstitial com-munity of practice' (Lave 1991, p. 78) comprised of oldtimer Local ESL students came to assume varying degrees of prominence in each of the eight ESL classes I observed. Combining critical ethnography with critical discourse analysis, I examined Local ESL students' displays of resistant social practice in close detail. These practices included leaving assigned materials 'at home'; not doing homework and completing assignments that required minimal effort (work-sheets) but not others (writing activities). The more overt, interactionally mediated practices included bargaining for reduced requirements on class-work; refusal to participate in instructional activities and the often delicate negotiations with teachers that resulted. There was also a cluster of practices in which Local ESL students engaged in public displays of difference or 'distinction' (Irvine and Gal, 2000) from their low-L2-English and newcomer ESL classmates. This took form in many ways, including mobilization of the category 'FOB.' It was also evident in Local ESL students' targeted use of a mock language variety I call 'Mock ESL.'

Mock ESL

Mock language is a speech style that indexes some form of outgroup or 'foreign' status. It is a racializing discourse that can be characterized by hyper-'marked' syntax and phonology, lexical borrowing and displays of pragmatic incompetence. Perhaps the best known work on mock language is Jane Hill's (e.g., 1998), on the Mock Spanish (e.g., 'no problemo [*sic*]' 'no way, José' or Arnold Schwarzenegger's 'hasta la vista, baby' in the movie *Terminator 2*) used by non-Spanish-speaking whites in the US Southwest.

Mock ESL shares similar semiotics to other mock language varieties but indexes an archetypal, pan-ethnic Foreigner, rather than a particular racial or ethnolinguistic group. In my study, I used occasions of Mock ESL to ground and elaborate my claims concerning the role of linguicism in producing the stigma of ESL; to demonstrate one means that Local ESL students produced 'distinction' from low-L2-proficient and newcomer classmates; and to illustrate how the 'mainstream/ESL' hierarchy evident outside the ESL programme was projected *within* it in terms of a respecified 'Local ESL/FOB' hierarchy (see below).

Space constraints prohibit an extensive data display or analysis, but even brief consideration of two data fragments highlights how critical discourse analysis can work to elaborate and ground critical ethnographic claims. The first fragment involves China and Raven, two Local ESL students.[2] It is the beginning of their ESL class, and their teacher is giving instructions for an assignment, and allotting the time to do it (15 minutes). China has been bargaining for twice that time. The fragment begins as China is mockingly justifying his need for this additional time: because he and Raven are ESL students (see the Appendix to this chapter for transcription conventions; transcripts are simplified).

China's style shift in lines 5 and 8 are examples of Mock ESL. In terms of prosody, both utterances are spoken in a higher pitch, with a light nasal tone, and both feature hyper-incorrect grammar. These features are in essence the embodied performance of the activity that China associates with the category 'ESL student' in line 8, 'we no English,' and the attribute that Raven assigns it

```
01. China: yeah [bu⁻
02. T:           [we (mu[st)
03. China:           [bu⁻    [bu⁻
04. T:                      [we have to hurry
05. China: ((higher pitch, light nasal tone)) but we E-S-L student!
                                    (([bʰʌ wi iesel studen]))
06. Raven: ((pidgin)) wi- wi so [dam!
                 we're- we're so dumb!
07. T:                         [that's okay!
08. China: ((higher pitch, light nasal tone)) we no English!
                                    (([wi no ɪŋɡelɪʃː]))
09. Raven: ((Pidgin)) haw du yu spel 'A'
                 how do you spell 'A'?
10. T:     ((to the class)) ten-thirty!
```

(in Pidgin) in line 6: 'so dumb'; this is expanded in line 9 with needing help to spell the letter 'A.' Thus, China animates a 'figure' (Goffman 1981) through Mock ESL: a low-L2-English-proficient, cognitively challenged newcomer, or 'FOB.' Although China has packaged his performance with several cues that he is mocking ESL, the teacher does not at first appear to realize this (line 7). She does moments later (line 10), however, orienting not only to the sardonic frame (Goffman 1974) keyed by China and Raven, but to their distinction from the 'FOB' category that they have indexed through this mocking performance.

The second fragment I consider involves Bush, a low-L2-proficient ESL student, and Mack Daddy, a Local ESL student of advanced English expertise. Bush has just volunteered to read to the class a sentence he has written for the vocabulary word 'moment.' However, his teacher has trouble understanding Bush, which provides Mack Daddy with an occasion to use Mock ESL.

```
01. Bush:       ((reading)) a cruel murderer have used a few
02.             moment to kill four little girl and buried her
03. T:          huh? used a what type of moment?
04. Bush:       a few moment
                (([ə feu mowme]))
05.             ((2.7)) ((T goes to Bush's desk, looks at his paper))
06. Mack Daddy: ((low pitch, nasal monotone)) I don't speak no English
                                    (([aI don spik now i:ŋlItʃ]))
07. T:          excuse me Mack?
08.             (1.7)
```

Bush's style shift to Mock ESL, similar to China's in the previous fragment, features syntactic 'error', and exaggerated, marked phonology indexical of 'foreign' English. Also similar is the convergence of propositional content with embodied performance to iconize both the category of low-L2-English-proficient ESL student, or FOB, and Bush, as its archetypal incumbent. In contrast, Mack Daddy's style shift points to his awareness that L2 'problems' such as Bush's are resources for a Mock ESL performance, and also his L2-English expertise and interactional competence, which are required to carry it out. Mack Daddy has, in other words, indexed his distinctiveness from Bush and from the FOB category to which Bush has been ascribed membership. The teacher orients to this display of distinction, and the ordering of categories it indexes: the marked 'FOB' in the subordinate position, and Mack Daddy's unmarked Local ESL counterpart in the superior. Although the teacher's line 7 utterance is a repair initiation, it is contextualized as a condemnation. This – and the fact that Mack Daddy does not respond (line 8) – suggest their orientations both to the sanctionability of this Mock ESL performance, and to the stigmatized status of ESL that it connotes.

The Local ESL/FOB Hierarchy and Fractal Recursivity

I conceptualized displays of distinction such as those in which Mock ESL was used as in part constituting a 'fractally recursive' (Irvine and Gal 2000) projection *within* the ESL programme of the mainstream/ESL hierarchy outside it, with 'Local ESL' in the unmarked position (in place of 'mainstream'), and 'FOB' in the marked subordinate (in place of 'ESL'). Fractal recursivity, a semiotic process proposed by Irvine and Gal (2000), 'involves the projection of [a language ideological] opposition, salient at some level of relationship, onto some another level' (p. 38). That is, the status asymmetry between ESL and mainstream students that was evident in the wider Tradewinds context was projected inward and respecified in the ESL classroom in practices such as those involving Mock ESL. However, just as the Local ESL/FOB hierarchy can be considered a fractally recursive projection of the mainstream/ESL hierarchy, the mainstream/ESL hierarchy can itself be considered a fractally recursive projection of oppositions ('American/Foreigner') in far more 'macro' (i.e., US) terms, that is, of *national* identities and *nationalist* language ideologies (cf. Lippi-Green 1997) (see Figure 10.2). In this respect, Local ESL students' displays of distinction were central to the reproduction in everyday ESL classroom conduct of the language ideologies and linguicism concerning immigrants, bi- and multilingualism, and assimilationism at Tradewinds, and more broadly, in the supralocal US context.

Praxis

I should note that there was a critical pedagogical intervention concerning linguicism and the stigma of ESL that I was collaboratively planning with one of the teacher-participants from the first, piloting year of research. However, due to several reasons, including uncertainty surrounding a proposed 40 per cent

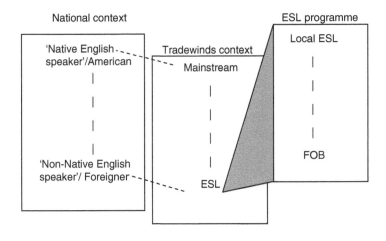

Figure 10.2 Fractally recursive 'mainstream/ESL' and 'Local ESL/FOB' hierarchies

budget reduction in ESL funding in Hawai'i, this teacher did not return to Tradewinds for the second year of the study. Although a much smaller-scale critical pedagogical 'unit' was planned instead, which connected ESL in the USA to the civil rights movement, and linguicism to other forms of discrimination, its implementation in the second year of the study was hastily planned, variably realized and ultimately, unsuccessful. In this respect, praxis in the Tradewinds study primarily involved cultural critique, rather than some form of collaborative, pedagogically oriented direct action, with the study instead working 'to situate and understand local events in the context of broader structural relations of power, [in an effort] to direct such understanding toward more expansive efforts at structural change' (Levinson 2001, p. 363; cf. Foley and Valenzuela 2005).

Conclusion

In this chapter, I have provided a brief discussion of empirical research in critical applied linguistics, focusing in particular on critical ethnography and critical discourse analysis. I have argued that using critical ethnography and critical discourse analysis complementarily can provide important benefits for the critical researcher: for example, critical ethnography allows critical discourse analyses to be more 'thickly described' (Geertz 1973) and deeply contextualized, and critical discourse analysis adds elements of rigour, analytic accountability, and elaboration of ethnographic description to critical ethnography. I demonstrated these arguments in an overview of a study I conducted, using critical ethnography to sketch (altogether too briefly) the rationale for the study, aspects of its context and certain practices constituting the Local ESL community of practice, while using critical discourse analysis to explicate the communicative resources, interactional occasioning and implications of one of these practices: use of Mock ESL. Using critical discourse analysis helped to provide warrants for research claims; working in such data-near terms not only added an important dimension of demonstrability and accountability to my analysis, but it also wound up elaborating my arguments – brought them to life, as it were – in ways that a critical ethnographic thematic analysis would likely have precluded.

Acknowledgements

My gratitude to Graham Crookes, John Willinsky, and the editors for comments on earlier drafts of this chapter.

Notes

1 Utterances in Pidgin in this chapter are transcribed phonemically, accompanied by italicized English glosses.
2 Students selected their own pseudonyms.

Resources for Further Reading

Blommaert, J. (2005), *Discourse: A Critical Introduction*. Cambridge: Cambridge University Press.
   This introduction to critical discourse analysis introduces theoretical frameworks and attendant methodological options available for critical discourse analytic work that go beyond, for example, the approach proposed by Fairclough. Blommaert draws on several different traditions from sociolinguistics and linguistic anthropology to provide a rich theoretical rationale and extensive methodological toolkit for undertaking critical discourse analysis. He demonstrates the approach in several thematically arranged chapters that include engaging critical analyses of discourse.
Canagarajah, A. S. (1999), *Resisting Linguistic Imperialism in English Teaching*. Oxford: Oxford University Press.
   This book-length critical ethnography, written by a leading scholar in critical applied linguistics, extends and elaborates his earlier (1993) study. The study is an important illustration of critical ethnography in applied linguistics and

provides beginning scholars interested in conducting a critical ethnography with a helpful model for conceptualizing one.

Levinson, B. A., Foley, D. E. and Holland, D. C. (eds) (1996), *The Cultural Production of the Educated Person: Critical Ethnographies of Schooling and Local Practice*. Albany, NY: State University of New York Press.

This edited anthology demonstrates the breadth and range of critical ethnography. Although it does not contain critical applied linguistics research, and is not methodologically oriented, it includes a large number of empirical studies undertaken in diverse educational contexts. It therefore provides useful examples of empirical research for scholars who are formulating their own critical ethnographic studies.

Norton, B. and Toohey, K. (eds) (2004). *Critical Pedagogies and Language Learning*. Cambridge: Cambridge University Press.

This edited anthology is a comprehensive representation of the state of contemporary critical L2 pedagogical research, and thus, of a major area in critical applied linguistics. The studies are wide-ranging and diverse, and are written by many well-known scholars. The book is theoretically engaging, and includes several chapters that are methodologically oriented. The volume is particularly useful for students interested in gaining an understanding of the range of work represented in critical L2 pedagogy.

Pennycook, A. (2001), *Critical Applied Linguistics: A Critical Introduction*. Mahwah, NJ: Lawrence Erlbaum Associates.

This is an accessible introduction to critical applied linguistics, written by a leading scholar in the area. Pennycook discusses a wide range of topics in applied linguistics, critical social theories and critical applied linguistics, and illuminates important complexities in these areas by contrasting different theoretical positions on them. The book, which is particularly helpful in its explication of theory, is also a model of critical reflexivity, subjecting its arguments to its own 'problematizing practice.'

References

Ahearn, L. M. (2001), 'Language and agency'. *Annual Review of Anthropology*, 30, 109–137.

Anderson, G. (1989), 'Critical ethnography in education: Origins, current status, and new directions'. *Review of Educational Research*, 59(3), 249–270.

Benesch, S. (2001), *Critical English for Academic Purposes: Theory, Politics, and Practice*. Mahwah, NJ: Lawrence Erlbaum Associates.

Blommaert, J. (2005), *Discourse: A Critical Introduction*. Cambridge: Cambridge University Press.

Bucholtz, M. and Hall, K. (2004), 'Language and identity', in A. Duranti (ed.), *Companion to Linguistic Anthropology*. Malden, MA: Blackwell, pp. 369–394.

Canagarajah, A. S. (1993), 'Critical ethnography of a Sri Lankan classroom: Ambiguities in student opposition to reproduction through ESOL'. *TESOL Quarterly*, 27, 601–626.

Carspecken, P. F. (1996), *Critical Ethnography in Educational Research: A Theoretical and Practical Guide*. New York: Routledge.

Crookes, G. and Lehner, A. (1998), 'Aspects of process in an ESL critical pedagogy teacher education course'. *TESOL Quarterly*, 32, 319–328.

Ellsworth, E. (1989), 'Why doesn't this feel empowering? Working through the repressive myths of critical pedagogy'. *Harvard Educational Review*, 59, 297–324.

Fairclough, N. (1992), *Discourse and Social Change*. Cambridge: Polity Press.

Foley, D. E. and Valenzuela, A. (2005), 'Critical ethnography: The politics of collaboration', in N. K. Denzin and Y. S. Lincoln (eds), *The Sage Handbook Of Qualitative Research* (3rd edn). Thousand Oaks, CA: Sage, pp. 217–234.

Geertz, C. (1973), 'Thick description: Toward an interpretive theory of culture', in C. Geertz (ed.), *The Interpretation of Cultures: Selected Essays*. New York: Basic Books, pp. 3–30.

Giddens, A. (1979), *Central Problems in Social Theory: Action, Structure, and Contradiction in Social Analysis*. Berkeley, CA: University of California Press.

Goffman, E. (1974), *Frame Analysis: An Essay on the Organization of Experience*. New York: Harper & Row.

—(1981), *Forms of Talk*. Philadelphia: University of Pennsylvania Press.

Hill, J. H. (1998), 'Language, race, and white public space'. *American Anthropologist*, 100, 680–689.

Irvine, J. T. and Gal, S. (2000), 'Language ideology and linguistic differentiation', in P. V. Kroskrity (ed.), *Regimes of Language: Ideologies, Polities, and Identities*. Santa Fe, NM: School of American Research Press, pp. 35–83.

Kincheloe, J. L. and McLaren, P. (2000), 'Rethinking critical theory and qualitative research', in N. K. Denzin and Y. S. Lincoln (eds), *Handbook of Qualitative Research* (2nd edn). Thousand Oaks, CA: Sage, pp. 279–313.

Lather, P. (1986), 'Issues of validity in openly ideological research: Between a rock and a soft place'. *Interchange*, 17(4), 63–84.

Lave, J. (1991), 'Situated learning in communities of practice', in L. B. Resnick, J. M. Levine and S. D. Teasley (eds), *Perspectives on Socially Shared Cognition*. Washington, DC: American Psychological Association, pp. 63–82.

Levinson, B. A., Foley, D. E. and Holland, D. C. (eds) (1996), *The Cultural Production of the Educated Person: Critical Ethnographies of Schooling and Local Practice*. Albany, NY: State University of New York Press.

Lippi-Green, R. (1997), *English with an Accent: Language, Ideology, and Discrimination in the United States*. London: Routledge.

Masemann, V. L. (1982), 'Critical ethnography in the study of comparative education'. *Comparative Education Review*, 26(1), 1–15.

May, S. (1997), 'Critical ethnography' in N. H. Hornberger and D. Corson (eds), *Encyclopedia of Language and Education. Volume 8: Research Methods in Language and Education*. Dordrecht, The Netherlands: Kluwer Academic Publishers, pp. 197–206.

McKay, S. L. and Wong, S.-L. C. (1996), 'Multiple discourses, multiple identities: Investment and agency in second-language learning among Chinese adolescent immigrant students'. *Harvard Educational Review*, 66, 577–608.

Miller, G. and Fox, K. J. (2004), 'Building bridges: The possibility of analytic dialogue between ethnography, conversation analysis, and Foucault', in

D. Silverman (ed.), *Qualitative Research: Theory, Method, and Practice* (2nd edn). London: Sage, pp. 35–55.

Morgan, B. (1997), 'Identity and intonation: Linking dynamic processes in an ESL classroom'. *TESOL Quarterly*, 31, 431–450.

Motha, S. (2006), 'Decolonizing ESOL: Negotiating linguistic power in US public school classrooms'. *Critical Inquiry in Language Studies*, 3(2–3), 75–100.

Norton, B. (2000), *Identity and Language Learning: Gender, Ethnicity, and Educational Change*. London: Longman.

Pennycook, A. (2001), *Critical Applied Linguistics: A Critical Introduction*. Mahwah, NJ: Lawrence Erlbaum Associates.

—(2003), 'Nostalgia for the real or refashioning futures: A response'. *Discourse & Society*, 14, 808–811.

—(2008), 'Critical applied linguistics and language education', in S. May and N. H. Hornberger (eds), *Encyclopedia of Language and Education: Volume 1: Language Policy and Political Issues in Education* (2nd edn). Boston: Springer, pp. 169–191.

Phillipson, R. (1988), 'Linguicism: Structures and ideologies in linguistic imperialism', in T. Skutnabb-Kangas and J. Cummins (eds), *Minority Education: From Shame to Struggle*. Philadelphia: Multilingual Matters, pp. 339–358.

Quantz, R. A. (1992), 'On critical ethnography (with some postmodern considerations)', in M. D. LeCompte, W. L. Millroy and J. Preissle (eds), *The Handbook of Qualitative Research in Education*. San Diego, CA: Academic Press, pp. 447–505.

Simon, R. and Dippo, D. (1986), 'On critical ethnographic work'. *Anthropology and Education Quarterly*, 17, 195–202.

Slembrouck, S. (2001), 'Explanation, interpretation and critique in the analysis of discourse'. *Critique of Anthropology*, 21, 33–57.

Talmy, S. (2005), 'Lifers and FOBs, Rocks and Resistance: Generation 1.5, Identity, and the Cultural Productions of ESL in a High School'. Unpublished doctoral dissertation, University of Hawai'i at Mānoa, Honolulu, HI.

—(2008), 'The cultural productions of the ESL student at Tradewinds High: Contingency, multidirectionality, and identity in L2 socialization'. *Applied Linguistics*, 29, 619–644.

—(2009), 'Forever FOB?: Resisting and reproducing the Other in high school ESL', in A. Reyes and A. Lo (eds), *Beyond Yellow English: Toward a Linguistic Anthropology of Asian Pacific America*. New York: Oxford University Press, pp. 347–365.

—(in press), 'Resisting ESL: Categories and sequence in a critically 'motivated' analysis of classroom interaction', in H. Nguyen and G. Kasper (eds), *Talk-in-interaction: Multilingual Perspectives*. Honolulu, HI: University of Hawai'i, National Foreign Language Resource Center.

Thomas, J. (1993), *Doing Critical Ethnography*. Newbury Park, CA: Sage.

Toohey, K. (2000), *Learning English at School: Identity, Social Relations, and Classroom Practice*. Clevedon, UK: Multilingual Matters.

Van Dijk, T. (2001), 'Critical discourse analysis', in D. Schiffrin, D. Tannen and H. E. Hamilton (eds), *The Handbook of Discourse Analysis*. Oxford: Blackwell Publishing, pp. 352–371.

Verschueren, J. (2001), 'Predicaments of criticism'. *Critique of Anthropology*, 21, 59–80.

Widdicombe, S. (1995), 'Identity, politics and talk: A case for the mundane and the everyday', in S. Wilkinson and C. Kitzinger (eds), *Feminism and Discourse: Psychological Perspectives*. London: Sage, pp. 106–127.

Wilkinson, S. and Kitzinger, C. (2008), 'Using conversation analysis in feminist and critical research'. *Social and Personality Psychology Compass*, 2, 555–573.

Appendix: Transcription Conventions

–	abrupt sound stop
[[	overlapping talk
( )	undecipherable/questionable transcription
(( ))	physical movement, characterizations of talk, coughing, etc.
(1.3)	pauses timed to tenths of a second

Part II:
Areas of Research

11 Researching Speaking

Rebecca Hughes

Chapter Overview

Speaking is a capacity that human beings draw on almost as easily and unconsciously as we breathe, and yet it is one that is richly complex to research. Spoken discourse is at the heart of both the most sophisticated and the most mundane of human activities. Everyday conversation is the social glue which underpins all human relationships. By the age of three a child who develops normally has gained a good day-to-day working vocabulary and by the age of five or six has grasped the basic linguistic and pragmatic skills required to develop their own identity and relationships within their family and the wider community (see Ochs and Sheifflin 2009 for an up-to-date survey of child language acquisition embedded in social and cultural contexts).

At a more abstract level the spoken language, from preliterate times to the present day, has been the originating and facilitating medium of a great deal of the creative, performative, political, educational and ideological developments through human history. Despite technological developments face-to-face speech remains a primary medium by which all humans collaborate about information and tasks, develop organizational behaviour and express and comprehend emotional life with others.

Yet despite (or perhaps because of) this pervasiveness and significance, research into spoken language remains a complex field to engage with, and is the focus for much debate in applied linguistics theory and practice. This complexity arises in part from the fact that, depending on the aspect of the spoken form being researched, the central questions being investigated may relate to the narrowest aspect of speech – for example, investigating a particular phonetic feature (as in Levy and Strange 2008 'Perception of French vowels by American English adults with and without French language experience') or the broadest, such as understanding the effects of the development of a literate culture in an oral society (see for example, the collection *The Making of Literate Societies*, Olson and Torrance 2001). The nature of the research techniques and strategies employed, and paradigms regarded as valid, will vary in line with the topic and outcomes of research which, as noted, may be extremely varied themselves.

In addition, the nature of the research will be strongly affected by the purposes for which it is undertaken and where it sits on the cline of theory and applications. One of the most tantalizing aspects of research into speech is that there is very little cross reference between areas with potentially overlapping interests. For example, the constraints on, and the nature of, lexical retrieval and articulation (how we come up with words and say them) have relevance to understanding the grammar of the spoken form. Speakers tend to construct utterances in predictably different ways from writers and this is in part due to the need to process the language being spoken in real time and with no potential for editing. However, the major advances in the understanding of spoken grammar have come from large studies of corpora (Svartvik 1990; Biber et al. 1999; Leech 2000; Carter and McCarthy 2006) and there is little interplay between the insights of speech processing which shape these grammatical choices and speech captured as text in the form of a corpus.

Equally, the work in psycho- or neuro-linguistics about unimpaired and impaired speech, or spoken language recognition is generally carried out in isolation from, for example, the needs of the second language learner or the norms of speech against which oral assessment is conducted. While these may seem distant areas from one another, taking an aspect of spoken language such as hesitations and reformulations (often listed in oral assessment criteria) and understanding the norms and constraints on spoken language in non-assessed contexts shows how there may be insights that have obvious relevance to each other.

Overall, therefore, in considering the focus of research into speaking, it has to be remembered that on the one hand the individual speaker and the society in which they produce their discourse are difficult for the researcher into speaking to disentangle and on the other the exact nature of the object of study is not as clear cut as it may seem at first glance. Much of the debate around approaches to researching speaking revolves around these issues, together with the fundamental issue of how to capture and analyse what is a transitory and dynamic medium without distortion.

Bearing in mind the necessary diversity of approaches to researching speaking outlined above, this chapter will aim to give an overview of some of the major approaches to research into speech and a brief summary of the typical methods by which investigations are undertaken.

Research Strategies and Techniques

Research into speaking is generally carried out via two main means: capturing and examining authentic speech data and capturing and examining elicited or non-authentic speech data. These areas are dealt with in more detail below but, due to its centrality in a number of research methods the section begins with some discussion of the role of transcription as a key tool in spoken language research.

A great number of approaches to spoken language research depend on being able to access conversational or other forms of speech data and make it available through time for analysis. These range from discourse and conversation analysis to ethnographic approaches to large spoken corpora. In psycholinguistics and second language acquisition studies the role of transcription is less central, however, even though, in the former there is often a role for elicited experimental data from subjects which needs to be captured in written form. This makes transcription one of the most key tools in spoken language research and one which any new researcher needs to take into consideration in setting up their methodological framework.

Transcription of Spoken Data

Many types of research into spoken language depend on capturing the data via not only electronic recording, but subsequently transcribing this into the static and more easily analysable written mode. Until the development of speech recognition software which can assist the automation of transcription to some extent, the transfer of speech data into the written mode was an extremely time-consuming process and one that needed to be factored in to the research project framework design both practically (it can take at least 6 minutes to make an accurate, basic transcription of a single minute of talk) and from a theoretical perspective.

A primary question in spoken language research is often therefore the type of transcription to be used. The decisions which a researcher needs to take about this can be regarded as relating to a basic process of materials gathering, and in some respects to developing an investigative tool. The reason for this is that writing down speech is not a neutral process and decisions as to what features to capture and how best to represent these in the static, visual medium of writing relate closely to the overall purpose of the investigation. All transcription conventions attempt to represent the acoustic information in some way but no system can capture the full breadth of linguistically salient information which even a short and apparently simple burst of speech contains.

The simplest conversation when transcribed and put under the microscope of analysis looks, to the untrained eye, chaotic. Here, for instance, is a two

147

person question and answer exchange transcribed for research into medical discourse and consulting skills (Ph = pharmacist, Pt = patient) (Salter et al. 2007):

1. Ph 05. Yeah okay and you're happy with the box that you are using
2. Pt 09. Yeah I can manage them (0.2) they ain't all the same some of them have
3. Pt 09. got a slide but you have to watch you don't un uncover more than one
4. Pt 09. hole=
5. Ph 05. =Yes yeah I've actually brought some with me here
6. Pt 09. You see
7. Ph 05. I think the one you mean is (0.2) is it like that (0.3) is it like that so you
8. Ph 05. have to be careful when you pull the *slides out*
9. Pt 09. *That's right* yeah they're the ones
10. Ph 05. Yeah
11. Pt 09. Yeah (0.3) so that just pull one pull pull down to them morning
12. Ph 05. Pull down to the one you want
13. Pt 09. And then the next dinner time
14. Ph 05. Yeah and make sure you only go so far with them=
15. Pt 09. =That's right
16. Ph 05. Yeah

A variety of transcription conventions have emerged over the years and the researcher using spoken data needs to familiarize themselves with these and decide on the level of detail and the salient features which it is necessary to capture in the study in question. A seminal chapter containing what has come to be known as *the Jefferson system* is shown in Sacks et al. (1978) and this has formed the basis of the transcription systems used in literally hundreds of other studies. Edwards and Lampert (1993) provide a thorough survey of transcription methods in relation to research frameworks. A good, and user friendly, summary of transcription conventions typically used in conversational analysis, discourse analysis and ethnographic studies can be found in ten Have (1999).

Parsing and Tagging

A very specific kind of transcription is used in corpus linguistics and speech recognition systems to capture not only acoustic information but also lexical and syntactic details. *Parsing* refers to the process by which spoken data is broken down into its grammatical constituents and *tagging* is the means by which these constituents, often down to the level of individual words and parts of words (morphemes), are labelled so that a computer can aid the researcher in the process of analysis. The development of sophisticated search engines that can seek and analyse data on the world wide web is expanding the breadth and depth of this work (Kilgarrif and Grefenstette 2003). However, a further stage in the development of multi-modal corpora and relevant tagging and searching devices is still needed for spoken language research to be carried out on a par with the simplicity and directness of written word searches and tools which have been around for decades such as concordancers.

Elicited Data and Experimental Approaches

As noted in the previous sections, for theoretical and methodological reasons, research into speech does not always or indeed necessarily take place directly on samples of spoken language as found in our daily lives. Those who do not use spontaneous spoken discourse fall broadly into two categories: those who seek to mimic authentic spoken data closely and elicit it in a more manageable way for analysis; those who step further away from contextualized speech data and construct experimental frameworks within which very precisely con- strained samples of speech can be analysed.

An example of the former approach would be the well-known approach referred to as a *map task experiment*. This is a technique to elicit dialogue in ways that are predictable and constrained, but at the same time create the need for explanation, clarification and convergence of understanding. Participants seek to share information of a route from A to B from two slightly different maps without showing them to each other. The maps are designed to have slight but important differences between them and this leads to a rich, spontaneous, dia- logue between the participants as they try to carry out the task of getting one or other of them to a specific destination. A corpus of these dialogues has been made publicly available at: http://www.hcrc.ed.ac.uk/maptask/index.html (accessed 19 April 2009).

Speech data are often gathered under much stricter experimental protocols, particularly when there is a very narrow research question being investigated. The approach involves, for example, a group of subjects who have a particular feature (dyslexic children, brain damaged patients, the elderly), a control group (children of similar age and background without dyslexia etc.) and a set of care- fully chosen prompts to elicit spoken data of the kind required by the investiga- tor. Altmann et al. (2008), in the realm of health sciences and communication, investigated the oral performance of dyslexic children by means of a strictly experimental approach that elicited a narrow sample of responses required by the research design. The careful construction of the prompts by means of which samples of speech were gathered, and their relationship to the research questions becomes clear in the following extract concerning their methods:

> In the current study, we presented participants with three-word stimuli that included a verb form and two nouns differing in animacy.[1] Noun stimuli consisted of a proper name and an inanimate noun chosen to be a good argument for a particular verb, so that a conceptual connection between the two could be easily established (e.g., kicked + football). Verb stimuli consisted of the past participles of three types of transitive verbs: control (CON) verbs comprised agent–patient verbs with regular morphology (e.g., stirred, kicked). Experimental verb types included agent–patient verbs with irregular (IRR) morphology (e.g., shaken, thrown) and theme–experiencer (TE) verbs with regular morphology (e.g., bored, confused). The two experimental verb types imposed different metalinguistic demands on participants. IRR verbs required participants to recognize that the past participle form could only be used in perfective sentences (e.g., had hidden), passive sentences (e.g., was hidden by), or in adjectival structures (e.g., the hidden X). Thus, to succeed in using IRR verbs participants had to detect the small orthographic/phonological differences signalling the morphological form, and be explicitly aware of the grammatical constraints inherent in this morphological form (Altmann et al. 2008, pp. 58–59).

Disciplines in linguistics that value elicited/experimental speech data, or approach speech from a decontextualized perspective and regard the norms of actual talk as less relevant include second language acquisition, psycholinguistics and speech processing, among others.

Authentic Data and Conversation Analysis Approaches

The sharp contrast between this type of approach and that used by researchers who prioritize authentic data is clear when compared to the influential method or indeed whole school or sub-discipline of applied linguistics, known as *Conversation Analysis* or 'CA'. Those who use elicited data of one kind or another often argue that this is necessary because even large samples of authentic data simply may not show the feature that the investigators are interested in. Those who begin from authentic spoken interaction turn this argument around and propose that even the apparently simplest and shortest example of a real exchange between situated interlocutors will provide a rich source of linguistic data. It is the starting point of such an approach to say that language is socially constructed, that meaning resides not so much in the words and clauses as in the understanding that emerges between speakers, that on a moment by moment basis speakers and hearers accommodate to one another in the achievement of conversational interaction. The detailed transcription, repeated hearings and interpretation by the researcher (often in discussion with others) of stretches of talk are the fundamental research tools of the CA tradition.

A guest editorial by Neilsen and Wagner (2007) in the *Journal of Pragmatics* provides an excellent overview and key references of the history of this influential approach from early studies situated in the field of sociology, through talk in institutional settings and what this reveals about individuals and organizations, to *interactional linguistics* and other newer branches. The role of authentic, situated, speech data is nicely summed up thus:

> Although CA research has engaged in new topics, settings, and disciplines, it has kept its identity and has acted as a discipline in its own right with a well-defined methodology and a strong analytic tradition in which new studies are written. Studies are carefully crafted collections of cases, sometimes assembled over many years due to low frequency. The cases are the basis for and the proof of the description of the recipies [sic] for social actions described in the studies. Herein lies the core of CA: testable sequential description of social actions, carried out on the basis of data, which have not been elicited but collected in the field (Neilsen and Wagner 2007, p. 442).

A useful and publicly available set of some of the seminal transcriptions used in the CA approach can be found at: *http://www.talkbank.org/CABank/* (accessed 19 April 2009).

Other research approaches that value actual spoken data at different levels of its production include: sociolinguistic and ethnographic approaches (which situate the research in a culture and a society and focus on interaction), corpus studies (which tend to focus more on word and clause level and the patterns that can be found in large bodies of speech data), and acoustic phonetics (which, at its most basic, deals with the stream of speech in terms of sounds as opposed to higher units such as words or clauses). The last two areas – particularly phonetic studies which have a very specialized set of measurement techniques, dedicated software, and equipment – provide a warning not to confuse the using of actual instances of speech data with a particular set of research methods. It is not the case that using real speech data equates to qualitative work. Samples of speech can be analysed in a number of ways and approaches that value authentic data can be placed on a spectrum moving from situated/qualitative (such as CA or ethnographic work) to decontextualized/quantitative (such as acoustic phonetics, frequency studies from large corpora).

151

Synthesis of Current Thinking and Research

Spoken language research is rather unusual in that many of the debates surrounding questions of theory are intertwined with the very practical issues touched on above of what data are regarded as acceptable as a basis for investigation and how these are best approached. These issues go to the heart of a very fundamental question indeed for researching speaking: 'What is speaking and how do you analyse it?'. In part the question under debate is the need (or not) for wholly authentic speech data to be the basis of spoken language research, and in part these conundrums relate to the much bigger question of the role of naturally occurring data in linguistic theory. A classic distinction in linguistics is that proposed by Noam Chomsky (1965) between *competence* (underlying aptitude in human beings for handling the language system) and *performance* (the tangible evidence of language used in the real world). This set the tone of debates from the 1960s onwards and is still seen by many as relevant – a 2007 issue of the *Modern Language Journal* is dedicated to questions still arising from the basic distinction posed 40 years earlier:

> Is acquiring a second language essentially a cognitive process situated in the mind of the individual learner? Or, is it, first and foremost, a social process because language learning necessarily occurs through interactive use with target language speakers? (Magnan 2007, p. 733).

Some of the complexities of research into spoken discourse therefore cross refer to ongoing debates in applied linguistics (for instance the interface between social and contextualized aspects of language and second language acquisition theory) (Larsen-Freeman 2007) or the debates surrounding the role of culture on the grammar of an individual language (Everett 2005). An individual researcher's position in relation to this central debate will inform what evidence they regard as valid and useful in their approach to researching speaking. These, in turn, relate to the stance of the researcher and the general framework or paradigm they regard as most compelling. Therefore, as outlined in the previous section, the techniques and methods in spoken language research are not only quite diverse, they are also sometimes somewhat 'loaded' in terms of how they relate to contesting views of language itself. All these points will influence a researcher's choices as to whether, for example, entirely natural or elicited speech data are preferable in a given study.

These methodological debates, in the same way as the theoretical ones outlined above, are not new and have been the locus of heated discussions since the 1960s and before. For instance, there is the well-known concept in applied linguistics called the *observer's paradox* which was first set out in a seminal chapter by William Labov (Labov 1966). This is based on the idea that when speech data is the object of study it can be influenced by the presence of a researcher in significant ways. Put simply, all of us will tend to behave differently if we think we are being observed and that what we are saying is being recorded for future analysis. Labov himself solved this problem by designing an ingenious method for his data gathering. By asking various shop assistants quickly for a particular item he elicited an unselfconscious answer ('4th Floor') that contained the particular spoken feature he was interested in.

Currently, there are two major trends which may bring spoken language research firmly into the centre of debates in applied linguistics once more. The first is the acknowledgment in second language acquisition and cognitive linguistics that the role of context and culture is difficult to exclude from theories that are to be meaningful rather than simply internally consistent. The role of the situated speaker particularly in the realm of SLA is gaining more attention (Mori 2007) and influential applications of research such as work on oral assessment in large and high stakes international examinations of second language use are also tending to push researchers to ask about the norms of spoken discourse in a variety or contexts (Hughes 2004).

The second area that is, and will continue to be, strongly influential is the role of new technologies on our capacity to capture, store and analyse large quantities of digitally recorded speech in audio and video formats. This trend is meeting up with two powerful drivers of change: the world wide web and commercial interests which require human-computer interactions to address spoken dialogue (currently mostly in restricted domains such as a call centre). Although still (at the time of writing) basically a text and image based medium, the web with its 'openness', data sharing potential, and sheer size allows groups of users to draw on spoken data in quantities that were simply unthinkable 5 years ago. A search on the term 'conversation' in the popular video clip site YouTube (http://www.youtube.com/results?search_query=conversation&page =1, accessed 24 March 2008) generated over 90,000 hits in 2008 and ten times this number by the following year. While some of these will include the mildly psychotic talking in monologue to their favourite tree this is one example of the richness of oral material which the web can provide. This trend for openly accessible multi-modal data may soon change the way that research into speaking is carried out in applied linguistics. For instance, the idea of the individual researcher recording data simply for a small, local, project and the data only being captured in the oral form may seem quite old-fashioned as large archives or open access sites of video materials become readily available online. Secondly, the notion of a private corpus of speech will become less and less attractive as researchers understand the benefits of sharing the workload of capture, transcription and aligning sound files with transcriptions.

These changes will happen all the sooner if some of the commercial interests (for instance, gaming or automation of responses to human interlocutors via a call centre) that are funding practical approaches to analysing dialogue are able to link up with applied linguistic research. This will be particularly powerful for researchers in the field if a means is found to search and to model dialogues in ways that make them as accessible as text and meaningful to computers. Work in this field is already quite sophisticated and in computational linguistics an array of publications and platforms are being produced to deal with human-machine interactions via the spoken medium. These range from a site where a 'chatbot' learns to speak to you purely from the input you provide: http://www.jabberwacky.com/ (accessed 19 April 2009) to academic papers presenting models of interactions between more than one speaker and a computer (Knott and Vlugter 2008), to analyses of spoken discourse in meetings that has been tagged, is available online for other researchers and is accessible together with software that allows it to be analysed from a multi-modal perspective: (http://corpus.amiproject.org/ accessed 19 April 2009). Some of these new approaches step outside the debates around the cognitive or cultural basis for language learning and may allow a more sophisticated and data-driven set of theories to emerge about spoken language in context.

Some Sample Studies

As has been noted throughout this chapter, speaking is a multifaceted human skill and there is no single research approach that can cover all the areas that interest the academic and wider community. Therefore this section presents two contrasting studies that are looking at the same area of speaking – the details of interactive behaviour – in order to give a sense of the diversity of approaches and some examples of the typical stages to projects in the field of spoken discourse. Speaking is distinguished by its high potential for interactivity, and spontaneous conversational data is the hardest of all for linguistic theory and for human-computer systems to model. Within speaking the mechanisms that allow smooth and seamless turn-taking have been an object of considerable attention. The case-studies presented here both look at turn behaviour as a central aspect of speech behaviour but are carried out by sharply contrasting means.

Sample Study 1: Durational Aspects of Turn-Taking in Spontaneous Face-to-Face and Telephone Dialogues (ten Bosch et al. 2004)

In this study ten Bosch and colleagues wanted to look at the differences in turn-taking behaviour in two contexts: face to face and on the telephone. Their approach was corpus based and rigorously quantitative. Using such a framework, it is crucial to match the data carefully and define the units that are being analysed extremely objectively. In part this is simply the conventions of the quantitative approach and in part it is due to the need for researchers to include sufficient information for other researchers to carry out similar studies and compare or challenge results. The researchers took comparable examples of speech in the two contexts from a pre-existing corpus and analysed the duration of pauses between speaker turns. They defined a 'turn' in a way that lent itself to the quantitative approach: utterances between silences (see also e.g., Koiso et al. (1998) for an influential study on Japanese in this area which uses the same technique). They introduce their definition thus:

> A study by Weilhammer and Rabold (2003) on durational aspects of turn-taking, which was based on task-oriented dialogue data, has shown that the logarithm of the durations of pauses and overlaps can be modeled by a Gaussian distribution.[2] In their analysis, the definition of turn was 'implicitly based' on the Verbmobil transcription conventions[3] (Burger 1997). Their definition of a turn states that 'a turn starts with the first word in the dialogue or with the first word breaking the silence that follows the previous turn'. Furthermore, 'the silence between two turns of one speaker is always overlaid by an utterance of the [interlocutor]'. The definition of a turn as used in the present study is very similar. (ten Bosch et al. 2004, p. 564)

In their discussion the authors acknowledge the limitations of this approach, suggesting the need for a 'functional' definition of the turn. However, the benefit of this approach is that it does allow very rigorous and objective cross-genre (in this case the telephone versus face-to-face mode) comparisons to be made. This is because the framework for the analysis is based on a unit that has been clearly defined and lends itself to measurement and to the analytical tools being used. One of their main findings was that pauses were of shorter duration in the telephone mode (see Figure 11.1).

The authors tentatively suggest that the lack of other cues to hold the floor (gaze and gesture, for instance), and the fact that the whole of the attention of the interlocutors is on the talk in hand may account for this.

Sample Study 2: Negotiating Negotiation: The Collaborative Production of Resolution in Small Claims Mediation Hearings (Garcia 2000)

The second study shows the application of conversation analytical approaches to a real-world problem: mediation and negotiation. In particular, the study deals with the need for neutrality on the part of any mediator and the

155

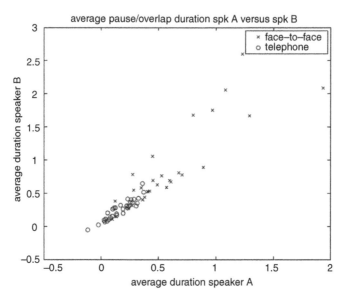

Figure 11.1 Scatter plot of the average pause duration. Each dialogue is represented by a single point in the scatter diagram, of which the coordinates are determined by the average pause duration for each speaker (ten Bosch et al. 2004, p. 568).

empowerment of the parties involved to reach a consensus for themselves. The CA approach is particularly useful in understanding how participants develop understanding between themselves in the process of interaction and was therefore seen as an appropriate paradigm by this researcher in contrast with earlier work on mediation which had tended to focus on outcomes rather than on the processes involved and how participants expressed consensus or resistance.

The analysis was based on 15 examples taken from a larger video-taped collection of mediation encounters, transcribed using *the Jefferson method* (see Sacks et al. 1978), and closely analysed using CA methods to allow a better understanding of the emergence, or not, of consensus and the power relations holding between the various parties. The analyses showed, in detail, how the trained mediator retains neutrality and the strategies employed by them to empower the individuals involved to create their own resolutions to the issues.

In Excerpt 9 the mediator asks specifically for a price for the camera, rather than requesting 'a solution'. By soliciting a price for the camera, the mediator is supporting the idea that a possible solution would be for Disputant C ('Pete') to purchase the camera.

Excerpt 9
552   M: so: (0.4) so wha:t would it co:st fer pete t' =
553   *pur*chase *thuh* *cam*ra*?

554   (3.6)
555   A: i'm willing tuh negotiate that.
               (Garcia 2000, p. 332)

In contrast to the first case study, the interpretive role of the researcher is presented in relation to close analysis of specific instances of talk in context, rather than objective quantitative results that 'speak for themselves'. Discussing the benefits of using the CA approach to help produce a better understanding of key issues in this area Garcia notes that it has tended to lack the interactional perspective and that the approach allows the research to show the specifics of how mediation works rather than dealing with abstractions.

These contrasting studies which end the chapter show something of the rich diversity of potential research on the spoken form and how it lends itself to a multiplicity of real world questions as well as being at the heart of some of the most contentious areas of linguistic theory.

Notes

1. 'Animacy' indicates the level of autonomous life the nouns showed. For example 'dog' or 'bird' will score more highly on this than 'stone' or 'stick'.
2. Gaussian distribution is a term from statistics also known as the normal or the bell curve. It is applied to the tendency for the distribution of data points in many samples – for example speech rates – to cluster around an average mid point with a small tail on each side of this peak showing higher or lower scores.
3. Verbmobil was a large artificial intelligence project in Germany looking at the automatic recognition of speech and translation into other languages.

Resources for Further Reading

Chafe, W. and Danielewicz, J. (1987), 'Properties of spoken and written language', in R. Horowitz and S. J. Samuels (eds), *Comprehending Oral and Written Language*. San Diego, CA: Academic Press, pp. 83–113.
    This remains one of the most accessible explanations of why speaking is different from writing and needs to be researched on its own merits.
De Beaugrande, R. (1994), 'Speech and writing in theory and in data', in S. Cmejrkova, F. Danes and E. Havlova (eds), *Writing vs Speaking: Language, Text, Discourse, Communication*. Tubingen: Gunter Narr Verlag, pp. 23–46.
    This chapter provides a challenging and stimulating statement of the need for research into speaking to be distinct from that into other modes.
Hughes, R. (forthcoming), *Teaching and Researching Speaking* (2nd edn). London: Longman.
    This book offers an overview of research into spoken language that is particularly aimed at the English language teaching community or those interested in the interface between teaching and research.

Stenström, A-B. (1990), 'Lexical items peculiar to spoken discourse', in J. Svartvik (ed.), *The London-Lund Corpus of Spoken English: Description and Research*. Lund Studies in English 82. Lund: Lund University Press, pp. 137–176.
This chapter gives a classic example of a corpus-based investigation of spoken language.

References

Altmann, L. J. P., Lombardino, L. J. and Puranik, C. (2008), 'Sentence production in students with dyslexia'. *International Journal of Language & Communication Disorders*, 43(1), 55–76.

Biber, D., Johansson, S., Leech, G., Conrad, S. and Finegan, E. (1999), *The Longman Grammar of Spoken and Written English*. London: Longman.

Carter, R. and McCarthy, M. (2006), *The Cambridge Grammar of English*. Cambridge: Cambridge University Press.

Chomsky, N. (1965), *Aspects of the Theory of Syntax*. Cambridge: Massachusetts Institute of Technology Press.

Edwards, J. A. and Lampert, M. D. (eds) (1993), *Talking Data: Transcription and Coding in Discourse Research*. Hillsdale, N.J.: Lawrence Erlbaum Associates.

Everett, D. L. (2005), 'Cultural constraints on grammar and cognition in Piraha'. *Current Anthropology*, 46(4), 621–646.

Hughes, R. (2004), 'Testing the visible: Literate biases in oral language testing'. *Journal of Applied Linguistics*, 1(3), 295–309.

Garcia, A. C. (2000), 'Negotiating negotiation: The collaborative production of resolution in small claims mediation hearings'. *Discourse and Society*, 11(3), 315–343.

Kilgarrif, A. and Grefenstette, G. (2003), 'Introduction to the web as corpus'. *Computational Linguistics*, 29(3), 333–347.

Knott, A. and Vlugter, P. (2008), 'Multi-agent human–machine dialogue: Issues in dialogue management and referring expression semantics'. *Artificial Intelligence*, 172, 69–102.

Koiso, H., Horiuchi, Y., Tutiya, S., Ichikawa, A. and Ken, Y. (1998), 'An analysis of turn-taking and backchannels based on prosodic and syntactic features in Japanese map task dialogs'. *Language and Speech*, 41(3–4), 295–322.

Labov, W. (1966), *The Social Stratification of English in New York City*. Washington: Center for Applied Linguistics.

Larsen-Freeman, D. (2007), 'Reflecting on the cognitive–social debate in second language acquisition'. *The Modern Language Journal*, 91, 773–787.

Leech, G. (2000), 'Grammars of spoken English: New outcomes of corpus-oriented research'. *Language Learning*, 50(4), 675–724.

Levy, E. S. and Strange, W. (2008), 'Perception of French vowels by American English adults with and without French language experience'. *Journal of Phonetics*, 36(1), 141–157.

Magnan, S. S. (2007), 'Presenting the focus issue'. *The Modern Language Journal*, 91(Focus Issue), 733–734.

Mori, J. (2007), 'Border crossings? Exploring the intersection of second language acquisition, conversation analysis, and foreign language pedagogy'. *The Modern Language Journal*, 91, 849–862.

Nielsen, M. F. and Wagner, J. (2007), 'Continuity and diversity in conversation analysis'. *Journal of Pragmatics*, 39(3), 441–444.

Ochs, E. and Sheifflin, B. B. (2009), 'Language acquisition and socialization: Three developmental stories and their implications', in A. Duranti (ed.), *Linguistic Anthropology: A Reader*. Oxford: Blackwell, pp. 296–328.

Olson, D. and Torrance, N. (2001), *The Making of Literate Societies*. Oxford: Blackwell.

Sacks, H., Schegloff, E. A. and Jefferson, G. (1978), 'A simplest systematics for the organization of turn-taking of conversation', in J. Schenkein (ed.), *Studies in the Organization of Conversational Interaction*. New York: Academic Press, pp. 7–57.

Salter, C., Holland, R., Harvey, I. and Henwood, K. (2007), 'I haven't even phoned my doctor yet.' The advice giving role of the pharmacist during consultations for medication review with patients aged 80 or more: Qualitative discourse analysis'. *British Medical Journal*, 334(7603): 1101.

Svartvik, J. (ed.) (1990), *The London Corpus of Spoken English: Description and Research*. Lund Studies in English 82. Lund: Lund University Press.

ten Bosch, L., Oostdijk, N. and de Ruiter, J. P. (2004), 'Durational aspects of turn-taking in spontaneous face-to-face and telephone dialogues'. *Text, Speech and Dialogue*. (Lecture Notes in Computer Science). Berlin: Springer, pp. 563–570.

ten Have, P. (1999), *Doing Conversation Analysis*. London: Sage Publications.

12 Researching Listening

Larry Vandergrift

It is probably self-evident to suggest that, of the four foundational language skills, listening is the least understood and the most difficult to investigate. The covert nature of the process and ephemeral nature of the input make the perceptual and comprehension processes involved in listening difficult to access. Research on listening in applied linguistics remains limited; however, recent studies have led to some new insights into the underlying cognitive processes, the teaching and the assessment of listening (see Vandergrift 2007). That being said, many questions still remain and, compared to the other skills, very few theoretical models have emerged.

In this chapter, I will begin with a very brief synopsis of current thinking and research on listening in applied linguistics. This will be followed by a critical overview of the range of methodologies that can be used to investigate the listening skill. I will conclude with a sample study that illustrates the use of some of these research methodologies.

Brief Overview of Listening

An understanding of listening must acknowledge the interplay of physiological and cognitive processes at different levels, as well as the influence of contextual factors. Recent reviews of research on listening (e.g., Rost 2002, 2006; Vandergrift

2004, 2007) highlight two fundamental cognitive processes required for comprehension: bottom-up and top-down processes. Listeners use bottom-up processes when they construct meaning from the incoming sound stream by gradually combining increasingly larger units of meaning from the phoneme-level up to discourse-level features to build comprehension of an utterance or a text. Listeners use top-down processes when they use context, prior knowledge (topic, genre, culture and other schema knowledge in long-term memory) and listener expectations to build a conceptual framework in which to slot the individual units of meaning retained from bottom-up processing to eventually arrive at a reasonable interpretation of the message. Although these processes occur simultaneously and in parallel fashion, the degree to which listeners use the one process more than the other will depend on the task or purpose for listening. Research on these cognitive processes suggests that listeners need to learn how to use both processes to their advantage, depending on their purpose for listening. Although the literature on listening instruction over the past years has tended to favour the development of top-down processes, there is currently a renewed interest in the contribution of perceptual processing (bottom-up processes) to successful listening comprehension (Field 2008).

The speed and effectiveness of these cognitive processes depend on the degree to which listeners can efficiently process what is heard. Native language listeners do this automatically, with little conscious attention to individual words. On the other hand, listeners learning a new language have limited linguistic knowledge; therefore, less of what they hear can be automatically processed. Depending on their level of proficiency or the difficulty level of the text, these listeners will need to consciously process some of the input and, given the limitations of working memory, comprehension either turns out to be incomplete or breaks down. To compensate for gaps in comprehension, skilled listeners can use their metacognitive knowledge about listening to orchestrate appropriate cognitive strategies, contextual cues and other relevant information available to them, to inference on what was not understood. When listeners are able to (1) analyse task requirements; (2) activate appropriate listening processes for the task; (3) make appropriate predictions; (4) monitor their comprehension; (5) problem solve to figure out the meaning of what they do not understand and (6) evaluate the success of their approach, they are using metacognitive knowledge for successful listening comprehension.

Listening involves more than cognitive processing, however. It can be constrained by affective factors such as anxiety which further limits how much information short-term memory can process at one time. Other learner variables that affect comprehension include background knowledge of the topic of the text, proficiency level in the target language, age, metacognitive knowledge about listening, strategy use, native language listening ability, working memory capacity and sound discrimination ability. The listening task itself, that is, the type of information and level of detail required and what the listener is expected to do with that information, can also affect the outcome of listening. Text characteristics such as speed of delivery, frequency of pausing and hesitations, accent and amount of informal language in the aural stream are further mitigating factors. In the case of texts that carry visual support, such as video, the speaker's actions and reactions, as well as the degree of congruency between the spoken and the visual, will also affect the level of comprehension. In the case of interaction with an interlocutor, the listener's sensitivity to paralinguistic cues (body language and non-verbal voice cues), as well as his/her power relationship to the interlocutor, play a significant role in comprehension. Moreover, a correct literal understanding of a message does not necessarily ensure accurate comprehension. Successful comprehension also requires listeners to apply pragmatic knowledge (see Roever this volume) to interpret the speaker's implied meaning, which may go beyond the literal meaning of the utterance. An awareness of the processes and variables related to listening success, and their interaction, is fundamental to an understanding of the listening construct. Since space limitations preclude a more detailed discussion of the listening construct and related variables, see Buck (2001), Rost (2002) and Vandergrift (2007) for more detailed discussions.

Research Methodologies for Investigating Listening

Rost (2002) suggests that two overlapping processes – learning to listen in a new language and listening to learn this new language – are involved in listening development. The distinction between product (listening to learn) and process (learning to listen) is a useful heuristic for the following discussion of the research methodologies for investigating listening. I will begin with a short discussion of methods for measuring listening ability, followed by an exploration and discussion of the different methodologies for investigating the product and the process of listening.

Measuring Listening Ability

Proficiency tests
Essential to conducting product-oriented research, listening test scores provide baseline data from which to measure growth in listening ability over time and/ or consequent to a pedagogical intervention. Test scores can also be used to assign a level of listening proficiency to participants in studies where proficiency in the target language is a variable under investigation. Although test scores may provide a more objective criterion for assigning proficiency level

than a grade, course level or teacher assessment, their generalizability is limited because they are either based on an in-house placement test instead of a more broad-based, standardized, objective measure (Berne 2004) or they may be assessing only particular aspects of listening ability (Buck 2001). Listening research can be strengthened and more broadly generalized through the use of valid and reliable tests referenced to internationally understood benchmarks such as the ACTFL Proficiency Guidelines (ACTFL 1999) or the Common European Framework of Reference for Languages (Council of Europe 2001), for example.

The advantage of listening tests as a comprehension measure for research purposes is that they are not labour-intensive and can be easily administered to large groups. The major challenge for listening test development and listening research, however, is the measurement of pure listening comprehension ability; that is, assessing comprehension without introducing reading or writing as confounding variables. Pure listening comprehension is most appropriately measured through aural prompts and verification options that are limited to non-verbal evaluation techniques such as selecting among a choice of pictures or objects, sequencing pictures or other graphics, drawing a picture, tracing on a map or performing a physical response. On the other hand, when using aural prompts to assess listening comprehension, memory becomes a confounding variable.

Free written recall protocols

Free recall protocols represent an alternative but more labour-intensive method for measuring aural comprehension of text content. Participants listen to a text and immediately afterwards write, in their native language, as much information as possible about what they understood. For example, Guichon and McLornan (2008) used recall protocols to measure differences in comprehension when an aural text was presented in four different conditions (audio alone, video with audio, video with audio and target language subtitles, and video with audio and native language subtitles) to different groups. After the first presentation of the text, students in each group wrote notes in the language of their choice, and after the second presentation, they prepared a detailed summary (recall protocols). The protocols were then analysed for the number of correct idea units, resulting in a score for each student and each group, to determine the level of listening success for each condition. Calculating a comprehension score is much more labour-intensive than administering a listening test, especially if a second rater independently verifies a certain percentage of the protocols to ensure reliability of the scores. However, recall protocols have the capacity to assess comprehension without using question prompts. Memory will be a confounding variable here as well, but perhaps less so if note taking and approximate spellings are allowed. An additional advantage to recall protocols as a measure of comprehension is their capacity for providing insights into the comprehension process. In fact, Guichon and McLoren (2008) opted for free recall protocols as a measure of comprehension in order to additionally examine student notes and summaries for evidence of native language interference and differences in cognitive overload for the different listening conditions.

Although listening test scores and recall protocols provide an objective measure for determining comprehension gains for research purposes, the reliability of the scores will be limited by the reliability of the test or, in the case of the written recall protocols, interrater reliability. In order for any measure of comprehension to be reliable for research purposes, scores may need to be adjusted to control for initial differences between groups; for example, listening ability or background knowledge of the text topic. Although listening test scores provide a product to identify a level of performance, they tell us nothing about the process; that is, how listeners arrive at the right answer or why comprehension breaks down.

Investigating the Product of Listening

Experimental research
Research on listening has traditionally focussed on the outcome, or the product of listening. In this line of research, student performance on a listening test is used to measure the success of a particular intervention. Two groups complete a pre-test; the experimental group experiences a different condition (such as exposure to an alternative pre-listening activity) from the control group. After the intervention, which may be long- or short term, both groups complete an immediate post-test to determine the effects of the experiment: did the intervention result in a statistically significant (see Phakiti this volume), higher score on the listening post-test by the experimental group over the control group? Sometimes, a delayed post-test is used to assess the long-term effects of the intervention, such as the retention of certain vocabulary items three months after the intervention. Generally, there is no interest in determining how the listeners used the experimental intervention to improve their comprehension.

Correlational research
Another line of product-oriented listening research involves determining the degree of relationship between different variables hypothesized to be related to listening success. In this case, listening test scores are correlated with the scores of an instrument that measures a personal variable in order to determine if there is a relationship between the two variables and the strength of that relationship. For example, student scores on a listening anxiety questionnaire or a sound

discrimination test are correlated with listening achievement scores to determine any potentially significant relationship. It is important to note, however, that although positive or negative correlations may point to interesting relationships between a given variable and listening success, it is not possible to claim causality between that variable and listening success. Uncovering the nature of the relationship between the variables requires careful interpretation and may be elucidated by more qualitative research methodologies such as interviews or stimulated recalls (of questionnaire data) that explore the listening process.

If the sample size is large enough, one can also simultaneously examine the relationship of a number of learner variables with listening success through multiple regression analysis (see Phakiti this volume for further discussion of this statistical test) and determine the effect of these variables on listening success (Vandergrift 2006). By regressing the scores of a number of independent variables (e.g., sound discrimination ability, first language listening ability, metacognitive awareness of listening) on the dependent variable (listening test scores), it is possible to determine the approximate percentage of variance that each independent variable might contribute to listening success (the dependent variable). This line of research, although interesting for what it might reveal about the predictive validity of hypothesized variables on listening ability, must be based on scores from reliable instruments and statistically significant relationships that are carefully interpreted.

Investigating the Process of Listening

Although a product-oriented approach to investigating listening can yield useful information about level of listening proficiency or potentially interesting relationships between listening ability and other learner variables, this line of research is not interested in exploring the problems listeners may experience in comprehension or the reasons motivating a student response on questionnaires. On the other hand, a process-oriented approach can provide potentially useful insights into the cognitive processes underlying listening comprehension. Process-oriented methodologies such as questionnaires, interviews, stimulated recalls, think-alouds, observation, diaries, tracking software and aural perception processing responses provide opportunities for participants to reveal, or researchers to uncover, listener decision-making processes during comprehension.

Questionnaires
Questionnaires (open- or closed-response) administered after a listening activity can provide insights into student awareness of the process of listening and, when used as a repeated measure, track any changes in awareness of the

listening process or listening attitudes, over time (e.g., Vandergrift et al. 2006). Closed-response questionnaires, or surveys, are particularly useful for collecting large amounts of data that can be compiled and analysed quickly. The reliability of this data, however, is dependant upon the reliability and validity of the instrument. Greater insights into the reason for student response to questionnaire items or to changes in item responses over time can be achieved with a stimulated recall where the listener is asked to reflect on any changes in response patterns on the same questionnaire (see the sample study below).

Interviews
Interviews, a more personable oral version of the open-ended response questionnaire, represent a more flexible but time-consuming method for eliciting data about listening. Individual or group interviews afford an opportunity to gain greater insights from a representative group of participants on important themes emerging from a large-scale survey; for example, concerning the difficulties students experience with listening in learning another language (e.g., Graham 2006). In particular, a semi-structured interview allows the researcher to diverge from the interview protocol to explore listener responses in greater detail. Interview sessions must be recorded, transcribed, coded and analysed. The reliability and validity of interview responses are enhanced when the participant is given the opportunity to read the transcripts to validate or correct them and, in the case of coding, when interrater reliability is at an acceptable level.

Stimulated recall protocols
Stimulated recall is a version of the individual interview where the researcher and the participant focus on another data set involving the participant, such as a video recording or questionnaire responses. In order to gain greater insight into listener behaviour or response, the researcher asks the participant to comment on a particular event in the video or an interesting pattern in questionnaire response. The reliability of the data, recorded and transcribed, is directly proportional to the proximity of the event under discussion and the interview. Although time consuming, stimulated recalls can also provide insights into listener decision-making processes as they navigate through support options while engaged in multimedia listening, for example (Grgurović and Hegelheimer 2007).

Diaries
Diaries are, first of all, tools for language learners to reflect on their language learning; however, they are also a useful research tool for gaining insights into learner awareness of listening processes, strategy development, listener anxiety, listening goals and actions taken to improve listening performance. Diaries can be entirely open-ended or guided by the researcher through given

prompts, and they are particularly fruitful when used over time. For example, Goh (1997) was able to document, over a ten-week period, the development of metacognitive knowledge about L2 listening. Classroom discussions based on reflection probes (e.g., Goh and Taib 2006) can also serve as the stimulus for subsequent diary writing. Although data gleaned from diaries, and any other kind of listening notes (e.g., Mareschal 2007), are constrained by ethical considerations (student permission) and lack of generalizability, they do provide interesting insights into metacognitive awareness about listening, strategy use and overall listening success.

Observation notes
Since listening is a covert process, observation is generally of limited value for investigating listening processes in uni-directional listening. However, observation of interviews, or other interactive situations, can provide some insights into listener behaviour in bi-directional listening. When recorded, these interviews can be reviewed by the researcher for evidence of the variable under investigation (e.g., number and type of clarification strategies). Review of the video recording with the research participant, using stimulated recall immediately after the interview, provides an opportunity to discover how the participant either clarified meaning or helped the interlocutor to advance the conversation (Farrell and Mallard 2006).

Think-aloud protocols
The research methodologies discussed so far have been retrospective in nature; that is, listeners comment and reflect on listening events that have taken place in the recent or distant past. Introspective methodologies, on the other hand, attempt to tap the thought processes of listeners while they are actually engaged in the listening event. After some initial training in the process, participants 'think aloud' at predetermined intervals while listening to a recorded aural text. The resulting data, the listener's voiced thoughts on what he/she is doing to comprehend, are recorded simultaneously and later transcribed. Introspection is the closest researchers can come to tapping thought processes while information is still available to the listener in short-term memory. Think-aloud protocols can be useful for shedding light on where and how listeners experience difficulties as they are listening (Goh 2002), the development of strategy use over time (e.g., Graham et al. 2008), or the differential use of visual and aural information to understand online academic lectures (e.g., Smidt and Hegelheimer 2004).

Tracking software
New technologies can provide further insights into the process of listening by tracking and analysing listener use of help functions while listening to a

recorded academic lecture (e.g., Grgurović and Hegelheimer 2007) or listener use of pauses, rewinds and fast forwards while working on an MP3 player (e.g., Roussel 2008). Greater insights into the motivation for listener behaviour can be gained, however, by complementing these methodologies with a stimulated recall as soon as possible after the listening event.

Aural perception processing responses
Aural perceptual processing investigates phenomena associated with the bottom-up dimension of listening, such as word segmentation skills. In this line of research, listeners hear a stimulus, a word or a short sentence (presented with no contextual cues), and are then asked to choose from among several options, the word or phrase they thought they heard, or write down what they thought they heard (recall protocol). The choice options are often built on potential error patterns (see Field 2004). Of interest are the errors made and what they might reveal about the listener's word segmentation strategies (e.g., influence of a native language segmentation strategy) and/or listener expectations. This line of research tends to be very micro in nature, excluding the macro-context of a text or communication that listeners generally use in real-life listening.

Triangulation of data
Although all of the research methodologies outlined above provide greater insights into the process of listening, their generalizability is often limited. In order to overcome this limitation, applied linguistics researchers investigating a construct as implicit as listening should try to use multi-method assessment to collect convergent data. Reliability and validity can be enhanced when data from more than one source are triangulated to provide a more complete picture of the listening construct; for example, complementing videotaped data with a stimulated recall on the video recording and a questionnaire (e.g., Cutrone 2005). In a recent doctoral thesis, Mareschal (2007) collected and analyzed data from a listening questionnaire, stimulated recalls on the questionnaire responses, listening notebooks, think-alouds, observation and a summative, open-response questionnaire to document how a self-regulatory approach to listening instruction influenced the listeners' self-regulatory ability, strategy use, metacognitive knowledge and listening success. Although these research methodologies provide greater insight into the process of listening, they are more labour-intensive with regard to collection and analysis of the data and less conducive to parsimonious reporting in order to demonstrate the trustworthiness and credibility of the research.

A Sample Study

The study I have chosen to illustrate some of the methodological considerations discussed in this chapter is a recent long-term, mixed-methods study

(Vandergrift and Tafaghodtari 2010) on teaching students how to listen, using a pedagogical cycle grounded in metacognitive theory. My interest in conducting this study emerged from a number of observations from the research literature. First, the results of long-term listening strategy instruction appear inconclusive and instruction in individual strategies does not appear to lead to overall listening improvement (Field 2001). Secondly, a number of recent studies suggest that skilled listeners appear to orchestrate cognitive and metacognitive strategies in an interconnected fashion (Goh 2002; Vandergrift 2004, 2007). Thirdly, the reading research literature is in general agreement that instruction in a repertoire of strategies is more effective than individual strategy instruction for teaching comprehension skills (Grabe 2004). Fourth, recent studies on listener metacognitive awareness suggest that systematically guiding language learners through the process of listening, as part of regular listening practice, can lead learners to practise the metacognitive processes involved in listening (see Vandergrift 2004, 2007). Finally, although the short-term effects of this process approach on student motivation and the development of metacognitive knowledge about listening have been demonstrated, the enduring effects of this approach on listening achievement still need to be empirically demonstrated (Berne 2004; Vandergrift 2004).

Methodological Considerations

The nature of this investigation led me, first of all, to design a carefully controlled quasi-experimental study to test the following hypotheses: (1) the experimental group receiving metacognitive instruction will outperform the control group; and, (2) the less-skilled listeners would make greater gains in listening achievement than their more-skilled counterparts. This constituted the product focus of the study. Secondly, in order to track the hypothesized growth in metacognitive knowledge about listening throughout the study and to gain greater insight into participant awareness of the process of listening, both groups completed a valid and reliable listening questionnaire (see Vandergrift et al. 2006, for information on the development and validation of this instrument). Finally, in an effort to gain an even deeper understanding of the development of listening processes, six participants from the experimental group were randomly selected to participate in a stimulated recall on differences in their questionnaire responses at the mid- and end-points of the study. These last two methodologies constituted the process focus of the study.

Participants were university students from six intact French as a second language classes, randomly assigned by class to either a control or experimental group. Participants were identified as less- or more-skilled listeners on the basis of their score on a listening test (Cronbach's alpha=0.90), also used as a post-test to measure growth in listening ability. Two instructors participated; one taught four different classes of low-intermediate learners and the other taught two different classes of high-beginners. To control for potentially confounding teaching variables, the same teacher taught both the control and the experimental group, and both groups listened to the same texts. All teaching sessions were observed by a research assistant to verify that the instructor respected the designated listening pedagogy for that group.

All participants completed the listening questionnaire at the beginning, mid- and end-points of the study, immediately after a listening activity. We hypothesized that the less-skilled listeners in the experimental group would demonstrate greater growth in the five factors related to metacognitive knowledge (i.e., Problem-Solving, Planning and Evaluation, Directed Attention, Mental Translation and Person Knowledge) than their more-skilled counterparts, and than both the more- and less-skilled participants in the control group. Participants selected for the stimulated recall sessions met with a research assistant twice: after the mid-point and at the end of the study. At the first session, the research assistant presented the participant with his/her beginning and mid-point questionnaire responses, and then discussed major discrepancies (2 point differences) in responses with the participant. During the second session, the participant was asked to discuss possible reasons for further discrepancies in responses based on the final completed questionnaire. All stimulated recall sessions were audio-recorded, transcribed verbatim, coded, and analyzed for emerging themes using the QSR-N*Vivo7.[1]

The study took place over a 13-week term. Each week, the classes listened to a different authentic-type text related to the topic of the teaching unit. The pedagogical cycle experienced by the experimental group, and the metacognitive processes underlying each step in the cycle, are described in detail in Vandergrift and Tafaghodtari (in press). Participants in the control group listened to the same texts the same number of times; however, they did not engage in prediction; they were not given an opportunity to discuss, predict or monitor their comprehension with a classmate; and, they did not engage in any whole-class reflection on strategy use.

Analyzing the Data

In order to confirm the first two hypotheses, a 2-factor ANCOVA (analysis of co-variance) was performed. Independent variables consisted of group (treatment and control) and the level of listening ability (less- and more-skilled), factorially combined. To control for any initial differences in listening ability, pre-listening test scores were used as covariate in the analysis. Results revealed that, overall, the experimental group outperformed the control group.

Furthermore, the less-skilled listeners who received metacognitive instruction outperformed the less-skilled listeners in the control group. In addition, the less-skilled listeners in the experimental group showed greater improvement than their more-skilled counterparts. Evidence for the third hypothesis was not as clear in terms of demonstrated growth in metacognitive knowledge about listening. Although listeners in the experimental group evidenced greater growth in all areas of metacognitive knowledge about listening, only growth in Problem-Solving and Mental Translation was statistically significant. The surprising finding about translation was later elucidated through the stimulated recall where it became evident that students were misinterpreting the concept of translation. The recall protocols also provided additional evidence for growth in the five areas of metacognitive knowledge. This study is a good example of research that is both product and process-oriented, using different research methodologies to explore the development of metacognitive knowledge for listening.

Conclusion

This chapter has presented an overview of methodologies for investigating listening in applied linguistics. The field is ripe for research. Emerging technologies and increased access to multi-modal online resources through high-speed internet and self-access centres, in particular, open up rich possibilities for teaching and researching listening (see Godwin-Jones 2007; Robin 2007). For more detailed information on areas for future research see Rost (2006) and Vandergrift (2007).

Note

1. N*Vivo is a qualitative research tool for classifying, sorting and arranging data in order to analyse them for patterns and to identify themes.

Resources for Further Reading

Buck, G. (2001), *Assessing Listening*. Cambridge, UK: Cambridge University Press.
  Although the emphasis of this volume is on the assessment of listening, the overview of theory and research on listening in the first two chapters is both comprehensive and accessible.
Field, J. (ed.) (2008), 'Listening'. *System*, 36 (1), 1–122.
  This special issue of *System* reports a range of studies related to listening: meaning construction, strategies, multi-modal video and testing, and perceptual processing.

Hubbard, P. (ed.) (2007), 'Technology and listening comprehension'. *Language Learning and Technology*, 11(1), 1–117. Available at: http://llt.msu.edu/vol11num1/default.html

This special issue of *Language Learning and Technology* is also dedicated to research on listening comprehension and technology. Of particular interest are three commentaries on the reported research and the possibilities of emerging technologies for teaching and researching listening.

Rost, M. (2002), *Teaching and Researching Listening.* London, UK: Longman.

This comprehensive volume provides an overview of teaching and researching listening. The third section introduces a number of research methodologies and frameworks, as well as concrete topics for action research.

Vandergrift, L. (2007), 'Recent developments in second and foreign language listening comprehension research'. *Language Teaching,* 40, 191–210.

This paper summarizes recent research and developments in listening from 2000 to 2007. It discusses areas requiring further research and argues for more in-depth studies probing the cognitive processes and contextual factors that influence listening.

References

American Council for the Teaching of Foreign Languages (ACTFL) (1999), 'ACTFL Proficiency Guidelines'. Retrieved 27 June 27 2008 from http://www.sil.org/lingualinks/languagelearning/OtherResources/ACTFLProficiencyGuidelines/contents.htm

Berne, J. E. (2004), 'Listening comprehension strategies: A review of the literature'. *Foreign Language Annals,* 37, 521–531.

Buck, G. (2001), *Assessing Listening.* Cambridge, UK: Cambridge University Press.

Council of Europe (COE) (2001), *A Common European Framework of Reference for Languages: Learning, Teaching and Assessment.* Cambridge: Cambridge University Press.

Cutrone, P. (2005), 'A case study examining backchannels in conversations between Japanese-British dyads'. *Multilingua,* 24, 237–274.

Farrell, T. C. and Mallard, C. (2006), 'The use of reception strategies by learners of French as a foreign language'. *The Modern Language Journal,* 90, 338–352.

Field, J. (2001), 'Finding one's way in the fog: Listening strategies and second-language learners'. *Modern English Teacher,* 9, 29–34.

—(2004), 'An insight into listeners' problems: Too much bottom-up or too much top-down?' *System,* 32, 363–377.

—(2008), 'Emergent and divergent: A view of second language listening research'. *System,* 36, 2–9.

Godwin-Jones, R. (2007), 'Digital video update: YouTube, Flash, High-Definition'. *Language Learning and Technology,* 11, 16–21.

Goh, C. (1997), 'Metacognitive awareness and second language listeners'. *ELT Journal,* 51, 361–369.

—(2002), 'Exploring listening comprehension tactics and their interaction patterns'. *System,* 30, 185–206.

Goh, C. and Taib, Y. (2006), 'Metacognitive instruction in listening for young learners'. *ELT Journal*, 60, 222–232.

Grabe, W. (2004). 'Research on teaching reading'. *Annual Review of Applied Linguistics*, 24, 44–69.

Graham, S. (2006), 'Listening comprehension: The learners' perspective'. *System*, 34, 165–182.

Graham, S., Santos, D. and Vanderplank, R. (2008), 'Listening comprehension and strategy use: A longitudinal exploration'. *System*, 36, 52–68.

Grgurović, M. and Hegelheimer, V. (2007), 'Help options and multimedia listening: Students' use of subtitles and the transcript'. *Language Learning and Technology*, 11, 45–66.

Guichon, N. and McLornan, S. (2008), 'The effects of multimodality on L2 learners: Implications for CALL resource design'. *System*, 36, 85–93.

Mareschal, C. (2007), 'Student Perceptions of a Self-Regulatory Approach to Second Language Listening Comprehension Development'. Unpublished doctoral thesis. University of Ottawa.

Robin, R. (2007), 'Learner-based listening and technological authenticity'. *Language Learning and Technology*, 11, 109–115.

Rost, M. (2002), *Teaching and Researching Listening*. London, UK: Longman.

—(2006), 'Areas of research that influence L2 listening instruction', in E. Uso-Juan, and A. Martinez-Flor (eds), *Current Trends in the Development and Teaching of the Four Language Skills*. Berlin: Mouton de Gruyter, pp. 47–74.

Roussel, S. (2008), 'Les stratégies d'autorégulation de l'écoute et leur influence sur la compréhension d'orale'. Unpublished doctoral dissertation. Université de Toulouse 2.

Smidt, E. and Hegelheimer, V. (2004), 'Effects of online academic lectures on ESL listening comprehension, incidental vocabulary acquisition and strategy use'. *Computer Assisted Language Learning*, 17, 517–556.

Vandergrift, L. (2004), 'Learning to listen or listening to learn?' *Annual Review of Applied Linguistics*, 24, 3–25.

—(2006), 'Second language listening: Listening ability or language Proficiency'? *Modern Language Journal*, 90, 3–17.

—(2007), 'Recent developments in second and foreign language listening comprehension research'. *Language Teaching*, 40, 191–210.

Vandergrift, L., Goh, C., Mareschal, C. and Tafaghodatari, M. H. (2006), 'The Metacognitive Awareness Listening Questionnaire (MALQ): Development and validation'. *Language Learning*, 56, 431–462.

Vandergrift, L. and Tafaghodtari, M. H. (2010), 'Teaching students how to listen does make a difference: An empirical study'. *Language Learning*, 60(2).

13 Researching Reading

Marie Stevenson

Chapter Overview	

This chapter gives an overview of key issues and research areas in second language reading research, and describes research techniques frequently used in this field. It also describes a sample study that uses verbal protocol analysis as a data collection technique in order to illustrate some of the methodological issues involved in collecting and analysing observational reading data.

Key Issues in Researching Reading

In contrast to writing, where the writer produces a text that can be examined and analysed, reading is essentially an internal activity, the relatively intangible product of which is a representation of the text that has been read in the mind of the reader. Probably for this reason, much reading research has traditionally been psycholinguistic in nature, focusing on gaining insight into the reader's internal cognitive processes. However, in recent decades reading research has broadened its focus by becoming more socially, culturally and multi-culturally oriented (Kamil et al. 2000). As a reflection of this, the more socio-culturally oriented term 'literacy' is currently sometimes used alongside 'reading'. It needs, however, to be pointed out that broader conceptualizations of literacy also exist, which, at the very least, include both reading and writing, and often also a variety of aspects of oral, aural and digital communication.

Within the field of applied linguistics, second language reading research has leaned heavily on first language reading research, by echoing – and even amplifying – its cognitive focus. And like first language reading research, second language reading research is shifting its focus – albeit to a lesser extent – to incorporate other perspectives, particularly socio-cultural ones. Reflecting this, the term 'multilingual literacy research' is sometimes used instead of 'second language reading research' (e.g., Fitzgerald 2003). Also similar to first language reading research, the bulk of second language reading research focuses on English – in this case as a second language, which has led to charges of a certain Anglocentrism in the research field (e.g., Bernhardt 2003).

Although first language and second language reading research share commonalities, there are issues specific to second language reading, largely relating to the fact that second language readers have access to more than one language and culture. An issue that has received considerable attention is *transfer*; that is, the extent to which skills that readers possess in their first language transfer to reading in a second language (Grabe and Stoller 2002). It is claimed that in L2 reading, below a certain threshold of proficiency in the second language, readers are unable to fully transfer the strategic skills, such as guessing meaning from context or making inferences, which they possess in their first language reading. This hypothesis is frequently referred to as the *threshold hypothesis*. Numerous studies have investigated transfer and/or the threshold hypothesis (e.g., Carrell 1991; Bernhardt and Kamil1995; Taillefer 1996; Lee and Schallert 1997; Yamashita 2002; van Gelderen et al. 2004). Some studies have emphasized the role of lack of L2 language knowledge in inhibiting transfer of reading ability from the first language to the second language, while others have emphasized the role of lack of second language linguistic processing skills, such as speed of word recognition and sentence parsing.

Despite assumptions that are sometimes made concerning the existence of a second language reading threshold, the empirical evidence is by no means conclusive. To give an example, in a longitudinal study conducted in three consecutive years, van Gelderen et al. (2007) examined both language knowledge and linguistic processing skills and their relationship to first language and second language reading comprehension. A key finding was that both first language reading comprehension and metacognitive knowledge were consistently strongly related to second language reading comprehension, and this was interpreted as indicating a large degree of transfer of reading ability from the first language to the second language. However, both language knowledge – in particular, vocabulary – and processing skills were also, though to a lesser extent, found to be related to second language reading comprehension. These findings were interpreted as indicating that these language factors are of impor-tance to reading comprehension, but do not necessarily constitute a barrier to the application of reading strategies in the second language. A complicating factor in drawing overall conclusions from the research about the existence of a threshold is that studies differ in the methods they have used to investigate this issue and in the characteristics of participants involved in the studies. Factors such as proficiency level, age and characteristics of the readers' first language are likely to strongly influence the degree of transfer from their first language to their second language.

Indeed, a second issue in second language reading research is how the processing of words, sentences and texts in the second language is influenced by characteristics of the reader's first language. For instance, it has been found that word identification processes in the second language are influenced by the characteristics of first language writing systems, such as whether they are alphabetic or non-alphabetic. Results of studies support the notion that word identification in an alphabetic L2, such as English, is easier for readers with an alphabetic first language than for readers with a non-alphabetic first language, such as Chinese or Arabic (see e.g., Wang and Koda 2007). At the text level, the extent to which the first language and the second language share similar text structure properties (i.e., rhetorical distance) has been shown to influence textual processing, with greater similarities facilitating the processing of key ideas and semantic relations (Koda 2005).

A third issue that has emerged concerns the effects of bilingualism on read-ing, and on the acquisition of literacy in the classroom. Recent psycholinguistic research has investigated how knowing two languages affects the neural activity in the brain during reading (e.g., Perfetti et al. 2007). Other research has focused on the development of bilingual children's reading ability (e.g., Bialystok, McBride-Chang and Luk 2005, 2007, 2008). One of the questions relating to this development is whether knowing two languages has a positive or a negative influence on the development of reading ability in either of the bilingual's languages. Studies have found that young bilinguals are more meta-linguistically aware than monolingual children in areas that underpin reading development, although according to Schwartz et al. (2005) the evidence for this advantage has not been conclusive. Schwartz et al. suggest that in light of the mixed outcomes of studies, it may be biliteracy, that is, the ability to read (and write) in two languages, rather than bilingualism per se that is crucial in deter-mining the course of the development of second language reading ability. They found that biliterate bilingual children outperformed both monoliterate bilin-gual children and monolingual children in terms of reading fluency and phono-logical awareness, but that there was little difference between the three groups in terms of their performance on linguistic measures.

Research Areas

Table 13.1 divides the field of second language reading research into six areas: linguistic, discoursal, strategic, affective, intermodal and sociocultural. For each area, one sample study is listed. The sample studies have been selected on the basis of recency, and also for representativeness of the kind of research topics common in a particular area. The studies chosen also reflect some of the diversity in research methods in second language reading research, ranging from qualitative case studies and small-scale observational studies to quantitative survey research and quasi-experimental studies. It should be noted that many of the studies described in this section reflect the aforementioned cognitive orientation of much L2 reading research. It should also be noted that within most of the areas, studies can be found that have an instructional focus, as they examine the effectiveness of a particular form of reading instruction or evaluate the effectiveness of a program incorporating a particular form of instruction. Testing and assessment of reading has not been included as an area, as it is seen as falling within the field of language testing, which is beyond the scope of this chapter.

Table 13.1 Research areas in L2 reading research

Research area	Examples	Sample study
Linguistic	e.g., vocabulary; word recognition; grammar	A quasi-experimental study on training learners' L2 word recognition (Fukkink et al. 2005)
Discoursal	e.g., text structure; background knowledge	A quantitative study on effects of text structure on L2 text recall (Chu et al. 2002)
Strategic	e.g., knowledge of and use of reading strategies	A verbal protocol study on using L1 in L2 reading (Upton and Lee Thompson 2001)
Affective	e.g., motivation; attitudes	A survey on reading attitudes in L1 and L2 (Yamashita 2007)
Inter-modal	e.g., relationship between reading and writing, listening or speaking	A quantitative study on reading and writing two types of texts (Carrell and Connor 1991)
Socio-cultural	e.g., home literacy environment; educational context	A case study on literacy practices of two Puerto Rican families in the US (Compton-Lilly 2007)

Linguistic Research into Second Language Reading

Linguistic research into second language reading focuses on lower order, language-related aspects of reading, such as vocabulary and grammar knowledge, and also on processing skills, such as word recognition and syntactic parsing. Word level aspects have been particularly prominent on the research agenda, specifically vocabulary knowledge and, in the past decade, word recognition skills. Research has found that vocabulary knowledge is the language knowledge component that is most strongly related to second language reading comprehension (Koda 2005), and studies have also focused on the role of reading in vocabulary development (e.g., Pulido 2007). Although some evidence has been found that word recognition skills are also important for second language reading (see Chikamatsu 2006), there is still uncertainty about the nature and size of this role. For example, Fukkink et al. (2005) conducted a classroom-based quasi-experimental study to investigate whether word processing skills could be trained and whether such training would lead to improvements in reading comprehension. They found that word recognition speeded up, but that these gains were not associated with gains in either reading speed or global comprehension.

Discoursal Research into Second Language Reading

Discoursal second language reading research focuses on higher order discourse processes involved in reading, such as the role that text structure and background knowledge play in the comprehension process. Some studies look at the effects of such aspects on comprehension. For example, Chu et al. (2002) found that when English texts were structured according to typical Chinese rhetorical conventions, Chinese learners of English had better recall than when texts were not structured in this way. Other studies look at online discourse processing, such as readers use of text structure information while actually reading texts. For example, Chen and Donin (1997) examined the effects of domain-specific knowledge on the processing of biology texts by Chinese readers of English. They found that domain-specific knowledge affected higher order conceptual and semantic processing more than it affected lower order linguistic processing.

Second Language Reading Strategy Research

Research in the area of reading strategies focuses on readers' knowledge and use of reading strategies in second language reading. Reading strategies are activities and behaviours that readers engage in to assist them in comprehending a text, such as predicting text content or guessing meaning from context. Strategies are thought to be related to metacognition, which is readers' ability to reflect on and control their reading processes. Some studies have examined the effects of reading strategy instruction on reading comprehension. For example, Kern (1989) found that strategy training led to strong gains in reading comprehension. Other studies have focused on the role that metacognitive knowledge plays in reading comprehension. For example, Schoonen et al. (1998) administered a questionnaire to Dutch high-school readers on their knowledge of reading goals, text structure and reading strategies. They found that for children in higher grades metacognitive knowledge played a greater role in both the first language (Dutch) and the second language (English) reading comprehension than at lower grades. Still other studies focus on the actual strategies that readers use, through online measurement of what readers do when they read in their first language and/or in their second language. For example, Upton and Lee-Thompson (2001) examined use of the first language when reading second language texts for Chinese and Japanese readers of English. They found that second language readers used their first language for a variety of strategic purposes, including predicting content and structure and monitoring their own reading behaviour.

Affective Factors in Second Language Reading

Research which examines affective aspects of second language reading focuses on aspects such as motivation and attitudes. Until very recently, little second language reading research had been carried out in this area (Mori 2002), and consequently the overall direction of the research is still taking shape. Topics that have recently been the subject of study are the components of second language reading motivation (Mori 2002), the relationship between motivation and reading comprehension (Kondo-Brown 2006), students' motivations for reading extensively (Takase 2007) and the relationship between first language and second language reading attitudes (Yamashita 2004, 2007). For example, in a survey of Japanese university student's attitudes towards reading in Japanese and English, Yamashita (2007) found that there was a relationship between attitudes to reading in L1 and second language, and that this relationship did not seem to be greatly affected by the level of second language proficiency.

Intermodal Second Language Reading Research

Intermodal second language reading research focuses on relationships between reading and the other modalities: writing, listening or speaking. Here again,

little second language research has been carried out so far, and the little that has been carried out is largely on reading-writing relations. Some work has been done on the transfer of reading and writing skills within and across first language and second language, with results showing that there is a degree of transfer both across skills and across languages (e.g., Carson et al. 1990). Looking solely at L2, Carrell and Connor (1991) examined the relationship between reading and writing of descriptive and persuasive texts by mixed first language groups in second language English using multiple measures for both skills. They found that the relationships between reading and writing varied as a function of text type, type of measure and level.

Sociocultural Research in Second Language Reading

Research in the area of socio-cultural aspects of reading has examined factors such as home literacy environment and educational context. This research has largely been carried out from an educational policy perspective by studying bilingual children for whom the language of schooling is not the same as the language in the home (Bialystok 2007). Much of the research has examined minority children in subtractive bilingual contexts, that is, contexts in which these children are disadvantaged, and has sought to identify factors in the social and educational environment that may compromise their ability to acquire literacy. For example, Compton-Lilly (2007) uses the notion of 'capital', taken from the sociologist, Bourdieu (see e.g., Bourdieu 1986), to examine the economic, social and cultural aspects of reading in the families of two elementary school children of Puerto-Rican background in the United States of America. She found that although the families did not possess much economic reading capital (e.g., computers, books) they were relatively rich in social capital (e.g., networks of relationships with family members, community and teachers), and that educators need to identify and utilize the unique funds of knowledge that children from various cultural backgrounds bring to classrooms.

There has been a call for more second language reading research to incorporate a socio-cultural perspective. Luke (2003) puts forward a multilingual literacy research agenda to examine issues such as how people use texts, discourses and literacies in homes, communities and schools and how the literacy resources that people have are recognized and incorporated into school-based literacy instruction. Fitzgerald (2003) makes a plea for a socio-cognitive approach to second language reading research in which social-cultural perspectives are combined with cognitive perspectives. As time goes by it is likely that an increasing number of studies will examine both cognitive and socio-cultural aspects of reading.

Research Techniques in Second Language Reading Research

This section gives a brief description of some of the most commonly used techniques in second language reading research, which is organized around the distinction between process and product-oriented techniques. Process-oriented techniques provide information about the reading process, that is, about what readers do when they read. In contrast, product-oriented techniques provide information on the product of reading, that is, on comprehension or its components. The description of techniques does not include interviews, surveys, diaries and logbooks, which are used in reading research as well as in many other fields of applied linguistics research, as these are already discussed in other chapters of this book.

Process-Oriented Techniques

Process-oriented techniques are used to infer readers' internal cognitive processes. These techniques may infer processes from observation (e.g., verbal protocols); from measurement of the time taken to respond to stimuli (e.g., speed measures); or from measurement of physiological responses, such as eye movements (i.e., eye-tracking) or the electrical activity of the brain (i.e., event-related potentials (ERPs)). Secondly language reading research has a strong tradition of using process measures in controlled, experimental settings, but there have also been abundant small-scale qualitative studies carried out, particularly using observational process measures. Below, three process-oriented techniques are described: verbal protocols, eye-tracking and speed measures.

Verbal protocols: Verbal protocols, also known as think-aloud protocols, are an observational technique that involve readers verbalizing thoughts about the text they are reading. Protocols may be directed towards gaining insight into a specific aspect of reading, such as deriving meaning from context, or they may be used to gain an overall picture of the strategies readers use in building a global representation of a text.

Verbal protocols can be collected either concurrently (i.e., while reading the text) or retrospectively (i.e., after reading the text). In concurrent collection, the thoughts that are verbalized are supposed to reflect the current content of short-term memory (Ericsson and Simon 1993). Although widely used, concurrent protocols have also been widely criticized for being disruptive to natural reading processes and for providing only a fragmentary representation of what actually goes on in a reader's mind when reading. While retrospective protocols are less potentially disruptive to reading processes, questions arise concerning the validity of the information obtained. Readers may not have accurate recall, and they are also more likely to provide explanations or interpretations, rather than reporting what they actually did. Some researchers have sought a compromise by placing marks at various points in a text, with readers verbalizing their thoughts every time they reach a mark. For a study on the issue of disruptiveness in verbal protocols, see Leow and Morgan-Short (2004).

Eye-tracking: Eye-tracking is a technique in which the reader wears a device that enables the measurement of eye movements made while reading. When reading, eyes make short, rapid, back or forth movements known as saccades, and short stops, known as fixations. Fixation time is taken to provide an indication of the time taken to process the point in the text to which the reader is attending the most (Rayner 1998). However, an important methodological issue is that there is not necessarily a one-to-one relationship between processing time and fixation time. For example, readers sometimes make multiple fixations on the same word; words may also be processed when they are not directly fixated, such as words above or below the fixated word; and processing may also occur during saccades (Irwin 1996). For a detailed consideration of methodological issues involved in eye-tracking research, see Rayner (1998). The bulk of eye-tracking research has examined first language reading, and to date only a handful of studies have examined second language reading (See Frenck-Mestre 2005). The use of eye-tracking in second language reading research is a field that is wide open for exploration in the coming years.

Speed measures: The speed with which processing is carried out is generally considered to be a reflection of readers' fluency. Common speed measures are the time taken to read the whole text (text level), speed of syntactic processing (sentence level), speed of word recognition (word level) and letter recognition (letter level). In many cases, measures include sentences or words that are in some way anomalous (e.g., nonsense sentences), and the speed of processing these elements may be compared to the speed of processing elements that do not contain anomalies. Reaction times for such measures are generally measured using computers.

A methodological issue is whether the measures used are context-specific or non-context specific (Stevenson 2005). Context-specific measurements are made within a textual context. For example, speed of syntactic processing may be measured by registering the speed at which readers read each sentence of a text. In contrast, non-context specific measurements are made in an isolated context. For example, fluency of sentence-level processing may be measured by registering the speed of reading sentences presented as isolated items that together do not form a text. Non-context specific methods, which select items from a general sample of words that are not taken from a specific text, are able to provide a measure of general processing skills, whereas measures that use items taken from a specific text can only make more limited claims concerning processing as it relates to specific texts. However, on the other side of the coin, using non-context specific measures leaves the researcher open to the criticism that little can be said about real online textual processing.

Product-Oriented Techniques

Product-oriented techniques measure comprehension of reading or of a component of reading. Below, these techniques are divided into comprehension measures, which seek to gain insight into the quality of the readers' mental representation of a text, and knowledge component measures, which seek to gain insight into the level of knowledge that a reader possesses concerning a component that is relevant to reading, such as vocabulary or grammatical knowledge.

Comprehension measures: Broadly speaking, comprehension measures can be sub-categorized into measures that require short responses and measures that require extended responses, referred to by Bachman and Palmer (1996) as extended production responses.

The classic short response measure is the multiple-choice comprehension test, which though much maligned, remains popular due to the ease with which it can be administered and scored. A major criticism that has been levelled against this testing format is that it measures test-taking skills more than it measures reading ability, as readers who have developed good guessing strategies may score well regardless of whether they have a good understanding of the text.

Another common short response measure is the cloze test, in which the reader is required to restore words in the text that have been deleted. The underlying rationale is that the semantic and syntactic constraints to which the reader must be sensitive in order to provide correct responses are also constraints that guide textual processing (Koda 2005). Alderson (2000) points out that there is a difference between a 'cloze test' and 'gap-filling' test, although the terms are often used interchangeably. According to Alderson, cloze tests are tests in which every n-th word is deleted, whereas in gap-filling tests the test constructor decides to delete certain words on the basis of grammatical or semantic criteria appropriate to the testing objective (e.g., deletion of verbs), thus giving the test constructor more control over what is measured. These kinds of tests have been criticized for being more sensitive to linguistic constraints than to underlying meaning and for only being capable of measuring local rather than global comprehension (Koda 2005). Many other kinds of short response formats exist, including short answer questions, yes/no questions, choosing from a heading bank for identified paragraphs and flow chart/ diagram completion.

Extended response measures, such as recall and summarization, are said to tap more directly into the reader's comprehension of the text, without the intervention of test questions. In free recall, the reader is asked to recall everything they can about the text. In cued recall, questions are used to guide the reader to recall particular aspects of the text. In summarization, the reader is asked to summarize the main ideas, either with or without the possibility of consulting the text. The scoring of extended response measures is more time-consuming and less 'objective' than the scoring of short response measures, as the resulting recall or summarization protocols require intensive coding.

Knowledge component measures: Knowledge component measures are used to disentangle the knowledge components that contribute to reading ability. These measures typically focus on lower-order linguistic aspects, such as vocabulary, grammar and spelling. However, they may also measure higher-order conceptual aspects, such as topic knowledge, or metacognitive aspects, such as knowledge of reading strategies. Studies that use what is known as the component skills approach may incorporate a battery of knowledge measures, as well as speed of processing measures and measures of global reading comprehension. This approach was used in the van Gelderen et al. (2007) study reported earlier in this chapter. Correlational statistical techniques, such as regression analysis, are frequently used to determine the strength of the relationship between the specific variables and reading comprehension measures.

A Sample Study

This section highlights methodological features of a verbal protocol study that was carried out to compare first and second language reading strategies (Stevenson et al. 2003). I have chosen a verbal protocol study, as in many protocol studies the methodological details have been scantily reported (Afflerbach 2000). Through this discussion, I hope to shed light on some of the methodological issues surrounding this widely used yet controversial technique. A brief description of the study will be given, followed by a discussion of methodological issues under the headings: texts, elicitation of verbalizations, modelling and instruction, and coding.

Description of the Study

The study examined the extent to which readers' strategy use transfers from the first language to the second language, by comparing the reading strategies of 22 Dutch junior high school students in L1 (Dutch) and a foreign language (English). I collected concurrent verbal protocols by recording each student thinking aloud while they read two texts in Dutch and two in English. In order to obtain more detailed information about strategy use than previous studies had been able to do, I classified the students' reading strategies in terms of three separate dimensions. The three dimensions in the coding scheme were Orientation of Processing (i.e., whether strategies are directed towards content or language); Type of Processing (i.e., whether strategies involve regulating the reading process, processing the meaning of the text or rereading the text) and linguistic Domain of Processing (i.e., whether strategies are directed towards texts elements at below-clause level, clause level or above-clause level). The results showed that the readers focused more on the language in the text in their foreign language (English), and that they did this by, in particular, regulating their reading process and using language strategies at clause level and above (i.e., by translating and paraphrasing chunks of text they did not understand). Thus, in contradiction to claims made by the threshold hypothesis, the readers appeared to be able to make good use of reading strategies in FL reading. Moreover, the readers did not appear to be inhibited in their foreign language in their use of strategies that focused on global text content.

Characteristics of Protocol Texts

If more than one text is to be read in a think aloud study, for many research purposes it is desirable to match the characteristics of the texts being used in the study. This means that the text characteristics may need to be adapted in order to make the texts more comparable. In my study, I selected four texts (2 Dutch, 2 English) in terms of text type: they were all argumentative texts. Topics were chosen that were similar but not overlapping (e.g., 'Children should wear school uniforms' (Dutch) and 'Boys and girls should be in separate classes some of the time' (English)). I then adapted the texts in terms of the number of arguments and sub-arguments. For example, the Dutch and English texts mentioned above were adapted so that they both contained one main argument, one counter-argument and one refutation. I also checked that there were no large discrepancies in the level of difficulty of the two texts by examining the mean sentence length, mean word length and the type token ratio. I gave the texts to several teachers and educationalists to ascertain whether they felt that the topics and levels of the texts were suitable for the target students.

Elicitation of Verbalizations

An important issue in verbal protocol studies is the manner in which verbalizations are elicited. I conducted an informal pilot study to determine the best way of doing this. I gave the two Dutch texts to be used in the study to a few students of the same age and grade as the students who would participate in the study. For one of the texts, students did not receive any prompting, and were free to verbalize spontaneously. For the other text, dots were placed in the text after every five sentences, and students were instructed to think aloud when they reached each dot. It became apparent that prompting influenced the kinds of verbalizations made. Prompted verbalizations frequently consisted of a summary of what had just been read, whereas when readers verbalized spontaneously they tended to voice the actual strategies they were using to help them understand the text. Therefore, I opted for spontaneous verbalization, but as a compromise I decided that if readers fell silent for more than 5 sentences they would be prompted verbally by asking 'what are you thinking about?' However, after the data was collected, it turned out that I had to exclude these prompted verbalizations from the data, as just as with the dots, they nearly always resulted in the readers summarizing part of the text.

Modelling and Instruction in the Use of Think Alouds

It is necessary to provide modelling and instruction in thinking aloud. A pressing issue is weighing up the amount of instruction against any time constraints. In my study, there were considerable time constraints, given that the students could only absent themselves from normal classes for one 40-minute lesson at a time, and that they needed to complete two reading tasks in this period. I decided to give each participant 15 minutes of instruction and practice immediately prior to reading the first text. I first modelled the technique myself, using a Dutch text similar to the texts in the study, and then asked the participant to use the same text to practice thinking aloud. The same verbalizations were modelled for all participants, and the model provided examples of different kinds of reading strategies. The participants were instructed to read the texts aloud and to voice their thoughts consistently. They were told that they were free to voice their thoughts in Dutch or English. They were also told that the text did not have to be read in a linear fashion: They could reread or omit any part of the text.

Coding Think Aloud Data

Developing a workable coding scheme is a central issue in the analysis phase of any protocol study. Traditionally, the first step in doing this has been to make a word-for-word transcription of the protocol recordings. However, I was lucky to be able to skip this very time-consuming step by using a computer program called Observer 3.0 to assist me in coding the protocols (Noldus Information Technology 1998). The program allowed me to code the data – by listening to the protocol recordings, stopping them at each point where a strategy ended, and typing codes into a format provided by the computer program. The program was also a useful coding tool in that it enabled me to record production measures, such as the time spent reading the text, and the time spent engaged in reading strategies.

It is important to be able to demonstrate that the coding scheme that is developed is reliable, that is, that it can be used by different people in a consistent way. Thus, it is necessary to have all or part of the data coded by more than one coder, and to use a statistical measure, such as Cohen's kappa (Cohen 1960), to calculate the interrater reliability. In my study, a research assistant and I independently encoded a quarter of the data. (For a formula for determining how much of the data in a particular study needs to be coded by more than one coder, see Siegel and Castellan 1988).

Obtaining an acceptable level of reliability can be surprisingly difficult. I learnt from experience the importance of having a coding scheme that is not overly complicated. A balance needs to be struck between, on the one hand, obtaining sufficiently detailed information, and on the other, not making the categories in the coding scheme so finely-grained that somebody else cannot distinguish between them. I also learnt that it was important for the coders to have an extended period of working and training together. The research assistant and I practised on protocols that would not be included in the reliability sample, adjusting categories in the coding scheme and discussing issues that arose as we went along. Discussing the coding scheme and practising coding turned out to be an invaluable step in developing a coding scheme that could be used reliably.

Resources for Further Reading

Grabe, W. and Stoller, F. L. (2002), *Teaching and Researching Reading*. London: Pearson Education Longman.
In addition to an overview of second language reading theory, this book provides an overview of cognitively oriented second language reading research and a framework for researching reading in the classroom.
Hulstijn, J., Schoonen, R. and van Gelderen, A. (2007), 'Unraveling the componential structure of second language skills,' *TESOL Quarterly*, 41, 186–192.
This article discusses some methodological features of three quantitative second language research projects in which the component skills approach is used.
Koda, K. (2005), *Insights into Second Language Reading: A Cross Linguistic Approach*. Cambridge: Cambridge University Press.
This book deals with the theoretical foundations of second language reading, and provides a detailed overview of components of reading, including relevant research.

Pressley, M. and Afflerbach, P. (1995), *Verbal Protocols of Reading*. Hillsdale, NJ: Lawrence Erlbaum.
This book provides a thorough overview of verbal protocol techniques, including the results of protocol studies and major methodological concerns.

References

Afflerbach, P. (2000), 'Verbal reports and protocol analysis', in M. L. Kamil, P. B. Mosenthal, P. D. Pearson and R. Barr (eds), *Handbook of Reading Research, Volume III*. Mahmah, NJ: Lawrence Erlbaum, pp. 163–179.

Alderson, J. (2000), *Assessing Reading*. Cambridge, UK: Cambridge University Press.

Bachman, L. F. and Palmer, A. S. (1996), *Language Testing in Practice: Designing and Developing Useful Language Tests*. Oxford, UK: Oxford University Press.

Bernhardt, E. (2003), 'Challenges to reading research from a multilingual world'. *Reading Research Quarterly*, 38, 112–117.

Bernhardt, E. B. and Kamil, M. L. (1995), 'Interpreting relationships between L1 and L2 reading: Consolidating the linguistic threshold and the linguistic interdependence hypotheses'. *Applied Linguistics*, 16, 15–34.

Bialystok, E. (2007), 'Acquisition of literacy in bilingual children: a framework for research'. *Language Learning*, 57(Supplementary 1), 45–77.

Bialystok, E., McBride-Chang, C. and Luk, G. (2005), 'Bilingualism, language proficiency, and learning to read in two writing systems'. *Journal of Educational Psychology*, 97, 580–590.

Bourdieu, P. (1986). 'The forms of capital', in J.G. Richardson (eds), *Handbook of Theory and Research for the Sociology of Education*. New York: Greenwood, pp. 241–258.

Carrell, P. (1991), 'Second language reading: Reading ability or language proficiency'. *Applied Linguistics*, 12, 159–179.

Carrell, P. L. and Connor, U. (1991), 'Reading and writing descriptive and persuasive texts'. *The Modern Language Journal*, 75, 314–324.

Carson, J. E., Carrell, P.L., Silberstein, S., Kroll, B. and Kuehn, P. A. (1990), 'Reading-writing relationships in first and second language', *TESOL Quarterly*, 24, 245–266.

Chen, Q. and Donin, J. (1997), 'Discourse processing of first and second language biology texts: Effects of language proficiency and domain-specific knowledge'. *Modern Language Journal*, 81, 209–226.

Chikamatsu, N. (2006), 'Developmental word recognition: A study of L1 English readers of L2 Japanese'. *The Modern Language Journal*, 90, 67–85.

Chu, H. J., Swaffar, J. and Charney, D. H. (2002), 'Cultural representations of rhetorical conventions: The effects on reading recall'. *TESOL Quarterly*, 36, 511–541.

Cohen, J. (1960), 'A coefficient of agreement for nominal scales'. *Educational and Psychological Measurement*, 20, 37–46.

Compton-Lilly, C. (2007), 'The complexities of reading capital in two Puerto-Rican families'. *Reading Research Quarterly*, 42, 72–98.

Ericsson, K. A. and Simon, H. A. (1993), *Protocol Analysis: Verbal Reports as Data*. Cambridge, MA: MIT press.

Fitzgerald, J. (2003), 'Multilingual reading theory'. *Reading Research Quarterly*, 38, 118–122.

Frenck-Mestre, C. (2005), 'Eye-tracking recording as a tool for studying syntactic processing in a second language: A review of methodologies and experimental findings'. *Second Language Research*, 21, 175–198.

Fukkink, R. G., Hulstijn, J. and Simis, A. (2005), 'Does training in second language word recognition skills affect reading comprehension? An experimental study'. *Modern Language Journal*, 89, 54–75.

Grabe, W. and Stoller, F. L. (2002), *Teaching and Researching Reading*. London: Pearson Education Longman.

Irwin, D. E. (1996), 'Integrating information across saccadic eye movements'. *Current Directions in Psychological Science*, 5, 94–100.

Kamil, M. L., Mosenthal, P. B., Pearson, P. D. and Barr, R. 'Preface', in M. L. Kamil, P. B. Mosenthal, P. D. Pearson and R. Barr (eds) (2000), *Handbook of Reading Research: Volume III*. Mahwah, NJ: Lawrence Erlbaum Associates, Publishers, pp. ix–xiv.

Kern, R. G. (1989), 'Second language reading strategy instruction: Its effects on comprehension and word inference ability'. *The Modern Language Journal*, 73, 135–149.

Koda, K. (2005), *Insights into Second Language Reading: A Cross-linguistic Approach*. Cambridge, UK: Cambridge University Press.

Kondo-Brown, K. (2006), 'Affective variables and Japanese L2 reading ability'. *Reading in a Foreign Language*, 18, 55–71.

Lee, J. W. and Schallert, D. L.(1997), 'The relative contribution of L2 language proficiency and L1 reading ability to L2 reading performance: A test of the threshold hypothesis in an EFL context'. *TESOL Quarterly*, 31, 713–739.

Leow, R. P. and Morgan-Short, K. (2004), 'To think aloud or not to think aloud: The issue of reactivity in SLA research methodology'. *Studies in Second Language Acquisition*, 26, 35–57.

Luke, A. (2003), 'Literacy and the other: A sociological approach to literacy research and policy in multilingual societies'. *Reading Research Quarterly*, 38, 132–141.

Mori, S. (2002), 'Redefining motivation to read in a foreign language'. *Reading in a Foreign Language*, 14, 91–110.

Noldus Information Technology b.v. (1998), Observer (Version 3.0), [Computer software]. Wageningen, the Netherlands: Noldus Information Technology b.v.

Perfetti, C. A., Liu, Y., Fiez, J., Nelson, J., Bolger, D. J. and Tan, L. (2007), 'Reading in two writing systems: Accommodation and assimilation of the brain's reading network'. *Bilingualism: Language and Cognition*, 10, 131–146.

Pulido, D. (2007), 'The relationship between text comprehension and second language incidental vocabulary acquisition: A matter of topic familiarity?'. *Language Learning*, 57(Supplementary 1), 155–199.

Rayner, K. (1998), 'Eye movements in reading and information processing: 20 years of research'. *Psychological Bulletin*, 124, 372–422.

Schoonen, R., Hulstijn, J. and Bossers, B. (1998), 'Language-dependent and language-independent knowledge in native and foreign language reading comprehension:

An empirical study among Dutch students in grades 6, 8 and 10'. *Language Learning*, 48, 71–106.

Schwartz, M., Leikin, M. and Share, D. L. (2005), 'Biliterate bilingualism versus mono-literate bilingualism'. *Written Language and Literacy*, 8, 179–205.

Siegel, S. and Castellan, N. J. (1988), *Nonparametric Statistics for the Behavioral Sciences*. Second edition. New York: McGraw-Hill.

Stevenson, M. (2005), 'Reading and Writing in a Foreign Language: A Comparison of Conceptual and Linguistic Processes in Dutch and English'. Unpublished doctoral dissertation. University of Amsterdam.

Stevenson, M., Schoonen, R. and de Glopper, K. (2003), 'Inhibition or compensation? A multi-dimensional comparison of reading processes in Dutch and English'. *Language Learning*, 53, 765–815.

Taillefer, G. (1996), 'L2 reading ability: Further insight into the short-circuit hypothesis'. *Modern Language Journal*, 80, 461–477.

Takase, A. (2007), 'Japanese high school students' motivation for extensive L2 reading'. *Reading in a Foreign Language*, 19, 1–18.

Upton, T. A. and Lee-Thompson, L. C. (2001), 'The role of the first language in second language reading'. *Studies in Second Language Acquisition*, 23, 469–495.

van Gelderen, A., Schoonen, R., de Glopper, K., Hulstijn, J., Simis, A., Snellings, P. and Stevenson, M. (2004), 'Linguistic knowledge, processing speed and metacognitive knowledge in first and second language reading comprehension: A componential analysis'. *Journal of Educational Psychology*, 96, 19–30.

Van Gelderen, A., Schoonen, R., Stoel, R. D., De Glopper, K. and Hulstijn, J. (2007), 'Development of adolescent reading comprehension in Language 1 and Language 2: A longitudinal analysis of constituent components'. *Journal of Educational Psychology*, 99, 477–491.

Wang, M. and Koda, K. (2007), 'Commonalities and differences in word identification skills among learners of English as a second language'. *Language Learning*, 57(Supplementary 1), 201–222.

Yamashita, J. (2002), 'Reading strategies in L1 and L2: Comparison of four groups of readers with different reading ability in L1 and L2'. *I.T.L. Review of Applied Linguistics*, 135–36, 1–35.

—(2004), 'Reading attitudes in L1 and L2, and their influence on extensive reading'. *Reading in a Foreign Language*, 16, 1–19.

—(2007), 'The relationship of reading attitudes between L1 and L2: An investigation of adult EFL learners in Japan'. *TESOL Quarterly*, 41, 81–105.

14 Researching Writing

Ken Hyland

Writing is fundamental to modern societies and is of overarching significance in all our lives: central to our personal experiences, life chances and social identities. Its complex, multifaceted nature, however, is difficult to pin down and as a result, many research approaches have emerged to help clarify both how writing works and the purposes it is employed to achieve. Research, in fact, has taken philosophical, historical, empirical and critical directions and encompassed a wide range of different interpretive and quantitative methods. In this chapter I briefly summarize and evaluate some of these and illustrate a sample study.

Assumptions, Writing and Research

First of all, it is important to recognize that writing research does not simply involve fitting suitable methods to particular questions. Methods are inseparable from theories and how we understand writing itself. For some people, writing is a product, an artefact of activity which can be studied independently of users by counting features and inferring rules. For others, it is a kind of cognitive performance which can be modelled by analogy with computer processing through observation and writers' on-task verbal reports. A third group sees it as the ways we make our social worlds and explore how writing connects us with readers and institutions in particular contexts. Different methods tell us different things about writing, but they always start with our preconceptions. Simplifying a complex picture, it is possible to group research methods according to their principal focus and whether they are concerned with illuminating our understanding of texts, writers or readers.

Text-Oriented Research

This views writing as an outcome of activity, as words on a page or screen and can be descriptive (revealing what occurs), analytical (interpreting why it occurs) or critical (questioning the social relations which underlie and are reproduced by what occurs). Texts can also be examined in a variety of ways, looking at particular features or their themes, cohesive elements or move structures. We can examine a text in isolation or as a sample from a single genre, time period or writer, and we can collect a number of texts together as a corpus and aggregate those features as representative of other texts.

Traditionally, research into texts followed views inherited from structuralism and implicit in the Transformational Grammar of Noam Chomsky. Texts were seen as *langue*, or a demonstration of the writer's knowledge of forms and grammatical rules rather than attempts to communicate, and methods were the means of revealing principles of writing independent of any actual contexts or users. From this perspective, writing improvement is measured by counting increases in features seen as important to successful writing and calculating the 'syntactic complexity' of texts by counting the number of words or clauses per T-unit and the number of T-units per sentence. There is, however, little evidence to show that syntactic complexity or grammatical accuracy are either the principal features of writing development or the best measures of good writing. Essentially, viewing texts in this way ignores their role as communicative acts and how they function as a writer's response to a particular communicative setting. Because all texts include what writers suppose their readers will know, and how they will use the text, no text can be fully explicit or universally 'appropriate'. Rather, they need to balance what needs to be said against what can be assumed.

Writer-Oriented Research

This emphasizes the actions of writers rather than the features of texts. Champions of this approach believe that writing constitutes a process, or at least a complex of activities, from which all writing emerges and that this is generalizable across contexts of writing. Interest here is on what good writers do when they write, principally so that these strategies can be taught to students. Early work assumed that writing is more of a problem-solving activity than an act of communication and drew on the tools and models of cognitive psychology and artificial intelligence to reveal how people engage in a writing task to create and revise personal meanings. More recent work has given greater emphasis to the actual performance of writing in a particular context, exploring what Nystrand (1987) calls the *situation of expression*, to investigate the personal and social histories of individual writers as they write in specific contexts.

The goal is to describe the influence of this context on the ways writers represent their purposes in the kind of writing that is produced. As Prior (1998, p. xi) observes:

> Actually writing happens in moments that are richly equipped with tools (material and semiotic) and populated with others (past present, and future). When seen as situated activity, writing does not stand alone as the discrete act of a writer, but emerges as a confluence of many streams of activity: reading, talking, observing, acting, making, thinking, and feeling as well as transcribing words on paper.

By using detailed observations of acts of writing, participant interviews, analyses of surrounding practices, and other techniques, researchers seek to develop more complete accounts of local writing contexts.

A range of methods have been employed to explore and elaborate the composing process, moving beyond text analysis to the qualitative methods of the human and social sciences. Case study research has been particularly productive, focusing on 'natural scenes' rather than on experimental environments, and often seeking to describe writing from an *emic* perspective, privileging the views of insiders or those participating in a situation. These studies have thus made considerable use of 'think aloud protocols', or writers' verbal reports while composing (e.g., Smagorinsky 1994), retrospective interviews (e.g., Nelson and Carson 1998) and task observation (e.g., Bosher 1998), sometimes involving keystroke recording during composing (e.g., Sullivan and Lindgren 2006). Often research is longitudinal, following students over an extended period (e.g., F. Hyland 1998) and uses multiple techniques which may include recall protocols, and analyses of several drafts.

However, while these descriptions give significant attention to the experiences of writers and to their understandings of the local features of the context they deal with as they write, concentrating on the local setting fails to capture the culture and event within which the action is embedded and which their writing must invoke. Texts do not function communicatively at the time they are composed but when they are read, as they anticipate particular readers and the responses of those readers to what is written. Texts evoke a social milieu which intrudes upon the writer and activates specific responses to recurring tasks and as a result most current writing research takes a more reader-oriented view to explore the ways writers see their audience and engage in cultural contexts.

Reader-Oriented Research

This looks beyond individual writers and the surface structures of products to see texts as examples of *discourse*, or language in use. Discourse approaches recognize that texts are always a response to a particular communicative setting and seek to reveal the purposes and functions which linguistic forms serve in texts. Here texts are not isolated examples of competence but the concrete expressions of social purposes, intended for particular audiences. The writer is seen as having certain goals and intentions, certain relationships to his or her readers, and certain information to convey, and the forms a text takes are resources used to accomplish these. Writing is therefore seen as mediated by the institutions and cultures in which it occurs and every text is embedded in wider social practices which carry assumptions about writer-reader relationships and how these should be structured. These factors draw the analyst into a wider paradigm which locates texts in a world of communicative purposes, institutional power and social action, identifying the ways that texts actually work as communication.

One way writers are able to construct an audience is by drawing on their own knowledge of other texts and by exploiting readers' abilities to recognize intertextuality between texts. This perspective owes its origins to Bakhtin's (1986) view that language is fundamentally dialogic, that a conversation between writer and reader is an ongoing activity. Writing reflects traces of its social uses because it is multiply linked and aligned with other texts upon which it builds and which it anticipates. 'Each utterance refutes, affirms, supplements, and relies on the others, presupposes them to be known and somehow takes them into account' (Ibid., p. 91). A key idea here is that of *genre*, a term for grouping texts together and referring to the repertoire of linguistic responses writers are able to call on to communicate in familiar situations. Genre reminds us that when we write we follow conventions for organizing messages because we want our readers to recognize our purposes. Research into genres therefore seeks to show how language forms work as resources for accomplishing goals, describing the stages which help writers to set out their thoughts in ways readers can easily follow and identifying salient features of texts which allow them to engage effectively with their readers.

An Overview of Methods

While I have divided methods up according to the paradigms with which they are mainly associated, much writing research combines several methods, often both quantitative and qualitative, to gain a more complete picture of a complex reality. In fact, the concept of *triangulation*, or the use of multiple sources of data, or approaches, can bring greater plausibility to the interpretation of results. It obviously makes sense to view research pragmatically, adopting whatever tools seem most effective and a researcher may, for example, gather student opinions about their writing practices through a questionnaire and supplement this with interview or diary data, and with the drafts of their essays, mixing methods to increase the validity of the eventual findings.

Another feature of writing research is that it tends to favour data gathered in naturalistic rather than controlled conditions. This is not to say that methods that elicit data through questionnaires, structured interviews or experiments are not employed or that they have nothing to tell us about writing. It is simply that there has been a strong preference for collecting data in authentic circumstances not specifically set up for the research, such as via classroom observations or analyses of naturally occurring texts. The main methods for researching writing are summarized in Figure 14.1 (Hyland 2003) and discussed briefly below.

Elicitation: Questionnaires and Interviews

These are the main methods for eliciting information and attitudes from inform-ants. *Questionnaires* are widely used for collecting large amounts of structured,

Questionnaires:	Highly focused elicitations of respondent self-reports about actions and attitudes
Interviews:	Adaptable and interactive elicitations of respondent self-reports
Verbal reports:	Retrospective accounts and think aloud reports of thoughts while composing
Written reports:	Diary or log accounts of personal writing or learning experiences
Observation:	Direct or recorded data of 'live' interactions or writing behaviour
Texts:	Study of authentic examples of writing used for communication in a natural context
Case studies:	A collection of techniques capturing the experiences of participants in a situation

Figure 14.1 Main data collection methods for researching writing (Hyland 2003, p. 253)

often numerical, easily analysable self-report data, while interviews offer more flexibility and greater potential for elaboration and detail. Both allow researchers to tap people's views and experiences of writing, but interviews tend to be more qualitative and heuristic and questionnaires more quantitative and conclusive. Questionnaires are particularly useful for exploratory studies into writing attitudes and behaviours and for identifying issues that can be followed-up later by more in-depth methods. One major use of questionnaires in writing research has been to discover the kinds of writing target communities require from students. Rogerson-Revell (2007), for example, used a questionnaire to shed light on participants' use of English in business meetings in a European company and to identify some of the language difficulties that can result.

Interviews offer more interactive and less predetermined modes of eliciting information. Although sometimes little more than oral questionnaires, interviews generally represent a very different way of understanding human experience, regarding knowledge as generated between people rather than as objectified and external to them. Participants are able to discuss their interpretations and perspectives, sharing what writing means to them rather than responding to preconceived categories. This flexibility and responsiveness means that interviews are used widely in writing research to learn more about *writing practices* (to discover the genres people write and how they understand and go about writing); about *teaching and learning practices* (to discover people's beliefs and practices about teaching and learning) and about *discourse-features* (to discover how text users see and respond to particular features of writing). Interviews are particularly valuable as they can reveal issues that might be difficult to predict, such as the kinds of problems that students might have in understanding teacher feedback (Hyland and Hyland 2001).

Introspection: Verbal and Written Reports

The use of *verbal reports* as data reflects the idea that the process of writing requires conscious attention and that at least some of the thought process involved can be recovered, either as a retrospective written or spoken recall or simultaneously with writing as a think aloud protocol.

Protocols involve participants writing in their normal way but instructed to verbalize all thinking at the same time so that information can be collected on their decisions, their strategies and their perceptions as they work. Think aloud data have been criticised as offering an artificial and incomplete picture of the complex cognitive activities involved in writing. For one thing, many cognitive processes are routine and internalized operations and therefore not available to verbal description while, more seriously, the act of verbal reporting may itself slow task progress or distort the process being reported on. But despite these criticisms, the method has been widely used, partly because the alternative is to deduce cognitive processes solely from subjects' behaviour, and this would obviously be far less reliable. Think aloud techniques have been extremely productive in revealing the strategies writers use when composing, particularly what students do when planning and revising texts. In one study, for example, de Larios et al. (1999) used the method to examine what students did when they were blocked by a language problem or wanted to express a different meaning, tracing the patterns they used in searching for an alternative syntactic plan.

Diaries offer an alternative way of gaining introspective data. These are first-person accounts of a language-using experience, documented through regular entries in a journal and then analysed for recurring patterns or significant events. Diarists can be asked to produce 'narrative' entries which freely introspect on their learning or writing experiences, or be set guidelines to restrict the issues addressed. These can be in the form of detailed points to note ('write about what you found most/least interesting about this class') or a loose framework for response ('note all the work you did to complete this task'). Alternatively, researchers may ask diarists to concentrate only on 'critical incidents' of personal significance or to simply record dates and times of writing. While some diarists may resent the time and intrusion involved, diaries provide a rich source of reflective data which can reveal social and psychological processes difficult to collect in other ways. Thus Nelson (1993) used diaries to discover how her students went about writing a research paper, following their trail through the library, how they evaluated sources and took notes, the conversations they had with others, decisions they made, and so on. This approach provided a rich account of writers' reflections, suggesting why they acted as they did and how they saw contextual influences.

Observations

While elicitation and introspective methods provide reports of what people *say* they think and do, observation methods offer actual evidence of it by systematic documentation of participants engaged in writing and learning to write. They are based on conscious noticing and precise recording of actions as a way of seeing these actions in a new light. Once again there are degrees of structure the researcher can impose on the data, from simply checking pre-defined boxes at fixed intervals or every time a type of behaviour occurs, to writing a full narrative of events. The most highly structured observations employ a prior coding scheme to highlight significant events from the mass of data that taped or live observation can produce (see Hyland 2003 for examples). All observation will necessarily privilege some behaviours and neglect others, as we only record what we think is important, but while a clear structure is easier to apply and yields more manageable data, such pre-selection may ignore relevant behaviour that wasn't predicted.

Observation is often combined with other methods, as in Camitta's (1993) three-year study of vernacular writing among adolescents. She observed and interviewed writers of different races and genders between the ages of 14 and 18 outside school, in free school time when they clustered in groups to talk and write, and in writing surreptitiously in class. She found that these students produced a wide variety of genres and that when writing was free of school constraints it generated considerable interest and much oral sharing.

Text Data

Finally, a major source of data for writing research is writing itself: the use of texts as objects of study. While texts can be approached in a variety of ways, most research now seeks to discover how people use language in specific contexts. The main approaches to studying written texts are currently genre and corpus analyses.

Genre Analysis

This embraces a range of tools and attitudes to texts, from detailed qualitative analyses of a single text to more quantitative counts of language features. Sometimes researchers work with a single text, either because it is inherently interesting or because it seems representative of a larger set of texts or particular genre. A major policy speech, a newspaper editorial or an important scientific article can offer insights into forms of persuasion, particular syntactic or lexical choices, or the views of text writers. More generally, a sample essay may shed light on students' uses of particular forms or the assumptions underlying different choices. Bhatia (1993) suggests some basic steps for conducting a genre analysis which emphasize the importance of locating texts in their contexts as presented in Figure 14.2.

Such an approach forms a *case study*, but while this is a widely recognized method, it raises questions about how far a single can be representative of a genre. Representativeness is strengthened if several texts are analysed, and corpus analyses, drawing on evidence from large databases of electronically encoded texts, are the main way of achieving this.

1 Select a text which seems representative of the genre you want to study.

2 Place the text in a situational context, i.e., use your background knowledge and text clues to guess where the genre is used, by whom, and why it is written the way it is.

3 Compare the text with other similar texts to ensure that it broadly represents the genre.

4 Study the institutional context in which the genre is used (through site visits, interviews, manuals, etc.) to better understand it's conventions.

5 Select a focus for analysis (moves, lexis, cohesion, persuasion, etc.) and analyse it.

6 Check your analysis with a specialist informant to confirm your findings and insights.

Figure 14.2 Steps in genre analysis (after Bhatia 1993, pp. 22–34)

Corpus Analysis

A *corpus* is simply a collection of naturally occurring language samples (often consisting of millions of words) which represent a speaker's experience of language in some restricted domain, thereby providing a more solid basis for genre descriptions. A corpus provides an alternative to intuition by offering both a resource against which intuitions can be tested and a mechanism for generating them. This enables analysts to depict what is usual in a genre, rather than what is simply grammatically possible, and helps to suggest explanations for why language is used as it is in particular contexts.

Corpus studies are therefore based on both qualitative and quantitative methods, using evidence of *frequency* and *association* as starting points for interpretation. *Frequency* is based on the idea that if a word, string or grammatical pattern occurs regularly in a particular genre or subset of language, then we can assume it is significant in how that genre is routinely constructed. *Association* refers to the ways features associate with each other in collocational patterns. A concordance programme brings together all instances of a search word or phrase in the corpus as a list of unconnected lines of text and so allows the analyst to see regularities in its use that might otherwise be missed. In other words, we can see instances of language *use* when we read these lines horizontally and evidence of *system* when we read them vertically, pointing to common usage in this genre.

In a study of the acknowledgement sections from 240 masters and doctoral dissertations, for example, I found a strong tendency to use the noun *thanks* in preference to other expressions of gratitude (Hyland 2004). Sorting concordance lines on the word to the left of this search word revealed this noun was modified by only three adjectives: *special, sincere* and *deep* with *special* making up over two-thirds of all cases. Figure 14.3 is a screen shot from the programme *MonoConc Pro* showing part of the results of this sorting.

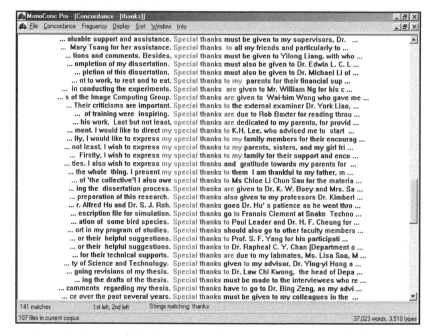

Figure 14.3 Special thanks pattern in Masters/Doctoral acknowledgements
(Hyland 2008, p. 546)

A Sample Study

To illustrate some of these ideas and to show what one approach to writing research looks like in practice, the remainder of this chapter reports on a study of Hong Kong undergraduates' writing I conducted a few years ago (Hyland 2002). I will discuss the main stages under four headings: framing issues, selecting methods, collecting data and analysing data.

Framing the issue: The study emerged from a sense that my undergraduate students had considerable problems constructing a credible representation of themselves and their work in their research writing. They seemed reluctant to claim an appropriate degree of authoritativeness in their texts and to get behind their statements, making their work seem anonymous and disembodied. I decided to pursue these impressions by investigating how these students used authorial pronouns, framing the issue by relating the use of first person to rhetorical identity. This sees identity as less a phenomenon of private experience than a need for affiliation and recognition in particular social networks. When we write in particular genres there is strong pressure to take on their forms and represent ourselves in a way valued by that community. This does not mean that writers simply slot into ready-made identities, but it limits individual manoeuvre. Newcomers, however, often find that the discourses of their disciplines support identities very different from those they bring with them from their home cultures, which prevent them from communicating appropriate commitments and undermine their relationship to readers.

Selecting methods: Framing pronoun use in terms of the constraints on rhetorical conventions of personality suggested two possible lines of inquiry. Basically, to adopt an ethnographic approach and focus on particular writers, investigating their personal and social histories and how these influenced their writing of academic assignments; or to look for preferred choices of pronoun use in a representative collection of student writing and interview writers about their choices. I decided on the latter, partly because I was more comfortable with the methods involved and partly because I wanted a wider picture of how they saw the demands of the task and chose to represent themselves in this context. A corpus approach offers a starting point for analysis by providing quantitative information about the relative frequency and use of self-mention, pointing to systematic tendencies in students' choices of meanings. To understand why writers made the choices they did I decided to support the text data with interviews, using focus groups as a way of reducing the threat to these L2 students.

Collecting data: To ensure that the text samples were representative of undergraduate research writing, I compiled a corpus of 64 final year project reports, a genre of 8,000 to 12,000 words and by far the most substantial piece of writing students do in their undergraduate careers. I obtained a broad cross-section of academic practice by collecting eight reports from each of eight different degree programmes, including sciences, engineering, social sciences, technology and business. This involved getting agreement from writers and electronic copies of their reports. I then computer-searched the corpus for the first person uses *I*, *me*, *my*, *we*, *us*, *our*, *mine* and *ours* using a commercially available concordance programme, and checked all cases to ensure they were exclusive first person uses.

While corpus analyses are excellent for telling us what writers do, to stop here runs the danger of reifying conventions rather than explaining them. I therefore conducted interviews with a supervisor from each field and with student writers. The supervisors were asked about their own writing, that of their students, and their impressions of disciplinary practices. The student interviews required more scaffolding and a more supportive environment and were conducted as focus groups of four or five students. All interviews had two parts. First, I asked participants to respond to features in selected texts as either writers or members of the readership for whom the texts were composed as a way of making explicit the tacit knowledge or strategies that they brought to acts of composing or reading. This was followed by more general observations of pronoun use to learn how respondents saw the practices of the cultures and communities that influenced their writing. All interviews were taped and written up as a summary immediately after the session and subsequently returned to several times, often with the assistance of the subjects.

Analysing data: The frequency counts showed 637 occurrences. In several sweeps of the data I also noted the surrounding text of the target words to identify recurring pragmatic functions. Checking concordance lines is a recursive procedure which involves trying to narrow down, expand and combine initial categories. This recursion allowed me to classify each instance as performing one of five functions, either stating a goal, explaining a procedure, stating results or claims, expressing self-benefits, or elaborating an argument. I validated the analysis by asking a colleague to independently code a sample of data.

In order to better understand student choices I compared the findings with those of expert writers using an existing corpus of 240 published research articles in cognate disciplines. These papers were selected from journals on students' reading lists and totalled 1.3 million words, twice as large as the student corpus in order to strengthen observations about expert practices, as opposed to those about a specific student population. Analysis of the two corpora showed that first person pronouns were substantially more frequent in the published corpus and that the students generally sought to downplay their authorial identity by consciously avoiding its most authoritative functions such as making a commitment to an interpretation or claim. In other words, they sought to deny ownership and responsibility for their views. I set out to investigate these findings further through the interviews.

I also approached the interview data recursively using a form of *content analysis*, beginning with obvious or recurring topics and looking for themes. Subsequent passes through the data helped to generate and refine categories, identify core ideas, find links and gradually build a picture of the data. I attended to the frequency with which particular ideas occurred, the strength of their expression, their distribution across the informants, and the rationale for the study. The data revealed a lot about beliefs and practices and raised issues concerning the students' intentions in using self-mention, their previous encounters with it in textbooks and class teaching, and their sense of its meanings. It showed that the students were sensitive to the effects of author pronouns and reluctant to accept its clear connotations of authority and commitment. They viewed the use of *I* with misgivings as it seemed to imply an identity they did not want. Together, analysis of the corpus and interview material suggested that culture and context shape our communicative practices in significant ways, influencing our preferences for structuring information, the relationships we establish with our readers, and how far we want to personally appear in our texts.

Conclusions

I have attempted to provide an overview of writing research approaches in this chapter. While space prevents elaboration, I hope to have shown that the questions we ask, the methods we adopt and the ways we interpret data, are all products of the ways we understand what writing is. Explanation involves selecting texts and features through the filter of our theories and research interests and sifting out the ways that writers' interests, beliefs, affiliations, experiences, values and practices appear to influence their writing. Because these are not things that can be directly observed, the researcher must select from a repertoire of interpretations rather than hit on the truth, but by grounding these interpretations in written and oral data we help to ensure that they are not pure speculation either. Ultimately, all we can claim for our research is that our findings are a plausible interpretation of some aspect of a given context of communication.

Resources for Further Reading

Baker, P. (2006), *Using Corpora in Discourse Analysis*. London: Continuum.
  This is an accessible guide to creating and analysing written corpora. Topics covered include corpus building, concordancing, keyness, frequency and dispersion.
Hyland, K. (2003), *Second Language Writing*. New York: Cambridge University Press.
  This is a teachers' guide to analysing and teaching L2 writing, with chapters on establishing students' needs, designing syllabuses, creating and sequencing tasks, and feedback and assessment. It contains a chapter on different writing research methods with examples.
Hyland, K. (2010), *Teaching and Researching Writing (2nd edn)*. London: Longman.
  This book is an overview of writing with an up-to-date discussion of theories on writing together with methods for research and teaching. It also contains ideas for writing research projects together with example studies.
Smagorinsky, P. (ed.) (1994), *Speaking about Writing: Reflections on Research Methodology*. Thousand Oaks, CA: Sage.
  Chapters in this book contain discussions and studies using a range of oral elicitation techniques including think-aloud protocols, retrospective accounts, ethnographic interviews and stimulated recall.
  There are also a number of free concordance tools on the web which allow you to search a range of academic, student, newspaper and literary corpora. The best of these are:
VLC Web Concordancer at: http://www.edict.com.hk/concordance/
CobuildDirect site at: http://www.collins.co.uk/corpus/CorpusSearch.aspx

References

Bakhtin, M. (1986), *Speech Genres and Other Late Essays*. Austin, TX: University of Texas Press.

Bhatia, V. K. (1993), *Analyzing Genre: Language Use in Professional Settings*. London: Longman.

Bosher, S. (1998). 'The composing processes of three southeast Asian writers at the post-secondary level: An exploratory study'. *Journal of Second Language Writing*, 7(2), 205–233.

Camitta, M. (1993), 'Vernacular writing: Varieties of literacy among Philadelphia high school students' in B. Street (ed.), *Cross-cultural Approaches to Literacy*. Cambridge: Cambridge University Press, pp. 228–246.

de Larios, J., Murphy, L. and Manchon, R. (1999), 'The use of restructuring strategies in EFL writing: A study of Spanish learners of English as a Foreign Language'. *Journal of Second Language Writing*, 8, 13–44.

Hyland, F. (1998), 'The impact of teacher written feedback on individual writers'. *Journal of Second Language Writing*, 7(3), 255–286.

Hyland, F. and Hyland, K. (2001), 'Sugaring the pill: Praise and criticism in written feedback'. *Journal of Second Language Writing*, 10(3), 185–212.

Hyland, K. (2002), 'Authority and invisibility: Authorial identity in academic writing'. *Journal of Pragmatics*, 34(8), 1091–1112.

— (2003), *Second Language Writing*. New York: Cambridge University Press.

— (2004), 'Graduates' gratitude: The generic structure of dissertation acknowledgements'. *English for Specific Purposes*, 23(3), 303–324.

— (2008), Genre and academic writing in the disciplines. *Language Teaching*. 41(4), 543–562.

Nelson, J. (1993), 'The library revisited: Exploring students' research processes', in A. Penrose and B. Sitcoe (eds), *Hearing Ourselves Think: Cognitive Research in the College Writing Classroom*. New York: Oxford University Press, pp. 60–80.

Nelson, G. and Carson, J. (1998), 'ESL students' perceptions of effectiveness in peer response groups'. *Journal of Second Language Writing*, 7(2), 113–131.

Nystrand, M. (1987), 'The role of context in written communication', in R. Horowitz and S. J. Samuels (eds), *Comprehending Oral and Written Language*. San Diego, CA: Academic Press. pp. 197–214.

Prior, P. (1998), *Writing/Disciplinarity: A Sociohistoric Account of Literate Activity in the Academy*. Mahwah, NJ: Erlbaum.

Rogerson-Revell, P. (2007), 'Using English for International Business: A European case study'. *English for Specific Purposes*, 26(1) 103–120.

Smagorinsky, P. (ed.) (1994), *Speaking about Writing: Reflections on Research Methodology*. Thousand Oaks, CA: Sage.

Sullivan, K. and Lindgren, E. (eds) (2006), *Computer Keystroke Logging and Writing*. London: Elsevier.

15 Researching Grammar

Neomy Storch

Grammar is a large and controversial topic in applied linguistics. In this chapter I focus on two distinct but related areas of research on second language (L2) grammar: (a) what constitutes knowledge of grammar and how we assess that knowledge, and (b) grammar instruction in L2 classes. The discussion of these two areas covers theoretical debates, methods of assessing grammatical knowledge and empirical findings. This is then followed by a description of a study which attempted to address some of the shortcomings identified in current research on grammar instruction. I conclude with outlining what I consider to be areas of L2 grammar that require additional research.

L2 Grammar Knowledge: What is it and How Do We Measure It?

Knowledge of grammar is said to consist of two types: explicit and implicit knowledge. According to N. Ellis (2005), these two types of knowledge are distinct and exist in separate parts of the brain. R. Ellis (2005) lists seven criteria that can be used to distinguish between explicit and implicit grammar knowledge. These criteria include, among others: level of awareness, accessibility and whether learners can verbalize the knowledge.

Broadly speaking, *explicit knowledge* is conscious knowledge about a language (rules, conventions of use) that learners can often verbalize. Accessing this knowledge is slow because it requires controlled processing. *Implicit knowledge*, on the other hand, is held unconsciously and can be accessed quickly and easily. It is the knowledge that learners draw on when comprehending or producing language in rapid, fluent communication. It is therefore implicit knowledge which is considered genuine knowledge of a language.

Thus when assessing grammatical knowledge or development in grammatical knowledge it is important to consider the kind of knowledge tested. According to Purpura (2004), tests which use constrained response type exercises (e.g., fill in the gap) test explicit knowledge. Implicit knowledge is tested via tasks requiring comprehension or production of language, in oral or written form. However, as R. Ellis (2005) points out, it is impossible to conclude with total certainty that when completing a particular test task the learner accesses only the type of knowledge that the test is designed to elicit.

In designing grammar tests, scoring is also an important consideration (Purpura 2004). Whereas scoring constrained response type exercises is fairly straightforward, assessing extended oral and written output is more complex and requires measures not only of accuracy, but also of syntactic complexity. This is because there may be a trade-off between accuracy and syntactic complexity. Some learners may achieve high scores of accuracy by using only simple sentences, whereas learners who use more complex sentences are perhaps more likely to make errors (Foster and Skehan 1996).

Extended written and oral output can be assessed using a qualitative or a quantitative approach. A qualitative approach employs a rating scale with discreet categories which describe the 'quality' of grammatical performance (Purpura 2004). The categories tend to describe global levels of accuracy (e.g., few errors overall) and syntactic complexity (e.g., a range of simple and complex sentences is evident). A quantitative approach to measuring accuracy is based on an error identification and count (Ellis and Barkhuizen, 2005). Measures of accuracy are computed by dividing the total number of errors by the total number of words produced, or by computing the accuracy of production units, such as T-units or clauses. A T-unit, a common unit in the analysis of writing and speaking, is a main clause plus whatever subordinate clauses are attached to it or embedded in it (Hunt 1966). Thus the accuracy of a student's written or oral output can be represented in terms of the percentage of error free T-units or the percentage of error free clauses (Wolf-Quintero et al. 1998). Other measures of accuracy focus on the accurate use of a particular grammatical structure, such as verbs or articles. Measures of syntactic complexity include the proportion of clauses to T-units, or the proportion of dependent clauses to all clauses (Wolf-Quintero et al. 1998).

L2 Grammar Instruction: Synthesis of Current Thinking and Research

Although grammar is considered central to language learning and language use, the role of grammar in L2 teaching is very controversial. The main controversy centres on whether grammar should be taught in L2 classes explicitly. *Explicit grammar instruction* means presenting and explaining a predetermined set of grammar rules, usually but not necessarily followed by practice. Three distinct positions can be identified in the applied linguistics literature: a zero position, a focus on forms (FonFs) and a focus on form (FonF) position. These positions are based on assumptions concerning whether explicit knowledge can become implicit knowledge.

The first position, the zero position, is represented by scholars such as Krashen (1981, 1993) who see very little merit in teaching grammar explicitly. In his comprehensible input hypothesis, Krashen (1981) argued that to acquire an L2 learners simply need exposure to language input that they can understand (i.e., comprehensible input). The hypothesis was based on claims that the same processes underlie first and second language acquisition as well as research findings (e.g., Bailey et al. 1974) which showed that all learners, regardless of first language, age or whether they were instructed or naturalistic learners, proceeded along the same order and sequence in the acquisition of certain grammatical structures. Thus Krashen (1981, 1993) argues that grammar instruction serves very little purpose. It provides learners, in his view, with explicit knowledge which may enable them to monitor and edit their language output (assuming certain conditions are met), but this explicit knowledge does not become part of the learner's implicit knowledge system. Other supporters of this position are scholars who refer to Chomsky's (1976) Universal Grammar (UG) and who claim that second language acquisition is innate and has nothing to do with explicit knowledge (e.g., Schwartz 1993). The teaching implication of this position is that language classrooms should only focus on meaning; on providing learners with plentiful exposure to authentic and comprehensible L2 input, initially via listening and reading activities, and once the learner is ready, with authentic production opportunities.

The second position is that adopted by scholars such as DeKeyser (1998) who see merit in explicit grammar instruction. DeKeyser claims that when explicit grammar instruction is sustained and followed by appropriate meaning-based practice, it will contribute to the development of implicit knowledge. Lightbown (1991) suggests that explicit knowledge can act as a priming mechanism to help learners notice structures in the L2 input. Similarly, although N. Ellis (2005) argues that the bulk of language learning occurs through usage, he suggests that learning begins with an explicit representation of linguistic forms. Thus, the teaching implications of this position are that explicit grammar instruction should precede practice. This stance is often referred to as Focus on Forms (FonFs).

The third position is that adopted by scholars who see some merit in grammar instruction, but only when it is reactive rather than predetermined. This approach, proposed by Long (1991, 1996), is referred to as Focus on Form (FonF). It draws on Schmidt's (1990) noticing hypothesis which posits that only language which is attended to (i.e., noticed) is processed. Pedagogically, a focus on form means spontaneous reaction to learners' language learning needs which occurs as learners engage in meaning-focused activities. These needs can be expressed as questions (e.g., clarification requests) or be evident in learners' errors. The teacher's role is to provide a brief explanation or correction which draws learners' attention to the problematic structure.

There are a few interesting points that should be noted about this debate. First, the three stances are largely theoretical, rather than based on solid empirical research. Furthermore, the term FonF has been re-defined and extended since its original formulation (Long 1991) and the distinction between FonF and FonFs has blurred. Ellis (2006), for example, distinguishes between incidental FonF and pre-emptive FonF. Incidental FonF, as in its original inception, is reactive and occurs spontaneously in response to a performance problem. Pre-emptive FonF, however, includes the use of tasks that are likely to elicit certain grammatical structures or predetermining the grammatical errors that will receive feedback (e.g., Doughty and Varela 1998) an approach which is closer to FonFs. Thus some authors (e.g., R. Ellis 2002; Garcia Mayo 2002; Lyster 2004) use the term form-focused instruction which seems to include elements of FonF and FonFs.

The available research evidence supports some form of grammar instruction. However, the evidence is largely indirect showing that in the absence of grammar instruction learners' grammatical accuracy may not develop. Perhaps the most convincing evidence comes from the French immersion programmes in Canada, where researchers (e.g., Harley and Swain 1984) have shown that despite exposure to rich and plentiful L2 input (as advocated by Krashen), L2 learners may become fluent but not accurate in their use of the L2. My own small-scale study (Storch 2007) provides further support for this claim. The study examined the writing of learners at the beginning and end of a semester's study (12 weeks). The participants in the study ($n = 20$) were enrolled in degree programmes. They were identified on an in-house diagnostic language test as needing further language support but, for a range of reasons, chose not to access the available language support services or enrol in ESL credit-bearing subjects.

The study found that after a semester of study in an English medium university, the learners' writing improved in terms of organization and development of ideas but that there was little improvement in grammatical accuracy.

The other often cited study in support of grammar instruction is the large meta-analysis by Norris and Ortega (2000) which showed that explicit instruction led to more substantial and enduring gains in learning than implicit instruction (extended exposure to the target forms). It should be noted, however, that most of the studies included in the Norris and Ortega meta-analysis relied on tests of explicit knowledge to show gains.

The current orthodoxy on L2 grammar instruction is an acceptance that some form of grammar instruction is beneficial but that grammar should not be the sole focus of L2 classes as in traditional language pedagogy. Rather, a growing number of scholars (see Hinkel and Fotos 2002) advocate a communicative approach to L2 instruction which integrates a focus on meaning and on grammar. In such an approach, the primary focus is on relevant content material or tasks which provide learners with opportunities for exposure to and authentic practice in producing grammatical structures. Consequently, research on grammar instruction now focuses on how best to teach grammar within a communicative, task-based approach and on what are the most effective ways of responding to grammatical errors in learners' language.

Research on How to Teach Grammar: Research on Tasks

Studies on how best to teach grammar attempt to investigate which communicative tasks and task conditions are most effective in drawing learners' attention to language. This research usually requires learners to work in pairs or small groups. Some researchers have focused on tasks which only require oral language output; others have investigated tasks which require learners to jointly produce written texts.

Studies on tasks requiring oral language output have, by and large, been informed by Long's interaction hypothesis (1991) which posits that interactions (e.g., clarification requests) not only serve to make input comprehensible but also draw learners' attention to linguistic problems and pushes them to modify their language, making it more grammatically accurate and appropriate. Thus research from this theoretical perspective has attempted to identify tasks and task conditions which are likely to maximize learners' interactions. For example, Pica et al. (1993) argue that jigsaw tasks (where each learner holds information vital to the task completion and only one solution is possible) are the most effective because information exchange between the participants is obligatory.

In tasks which require learners to jointly produce written output, researchers audio record the learners' talk as they complete the tasks and the transcribed talk is then analysed for the amount of attention to grammatical structures that the tasks elicit. The unit of analysis that has often been employed in this kind of research is the *Language Related Episode* (LRE). This episode is defined as any part of a dialogue where learners talk about the language they are producing, question their language use, self and other correct (Swain and Lapkin 1998). Adopting a Vygotskian (1986) sociocultural theoretical perspective, Swain (2000) argues that these episodes are sites of language learning because learning arises in dialogue. From this theoretical perspective, speaking is perceived as a cognitive activity which externalizes thoughts. Once externalized, the thought can be analysed, questioned and reflected upon (Swain and Lapkin 2003). This activity of talking about language, referred to more recently by Swain (2007) as '*languaging*', affords learners opportunities to learn from each other and consolidate their language knowledge.

The following excerpt is taken from a study (Storch 2005) where learners composed a text in pairs. It provides an example of an LRE showing evidence of learners externalizing their thoughts about the choice of a verb form. The learners offer suggestions (line 162), counter suggestions (lines 163, 164) and finally, by pooling their linguistic resources, reach a correct grammatical decision about the verb form required in this instance.

Excerpt 1:   Example of an LRE
162   M: . . . the Vietnamese and the Laotian are
163   C: improve
164   M: have the, yeah, have, have improved yeah
165   C: yes

A number of studies have attempted to compare the effectiveness of various communicative written tasks. For example, Swain and Lapkin (2001) compared the efficacy of a dictogloss and a jigsaw task. The dictogloss task, originally designed by Wajnryb (1990), requires learners to reconstruct a text using notes taken when the teacher dictates the text. The jigsaw in this study was based on a series of eight pictures. Each learner held four pictures and thus the task required the learners to arrange their pictures in a sequence and write out a story based on the pictures. The study found that both tasks were equally effective as they generated a similar number of LREs. Others (e.g., Storch 1998; Garcia Mayo 2002) found that a text reconstruction task, where learners are provided with content words but need to insert the necessary function words or change word forms, elicited more LREs than traditional grammar exercises (e.g., fill in the blanks) and more than the jigsaw and dictogloss (De La Colina and Garcia Mayo 2007).

A related area of research on tasks is how task implementation variables affect learners' attention to language. For example, Leeser (2004) examined how proficiency pairing affects learners' focus on grammar in the learning of

Spanish. In his study 21 pairs of learners completed a dictogloss task. The learners were grouped according to their L2 (Spanish) proficiency forming seven pairs each of high-high (H-H), high-low (H-L) and low-low (L-L) learners. Leeser found that the H-H learners produced the highest number of LREs, followed by H-L and finally L-L dyads. The implications of these findings are that mixed proficiency pairing may be more conducive to learning than pairing low-proficiency learners (L-L). However, in his Ph.d. study conducted in EFL classes in Saudi Arabia, Aldosari (2008) found that it is not only proficiency grouping which determines the quantity of LREs, but also the role relationship learners form when working in pairs. Employing a model of pair relationships (Storch 2002), Aldosari found that learners of the same proficiency level (high-high and low-low) were more likely to form collaborative relationships where both learners were involved in deliberating over L2 choices. In mixed proficiency pairs (high-low) one learner was more likely to assume an assertive role and dominate the activity. In such dominant-passive pairs, there were fewer deliberations over language use and hence fewer LREs.

The assumption that underlies many studies investigating the effectiveness of various tasks is that those tasks or task conditions which elicit more interaction (e.g., more comprehension checks) or more deliberations about language (i.e., more LREs) are more effective for language development. However, as Nakahama et al. (2001) have pointed out, researchers also need to examine the language the learners produce during their interaction, to consider for example, the length, complexity and accuracy of the learners' utterances. There is also a need, as I have noted elsewhere (Storch 2008), to examine the quality of engagement with language evident in the LREs. An LRE may be short, composed only of one or two turns, or quite long involving multiple turns. These qualitative differences in the level of engagement and their potential impact on language learning have not been sufficiently investigated. Another shortcoming of the research on the effectiveness of oral and written tasks is that there are very few studies which have investigated whether interactions or deliberations over language lead to development in implicit grammatical knowledge as measured by some form of a post-treatment test. The handful of studies that have attempted to address this gap in research have thus far either used constrained responses exercises such as multiple choice or true/false type exercises (e.g., Swain and Lapkin 2001) thus measuring explicit rather than implicit knowledge, or have been small scale (e.g., Storch 2002).

Research on How to Teach Grammar: Feedback on Errors

Another pedagogical intervention which aims to improve learners' grammatical accuracy is *corrective feedback*. Corrective feedback (feedback on errors) is pervasive in L2 classrooms. It is provided on both oral and written language production, and can take a number of different forms.

Feedback on Oral Production

Feedback on oral language can be implicit or explicit. *Implicit feedback* occurs when the corrective intent of the feedback is covert, as in the case of a *recast* or a clarification request (e.g., sorry?). A recast consists of a reformulation of the learner's incorrect utterance while maintaining the meaning of the original utterance. *Explicit feedback* means an overt correction of erroneous utterances with or without explanations. The following examples illustrate the difference between implicit and explicit feedback.

Example of implicit feedback (recast)
Learner: Last night, I go to the movies.
Teacher: Oh, last night you went to the movies.

Example of explicit feedback (overt correction with explanation)
Learner: Last night, I go to the movies.
Teacher: No, you say last night I went to the movies because last night means in the past.

Research on recasts has shown that it is perhaps the most prevalent form of teacher feedback (Lyser and Ranta 1997; Ellis et al. 2001), even in meaning-focused classes. However, the effectiveness of this form of feedback is inconclusive. Using *uptake* (learners repeating the correct model provided in the recast immediately after receiving the recast) as a measure of effectiveness, studies have shown that uptake is lower following recasts than following explicit feedback (Lyster and Ranta 1997; Lyster 2004). These findings are disputed by Mackey and Philp (1998) who question the use of immediate uptake as a measure of effectiveness. Uptake may occur in subsequent turns rather than in the immediate next turn or, as shown by Ohta (2000), the uptake may not be vocalized. However, perhaps the more important consideration in this discussion of uptake is whether uptake is necessarily evidence of learning or whether it does indeed lead to learning. Uptake is a repetition, and repetitions may be quite mechanical without much attention invested in the act (Panova and Lyster 2002) or could be used to serve a number of important social rather than just cognitive functions (Duff 2000).

Unlike descriptive studies of feedback, Loewen's (2005) study investigated the efficacy of recasts by using a post-test design. Following 17 hours of observation in 12 different ESL classes, Loewen developed individualized tests where learners were asked to recall the linguistic information provided to them in class. The study found a relatively high recall rate: 60 per cent in the short term (1–3 days after the feedback was provided), and 50 per cent two weeks later. However it is questionable whether ability to recall translates into ability to use the structures correctly in free production (i.e., implicit knowledge).

Feedback on Written Production

The debate about the efficacy of written feedback resembles to some extent the debate about explicit grammar instruction. At one extreme are researchers who have argued that there is no merit whatsoever in feedback on grammar in L2 writing (e.g., Truscott 1996, 2007); whereas others (e.g., Ferris 1999, 2006) have argued that such feedback is beneficial. However, scholars on both sides of the debate agree that a more definitive stance on the merit of feedback requires additional research on written feedback (Truscott 1999; Ferris 2002, 2004).

Like feedback on oral production, feedback on writing can take different forms. It can range from indirect feedback, such as editing symbols in the margins (e.g., X) or underlining the erroneous structure, with or without a symbol indicating the type of error, to more direct forms such as writing the correct version above the incorrect one.

Research on feedback has tended to focus on the efficacy of different forms of feedback, different ways of providing feedback, as well as the efficacy of different feedback providers (teacher, peer and self-editing). For example, the study by Bitchener et al. (2005) compared the effectiveness of explicit corrective feedback with and without a five-minute individual conference and no feedback. Three errors were targeted in the feedback conditions: prepositions, simple past tense and use of definite articles. The study found that, although the combined feedback condition (written plus conference) was most effective, gains in accuracy did not show a linear upward trend. Furthermore, the structure targeted by the feedback was an important consideration, with prepositions showing least response to feedback.

The overwhelming conclusion that can be drawn about the efficacy of written feedback is the complexity of this issue. Researchers need to take into consideration not only how the feedback is provided, but also factors such as which grammatical structures are targeted in the feedback, the learners L2 proficiency and their language learning aptitude (Sheen 2007). We also need longitudinal studies with clearly identified and defined measures of effectiveness, and above all studies which collect qualitative data which could provide some insights into how learners process the feedback they receive. The following study attempted to incorporate some of the factors mentioned above.

A Sample Study

The sample study is part of a large-scale project which investigated the efficacy of different forms of written feedback in the short and long term and the impact of a number of variables including proficiency level, task type and mode of composing (individually versus in pairs).[1]

The study examined the efficacy of two forms of feedback on writing: reformulation and editing. *Reformulation* is a technique whereby a native speaker rewrites the text produced by the learner correcting all grammatical errors while preserving the learner's ideas. Editing in this study involved providing learners with a symbol which located their error (e.g., underlining, insertion symbol), and an abbreviation which explained the type of error (e.g., C stood for word choice). All participants who received editing feedback were given a key to the symbols and abbreviations used.

The participants in this study were university students whose ESL proficiency was deemed to be advanced (based on IELTS scores). The participants ($n = 48$) formed two groups: one group of 12 pairs received feedback in the form of reformulations, the other group received feedback in the form of editing. All pairs were self-selected and students were paid for their participation. Both forms of feedback were given by the same research assistant, a native speaker who was an experienced ESL teacher.

The participants were required to attend on three different days. On each occasion, they were required to write a report (data commentary) based on a graphic stimulus, showing rainfall patterns in different cities in the world. On Days 1 and 5 (session 1 and 2) they worked in pairs and their pair talk was audio recorded. On Day 28 they worked individually. Data collected on Day 28 enabled us to investigate the impact of feedback on writing completed beyond the immediate revision session (Day 5), and thus measured development in implicit knowledge over time. Figure 15.1 below summarizes what each session involved.

Day	Duration	Task
Day 1	30 min	Students compose a short report in pairs
Day 5, session 1	15 min	Pairs receive and discuss the feedback on their report
Day 5, session 2	30 min	Version containing feedback removed. Pairs given an unmarked version of the text produced on Day 1 and are asked to rewrite it.
Day 28	20 min	Individual learners write a short report based on the same prompt as that used on Day 1.

Figure 15.1 Study design

The following excerpts illustrate the original versions written by the participants and the form of feedback they received. Excerpt 2 provides an example of a reformulation. The reformulation contains two changes: deletion of an indefinite article (an) and changing the word rainfall to rainfalls.

Excerpt 2: Reformulations
Original:
This chart illustrates an average rainfall in each season in the year 2000.

Reformulated version:
This chart illustrates average rainfalls in each season in the year 2000.

Excerpt 3 illustrates the form of editing that participants received. In this example, three errors were identified in the original version: an omission (denoted by an insertion symbol), an error in choice of prepositions (C) and in word form (F).

Excerpt 3: Editing feedback
Original version:
The rainfall in Lagos city is 240 mm on average in summer, which the highest amongst the other season.

Edited version:
The rainfall in Lagos city is 240 mm on average in summer, which ∧ the
             C   F
highest *amongst* the other *season*.

Analysis of the Data

All written reports (produced by the pairs on Days 1 and 5 and by individual learners on Day 28) were analysed for fluency (length in words), grammatical accuracy and grammatical complexity. Grammatical accuracy measures included the percentage of error free T-units and of error free clauses. Complexity measures included clauses per T-unit ratios. The example below (Excerpt 4), taken from our data, shows a T-unit composed of two clauses separated by a slash. Only the first clause was coded as error free.

Excerpt 4: an example of a T-unit, clauses and accuracy analysis
Beijing has about 160mm of rain in summer /which is around 16 times than that in winter (10mm)

Audio recorded and transcribed pair talk (collected on Day 5 in both sessions) were analysed for Language Related Episodes (LREs). LREs were coded for the nature of engagement, distinguishing between single turn and multi-turn LREs, for their focus (lexis, grammar, mechanics) and for whether the decision reached in the deliberations was correct.

Findings

Analysis of the learners' writing showed that accuracy measures showed the most change over time. Reports written on Day 5 were more accurate than those written on Day 1. Thus both editing and reformulations led to similar gains in accuracy in the short term (see Table 15.1). However, when we compared accuracy scores on Day 5 with mean accuracy scores on Day 28, we found that the gains were more enduring for the students who received reformulations.

Analysis of the pair talk transcripts showed that LREs dealt with a range of grammatical (and lexical) items, not limited to the items which received corrective feedback, and a large proportion (over 75%) of the LREs were resolved correctly. More importantly, editing seemed to generate a larger number of LREs than reformulations, particularly during the processing session on day 5, and these LREs tended to be longer (see Table 15.2).

Table 15.1 Mean accuracy scores on Day 1, 5, and 28

	Day 1	Day 5	Day 28
Reformulation			
Error-free T units per T unit	51.47	66.43	61.46
Error-free clauses per clause	60.44	75.11	68.79
Editing			
Error-free T units per T unit	54.47	68.22	58.37
Error-free clauses per clause	64.02	74.74	66.84

Table 15.2 LREs Generated on Day 5

	No. of LREs	Multi-turn LREs	%
Reformulation			
Processing	134	98	73.13
Rewriting	225	187	83.11
Total	**359**	**285**	**79.38**
Editing			
Processing	190	159	83.68
Rewriting	220	206	93.64
Total	**410**	**365**	**89.02**

We were somewhat puzzled by our findings: editing generated greater attention to form (as evident by the larger number and lengthier LREs) than reformulations, yet the impact of reformulation on writing accuracy seemed longer lasting. A closer analysis of the learner talk provided a possible explanation. The analysis revealed that a number of pairs who received reformulations proceeded to memorize and reproduce the reformulated text. These findings suggest that we may need to re-examine the role of memorization in second language acquisition (see also Lantolf and Thorne, 2006). Furthermore, these findings highlight the need to consider qualitative data very carefully.

Conclusion

For students interested in doing research on grammar, particularly those who are or plan to become language teachers, the most pressing research topics concern the most effective ways (in terms of tasks and feedback) of teaching grammar. Future studies on tasks need to consider not only how much attention to grammar different tasks generate, but also the quality of students' language output (oral or written) when completing such tasks. We also need to investigate whether learners' interactions and engagement with grammar lead to improved grammatical ability by using tests of implicit grammatical knowledge (i.e., extended speaking and/or writing). Similarly, future research on feedback needs to investigate the impact of feedback on learners from different L2 proficiency levels, whether feedback may be more effective on some grammatical structures than on others, for some learners more so than for others and the effect of feedback on grammatical accuracy in the long term, as effects may not be apparent immediately.

In terms of research methodology, we need studies which collect different types of data (e.g., learners' output, interviews, think aloud protocols) and analyse data using quantitative and qualitative analyses. Whereas quantitative analysis would employ various measures of grammatical and syntactic complexity, qualitative analysis would consider aspects such as learners' engagement with language. Case studies (see Casanave, this volume) may be particularly appropriate to investigate feedback as they enable researchers to collect rich, detailed data on the feedback provided, on how learners engage with the feedback, and on learners' goals and attitudes to the feedback. Such studies could provide researchers and teachers with clearer insights and explanations about the efficacy of different forms of grammar instruction and corrective feedback. Furthermore, to date studies on tasks and task implementation as well as on feedback have tended to be conducted largely in ESL and EFL contexts. There is clearly a need for research on grammar in classes that teach languages other than English.

Note

1. The study was funded by an Australian Research Council Discovery Grant # DP 0450422 awarded to Wigglesworth, G. and Storch, N. (2004–2006).

Resources for Further Reading

Ellis, R. (2006), 'Current issues in the teaching of grammar: An SLA perspective'. *TESOL Quarterly*, 40, 83–107.

    This article considers eight key questions relating to grammar pedagogy. These questions include, for example, what grammatical structures to teach, at what L2 proficiency should grammar instruction be introduced, and whether to integrate grammar into communicative activities or to teach it separately. In discussing the questions, Ellis provides insights from theory and research, and highlights issues which require further investigation.

Ellis, R. and Barkhuizen, G. (2005), *Analysing Learner Language*. Oxford: Oxford University Press.

    This book is particularly useful for those wishing to analyse language output. It describes different types of analyses that can be undertaken, different measures that can be employed to assess grammatical accuracy and complexity, and provides concrete examples of such analyses and measures.

Ferris, D. (2002), *Treatment of Error in Second Language Student Writing*. Ann Arbor: University of Michigan Press.

    Ferris's book provides a comprehensive overview of some of the key issues related to the topic of written feedback. These issues include why error treatment is necessary for L2 learners and how to respond to learner errors.

Hinkel, E. and Fotos, S. (eds) (2002), *New Perspectives on Grammar Teaching in Second Language Classrooms*. Mahwah, NJ: Lawrence Erlbaum.

    This edited volume includes articles by leading researchers on grammar, thus providing a broad coverage of current thinking and research on grammar. Topics covered include theoretical arguments for teaching grammar and practical suggestions on how to teach grammar in ESL/EFL classrooms.

Purpura, J. (2004), *Assessing Grammar*. Cambridge: Cambridge University Press.

    This is a very accessible text which discusses factors which need to be taken into consideration in designing grammar tests. It provides clear examples of various grammar tests and response types.

References

Aldosari, A. (2008), 'The Influence of Proficiency Levels, Task Type, and Social Relationships on Pair Interactions: An EFL Context'. Unpublished Ph.D. dissertation, University of Melbourne, Australia.

Bailey, N., Madden, C. and Krashen, S. (1974), 'Is there a "natural sequence" in adult second language learning?' *Language Learning*, 24, 235–243.

Bitchener, J., Yong, S. and Cameron, D. (2005), 'The effects of different types of corrective feedback on ESL student writing'. *Journal of Second Language Writing*, 14, 191–205.

Chomsky, N. (1976), *Reflections on Language*. London: Temple Smith.

De la Colina, A. A. and Garcia Mayo, M. P. (2007), 'Attention to form across collaborative tasks by low-proficiency learners in an EFL setting', in G. Mayo (ed.), *Investigating Tasks in Formal Language Learning*. Clevedon, UK: Multilingual Matters, pp. 91–116.

DeKeyser, R. (1998), 'Beyond focus on form: Cognitive perspectives on learning and practicing second language grammar', in C. Doughty and J. Williams (eds), *Focus on Form in Classroom Second Language Acquisition*. New York: Cambridge University Press, pp. 42–63.

Doughty, C. and Varela, E. (1998), 'Communicative focus on form', in C. Doughty and J. Williams (eds), *Focus on Form in Classroom Second Language Acquisition*. Cambridge: Cambridge University Press, pp. 114–138.

Duff, P. A. (2000), 'Repetition in foreign language classroom interaction', in J. K. Hall and L. S. Verplaetse (eds), *Second and Foreign Language Learning through Classroom Interaction*. Mahwah, NJ: Lawrence Bloom, pp. 109–138.

Ellis, N. (2002), 'Does form-focused instruction affect the acquisition of implicit knowledge?' *Studies in Second Language Acquisition*, 24, 223–236.

—(2005), 'At the interface: Dynamic interactions of explicit and implicit language knowledge'. *Studies in Second Language Acquisition*, 27, 305–352.

Ellis, R. (2002), 'Does form-focused instruction affect the acquisition of implicit knowledge'? *Studies in Second Language Acquisition*, 24, 223–236.

Ellis, R. (2005), 'Measuring implicit and explicit knowledge of a second language. A psychometric study'. *Studies in Second Language Acquisition*, 27, 141–172.

—(2006), 'Current issues in the teaching of grammar: An SLA perspective'. *TESOL Quarterly*, 40, 83–107.

Ellis, R. and Barkhuizen, G. (2005), *Analysing Learner Language*. Oxford: Oxford University Press.

Ellis, R., Basturkmen, H. and Loewen, S. (2001), 'Learner uptake in communicative ESL lessons'. *Language Learning*, 51, 281–318.

Ferris, D. (1999), 'The case for grammar correction in L2 writing classes: A response to Truscott (1996)'. *Journal of Second Language Writing*, 8, 1–10.

—(2002), *Treatment of Error in Second Language Student Writing*. Ann Arbor: University of Michigan Press.

—(2004), 'The "Grammar Correction" debate in L2 writing: Where are we, and where do we go from here? (and what do we do in the meantime . . .?)', *Journal of Second Language Writing*, 13, 49–62.

—(2006), 'Does error feedback help student writers? New evidence on the short-and long-term effects of written error corrections', in K. Hyland and F. Hyland (eds), *Feedback in Second Language Writing. Contexts and Issues*. Cambridge: Cambridge University Press, pp. 81–104.

Foster, P. and Skehan, P. (1996), 'The influence of planning and task type on second language performance'. *Studies in Second Language Acquisition*, 18, 299–323.

Garcia Mayo, M. P. (2002), 'Interaction in advanced EFL pedagogy: A comparison of form-focused activities'. *International Journal of Educational Research*, 37, 323–341.

Harley, B. and Swain, M. (1984), 'The interlanguage of immersion students and its implications for second language teaching', in A. Davies, C. Criper and H. Howatt (eds), *Interlanguage*. Edinburgh: Edinburgh University Press, pp. 291–311.

Hinkel, E. and Fotos, S. (eds) (2002), *New Perspectives on Grammar Teaching in Second Language Classrooms*. Mahwah, NJ: Lawrence Erlbaum.

Hunt, K. (1966), 'Recent measures in syntactic development'. *Elementary English*, 43, 732–139.

Krashen, S. (1981), *Second Language Acquisition and Second Language Learning*. Oxford: Oxford University Press.

—(1993), 'The effects of grammar teaching. Still peripheral'. *TESOL Quarterly*, 27, 717–725.

Lantolf, J. P. and Thorne, S. L. (2006), *Sociocultural Theory and the Genesis of Second Language Development*. Oxford: Oxford University Press.

Leeser, M. J. (2004), 'Learner proficiency and focus on form during collaborative dialogue'. *Language Teaching Research*, 8, 55–81.

Lightbown, P. (1991), 'What have we here? Some observations on the influence of instruction on L2 learning', in R. Philipson, E. Kellerman, L. Selinker, M. Sharwood Smith, and M. Swain (eds), *Foreign Language Pedagogy Research: A Commemorative Volume for Claus Faerch*. Clevedon, UK: Multilingual Matters, pp. 197–212.

Loewen, S. (2005), 'Incidental focus on form and second language learning'. *Studies in Second Language Acquisition*, 27, 361–386.

Long, M. (1991), 'Focus on form: A design feature in language teaching methodology', in K. DeBot, R. Ginsberg, and C. Kramsch (eds), *Foreign Language Research in Cross-Cultural Perspectives*. Amsterdam: John Benjamins, pp. 39–52.

—(1996), 'The role of the linguistic environment in second language acquisition', in W. C. Ritchie and T. K. Bhatia (eds), *Handbook of Language Acquisition: Second Language Acquisition* (Vol. 2). New York: Academic Press, pp. 413–468.

Lyster, R. (2004), 'Differential effects of prompts and recasts in form-focused instruction'. *Studies in Second Language Acquisition*, 26, 399–432.

Lyster, R. and Ranta, L. (1997), 'Corrective feedback and learner uptake'. *Studies in Second Language Acquisition*, 19, 37–66.

Mackey, A. and Philp, J. (1998), 'Conversational interaction and second language development: Recasts, responses and red herrings'. *The Modern Language Journal*, 82, 338–356.

Nakahama, Y., Tyler, A. and Van Lier, L. (2001), 'Negotiation of meaning in conversational and information gap activities: A comparative discourse analysis'. *TESOL Quarterly*, 35, 377–432.

Norris, J. and Ortega, L. (2000), 'Effectiveness of L2 instruction: A research synthesis and quantitative meta-analysis'. *Language Learning*, 50, 417–428.

Ohta, A. (2000), 'Rethinking recasts: A learner-centered examination of corrective feedback in the Japanese language classroom', in J. K. Hall and L. S. Verplaetse (eds), *Second and Foreign Language Learning through Classroom Interaction*. Mahwah, NJ: Lawrence Erlbaum, pp. 47–72.

Panova, I. and Lyster, R. (2002), 'Patterns of corrective feedback and uptake in an adult ESL classroom'. *TESOL Quarterly*, 36, 573–595.

Pica, T., Kanagy, R. and Falodun, J. (1993), 'Choosing and using communication tasks for second language instruction and research', in G. Crookes and S. Gass (eds), *Task and Language Learning*. Clevedon, UK: Multilingual Matters, pp. 9–34.

Purpura, J. (2004), *Assessing Grammar*. Cambridge: Cambridge University Press.

Schmidt, R. (1990), 'The role of consciousness in second language learning'. *Applied Linguistics*, 11, 129–158.

Schwartz, B. (1993), 'On explicit and negative data effecting and affecting competence and linguistic behaviour'. *Studies in Second Language Acquisition*, 15, 147–163.

Sheen, Y. (2007), 'The effect of focused written corrective feedback and language aptitude on ESL learners' acquisition of articles'. *TESOL Quarterly*, 41, 255–283.

Storch, N. (1998), 'Comparing second language learners' attention to form across tasks'. *Language Awareness*, 7, 176–191.

—(2002), 'Patterns of interaction in ESL pair work'. *Language Learning*, 52, 119–158.

—(2005), 'Collaborative writing: Product, process and students' reflections'. *Journal of Second Language Writing*, 14, 153–173.

—(2007), 'Development of L2 writing after a semester of study in an Australian university'. *Indonesian Journal of English Language Teaching*, 2, 173–189.

—(2008), 'Metatalk in a pair work activity: Level of engagement and implications for language development'. *Language Awareness*, 17, 97–114.

Swain, M. (2000), 'The output hypothesis and beyond: Mediating acquisition through collaborative dialogue', in J. P. Lantolf (ed.), *Sociocultural Theory and Second Language Learning*. Oxford: Oxford University Press, pp. 97–114.

—(2007, April), 'Talking It Through': Languaging as a Source of Learning. Plenary paper presented at the meeting of Social and Cognitive Aspects of Second Language Learning and Teaching, Auckland, New Zealand.

Swain, M. and Lapkin, S. (1998), 'Interaction and second language learning: Two adolescent French immersion students working together'. *Modern Language Journal*, 82, 320–337.

Swain, M. and Lapkin, S. (2001), 'Focus on form through collaborative dialogue: Exploring task effects', in M. Bygate, P. Skehan, and M. Swain (eds), *Researching Pedagogic Tasks: Second Language Learning, Teaching and Testing*. London: Longman, pp. 99–118.

Swain, M. and Lapkin, S. (2003), 'Talking it through: Two French immersion learners' response to reformulation'. *International Journal of Educational Research*, 37, 285–304.

Truscott, J. (1996), 'The case against grammar correction in L2 writing classes'. *Language Learning*, 46, 32–369.

—(1999), 'The case for "the case for grammar correction in L2 classes": A response to Ferris'. *Journal of Second Language Writing*, 8, 111–122.

—(2007), 'The effect of error correction on learners' ability to write accurately'. *Journal of Second Language Writing*, 16, 255–272.

Vygotsky, L. S. (1986), *Thought and Language*. Cambridge, MA: MIT Press.

Wajnryb, R. (1990), *Grammar Dictation*. Oxford: Oxford University Press.

Wolf-Quintero, K., Inagaki, S. and Kim, H. (1998), *Second Language Development in Writing: Measures of Fluency, Accuracy and Complexity*. Honolulu, Hawai'i: University of Hawai'i at Manoa.

16 Researching Vocabulary

David Hirsh

Chapter Overview

Vocabulary has become a well-researched area within second language studies, with particular research interest in investigating key questions which could inform the vocabulary learning and teaching process. This chapter will highlight the main lines of enquiry which vocabulary research has to take account of, present research methods and tools associated with good vocabulary research, discuss some key challenges facing vocabulary researchers and conclude by presenting a study which aimed to take account of some of these issues.

Current Thinking and Related Research

Determining What is a Word

A suitable place to begin a discussion of important thinking and research in vocabulary studies is to look at what is a *word*. The current thinking is that words are, from a teaching and learning perspective, most suitably treated as *word families*. A word family is a group of word forms derived from a core word and conveying a core meaning or meanings. Researchers need to deal objectively

Inflexed forms	Derived forms	
– s	un –	– ity
– ed	pre –	– ness
– ing	anti –	– ful

Figure 16.1 Common inflexed and derived forms (Bauer and Nation 1993, pp. 253–279)

with what constitutes a word family. Bauer and Nation (1993) provide guidelines for determining word family membership in the form of commonly occurring, productive and regular inflexed and derived forms which a language learner could reasonably be expected to recognize when applied to a word they already know. The guidelines would group *contribute, contributes, contributed, contributing, contribution, contributions, contributor* and *contributors* into one word family. Examples of some commonly used inflexed and derived forms appear in Figure 16.1.

Schmitt and Zimmerman (2002) tested the extent to which knowledge of one member of a word family facilitates easy recognition of other members of the family, with a particular interest in productive uses of words. They found that knowledge of other word family members was linked to familiarity with derived forms, and that knowledge of derived forms increased with general language proficiency. Mochizuki and Aizawa (2000) were similarly interested in knowledge of affixes (synonymous with derived forms here), and found moderate correlations between the vocabulary size of second language learners and their knowledge of prefixes (0.58) and suffixes (0.54).

Conditions for Vocabulary Learning

Another major issue for vocabulary researchers is how words are learnt. There is some contention regarding the merits of direct learning of vocabulary as opposed to incidental learning, where the learning is not deliberate, but rather through exposure to and use of language. The backdrop for this debate is studies which have examined conditions which promote vocabulary learning and strategies that enhance vocabulary learning and retention (see Laufer and Hulstijn 2001). Nation (2001) sees an important role for both incidental learning and direct learning of vocabulary in second language programs, and makes the important point that, in both cases, the quality of learning is dependent upon what happens when a new word is met.

Nation (2001) has identified three key conditions which increase the quality of vocabulary learning in the case of direct learning. These are *noticing, spaced retrieval* and *generative use*. *Noticing* highlights the need for the learner to focus on a new word as a specific language learning goal, *spaced retrieval* highlights the value of recalling the new word's meaning at a later time and *generative use* highlights the importance of using a newly learned word productively in writing or speaking. The quality of both incidental and direct vocabulary learning are conditional on the amount of learner involvement while processing words. Laufer and Hulstijn (2001) have identified three key dimensions which have been linked to learner involvement during incidental vocabulary learning. They are *need* (motivational need to use a new word), *search* (attempt to find the word meaning or form) and *evaluation* (comparison of the new word with known words). The themes of *learner involvement* and *deep processing* are frequent in studies of vocabulary learning, and are evident in Laufer and Hulstijn's (2001) *Involvement Load Hypothesis*, which states that the effectiveness of word retention is dependent upon the amount of motivation and cognitive loading associated with the task in which words are learnt. The hypothesis builds on studies such as Newton (1995) which investigated the effect of nego-tiation of word meaning in group interactive tasks, finding negotiated words were retained better than words not negotiated, and Joe (1995) who investi-gated the effect of generated use of new words in learner language, finding that generated words were retained better than words not generated.

More recently, Kim (2008) investigated the effect of different levels of task-induced involvement on initial word learning and subsequent word retention, and found that tasks which had higher levels of learner involvement resulted in improved initial word learning and improved word retention. Following a similar line of enquiry, Min (2008) investigated the impact of reading and vocabulary-focused activities on vocabulary learning and retention, finding that tasks that induced higher involvement loads resulted in enhanced vocabu-lary learning, and thus greater vocabulary gains over time.

Categories of Words

Another major issue in vocabulary research is how words are categorized into groups. Not all words are equal when it comes to language use, with common distinctions made between *high frequency* words, *academic* words, *technical* words and *low frequency* words. The 2,000 most frequently occurring words in English, termed high frequency vocabulary, are regarded as critical for communication in English. They provide 90 per cent lexical coverage (the percentage of word occurrences used from this list) of conversation (Nation 2001), up to 90 per cent coverage of fiction (Hirsh and Nation 1992) and about 80 per cent coverage of newspapers (Hwang and Nation 1989), and are widely accepted as the starting point for second language vocabulary learning.

Beyond high frequency words, research has focused on specialized groups of words. Academic vocabulary occurs frequently in academic texts across a range of subject areas. Technical words are associated with specific subject areas. A further category, low frequency words, is a default term describing words which do not appear frequently in a text or sample of language being looked at. Many specialized technical terms would be regarded as low frequency when occurring in contexts outside their subject area. Technical vocabulary is a relatively under-researched area in light of its important role in specialized reading (see Chung and Nation 2003).

Vocabulary Size

A further important issue for vocabulary researchers is counting and grouping words: the number of words in English, the most useful words for different communicative tasks and the vocabulary size of groups of users. This has identified thresholds for effective language use, and has given rise to the concept of a vocabulary gap in second language learning.

One line of enquiry has examined vocabulary size for first and second language users. Goulden et al. (1990) estimate that there are 117,000 word families in English, of which their participant group of English as a first language university students knew on average 17,200, suggesting acquisition of 1,000 new words during each year of schooling and a very large number of words never learnt and in many cases never met in spoken or written language. A considerably lower vocabulary size of 1,200 word families was determined by Nurweni and Read (1999) for a group of second language college students in Indonesia.

Another line of enquiry has examined the vocabulary size required for specific uses of language. Studies of this type have assumed that, although a language user needs to be familiar with 95 per cent of the words in a spoken or written text (i.e., 19 out of 20 word occurrences) for satisfactory comprehension (Laufer 1989), closer to 98 per cent of the words (i.e., 49 out of 50) is required for more pleasurable and effective language use (Hu and Nation 2000). Below the 95 per cent threshold, there is likely to be inadequate familiar language for the meaning of unknown words to be determined based on contextual clues. Laufer (1992) identified a turning point in second language reading comprehension occurring at the 3,000 word level, suggesting this as a minimum threshold for reading. Nation (2006), aiming for 98 per cent lexical coverage, estimated 6,000–7,000 word families required for listening to movies and discussions, and 8,000–9,000 word families required for reading novels and newspapers. A middle-ground benchmark of 4,000 word families has been suggested (see Alderson 2007).

Researchers have sought to identify stages of vocabulary knowledge beyond the 2,000 word list to address the vocabulary gap between second language vocabulary size and the vocabulary required for effective use of English in different contexts. The focus has largely been on prioritizing, that is to identify the words that provide the best return in terms of comprehension and communicative quality. Studies of this type have examined word occurrence in specific uses of English to identify core vocabularies.

A series of studies have focused on the vocabulary of academic study as one area of language learning. One approach has been to identify commonly used academic words. Coxhead (2000) identified 570 candidates for an Academic Word List, representing words occurring frequently in first-year undergraduate reading in a broad range of subject areas. Another approach has been to identify the vocabulary for specific areas of study. Ward (1999) followed this approach to identify the most useful vocabulary for reading undergraduate engineering texts, while Coxhead and Hirsh (2007) developed a word list for science students. These approaches represent targeted vocabulary lists which would provide good return for learning effort for specific groups of learners.

Aside from interest in vocabulary gaps and growth, there is research interest in vocabulary loss (or attrition). The study of vocabulary attrition for participants no longer using a language draws on data collected at intervals of months or even years to chart a pattern of lexical loss over time. Min (2008) found significant vocabulary loss three months after language instruction ended, with indications that most receptive and productive word knowledge became partially known words, suggesting that only formal knowledge of most target vocabulary is retained. Related to this line of enquiry is interest in how words are stored in memory, and the impact loss of one word has on the recall and use of other words (see Meara 2004), and mirrors interest in how knowledge of one word impacts on the learning of others (see Laufer 1990). This view of vocabulary knowledge as interrelated challenges the more simplistic methodologies based on the counting of isolated word items.

Receptive and Productive Knowledge

There are two remaining issues to be highlighted here for vocabulary researchers. The first concerns the widely accepted view that people know more words than they use. A clear distinction is made in vocabulary research between receptive and productive vocabulary knowledge (see Laufer 1998). Receptive knowledge of words relates to word recognition in written and spoken texts, and tests of receptive vocabulary knowledge assess the ability to attach a meaning to a word in written form, or to transcribe words presented in oral language.

Productive knowledge of words relates to word use in meaningful contexts, either written or spoken.

Tests of receptive and productive vocabulary knowledge measure different forms of word knowledge and require different units of measurement (Nation 2008, personal communication, 18 April). It can be assumed that receptive knowledge of a word form or type (e.g., *succeed*) indicates receptive knowledge of other members of the word family (i.e., *succeeds, success, successes, succeeding, succeeded, successfully, unsuccessful, unsuccessfully*). Productive knowledge, on the other hand, concerns retrieval from memory of a single word type (or *lemma*). It cannot be assumed that productive knowledge of one word form indicates productive knowledge of other word forms in the word family. This is because people do not productively use all the words they know. Thus, while measures of receptive knowledge should count and report in *word family* units, productive knowledge measures should count and report in *word type* units.

The Company Words Keep

The final issue to be discussed here regarding vocabulary research is how words appear in the language. Vocabulary lists present words in isolation, detached from meaningful contexts and the words they appear commonly with in spoken or written language. In contrast, concordance data displays words in context, with scope through use of corpora to focus on a word's use in specific contexts. A researcher could examine how a word is commonly used in a particular kind of text (e.g., newspapers) or in a particular subject area (e.g., nursing). Differences between spoken and written uses of a word can be examined, as can differences in word use between groups of language users. The range of data available depends on the nature of the corpus, and the complexity of the word analysis programs used. One line of enquiry in this area is the investigation of *lexical bundles*, or recurring multiword sequences, also referred to as *lexical phrases* and *lexical chunking*. Lexical bundles are frequently occurring sequences of words such as *has to do with, one of the things* and *you're never going to believe this*, differing from idiomatic expressions such as *in a nutshell*, and assuming important discourse functions in the language (see Biber and Barbieri 2007).

Research Stages and Related Test Instruments

This section looks at a sample of research tools and test instruments associated with some of the main lines of enquiry in vocabulary research.

Investigating Depth of Vocabulary Knowledge

One test instrument draws on elements of Nation's (2001) well-established model of word knowledge at three levels: *form* (spelling, sound, word parts), *meaning* (associations) and *use* (grammar, collocations, constraints on use). Read (1998) developed a word associates test to allow investigation of the semantic associations between words, as an indicator of depth of word knowledge. This tool focuses on identifying words with a meaning associated with a target word item, and requires test-takers to select suitable responses from those provided. Distractor items which have no association with the target word are included in the possible choices. Two examples of this test format are provided in Figure 16.2.

In the examples given in Figure 16.2, knowledge of word associations for the target words *sudden* and *common* are being tested. In this test format, the group of four adjectives in the left hand box includes two words which are synonyms of the target word or represent one aspect of the target word meaning (e.g., sudden-quick; sudden-surprising; common-ordinary; common-shared), and two distractor items. The group of four nouns in the right hand box includes two collocates of the target word, meaning that the two words occur together frequently in the language (e.g., sudden change; sudden noise; common boundary; common name), and two distractor items.

Investigating Vocabulary Demands for Specific Uses

Computer-based programs can be used to examine the lexical demands of communicative tasks such as reading, writing or listening, by determining how many words are required for the task. Research in this area involves preparing an electronic version of a text, spoken or written, to be analysed, and examining word occurrence in the text using a computer program. *Range* (Heatley and

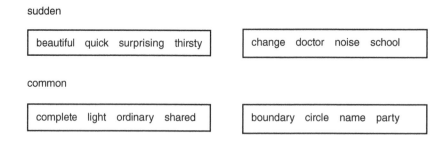

sudden

| beautiful   quick   surprising   thirsty |

| change   doctor   noise   school |

common

| complete   light   ordinary   shared |

| boundary   circle   name   party |

Figure 16.2 Sample items from the word associates test (Read 1998, p. 46)

Word list	Percentage coverage (%)
one (first 1,000 words)	72
two (second 1,000 words)	4
three (academic words)	10
other words	14
Total	**100**

Figure 16.3 Lexical profile of a sample of second language writing

Nation 1998) is a program designed to list words and their frequency of occurrence in a text according to word family lists: the 1,000 most frequently occurring words in English, the second 1,000 most frequently occurring words, and academic words. Words occurring in a text which are not from these three word lists are reported as *other words*. An example of a results summary for a sample of text produced by a second language writer using Range appears in Figure 16.3.

Figure 16. 3 shows how Range has been used to statistically present word use in the text, indicating that 72 per cent of all words in the text were words from the first 1,000 word level, while 4 per cent of words were from the second 1,000 word level and 10 per cent of words in the text were academic words. The combined lexical coverage of high frequency (the first and second thousand words) and academic vocabulary for a text is the added values for these three levels, in this case 86 per cent. The remaining 14 per cent of words shown in Figure 16.3 as *other words* could be misspelt words, proper nouns, technical words related to the subject area of the text or low frequency words.

Investigating Vocabulary Size

A series of test instruments have been developed to enable researchers to reliably investigate how many words a group of language users know. Tests tend to distinguish between receptive vocabulary knowledge and productive vocabulary knowledge, with tests developed to measure productive vocabulary knowledge in both controlled (measurement of correct elicitation of target items) and free (no specific target items being elicited) formats. This gives rise to three widely used formats for vocabulary size measurement: receptive, controlled productive and free productive (see Laufer 1998) as presented in Figure 16.4.

A test instrument designed to measure receptive vocabulary size is the *Vocabulary Levels Test* (Nation 1983). This employs a word-meaning format to

controlled productive

receptive ------------------ <

free productive

Figure 16.4 Types of vocabulary knowledge (adapted from Zhong 2008, p. 13)

Choose the right word to go with each meaning. Write the number of that word next to its meaning.

1. copy

2. event   __ end or highest point

3. motor   __ this moves a car

4. pity   __ thing made to be like another

5. profit

6. tip

Figure 16.5 Sample of the 2,000 word section of the Vocabulary Levels Test (Schmitt et al. 2001, p. 82)

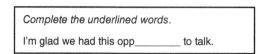

Complete the underlined words.

I'm glad we had this opp_____ to talk.

Figure 16.6 Sample of the 2,000 word section of the Controlled Productive Vocabulary Levels Test (Laufer and Nation 1999, p. 46)

assess word meaning recognition at five word levels: 2,000, 3,000, 5,000, 10,000 and academic words. An example of a test item from the 2,000 word section of a version of this test format appears in Figure 16.5.

A test instrument designed to measure productive vocabulary knowledge in a controlled format is the *Controlled Productive Vocabulary Levels Test* (Laufer and Nation 1999). This assesses the ability to complete the missing letters in a target word presented in a sentence at five word levels: 2,000, 3,000, 5,000, 10,000, and academic vocabulary. An example of a test item from the 2,000 word section appears in Figure 16.6.

A tool designed to measure lexical richness in a student's writing is the *Lexical Frequency Profile* (Laufer and Nation 1995). This instrument statistically

1. attack   war, castle, guns, armour

Figure 16.7 Lex30 test item and sample answers (Meara and
Fitzpatrick, 2000, p. 28)

compares the proportion of high frequency words and academic words in a
sample of writing through computer analysis of word use in the text.

Another test instrument designed to measure productive vocabulary knowledge in a free way is Lex30 (Meara and Fitzpatrick 2000). In this test, participants are instructed to list words associated with a high frequency prompt
word. All the words produced by an individual test-taker are examined in
terms of word frequency, that is, the proportion of words within and outside
the 2,000 word list, to indicate lexical richness. An example of words listed by a
test-taker which are associated with the target word *attack* are indicated in
Figure 16.7. These words are *war, castle, guns* and *armour*, indicating that the
test-taker thought of these words when prompted by the target word.

New methodologies in vocabulary size assessment will continue to be developed in the search for more robust reporting.

Investigating Vocabulary Growth

Methodologies have been developed to allow researchers to investigate how
many words are learnt or acquired during a certain period, such as a semester
or a year of study. Two main approaches have been used. One approach is to
compare the vocabulary size of groups of learners representing different stages
of learning, such as the fifth (grade 5) and sixth (grade 6) years of schooling, in
the same learning environment. Laufer (1998) used this approach in a study of
the productive vocabulary knowledge growth of grade 10 (aged 16 years) and
grade 11 (aged 17 years) second language high school students in Israel. Another
approach is to collect data from one group of learners at two different stages of
learning (e.g., 12 weeks apart) using a pre-test and post-test format. Horst and
Collins (2006) used this approach at intervals of 100 hours of instruction with
second language elementary school students in Quebec. In either approach,
decisions need to be made on which vocabulary knowledge test instruments
(receptive, controlled productive or free productive) to employ.

Investigating Strategies in Vocabulary Learning and Vocabulary Use

An area of vocabulary research which has involved rich data collection
is strategy use, with the focus largely on determining which vocabulary

231

learning strategies are associated with effective vocabulary learning and effective vocabulary use. Methodologies used in such studies include *participant questionnaires*, focusing on strategies used and their effectiveness, *student logs*, comprising written reflections of strategy use while reading, and *think-aloud protocols*, where participants explain processes as they use the language.

Gu (2003) investigated vocabulary strategy use of two successful adult English as a foreign language learners at three stages of an intensive reading task: meeting new words, committing words to memory and use of new words. The study was designed to determine which strategies were used by participants as they encountered new words in a text on pollution in Athens which, it was estimated by the researcher, contained about one new word in 50 (i.e., the participants would know 98 per cent of the words in the text). Think-aloud protocols and follow-up interviews were used to focus on task-specific as well as more general vocabulary learning strategy use. The findings indicated that both learners displayed high levels of motivation to learn new words, and employed a wide range of metacognitive and cognitive strategies. Metacognitive strategy use included self-initiation to learn beyond what was required, conscious selection of strategy use, and applying criteria such as relevance, interest and importance in selecting words to learn. Cognitive strategy use included using contextual clues, negotiating between dictionary meaning and contextual meaning and using newly learnt words productively.

Analysis of Lexical Bundles

The last type of research tool discussed here is concerned with studies of how individual words are used in different linguistic contexts. While vocabulary lists present words in isolation, research on lexical bundles explores the way words are used in the language, with particular interest in identifying recurring groups of words which could be used as a model for language learners and language assessment. Research of this type requires access to a corpus of language and appropriate software. The focus for the research will indicate the type of corpus and program required, and the parameters of the analysis. Oxford Wordsmith Tools (Oxford University Press 2008) is one program available to researchers which reports concordance data from which recurring lexical bundles could be identified. An example of data from a concordance results file for *issue* appears in Figure 16.8.

Challenges Associated with Vocabulary Research

Vocabulary researchers are faced with some predictable challenges, each with appropriate responses. One challenge inherent in research involving

```
social and economic issues

public moral issues

environmental issues

the key issues
```

Figure 16.8 Concordance data on the word *issue* (Thurstun and
Candlin 1997, p. 2)

participants is minimizing the effect of participant reorientation to suit the
study focus or goals. Reorientation, in this sense, describes the process of study
participants temporarily changing their behaviour because of the study. This is
called the *Hawthorne Effect* (Landsberger 1958), and can occur if information
about the study is shared with learners prior to or during collection of data.
Studies of vocabulary learning strategy use and classroom vocabulary learning
would be particularly susceptible to reorientation on the part of language learners and their teachers. There is an ethical requirement for informed and voluntary participation in studies of this type. Careful consideration should thus be
placed to the information being shared with the participants (e.g., learners) and
their teachers and the timing of this.

When using parallel pre-tests and post-tests, preventive measures to
minimize the impact of the pre-test on subsequent vocabulary learning can
include: collection of all copies of pre-tests; not communicating test results with
participants or teachers during the survey period between the two sets of tests
(pre and post) and not indicating to participants or teachers the relationship
between the pre-tests and post-tests.

Another challenge in studies of participant vocabulary knowledge relates to
the use of test instruments and the data they generate. Researchers face dual
concerns of sampling a sufficient number of vocabulary items to address
reliability and validity needs, while minimizing the effect of participant test
fatigue. Vocabulary levels tests sampling receptive knowledge at five levels of
vocabulary (2,000, 3,000, 5,000, 10,000 and academic vocabulary) and including
30 test items per vocabulary level, can be completed within 30 minutes. This test
format represents a response to these dual concerns.

A further challenge in vocabulary research can occur in the measurement of
vocabulary growth. Such studies use pre-tests and post-tests to indicate changes
in performance on the test instruments. These tests need to be comparable in
what they test and how they test it, in order for meaningful comparisons to be
made. Use of test instruments in longitudinal studies of vocabulary growth
should be subject to reliability assessment, particularly where multiple versions
of a test format are used on the assumption that the test versions are parallel,
that is that they measure similar aspects of knowledge at a similar level. Xing

and Fulcher (2007) have indicated that the 2,000, 3,000 and academic vocabulary levels of two different versions of the receptive vocabulary levels test are highly correlated, that is they can be used reliably in a parallel format, but that the 5,000 word-level versions are not parallel (i.e., one version is more difficult), and thus are in need of revision.

A Sample Study

I have selected a vocabulary study to show how it took account of a number of issues, methods and challenges in the research design. The study (Zhong 2008) was conducted by one of my research students, Hua Zhong. She was interested in investigating vocabulary learning in a high school setting in China, employing pre-tests and post-tests for a single group of participants. The constraints of the study period restricted the duration of the study period to 10 weeks. She was interested in both receptive and productive knowledge of words at four word levels (2,000, 3,000, 5,000 and academic vocabulary). The study built on earlier findings that receptive and productive vocabulary knowledge grow at different rates (see Laufer 1998).

The study dealt with a series of methodological issues. It employed the use of identical pre-tests and post-tests, and thus one key concern was to ensure that the pre-tests had minimal impact on the English language learning program during the 10-week study period. The test instruments used were the receptive vocabulary levels test (Nation 1983) and controlled productive vocabulary levels test (Laufer and Nation 1999). A pilot test was conducted to determine which test items in these two test instruments would be suitable for the selected group of learners in terms of content and language level. Marking criteria were developed to ensure reliability and objectivity in making decisions on whether partial words were satisfactorily completed in the controlled productive vocabulary levels test. Procedures for data analysis were developed and pilot tested to ensure findings were empirically sound. Each of these issues is discussed.

One feature of the study was its longitudinal nature, conducted during 10 weeks of the school semester. It was decided that vocabulary learning during this 10-week period could be measured most accurately if the pre-tests and post-tests were the same, and analysis was made of one group of learners at two stages of their learning. The thinking was that if data from the pre-tests and post-tests were fully comparable, then differences between the test scores could be used as indicators of vocabulary learning.

It was realized that the study participants and their teacher could not be told about the relationship between the pre-tests and post-tests until the completion of the study, for fear of the pre-tests being regarded as a vocabulary learning goal for the subsequent 10 weeks. As preventive measures, the researcher ensured that all copies of the pre-tests were collected, and that no pre-test results were passed on to the teacher or research participants until completion of the study.

Another feature of the study was its focus on a homogenous study population of high school students learning English as a foreign language in China. The study employed a pilot test with a small number of Chinese background participants who had a similar language proficiency to the main participant group. The pilot test was designed to check that the test instruments were appropriate for this participant group in terms of content and language level. The pilot test indicated which test items were unsuitable, and which word levels of the existing test instruments (2,000, 3,000, 5,000, 10,000 and academic words) would be applicable to the study, and in particular whether the 10,000 word level should be used. It became clear that the 10,000 level would be unlikely to generate any useful data due to anticipated low levels of both initial vocabulary knowledge and subsequent vocabulary learning over 10 weeks for this participant group.

The pilot test was also used to generate a small amount of raw data which the researcher used to refine procedures for ensuring objectivity in marking decisions in the case of the controlled productive vocabulary levels test where variable answers were possible for each test item. Guidelines were developed and tested to standardize marking decisions to take account of differences in the spelling and grammatical form (e.g., singular or plural noun forms) of target vocabulary items. Minor spelling mistakes and grammatical errors were ignored on this basis: for spelling, one missing, added or wrong letter per word, or two adjacent letters in the wrong order were ignored; for grammar, errors in suffix endings involving *–ed*, *–s*, and *–ing* were ignored. The intention of the marking guidelines was to focus on vocabulary knowledge while dealing objectively with variations in form and accuracy of productive use.

Another feature of the study was its small participant size for quantitative research. From 83 students approached, 64 gave their consent to participate in the study indicating a 77.1 per cent participation rate. From this, 41 participants completed all the required tests allowing their data to be utilized in the study. This indicated a 35.9 per cent attrition rate. The number of participants in the study impacted on the statistical tools to be used in the data analysis. Taking account of the small number of participants, the researcher employed descriptive statistics to describe the trends and patterns evident in the data, in the form of mean scores and ratios. Parametric techniques, widely used to enable generalizations to be made regarding the data, were not used in the study due to the small sample size and to the abnormal distribution of data indicated through descriptive statistics to compare scores for mean, median and mode.

The adjustment of the methodology to suit the study enabled meaningful findings to be generated. They indicated significant levels of useful vocabulary growth, particularly of academic vocabulary, as well as overall higher levels of growth for productive vocabulary knowledge than for receptive vocabulary knowledge during the 10 weeks. The researcher was able to relate the study findings to previous research in the area, having employed similar principles and methodologies to earlier studies of this type, while having ensured that issues of reliability and validity were built into the research model.

Resources for Further Reading

Bogaards, P. and Laufer, B. (eds) (2004), *Vocabulary in a Second Language*. Amsterdam: John Benjamins.
  The editors of this book have assembled eleven chapters, primarily from papers presented at the Second Language Vocabulary Acquisition Colloquium held at Leiden University in 2002. The volume provides a host of new insights into experimental research covering the areas of selection, acquisition and testing of vocabulary.
Nation, I. S. P. (2001), *Learning Vocabulary in Another Language*. Cambridge: Cambridge University Press.
  Paul Nation provides a thorough overview of research on vocabulary spanning decades, providing insights on theory and practice, case studies and large-scale empirical studies, which inform contemporary approaches to the teaching and learning of vocabulary.
Read, J. (2000), *Assessing Vocabulary*. Cambridge: Cambridge University Press.
  Assessing Vocabulary focuses on a broad range of assessment tools and procedures for investigating vocabulary learning, knowledge and use. The book highlights and evaluates key studies, examines the role of corpus analysis and identifies areas for future research in vocabulary assessment.
Schmitt, N. and McCarthy, M. (eds) (1997), *Vocabulary: Description, Acquisition and Pedagogy*. Cambridge: Cambridge University Press.
  This edited volume presents 15 papers covering the theory and practice of vocabulary teaching and learning, with relevant chapters on approaches to research in key areas of vocabulary studies such as word knowledge and lexical chunks.

Online Resources

Compleat Lexical Tutor (see www.lextutor.ca)
  Tom Cobb has assembled a range of online tools and resources with open access for language researchers, teachers and learners. The site includes vocabulary levels tests, lexical profile software, concordance software with accompanying corpora and information on word lists.
Range (available from http://www.victoria.ac.nz/lals/staff/paul-nation/nation.aspx)
  Range is a computer-based program designed to report on word occurrence in written texts at set vocabulary levels. Paul Nation has provided on his web-page

an open-access link to two downloadable versions of Range, each with corresponding word lists and instruction files, including word lists developed from the British National Corpus.

List of corpora – An open-access list of English language corpora such as the British National Corpus (BNC) is available at http://www.athel.com/English_corpora.html.

References

Alderson, J. C. (2007), 'Judging the frequency of English words'. *Applied Linguistics*, 26, 383–409.

Bauer, L. and Nation, P. (1993), 'Word families'. *International Journal of Lexicography*, 6, 253–279.

Biber, D. and Barbieri, F. (2007), 'Lexical bundles in university spoken and written registers'. *English for Specific Purposes*, 26, 263–286.

British National Corpus (see http://www.natcorp.ox.ac.uk/)

Chung, T. and Nation, P. (2003), 'Technical vocabulary in specialized texts'. *Reading in a Foreign Language*, 15, 103–116.

Coxhead, A. (2000), 'A new academic word list'. *TESOL Quarterly*, 34, 213–238.

Coxhead, A. and Hirsh, D. (2007), 'A pilot science-specific word list'. *French Review of Applied Linguistics*, 7, 65–78.

Goulden, R., Nation, P. and Read, J. (1990), 'How large can a receptive vocabulary be?' *Applied Linguistics*, 11, 341–363.

Gu, P. (2003), 'Fine brush and freehand: The vocabulary-learning art of two successful Chinese EFL learners'. *TESOL Quarterly*, 37, 73–104.

Heatley, A. and Nation, P. (1998), Range. School of Linguistics and Applied Language studies, Victoria University of Wellington.

Hirsh, D. and Nation, P. (1992), 'What vocabulary size is needed to read unsimplified texts for pleasure?' *Reading in a Foreign Language*, 8, 689–696.

Horst, M. and Collins, L. (2006), 'From *faible* to strong: How does their vocabulary grow?' *Canadian Modern Language Review*, 63, 83–106.

Hu, M. and Nation, P. (2000), 'Unknown vocabulary density and reading comprehension'. *Reading in a Foreign Language*, 13, 403–430.

Hwang, K. and Nation, P. (1989), 'Reducing the vocabulary load and encouraging vocabulary learning through reading newspapers'. *Reading in a Foreign Language*, 6, 323–335.

Joe, A. (1995), 'Text-based tasks and incidental vocabulary learning'. *Second Language Research*, 11, 149–158.

Kim, Y. (2008), 'The role of task-induced involvement and learner proficiency in L2 vocabulary acquisition'. *Language Learning*, 58, 285–325.

Landsberger, H. (1958), *Hawthorne Revisited: Management and the Worker, Its Critics, and Developments in Human Relations in Industry*. Ithaca, NY: Cornell University.

Laufer, B. (1989), 'What percentage of text-lexis is essential for comprehension?' in C. Lauren and M. Nordman (eds), *Special Language: From Humans Thinking to Thinking Machines*. Clevedon: Multilingual Matters, pp. 316–323.

—(1990), 'Words you know: How they affect the words you learn', in J. Fisiak (ed.), *Further Insights into Contrastive Analysis*. Amsterdam: John Benjamins Publishing Company, pp. 573–593.

—(1992), 'How much lexis is necessary for reading comprehension?' in P. Arnaud and H. Bejoint (eds), *Vocabulary and Applied Linguistics*. London: Macmillan, pp. 126–132.

—(1998), 'The development of passive and active vocabulary in a second language: Same or different?' *Applied Linguistics*, 19, 255–271.

Laufer, B. and Hulstijn, J. (2001), 'Incidental vocabulary acquisition in a second language: The effect of task-induced involvement load'. *Applied Linguistics*, 22, 1–26.

Laufer, B. and Nation, P. (1995), 'Vocabulary size and use: Lexical richness in L2 written production'. *Applied Linguistics*, 16, 307–322.

—(1999), 'A vocabulary size test of controlled productive ability'. *Language Testing*, 16, 33–51.

Meara, P. (2004), 'Modelling vocabulary loss'. *Applied Linguistics*, 25, 137–155.

Meara, P. and Fitzpatrick, T. (2000), 'Lex30: An improved method of assessing productive vocabulary in an L2'. *System*, 28, 19–30.

Min, H. (2008), 'EFL vocabulary acquisition and retention: Reading plus vocabulary enhancement activities and narrow reading'. *Language Learning*, 58, 73–115.

Mochizuki, M. and Aizawa, K. (2000), 'An affix acquisition order for EFL learners: And exploratory study'. *System*, 28, 291–304.

Nation, P. (1983), 'Testing and teaching vocabulary'. *Guidelines*, 5, 12–25.

—(2001), *Learning Vocabulary in Another Language*. Cambridge: Cambridge University Press.

—(2006), 'How large a vocabulary is needed for reading and listening?' *Canadian Modern Language Review*, 63, 59–82.

Newton, J. (1995), 'Task-based interaction and incidental vocabulary learning: A case study'. *Second Language Research*, 11, 159–177.

Nurweni, A. and Read, J. (1999), 'The English vocabulary knowledge of Indonesian university students'. *English for Specific Purposes*, 18, 161–175.

Oxford University Press (2008), Oxford Wordsmith Tools 4.0 (see http://www.lexically.net/downloads/version4/html/index.html).

Read, J. (1998), 'Validating a test to measure depth of vocabulary knowledge', in A. Kunnan (ed.), *Validation in Language Assessment*. Mahwah, NJ: Erlbaum, pp. 41–60.

Schmitt, N. and Zimmerman, C. (2002), 'Derivative word forms: What do learners know?' *TESOL Quarterly*, 36, 145–171.

Schmitt, N., Schmitt, D. and Clapham, C. (2001), 'Developing and exploring the behaviour of two new versions of the Vocabulary Levels Test'. *Language Testing*, 18, 55–88.

Thurstun, J. and Candlin, C. (1997), *Exploring Academic English: A Workbook for Student Essay Writing*. Sydney: National Centre for English Language Teaching and Research.

Ward, J. (1999), 'How large a vocabulary do EAP engineering students need?' *Reading in a Foreign Language*, 12, 309–324.

Xing, P. and Fulcher, G. (2007), 'Reliability assessment for two versions of Vocabulary Levels Tests'. *System*, 35, 182–191.

Zhong, H. (2008), 'Vocabulary size development: A study of Chinese high school students'. Unpublished MEd TESOL dissertation, Sydney: University of Sydney.

17 Researching Pragmatics

Carsten Roever

Chapter Overview

Pragmatics as a field is a broad area, and is investigated through an equally wide range of research approaches. The study of pragmatics traditionally focuses on the relationship between language use and context, that is, how features of the external, real-world context are reflected in the language used. Such context incorporates the physical context, which is reflected through deictic expressions (this, there, mine), the interpersonal context, including the interlocutors' shared history and their relationship in terms of acquaintance-ship and power differential, and the social context with its rules of appropriate conduct.

Pragmatics research in applied linguistics is mostly concerned with the relationship between language use on the one hand and the social and inter-personal context of interaction on the other. Specifically, the field of cross-cultural pragmatics investigates differences in pragmatics based on first language background, whereas interlanguage pragmatics investigates how second language learners' knowledge and ability for use of target language pragmatics develops.

Research approaches in pragmatics range from the recording of authentic, unelicited discourse, via elicitation of discourse to elicitation of metapragmatic knowledge. Some psycholinguistic research has also recently appeared, for example, by Holtgraves (2007) and Taguchi (2008).

Typical Stages in This Research

Stage 1: Which Aspect of Pragmatics is to be Investigated?

The first decision to be made in this research is what aspect of pragmatics to investigate. Traditionally, the major focus has been on speech acts, and of the speech acts investigated, requests and apologies have been the most frequently researched ones (e.g., Trosborg 1995; Achiba 2002; Jung 2004; Biesenbach-Lucas 2007; Cohen and Shively 2007; Felix-Brasdefer 2007; Warga and Scholmberger 2007). Other speech acts include refusals (Gass and Neu 1996; Barron 2003; Felix-Brasdefer 2004; Kwon 2004), compliments and compliment responses (Lorenzo-Dus 2001; Golato 2003; Yu 2004; Tran 2006), suggestions (Bardovi-Harlig and Hartford 1990, 1993, 1996), advice (Hinkel 1997; Matsumura 2001, 2003, 2007; Decapua and Dunham 2007), agreement and disagreement (Porter, 1986; Salsbury and Bardovi-Harlig 2001), complaints (Trosborg 1995), expressions of gratitude (Eisenstein and Bodman 1993) and some others.

Of course, pragmatics does not only consist of speech acts but research into other aspects of pragmatics is less common though no less important. Politeness has been investigated with and without regard to specific speech acts (Bardovi-Harlig and Griffin 1996; Bardovi-Harlig and Dörnyei 1998; Niezgoda and Röver 2001), and implicature, which describes indirect, implied language use, has also received some attention although mostly from a pedagogical and assessment angle (Bouton 1988, 1994, 1999; Roever 2005, 2006, 2007). Routine formulae have been more widely investigated (Wildner-Bassett 1986; House 1996; Kanagy 1999; Davis 2007) and have also been of interest to researchers working in general second language acquisition (Myles et al. 1996; Jiang and Nekrasova 2007; Taguchi 2007).

Other aspects of interaction and discourse, such as opening and closings and sequence organization, are more commonly investigated through other discourse analytic approaches, most commonly Conversation Analysis (for an introduction, see Hutchby and Wooffitt, 2008).

Stage 2: What Independent Variables are to be Investigated?

Pragmatics research in applied linguistics can be divided into two large camps and a smaller cluster of other studies. The large research areas concern *cross-cultural pragmatics* and *interlanguage pragmatics*. Cross-cultural pragmatics typically makes membership in a cultural group, usually defined as an L1 group, the independent variable[1] and compares differences between the groups.

Acquisition of second language pragmatics is not a concern in these studies. The largest study in cross-cultural pragmatics was the Cross-Cultural Speech Act Realization Patterns (CCSARP) project (Blum-Kulka et al. 1989), which collected L1 and L2 request and apology data from 1,946 participants with Discourse Completion Tasks (DCTs), covering seven native and three target languages. One problem with cross-cultural pragmatics research is the type of conclusions to be drawn from findings. A difference between two cultural groups in their speech act realization or the cultural norms underlying their pragmatic performance does not necessarily mean that communication between them will be problematic or flawed. It simply means that a difference exists which may or may not impact communication.

The second major type of research is interlanguage pragmatics research, also known as acquisitional or developmental pragmatics research. In this research tradition, the focus is on the acquisition of pragmatic competence in a target language, so the independent variable in such studies is a factor that is hypothesized to affect L2 pragmatic competence, most commonly L2 proficiency or exposure to the L2 environment. The independent variable can simply be native-speaker status, and would then involve a comparison between learners' and native speakers' performance on the research instrument. Alternatively, the independent variable can have various levels, for example, low proficiency, mid-proficiency and high-proficiency learners can be compared in a "pseudo-longitudinal" design, which hopes to predict developmental trajectories. Similarly, learners with different levels of exposure can be compared, for example, no exposure, 5 months in the L2 country, 10 months in the L2 country (e.g., Grieve 2007). Often, there is also a native speaker comparison group to establish a baseline of native speaker performance with which learners are then contrasted.

Stage 3: What Research Instrument is to be Used?

The most commonly used research instruments in pragmatics research are Discourse Completion Tasks (DCTs), role plays, metapragmatic judgements and multiple choice instruments. Other less commonly used research approaches include interviews, observations and the collection of natural data. In this section, the two most frequently used research tools will be discussed: DCTs and role plays. For discussion of other possible instruments, see Kasper and Rose (2002).

Discourse Completion Tasks

DCTs used to be the standard way of collecting data in interlanguage and cross-cultural pragmatics research because they allow rapid and targeted collection of a large amount of data. However, recent critiques of DCT research by Golato (2003), Kasper (2006) and Meier (1998) have made the uncritical use of DCTs impossible, and researchers must now make a case for the use of a DCT as a research instrument.

A DCT traditionally consists of a situational prompt, which is followed by a gap for the participant to enter their response. The prompt is a situation description that provides background on the setting that the imaginary interaction occurs in, as well as on the imaginary interlocutor. Prompts can be more or less detailed, and their level of detail has been found to influence participants' responses (Billmyer and Varghese 2000). It is very important in the design of the prompt to assign the participants roles that they can identify with and describe situations that are familiar to them. In addition to the prompt, the gap can be preceded by an opening utterance of the imaginary interlocutor, and followed by a rejoinder. Research has shown a noticeable effect of rejoinders on production (Johnston et al. 1998) but little effect of preceding utterances (Goh 2006). A DCT item might therefore look as in Figure 17.1 (the parts in brackets are optional).

The relationship with the imaginary interlocutor is crucial, and DCT situations are usually constructed to incorporate some of the context variables identified by Brown and Levinson (1987) as influencing politeness in conversation: *power, social distance* and *degree of imposition*.

Power concerns the relative power difference between the participant and the imaginary interlocutor, and can have three basic settings: high power (of the imaginary interlocutor), equal power, low power. In the example shown in Figure 17.1, power would be equal. Examples of high power interlocutors for student participants are professors, landlords, employers or police officers, but it can be difficult to find lower-power interlocutors if participants are students and do not have much experience being in positions of power. Possibilities include casting the participant as an assistant manager of a small shop who is talking to an employee, or as a graduate assistant/tutor talking to a student.

> You need to print out a letter but your printer is not working. You decide to ask your housemate Jack if you can use his printer. Jack is in his room reading a book as you walk in.
>
> [Jack: Hey, how are you?]
>
> You: _____
>
> [Jack: Sure, go for it.]

Figure 17.1 Example of DCT item

Depending on the target culture, they could also be cast as talking to a younger relative.

Social distance is the degree of shared group membership and/or acquaintanceship. In the DCT example in Figure 17.1, social distance would be considered low as housemates tend to know each other fairly well. High social distance pertains to interlocutors that the participant does not know and has little in common with, for example, strangers on the bus, customers in a shop, a professor they do not know. Medium social distance might apply to interlocutors who are vaguely but not well known or who share group membership with the participant without much personal knowledge, for example, a colleague in another department, a fellow student of the same age that the participant has never talked to or a distant relative.

Imposition differs somewhat by speech act. In a request, like the example in Figure 17.1, it is the cost to the imaginary interlocutor of complying with the participant's request. Such cost can be in terms of time, money, effort or inconvenience. The example above would be considered a low-imposition situation, with high-imposition examples including borrowing a large amount of money, asking for a ride to a distant airport, borrowing a laptop that the interlocutor also urgently needs or asking for help with a difficult and time consuming move. In apologies, imposition is the severity of offence, that is, the cost of the damage to the interlocutor caused by the participant's (imaginary) action or the severity of violation of a norm. Low-imposition apology situations include almost but not actually breaking an item, losing or destroying something cheap that belongs to the interlocutor (a magazine, a pencil) or bumping into somebody without causing any damage. In high imposition apology situations, the participant might be cast as destroying a valuable possession of the interlocutor's (a camera, a laptop), spilling red wine on a light carpet or bumping into the interlocutor and knocking them over.

All three context variables (power, social distance and degree of imposition) are measured on a continuum, and they are not all-or-nothing propositions. In addition, there may be culture-specific variables, such as age or gender that may affect responses. It is recommended that researchers check prior to data collection whether their own intuitions about context variables and other variables match the target participants' views.

DCTs are usually designed so that they systematically incorporate combinations of contextual variables (and other variables, where applicable). However, researchers frequently have to make choices as to which context variables they will focus on in their study because even if the three context variables identified by Brown and Levinson were only varied dichotomously, this would lead to eight possible variable combinations, as shown in Table 17.1.

Table 17.1 Combinations of power, imposition, and social distance if varied dichotomously

	Power (P)	Imposition (I)	Social Distance (D)
1	High (+)	High (+)	High (+)
2	High (+)	High (+)	Low (–)
3	High (+)	Low (–)	High (+)
4	High (+)	Low (–)	Low (–)
5	Equal (+/–)	High (+)	High (+)
6	Equal (+/–)	High (+)	Low (–)
7	Equal (+/–)	Low (–)	High (+)
8	Equal (+/–)	Low (–)	Low (–)

If some variables are considered to have multiple levels, the number of possible combinations would increase according to the following formula:

number of combinations = levels of power * levels of imposition * levels of social distance * levels of additional variable x * levels of additional variable y etc.

So in a study that incorporates a medium social distance setting in addition to varying power and imposition dichotomously and also looks at gender of the imaginary interlocutor as a variable (male/female), eight different combinations would result. Given that each combination of context variables should be represented by at least two DCT items (better three or four), it is often not possible to vary more than two variables (either two context variables or a context variable and another variable) in a given study. To avoid fatigue and inauthentic responses, participants should not be expected to complete more than 20 DCT situations, preferably no more than 12. Care must be taken to ensure that the other context variables and possible other variables are controlled and kept equal for all situations. So if power and imposition are varied, social distance needs to be kept constant for all situations (usually low), and there must be reason to assume that other possible variables do not have much of an influence, or they must be systematically controlled as well. Keeping variables constant limits the range of conclusions that can be drawn from the study, but this trade-off between practicality and external validity is common and unavoidable.

Role Plays

Design considerations for role plays are similar to DCTs in terms of the context variables of power, social distance and degree of imposition. For role plays as well, researchers vary one or more of these context variables, and design role play situations so as to include different combinations of them. However, since role plays are much more resource intensive, time consuming and tiring for researcher and participants alike, the number of situations will generally be smaller and not exceed six. The major obvious difference between role plays and DCTs is that role plays involve extended conversations between the interlocutor and the participant. This allows speech acts to unfold over several turns and data resembles authentic conversation more than in a DCT. Also, role plays elicit ability for use rather than knowledge like DCTs, because participants have to produce language under the pressures and constraints of a communicative situation.

However, it is important to note that role plays are not the same as authentic conversations. Most importantly, participants are aware of the simulated nature of role plays, which have no stakes attached, unlike authentic conversation, and role plays do not impact real-world outcomes and/or relationships. Participants therefore do not have the same motivations as they would in authentic interactions. In addition, role plays tend to be conducted in controlled environments to enable recording, so facilitative and inhibiting effects of the natural environment are lacking, such as background noise, visual cues or model interactions by others.

Another consideration in role plays concerns interlocutor effects. While interactions in role plays develop more naturally than they ever could in DCTs, comparability between different interactions is limited due to the co-constructed nature of conversation. However, interlocutors can try to keep their conversations with participants fairly similar by following broad guidelines. For example, in exchanges where participants are meant to make a request, interlocutors might follow a strategy of not immediately acceding to the request but introducing a complication, which then leads to a successful solution having to be negotiated. Such complicating strategies lengthen the interaction and thereby force participants to display more of their pragmatic competence, but at the same time, they may not be feasible for low-proficiency learners, whose L2 proficiency may be too limited to support lengthy negotiations.

Another possibility interlocutor effect relates to the plausibility of the role taken on by the interlocutor. Interlocutors frequently perform a variety of very different roles to accommodate different context variable settings. For example, if the variable 'power' is varied and the participant is a graduate student, the interlocutor might play a professor (P+), a fellow graduate student (P=) and an employee in the video store where the participant is cast as the manager (P–)[2]. Participants have to suspend disbelief to imagine the interlocutor's portrayed persona as real, and this increases their awareness of the simulated and non-authentic nature of role plays.

Besides these caveats, role plays also have logistical limitations. Unlike DCTs, which can be administered to large groups of participants in far-flung locations, role play data has to be collected in individual sessions between participants and researcher/confederate, which increases time and costs.

The eventual decision as to whether a DCT or a role play is more suitable for a given study depends primarily on the types of conclusions to be drawn from the study. If researchers are interested in isolated pieces of participants' knowledge that do not require discourse unfolding over various turns, DCTs are appropriate. For example, studies on address terms, formulaic expressions, or investigations of the repertoire of semantic formulae participants know, can rely on DCTs. However, if ability for use or complex speech acts are to be investigated, or participants' ability to construct extended discourse, role plays are preferable. For examples, investigations of how participants realize speech acts in discourse need to employ role plays rather than DCTs.

Stage 4: How Will the Data be Analysed?

Data analysis of the most frequently investigated speech acts, request and apology, traditionally follows the coding scheme developed originally in the Cross-Cultural Speech Act Realization Patterns project (CCSARP; Blum-Kulka et al. 1989) and later modified by several authors, most notably Trosborg (1995) and Hudson et al. (1995). The CCSARP coding scheme and its derivatives atomize speech acts into head acts and supportive moves, and can code for modifications within both. The unit of coding is 'strategy', and as an example take the following apology situation and participant response (from Roever 2000):

> *Rushing to get to class on time, you run around the corner and bump into another student almost knocking him down. The other student is male, about your age, but you don't know him.*
>
> Oh my gosh! I'm so sorry. Are you okay? I'm late and I guess I wasn't watching where I was going. Are you sure you're okay?

According to CCSARP, this utterance would be segmented and coded as follows:

> 'Oh my gosh!' = Alerter
> 'I'm so sorry.' = Illocutionary force indicating device (IFID) with intensifying adverbial
> 'Are you okay?' = Concern for the hearer

'I'm late and I guess I wasn't watching where I was going.' = Taking
on responsibility
'Are you sure you're okay?' = Concern for the hearer

The frequency of strategies is counted and compared between the groups of
interest, for example, native speakers and L2 learners. Such comparisons can be
done simply by contrasting different frequency counts or using an inferential
statistical procedure such as chi-square, which indicates a relationship between
group membership and the frequency of use of a certain strategy.

There has, however, recently been increasing criticism of the atomistic
CCSARP approach because it does not handle extended interactions well and
because the categories are not always well-defined (Meier 1998; Kasper 2006).
For role play data, it can also be difficult to identify the actual head act as many
types of supportive moves already have some degree of the target illocutionary
force. Al-Ghatani and Roever (2009) suggest a head act identification based on
the next-turn proof procedure from Conversation Analysis (Sacks et al. 1974).
They also developed a revised classification system of head acts based on formal properties, rather than politeness levels. However, they still employ a system of frequency counts to compare groups. Houck and Gass (1996) offer a
different approach to the analysis of role play data, using a classification system
to group response types without atomizing them at the level of strategy.

The ultimate goal of the analysis is to compare the different levels of the
independent variable, for example, NS vs. NNS or NNS of different proficiency
or exposure levels. Different combinations of context variables and their effect
also need to be explored, possibly nested within the other independent variable. Differences between groups and context variable combinations are then
described and interpreted.

A Sample Study

In an interlanguage pragmatics study, Byon (2004) investigated knowledge of
Korean requests by native English speaking Korean as a foreign language (KFL)
learners in the United States of America, and compared their responses with
Korean native speaker and American English native speaker data. While the
focus of his paper was on the learners, he included native speakers of both languages to facilitate the identification of transfer effects. Byon used a DCT and
systematically varied the context variables Power (higher/equal/lower) and
Social Distance (high/low). This generated six possible combinations of context
variables, and he used two items per combination, leading to a 12-item DCT.
He validated his DCT by having a small sample of native Korean and native
English speakers evaluate the plausibility of the situations and the degree of

imposition. He found that the situations were plausible and that imposition was rated similarly in both speech communities, although he does not provide these ratings in the paper.

It is worth noting that Byon did not keep imposition constant (i.e., always low or always high) for his situations, neither did he claim that he did. For example, both his +P/+D situations are clearly not low imposition, requiring participants to ask a professor to allow them into a class where registration has already closed, or to ask a professor to schedule a special exam sitting for them so they can attend a relative's wedding. In contrast, his =P/+D situations are certainly low imposition, requiring participants to ask a passing student for a dorm location, or to ask a passing student to take a picture of the participant and a visiting friend. The imposition of another situation depends on (unmentioned) context variables when the participant needs to ask a roommate to borrow his/her computer for an evening to complete an assignment. If the roommate also needs the computer, this is a high-imposition situation, but if the roommate is going to be out for the evening and does not need it, it is much lower imposition. However, no such background information is given. These inconstant imposition settings do not matter much if only groups are compared and context variable effects are not investigated, but since Byon does investigate them, not keeping imposition constant introduces an intervening variable and makes the results and any conclusions drawn from them less defensible.

Byon investigated two independent variables:

- language background, with three levels: native Korean speaker, learner of Korean, native English speaker
- context variables, with six levels: +P/+D, =P/+D, –P/+D, +P/–D, =P/–D, –P/–D

His dependent variable was use of request strategies.

Byon recruited 50 female participants for each of his three groups. He screened his KFL participants to make sure they had sufficient Korean proficiency to answer the questionnaire but he eliminated potential participants who had spent extended periods in Korea to keep the sample homogenous. He further limited his sample to female participants in order to avoid gender effects but did not specify what these gender effects might be. While such limitations of the sample group are legitimate and often necessary to avoid having to consider too many variables for too small a sample, limiting the sample to a subset of the target population reduces the range of conclusions that can be drawn from the study. Strictly speaking, Byon's conclusions should be limited to female language users, and for learners of Korean, they should be limited to learners in a foreign language situation.

Byon administered his DCT to his participants and then analysed the data in a series of steps. He started out using the CCSARP and the coding scheme developed by Hudson et al. (1995) and adapted these existing schemes for his data. Such adaptation is commonly necessary because pre-existing coding schemes often do not represent a new data set well and need even more revision if the data set consists of a target language different from the one used in the creation of the prior coding schemes. In adapting the scheme, the original scheme is first applied to the data, exemplars that do not fit are identified and new categories are created to accommodate them, while deleting categories that do not occur in the data set.

Byon reports his results by first providing an inventory of the strategies used with examples, and then shows total frequencies for each strategy across all situations by group. In the next section, he compares the most frequent supportive moves for the three groups, and discusses selected differences that are particularly striking or pedagogically relevant. It is often impossible and unnecessary to discuss all differences and similarities, so researchers need to focus on the ones that are of most theoretical or practical interest.

Next, Byon analyses the effect of the context variables Power and Distance to understand the level of sociopragmatic awareness (sensitivity to contextual features) learners have attained. He finds, for example, that the native speakers used more indirect strategies when talking to someone higher in power but more direct strategies when talking to someone lower in power. The KFL learners on the other hand used indirect strategies in both cases. This can indicate that the KFL learners do not understand the sociopragmatic rules of Korean conversation about using directness/indirectness, in other words, their sociopragmatic knowledge is not adequately mapped to their pragmalinguistic knowledge. It can, however, also indicate that the learners construed the social relationships in a non-Korean way and did not consider a junior student club member or younger roommate as less powerful than themselves. This shows that they do not have a comprehensive understanding of social relationship structures in Korean society but does not allow the researcher to draw conclusions about the relationship between their sociopragmatic and pragmalinguistic knowledge. To ensure that effects of social variables are due to sociopragmatic-pragmalinguistic mapping rather than differences in knowledge about social structures and relationships, researchers should ask a pilot sample of participants from both speech communities to rate power and distance, just as Byon did for implicature.

In the final section of his presentation and discussion of results, Byon compares the use of request head acts between groups and under different context conditions, and explains findings in terms of transfer effects.

Byon's study is a fairly typical interlanguage pragmatics study conducted in a traditional, speech act oriented way. Among its major strengths is Byon's focus on Korean as a target language, which adds to the still very spotty knowledge base of the acquisition of pragmatics in languages other than English. Byon's careful checking of the plausibility of his situations and his development of a coding scheme that is based on previous work but fits his own data set are also strong points of his study. One of the major methodological issues in Byon's paper is the impact of imposition, which was not kept constant for all situations. This makes findings on the effect of context variables somewhat questionable. Similarly, he did not ensure that all groups had similar perceptions of power and distance, so he cannot draw conclusions about the structure of learners' pragmatic knowledge. Finally, the use of DCTs imposes limitations on the type of data to be collected, and Byon's conclusions must be seen as limited to pragmatic knowledge about speech act formulae rather than ability for use in discourse.

This illustrates an important methodological shortcoming of much traditional interlanguage and cross-cultural pragmatics research. For work in these areas to progress and allow more tenable conclusions to be drawn about learners' ability to deploy pragmatic knowledge in interaction, the focus of future research should be more squarely on collecting interactive data. This does not mean that DCT research no longer has a place in interlanguage pragmatics work, but only that researchers need to face up to the challenges and opportunities inherent in investigating longer stretches of discourse, be they real or role played.

Notes

1. The independent variable is a factor that distinguishes groups of participants or tasks from each other, and is hypothesized to cause the outcome.
2. There is some confusion in the literature with regard to the meaning of P–. It can mean that the interlocutor is in the lower power position, or it can mean that there is no power differential. In this paper, P– means that the interlocutor is in the lower power position, and P = means that there is no power differential. P+ always indicates that the interlocutor is higher in power.

Resources for Further Reading

Blum-Kulka, S., House, J. and Kasper, G. (eds) (1989), *Cross-cultural Pragmatics: Requests and Apologies*. Norwood, NJ: Ablex.
   Though a bit outdated, this is still the 'grandfather' of the cross-cultural pragmatics research literature. The use of DCTs limits this study a bit, and Kasper herself is now critical of some of the categorizations used (Kasper 2006), but the CCSARP manual is still an invaluable and highly influential tool.

Golato, A. (2003), 'Studying compliment responses: A comparison of DCTs and recordings of naturally occurring talk'. *Applied Linguistics*, 2003, 24(1), 90–121.

Golato's paper was extremely influential in showing the limits of the DCT research by contrasting DCT data with authentic real-world data. It illustrates very well how cautious researchers have to be in interpreting data, and how the use of certain research instruments shapes the data we obtain.

Hudson, T., Detmer, E. and Brown, J. D. (1995), *Developing Prototypic Measures of Cross-cultural Pragmatics* (Technical Report #7). Honolulu, HI: University of Hawa'ii, Second Language Teaching and Curriculum Center.

This is a description of the development and validation of a variety of research instruments for assessment purposes. It is useful as an example of how careful and thoughtful development of research tools should be conducted.

Kasper, G. and Rose, K. R. (2002), *Pragmatic Development in a Second Language*. Oxford: Basil Blackwell. Chapter 3: Approaches to developmental pragmatics research.

This is the most recent treatment of research instruments in interlanguage pragmatics research by Kasper and Rose. It is rather theoretical, that is, not a 'how-to' guide, but gives valuable background on what can and cannot be accomplished by using various research tools.

References

Achiba, M. (2002), *Learning to Request in a Second Language: Child Interlanguage Pragmatics*. Clevedon, England: Multilingual Matters.

Al-Ghatani, S. M. and Roever, C. (2009), 'Development of Requests by Saudi Learners of Australian English'. Manuscript submitted for publication.

Bardovi-Harlig, K. and Hartford, B. (1990), 'Congruence in native and nonnative conversations: Status balance in the academic advising session'. *Language Learning*, 40, 467–501.

Bardovi-Harlig, K. and Hartford, B. S. (1993), 'Learning the rules of academic talk: A longitudinal study of pragmatic development'. *Studies in Second Language Acquisition*, 15, 279–304.

Bardovi-Harlig, K. and Hartford, B. S. (1996), 'Input in an institutional setting'. *Studies in Second Language Acquisition*, 18, 171–188.

Bardovi-Harlig, K. and Dörnyei, Z. (1998), 'Do language learners recognize pragmatic violations? Pragmatic vs. grammatical awareness in instructed L2 learning'. *TESOL Quarterly*, 32, 233–259.

Bardovi-Harlig, K. and Griffin, R. (2005), 'L2 pragmatic awareness: Evidence from the ESL classroom'. *System*, 33(3), 401–15.

Barron, A. (2003), *Acquisition in Interlanguage Pragmatics: Learning How to Do Things with Words in a Study Abroad Context*. Amsterdam: John Benjamins.

Biesenbach-Lucas, S. (2007), 'Students writing emails to faculty: An examination of E-politeness among native and non-native speakers of English'. *Language Learning and Technology*, 11(2), 59–81.

Billmyer, K. and Varghese, M. (2000), 'Investigating instrument-based pragmatic variability: Effects of enhancing Discourse Completion Tasks'. *Applied Linguistics*, 21(4), 517–552.

Blum-Kulka, S., House, J. and Kasper, G. (eds) (1989), *Cross-cultural Pragmatics: Requests and Apologies*. Norwood, NJ: Ablex.

Bouton, L. (1988), 'A cross-cultural study of ability to interpret implicatures in English'. *World Englishes*, 17, 183–196.

—(1994), 'Conversational implicature in the second language: Learned slowly when not deliberately taught'. Journal of Pragmatics, 22, 157–167.

—(1999, March), *The Amenability of Implicature to Focused Classroom Instruction*. Paper presented at TESOL 1999, New York, NY.

Brown, P. and Levinson, S. D. (1987), *Politeness: Some Universals in Language Usage*. New York: Cambridge University Press.

Byon, A. S. (2004), 'Sociopragmatic analysis of Korean requests: Pedagogical settings'. *Journal of Pragmatics*, 36(9), 1673–1704.

Cohen, A. D. and Shively, R. L. (2007), 'Acquisition of requests and apologies in Spanish and French: Impact of study abroad and strategy-building intervention'. *The Modern Language Journal*, 91(2), 189–212.

Davis, J. M. (2007), 'Resistance to L2 pragmatics in the Australian ESL context'. *Language Learning*, 57(4), 611–649.

Decapua, A. and Dunham, J. F. (2007), 'The pragmatics of advice giving: Cross-cultural perspectives'. *Intercultural Pragmatics*, 4(3), 319–342.

Eisenstein, M. and Bodman, J. (1993), 'Expressing gratitude in American English', in G. Kasper and S. Blum-Kulka (eds), *Interlanguage Pragmatics*. Oxford: Oxford University Press, pp. 64–81.

Felix-Brasdefer, J. C. (2004), 'Interlanguage refusals: Linguistic politeness and length of residence in the target community'. *Language Learning*, 54(4), 587–653.

—(2007), 'Pragmatic development in the spanish as a FL classroom: A cross-sectional study of learner requests'. *Intercultural Pragmatics*, 4(2), 253–286.

Gass, S. M. and Neu, J. (1996) (eds), *Speech Acts Across Cultures: Challenges to Communication in a Second Language*. Berlin: Mouton de Gruyter.

Goh, I. (2006), 'Design Variation: Opening Prompts in Discourse Completion Tasks'. Unpublished master's thesis, University of Melbourne, Victoria, Australia.

Golato, A. (2003), 'Studying compliment responses: A comparison of DCTs and recordings of naturally occurring talk'. *Applied Linguistics*, 24(1), 90–121.

Grieve, A. (2007, March), The Acquisition of Pragmatic Markers by German Study Abroad Adolescents. Paper presented at the 17th International Conference on Pragmatics and Language Learning, University of Hawai'i at Manoa, Honolulu, Hawai'i.

Hinkel, E. (1997), 'Appropriateness of advice: DCT and multiple choice data'. *Applied Linguistics*, 18, 1–26.

Holtgraves, T. (2007), 'Second language learners and speech act comprehension'. *Language Learning*, 57(4), 595–610.

Houck, N. and Gass, S. M. (1996), 'Non-native refusal: A methodological perspective', in S. M. Gass and J. Neu (eds), *Speech acts across cultures: Challenges to communication in a second language*. Berlin: Mouton de Gruyter, pp. 45–64.

House, J. (1996), 'Developing pragmatic fluency in English as a foreign language: Routines and metapragmatic awareness'. *Studies in Second Language Acquisition*, 18, 225–252.

Hudson, T., Detmer, E. and Brown, J. D. (1995), Developing Prototypic Measures of Cross-cultural Pragmatics (Technical Report #7). Honolulu, HI: University of Hawaii, Second Language Teaching and Curriculum Center.

Hutchby, I. and Woffitt, R. (2008), *Conversation Analysis*. Cambridge: Polity.

Jiang, N. and Nekrasova, T. M. (2007), 'The processing of formulaic sequences by second language speakers'. *The Modern Language Journal*, 91(3), 433–445.

Jung, E. H. (2004), 'Interlanguage Pragmatics: Apology speech acts', in C. L. Moder and A. Martinovic (eds), *Discourse Across Languages and Cultures*. Amsterdam: John Benjamins, pp. 99–116.

Kanagy, R. (1999), 'Interactional routines as a mechanism for L2 acquisition and socialization in an immersion context'. *Journal of Pragmatics*, 31(11), 1467–1492.

Kasper, G. (2006), 'Speech acts in interaction: Towards discursive pragmatics', in K. Bardovi-Harlig, J. C. Felix-Brasdefer and A. S. Omar (eds), *Pragmatics and Language Learning: Vol. 11*. University of Hawai'i at Manoa: National Foreign Language Resource Center, pp. 281–314.

Kasper, G. and Rose, K. R. (2002), *Pragmatic Development in a Second Language*. Oxford: Basil Blackwell.

Johnston, B., Kasper, G. and Ross, S. (1998), 'Effect of rejoinders in production questionnaires'. *Applied Linguistics*, 19(2), 157–182.

Kwon, J. (2004), 'Expressing refusals in Korean and in American English'. *Multilingua*, 23(4), 339–364.

Lorenzo-Dus, N. (2001), 'Compliment responses among British and Spanish university students: A contrastive study'. *Journal of Pragmatics*, 33(1), 107–127.

Matsumura, S. (2001), 'Learning the rules for offering advice: A quantitative approach to second language socialization'. *Language Learning*, 51, 635–679.

—(2003), 'Modelling the relationships among interlanguage pragmatic development, L2 proficiency, and exposure to L2'. *Applied Linguistics*, 24(4), 465–491.

—(2007), 'Exploring the aftereffects of study abroad on interlanguage pragmatic development'. *Intercultural Pragmatics*, 4(2), 167–192.

Meier, A. J. (1998), 'Apologies: What do we know?' *International Journal of Applied Linguistics*, 8, 215–231.

Myles, F., Hooper, J. and Mitchell, R. (1998), 'Rote or rule? Exploring the role of formulaic language in classroom foreign language learning'. *Language Learning*, 48(3), 323–364.

Niezgoda, K. and Röver, C. (2001), 'Pragmatic and grammatical awareness: A function of the learning environment?', in K. R. Rose and G. Kasper (eds), *Pragmatics in Language Teaching*. New York: Cambridge University Press, pp. 63–79.

Porter, P. A. (1986), 'How learners talk to each other: Input and interaction in task-centered discussions' in R. R. Day (ed.), *Talking to Learn: Conversation in Second Language Acquisition*. Rowley, MA: Newbury House, pp. 200–222.

Roever, C. (2000), Rejoinders in Production Questionnaires Revisited. Unpublished manuscript, University of Hawai'i at Manoa.

—(2005), *Testing ESL Pragmatics*. Frankfurt: Peter Lang.

—(2006), 'Validation of a web-based test of ESL pragmalinguistics'. *Language Testing*, 23, 2, 229–256.

—(2007), 'DIF in the assessment of second language pragmatics'. *Language Assessment Quarterly*, 4(2), 165–189.

Sacks, H., Schegloff, E. A. and Jefferson, G. (1974), 'A simplest systematics for the organization of turn-taking for conversation'. *Language*, 50(4), 696–735.

Salsbury, T. and Bardovi-Harlig, K . (2001), '"I know your mean, but I don't think so": Disagreements in L2 English', in L. F. Bouton (ed.), *Pragmatics and Language Learning: Vol. 10*. Urbana-Champaign, IL: Division of English as an International Language, University of Illinois, Urbana-Champaign, pp. 131–151.

Taguchi, N. (2007), 'Chunk learning and the development of spoken discourse in a Japanese as a foreign language classroom'. *Language Teaching Research*, 11(4), 433–457.

—(2008), 'Cognition, language contact, and the development of pragmatic comprehension in a study-abroad context'. *Language Learning*, 58(1), 33–71.

Tran, G. Q. (2006), *The Nature and Conditions of Pragmatic and Discourse Transfer Investigated through Naturalized Role-Play*. Munich, Germany: Lincom Europa.

Trosborg, A. (1995), *Interlanguage Pragmatics: Requests, Complaints, and Apologies*. Berlin: Mouton de Gruyter.

Warga, M. and Scholmberger, U. (2007), 'The acquisition of French apologetic behavior in a study abroad context'. *Intercultural Pragmatics*, 4(2), 221–251.

Wildner-Bassett, M. (1986), 'Teaching and learning "polite noises": Improving pragmatic aspects of advanced adult learners' interlanguage', in G. Kasper (ed.), *Learning, Teaching and Communication in the Foreign Language Classroom*. Aarhus, Denmark: Aarhus University Press, pp. 163–178.

Yu, M. (2004), 'Interlinguistic variation and similarity in second language speech act behavior'. *The Modern Language Journal*, 88(1), 102–119.

18 Researching Discourse

Brian Paltridge and Wei Wang

Chapter Overview

There are now many introductory books on linguistics. These books typically describe the sounds of a language, the ways that words are formed, the meanings of words and the sentence structure of a language. All of these are important in the description of languages. Many of these books, however, do not go beyond this, and do not help us understand why we make particular language choices and what we mean by these choices. This is what discourse analysis aims to do. It can help us explain the relationship between what we say and what we mean in particular spoken and written contexts. It can also give us the tools to look at larger units of texts such as conversational and textual organizational patterns that are typical of particular uses of language, or *genres* (Martin 1984; Swales 1990). Discourse analysis also looks at social and cultural settings of language use to help us understand how it is that people come to make particular choices in their use of language. This chapter will outline some of the ways in which spoken and written discourse may be examined. It will then present a sample study which looks at one particular aspect of discourse, the discourse structure of texts.

Approaches to the Analysis of Discourse

There are a number of ways in which discourse analysis might be carried out. Discourse analysts might, for example, examine paragraph structure, the organization of whole texts, and typical patterns in conversational interactions such as the ways speakers open, close and take turns in a conversation. They might also look at vocabulary patterns across texts, words which link sections of texts together, and the ways items such as *it* and *they* point backward or forward in a text; that is the use of *conjunction* and *reference* items (Halliday and Hasan 1976) in a text. Discourse analysts may also look at the broader social context of language use and how this impacts on what is said and how it is said in a written or spoken text. Discourse analysts also consider how the use of language both presents and constructs certain world views as well as how, through the use of language, we present who we are, or how we want people to see us.

A number of aspects of language use considered under the heading of discourse analysis are also discussed in the area known as *pragmatics* (see Thomas 1995; Roever this volume). Pragmatics is especially interested in the relationship between language and the context. This includes the study of how the interpretation of language depends on knowledge of the world, how speakers use and understand utterances, and how the structure of sentences is influenced by relationships between speakers and hearers. Pragmatics, thus, is interested in what people mean by what they say, rather than what words or phrases might, in their most literal sense, mean by themselves (Yule 1996). Pragmatics is sometimes contrasted with *semantics* which deals with literal or sentence meaning; that is, meaning without reference to users or purpose of communication.

Discourse analysis, then, in the sense we will be considering it here, focuses on:

- linguistic patterns which occur across stretches of spoken and written texts
- knowledge about language beyond the word, clause, phrase and sentence that is needed for successful communication
- what people mean by what they say, and how they work out that understanding
- the relationship between language and the social and cultural contexts in which it is used
- the way in which language constructs different views of the world and different understandings.

Clearly, some of the features of what for some people fall under the term discourse analysis may also be considered in other areas of analysis as well. For example, the notion of turn taking is discussed by Levinson (1983) and

Research Methods in Applied Linguistics

Mey (2001) under the general topic of pragmatics, but is also referred to extensively in the literature on discourse analysis and, in particular, in the area known as *conversation analysis* (Hutchby and Wooffitt 1998; Seedhouse 2005). Equally, some aspects of interest in discourse analysis, such as the study of *speech acts* (Austin 1962; Searle 1969), are sometimes discussed in the area of semantics. This chapter will discuss, under the general term discourse analysis, aspects of language analysis and use which at times are also considered under the area of pragmatics.

Key Areas of Influence in Discourse Analysis

A number of different approaches to the analysis of discourse have had an influence in the area of applied linguistics. There are various ways in which these approaches could be described. One way is in terms of some of the people who have been influential in this area. The section that follows will give an overview of key researchers in the areas of speech act theory, conversation analysis, genre analysis, contrastive rhetoric and critical discourse analysis.

Speech Act Theory

A key person in the area of discourse analysis is the philosopher John Austin whose book *How to do Things with Words* (1962) laid the ground for what has come to be called *speech act theory*. Austin's work was further developed and systematized by the American philosopher John Searle (1969) who studied with Austin at Oxford University. Austin and Searle argued that in the same way that we perform physical acts, such as having a meal or closing a door, we can also perform acts by using language. We can use language, for example, to give orders, to make requests, to give warnings or to give advice. People, thus, 'do things with words' in much the same way as they perform physical actions.

Cross-Cultural Pragmatics

The area of research which investigates the use of speech acts across cultures is commonly referred to as *cross-cultural pragmatics* (Rose and Kasper 2001). Researchers have observed that degrees of social distance and power between speakers are important factors in terms of how a particular speech act might be expressed. This varies, however, across cultures and may interact with other factors such as how much use of the particular speech act imposes on the other person, the age of participants involved in the interaction, the gender of the speaker or hearer and culture-specific hierarchies and roles particular to interaction. An important contribution to cross cultural pragmatics research is the work of Anna Wierzbicka (2003) who argues that differences in the use of language are due to differences in cultural norms and assumptions. In her view, to understand the use of language across cultures 'it is essential to not only know what the conventions of a given society are but also how they are related to cultural values' (Wierzbicka 2003, p. xv).

Conversational Implicature

Another key figure in the area of pragmatics and discourse is the philosopher Paul Grice (1975) whose work on the way people cooperate with each other in conversational interactions has been extremely important. Grice introduced the term *conversational implicature* to describe the process by which we derive meanings from the situation in which language is used; that is, the way we work out what is meant by what someone says. Authors such as Celce-Murcia and Olshtain (2000) and Cutting (2008) have discussed practical implications of this view showing how crucial this notion is to understanding how conversational interactions work and the linguistic choices that people make as they interact with each other.

Politeness and Face

Two further key notions in the area of discourse analysis are *politeness* and *face*. An influential work in this area is Brown and Levinson's (1987) *Politeness: Some Universals in Language Usage*. In their view, politeness is based on the notions of *positive face* and *negative face*. Positive face refers to a person's need to be accepted, or liked, by others, and to be treated as a member of a group knowing that their wants are shared by others. Negative face refers to a person's need to be independent and not imposed on by others. Other important work in this area includes Mills (2003) on gender and politeness and Watts (2003) who presents a view of politeness in terms of politic, or strategic, verbal behaviour. Recent politeness research has also taken up the notion of *communities of practice* (Wenger 1998) in their discussions of politeness; that is, the discourse expectations of the particular community, or group and the local conditions in which the communication is taking place.

Conversation Analysis

There is also the important contribution of people working in the area of *conversation analysis* such as Sacks et al. (1974) who have explored conversational norms and recurring patterns in spoken interactions. Conversation analysts are interested, in particular, in how social worlds are jointly constructed and recognized by speakers as they take part in conversational discourse. Early work in conversation analysis looked mostly at everyday spoken interactions such as chat and casual conversation. This has since been extended, however, to include spoken discourse such as doctor-patient consultations, legal hearings, news interviews, psychiatric interviews, interactions in courtrooms and classrooms, and gender and conversational interactions. For conversation analysts, ordinary conversation is the most basic form of talk and the main way in which people come together, exchange information and maintain social relations. It is, further, from this form of talk that all other talk-in-interaction is derived. A key feature of work in the area of conversation analysis is the tracing of how participants in a conversation 'interpret each others' actions and develop a shared understanding of the progress of the interaction' (Seedhouse 2005, p. 166); that is, how participants understand and respond to each other in their talk and how, from this understanding, sequences of talk develop (Hutchby and Wooffitt 1998). Researchers in the area of *discursive psychology* (Edwards 2005; Wetherell 2007) have extended this work by looking at issues such as discourse and identity (Benwell and Stokoe 2006), discourse and gender (Weatherall 2002; Speer 2005; Edley and Wetherell 2008) and racial discourse (Wetherell and Potter 1992; Stokoe and Edwards 2007).

Genre Analysis

Two linguists who have been especially influential in the area of discourse analysis are Michael Halliday and Ruqaiya Hasan. Halliday's notion of language as a system of choices and his views on the social functions of language (Halliday 1973; Halliday and Hasan 1989) are important in the area of discourse analysis. Their work has been extremely influential in the development of the *Sydney genre school* (Hyon 1996), a group of linguists and language educators who have examined a range of different texts and applied these analyses in various educational settings. Halliday and Hasan's (1976) work on *patterns of cohesion* – that is, the relationship between grammatical and lexical items in texts such as *reference* items, *conjunction* and *ellipsis* – has also made an important contribution to the area of discourse analysis. While the Australian genre work has typically looked at written texts, the observations they have made are equally applicable to spoken texts. Thornbury and Slade (2006), for example, take a genre perspective on the grammar of conversation, as do Eggins and Slade (1997) in their work on the analysis of casual conversation.

Martin (1984, p. 25), from the Sydney genre school, describes genre as 'a staged, goal-oriented, purposeful activity in which speakers engage as members of our culture'. This view draws on Halliday's work and that of the anthropologist Malinowski and, in particular, the view that 'contexts both of situation and of culture [are] important if we are to fully interpret the meaning of a text' (Martin 1984, p. 25). Examples of genres examined in this perspective include service encounters, research reports, academic essays, casual conversations and *micro-genres* (Martin 1997) such as descriptions, reports, recounts, procedures and expositions, described in terms of their discourse, or *generic structures* and genre-specific language features.

English for specific purposes genre studies are based largely on Swales' (1990; 2004) work on the discourse structure and linguistic features of texts. Swales uses the notion of *moves* to describe the discourse structure of texts. These studies have had a strong influence in the teaching of English for Specific Purposes, and especially the teaching of academic writing to second language graduate students. Genre studies in composition studies, and in what is often called the *new rhetoric* (Freedman and Medway 1994), has been influenced in particular by a paper written by the speech communications specialist Carolyn Miller (1984) titled 'Genre as social action' and has been discussed, in particular, in relation to first-year undergraduate writing and professional communication in North American settings (see e.g. Bawarshi 2003; Devitt 2004). Here, discussion is more on social and contextual aspects of genres, rather that the language or discourse structures of texts.

Critical Discourse Analysis

A number of researchers such as Fairclough (1995, 2003), Wodak (Fairclough and Wodak 1997; Wodak and Chilton 2005), van Dijk (2001) and van Leeuwen (2008) have considered the use of language from a particularly critical perspective; that is, how discourse is shaped by relations of power and ideology, and the effects discourse has upon social identities, relations, knowledge and beliefs. This perspective, *critical discourse analysis*, starts with the assumption that language use is always social and that discourse both reflects and constructs the social world. A critical analysis might explore issues such as gender (see Sunderland this volume), ideology, and identity (see Block this volume) and how these are reflected in particular texts. The analysis might commence with an analysis of the use of discourse and move from there to an explanation and interpretation of the discourse. From here, the analysis might proceed to deconstruct and challenge the texts, tracing ideologies and assumptions underlying the use of discourse, and relating these to different views of the world, experiences and beliefs (Clark 1995).

Contrastive Rhetoric

The area of research known as *contrastive rhetoric* (Connor 1996) compares genres in different languages and cultures. Many studies in this area have focused on written genres. Contrastive rhetoric has its origins in the work of Kaplan (1966) who examined different patterns in the academic essays of students from a number of different languages and cultures. Although Kaplan has since revised his strong claim that differences in academic writing are the result of culturally different ways of thinking, many studies have found important differences in the ways in which texts are written in different languages and cultures. Other studies, however, have found important similarities in writing across cultures. Kubota (1992; Kubota and Lehner 2004), for example, argues that just as Japanese expository writing has more than one rhetorical style, so too does English, and that it is misleading to try to reduce rhetorical styles to the one single norm. Contrastive rhetoric has, in more recent years, moved to emphasize the social situation of writing rather than just discourse patterns across cultures. This has lead to the area now known as *intercultural rhetoric* (Connor 2004) where writing is examined in relation to the intellectual history and social structures of different cultures.

In summary, each of these areas of research and others, such as the use of corpus approaches to discourse analysis (Conrad 2002; Baker 2006), multimodal discourse analysis (Kress and van Leeuwen 2001; O'Halloran 2004), other ways of theorizing discourse (Mills 1997; Wetherall et al. 2001; Jorgensen and Phillips 2002) and the use of systemic functional tools for analysis (Hasan et al. 2005, 2007), has given us insights into the organization and interpretation of spoken and written discourse. What each of these views reveals is, in part, a result of the perspective the researchers have taken, and the questions they have asked. There are many ways, then, in which one could, and can approach discourse analysis.

A Sample Study

The rest of this chapter discusses a discourse analysis project that drew on a number of research techniques to answer its set of questions. The study (Wang 2007, 2008a, 2008b) examined newspaper commentaries on the events of September 11 that were published in China and Australia in the months that followed on from these events. This study aimed to explore how the texts were written from a discourse point of view, as well as possible reasons for the ways in which they were written.

Research Perspectives

The study drew on four research perspectives: contrastive rhetoric (Connor 2004), the new rhetoric view of genre (Freedman and Medway 1994), the

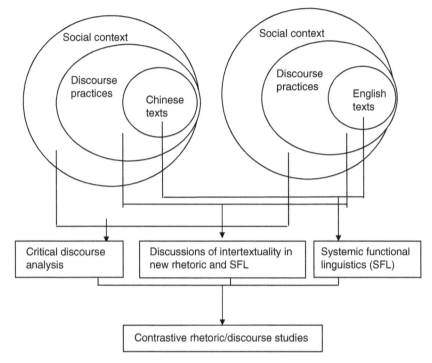

Figure 18.1 Theoretical framework for the study (Wang 2007, p. 60)

systemic functional view of genre (Martin 1997, 2002; Martin and Rose 2007) and critical discourse analysis (Fairclough 1995, 2003; Fairclough and Wodak 1997). The framework presented in Figure 18.1 summarizes the perspectives that were drawn on to examine the two sets of texts and the relationship between the texts and the socio-cultural contexts in which they were produced.

Contrastive rhetoric was the major starting point for the study in that it explored similarities and differences in rhetorical patterns between the two sets of texts under examination. The project drew on the new rhetoric view of genre in its discussion of the texts and the relationship between the texts and the social world that the writers and readers of the texts inhabit. The systemic functional view of genre was drawn on to examine textual features of genres. Work in the area of critical discourse analysis was drawn on to explore the social, political and contextual factors which contribute to the construction of the texts. The study, thus, aimed to describe not only linguistic characteristics of the texts but also considered how the texts had been produced and consumed in the particular socio-cultural context in which they were written.

Data Collection

Twenty-five Chinese newspaper commentaries published during the first three months after September 11, 2001 were selected from newspapers in Mainland China and 25 newspaper commentaries from Australian newspapers were chosen as the focus of the study. The number and sources of the texts are shown in Appendix 1.

An important focus of the data collection was to establish a *'tertium comparationis'* (a comparable platform) (Connor and Moreno 2005, p. 155) for the two sets of newspaper to be examined. Texts were chosen from Chinese and Australian newspapers taking into consideration geographic and demographic features that seemed to be comparable between the two countries. The newspapers were put into three broad groups: National General, National Specialist and State/Provincial (The principal administrative division in China is a province, while in Australia it is a State). Seven Australian and 16 Chinese newspapers were matched to these categories (see Appendix 1).

To establish a balance between the two sets of data, 25 Chinese newspaper commentaries published during the first three months after September 11, 2001 were selected from the Mainland China newspapers and 25 newspaper commentaries were selected from the Australian newspapers. The criteria for selection were first, that the commentaries must be close to the date of September 11, 2001; and second, that the commentaries focus on the issue of terrorism or the terrorist attacks of September 11. The total of 50 commentaries were considered both manageable and of sufficient range for both the linguistic and contextual analysis of the data.

Analysis of the Data

The newspaper commentaries were examined at three levels of analysis, namely, textual, intertextual and contextual. At the textual level, the analysis aimed to identify similarities and differences in terms of micro-genres, generic structures and rhetorical structures (Martin 1997) of the two sets of texts. A *micro-genre* is a section of a text (or whole text) which represents a type of text such as exposition, discussion, or problem-solution etc. *Generic structure* refers to the stages through which a text moves in order to achieve its particular goal (Martin 1984) such as, in the case of newspaper commentaries, headline, subheadline, body and conclusion. *Rhetorical structure* refers to discourse structures which realize rhetorical functions in the texts such as thesis statement, arguments, evidence and conclusions etc. To do this, the texts were first of all assigned to micro-genre categories (White 2005; Martin and Rose 2008) such as exposition,

Table 18.1 Examples of generic structures and rhetorical structures

Genre	Generic structure	Micro-genre	Rhetorical structure
Newspaper commentary	Heading ^ Name of author ^ Introduction ^ Body ^ Conclusion ^	Exposition (Explanation)	Thesis ^ Orientation ^ Thesis Reiteration ^ Facts ^ Reasons ^ Solutions ^ Conclusion
Newspaper commentary	Heading ^ Name of author ^ Introduction ^ Body ^ Conclusion ^	Exposition (Argument)	Thesis ^ Argument 1 ^ Argument 2 ^ Argument 3 ^ Conclusion 1 ^ Argument 1 ^ Argument 2 ^ Argument 3 ^ Conclusion 2

Note: ^ = followed by

argument, explanation, discussion etc. Next the individual texts were analysed to identify their generic and rhetorical structures. Table 18.1 shows the typical structure of two of the key micro-genres found in the study, exposition (explanation) and exposition (argument). The textual analysis of one of the English texts, an exposition (argument), is shown in Appendix 2.

At the intertextual level, the study examined how the writers employed outside sources to construct their texts by drawing on frameworks for analysis from the new rhetoric (Bazerman 2004) and systemic functional linguistics (White 2005). At the contextual level, the study investigated the role of the mass media and opinion discourses in the two socio-cultural contexts and how this lead to different representations of terrorism in the texts (see Wang 2007, 2008a, 2008b for further details on this).

Findings of the Study

The study found that the Chinese writers frequently used explanatory expositions in their newspaper commentaries whereas the Australian writers used argumentative expositions. The study found, further, that the Chinese commentaries focused mainly on explaining terrorism, advocating an anti-terrorist battle under the leadership of the UN and discussing the possible impacts of the events of September 11 on the world economy. The Australian commentaries on terrorism debated the rhetoric of 'us' vs. 'them', and whether a humanitarian approach should be adopted to combat terrorism. These findings are very much in line with the role of the press in China as the public voice of the government and in Australia as a public forum for discussion; that is, the very different roles that newspaper commentaries play in the different social and cultural settings.

The study showed, then, that newspaper commentaries on terrorism in China and Australia are constructed in different ways. It also showed that many of these differences can be traced back to the different socio-cultural settings in which the texts occur. It did this by drawing together textual and contextual views on the texts as a way of aiming to understand not only what the writers do, but also why they do what they do.

Resources for Further Reading

Cameron, D. (2001), 'What is discourse and why analyse it?' Chapter 1. *Working with Spoken Discourse*. London: Sage.
  While the focus of Cameron's book is on spoken discourse, it covers many issues that are of equal relevance to the analysis of written discourse. Cameron's first chapter discusses meanings of the term 'discourse' and goals and purposes in analysing discourse. The later part of this chapter talks about how social reality is discursively constructed as people talk about things using the ways of speaking (or discourses) that they have access to.

Jaworski, A. and Coupland, N. (2006), 'Introduction: Perspectives on discourse analysis', in A. Jaworski and N. Coupland (eds), *The Discourse Reader*. London: Routledge, pp. 1–37.
  Jaworski and Coupland's introduction to their book provides further details on a number of topics that have been presented in this chapter. This includes definitions of the term 'discourse', traditions in the analysis of discourse, speech act theory and pragmatics, conversation analysis, the social constructionist view of discourse analysis and critical discourse analysis. Strengths and limitations of discourse studies are also discussed.

Paltridge, B. (2006), *Discourse Analysis*. London: Continuum.
  This book elaborates on many of the topics touched on in this chapter. There are chapters on discourse and society, discourse and pragmatics, discourse and genre and discourse and conversation analysis. Grammar is considered from a discourse perspective, as are corpus and critical approaches to the analysis of discourse.

Schiffrin, D., Tannen, D. and Hamilton, H. (2001), *The Handbook of Discourse Analysis*. Oxford: Blackwell.
  The Handbook of Discourse Analysis is an extremely comprehensive set of chapters written by leaders in the field on the analysis of spoken and written discourse. Discourse is considered from linguistic, theoretical, social, contextual, cultural and disciplinary points view.

Wray, A. and Bloomer, A. (eds) (2006), *Projects in Linguistics: A Practical Guide Researching Language*, (2nd edition). London: Hodder Arnold/New York: Oxford University Press.
  Wray and Bloomer's book provides advice on how to choose a research topic, how to collect data, how to analyse data and how to write up the results. Many ideas are given for possible research projects and lists of key references are provided for following up on each of the topics discussed.

References

Austin, J. L. (1962), *How to Do Things With Words*. Oxford: Clarendon Press.
Baker, P. (2006), *Using Corpora in Discourse Analysis*. London: Continuum.
Bawarshi, A. (2003), *Genre and the Invention of the Writer*. Logan, UT: Utah State University Press.
Bazerman, C. (2004), Intertextuality: How texts rely on other texts, in C. Bazerman and P. Prior (eds), What Writing Does and How it Does it: An Introduction to Analyzing Texts and Textual Practices. Mahwah, NJ: Lawrence Erlbaum, pp. 83–96.
Benwell, B. and Stokoe, E. (2006), *Discourse and Identity*. Edinburgh: Edinburgh University Press.
Brown, G. and Levinson, S. (1987), *Politeness. Some Universals in Language Usage*. Cambridge: Cambridge University Press.
Celce-Murcia, M. and Olshtain, E. (2000), *Discourse and Context in Language Teaching. A Guide for Language Teachers*. Cambridge: Cambridge University Press.
Clark, R. J. (1995), 'Developing critical reading practices', *Prospect*, 10, 65–80.
Connor, U. (1996), *Contrastive Rhetoric: Cross-cultural Aspects of Second Language Writing*. Cambridge: Cambridge University Press.
—(2004), 'Intercultural rhetoric research: Beyond texts', *Journal of English for Academic Purposes*, 3, 291–304.
Connor, U. and Moreno, A. (2005), 'Tertium comparationis: A vital component in contrastive rhetoric research.', in P. Bruthiaux, D. Atkinson, W. G. Eggington, W. Grabe and V. Ramanathan (eds), *Directions in Applied Linguistics*. Clevedon, England: Multilingual Matters, pp. 153–164.
Conrad, S. (2002), 'Corpus approaches for discourse analysis', *Annual Review of Applied Linguistics*, 22, 75–95.
Cutting, J. (2008), *Pragmatics and Discourse*. Second edition. London: Routledge.
Devitt, A. (2004), *Writing Genres*. Carbondale, IL: Southern Illinois University Press.
Edley, N. and Wetherell, M. (2008), 'Discursive psychology and the study of gender: A contested space', in K. Harrington, L. Litosseliti, H. Saunston and J. Sunderland (eds), *Language and Gender Research Methodologies*. London: Palgrave Macmillan, pp. 119–138.
Edwards, D. (2005), 'Discursive psychology', in K. L. Fitch and R. E. Sanders (eds), *Handbook of Language and Social Interaction*. Mahwah, NJ: Erlbaum, pp. 257–293.
Eggins, S. and Slade, D. (1997), *Analysing Casual Conversation*. London: Cassell. (Republished 2005, London: Equinox Publishers).
Fairclough, N. (1995), *Critical Discourse Analysis*. London: Longman.
—(2003), *Analyzing Discourse: Textual Analysis for Social Research*. London: Routledge.
Fairclough, N. and Wodak, R. (1997), 'Critical discourse analysis: An Overview', in T. A. van Dijk (ed.), *Discourse as Social Interaction*. London: Sage, pp. 67–97.
Freedman, A. and Medway, P. (eds) (1994), *Genre and the New Rhetoric*. London: Taylor and Francis.
Grice, H. P. (1975), 'Logic and conversation', in P. Cole and J. L. Morgan (eds), *Syntax and Semantics 3: Speech Acts*. New York: Academic Press. Reprinted in A. Jaworski and N. Coupland (1999), *The Discourse Reader*. London: Routledge, pp. 76–88.

Halliday, M. A. K. (1973), *Explorations in the Functions of Language*. London: Edward Arnold.

Halliday, M. A. K. and Hasan, R. (1976), *Cohesion in English*. London: Longman.

—(1989), *Language, Context and Text: Aspects of Language in a Social-Semiotic Perspective*. Oxford: Oxford University Press.

Hasan, R., Matthiessen, C. and Webster, J. (eds) (2005), *Continuing Discourse on Language. A Functional Perspective*. Vol 1. London: Equinox.

—(2007), *Continuing Discourse on Language. A Functional Perspective*. Vol 2. London: Equinox.

Hutchby, I. and Wooffitt, R. (1998), *Conversation Analysis: Principles, Practices and Applications*. Cambridge: Polity Press.

Hyon, S. (1996), 'Genre in three traditions: Implications for ESL,' *TESOL Quarterly*, 30, 693–722.

Jorgensen, M. and Phillips, L. (2002), *Discourse Analysis as Theory and Method*. London: Sage.

Kaplan, R. B. (1966), 'Cultural thought patterns in intercultural education', *Language Learning*, 16, 1–20.

Kress, G. and van Leeuwen, T. (2001), *Multimodal Discourse: The Modes and Media of Contemporary Communication*. London: Hodder Arnold.

Kubota, R. (1992), *Contrastive rhetoric of Japanese and English: a critical approach*. Doctoral dissertation, Department of Education, University of Toronto.

Kubota, R. and Lehner, A. (2004), 'Toward critical contrastive rhetoric'. *Journal of Second Language Writing*, 13, 7–27.

Levinson, S. (1983), *Pragmatics*. Cambridge: Cambridge University Press.

Martin, J. R. (1984), 'Language, register and genre', in F. Christie (ed.), *Language Studies: Children's Writing: Reader*. Geelong, Vic: Deakin University Press, pp. 21–29. Reprinted with revisions in A. Burns and C. Coffin (eds) (2001), *Analyzing English in a Global Context*. London: Routledge, pp. 149–166.

—(1997), 'Analysing genre: Functional parameters', in F. Christie and J. R. Martin (eds), *Genre and Institutions: Social Processes in the Workplace and School*. London and New York: Continuum, pp. 3–39.

—(2002), 'Meaning beyond the clause: SFL perspectives', *Annual Review of Applied Linguistics*, 22, 52–74.

Martin, J. R. and Rose, D. (2007), *Working with Discourse: Meaning Beyond the Clause*. Second edition. London: Continuum.

—(2008), *Genre Relations: Mapping Culture*. London: Equinox.

Miller, C. R. (1984), 'Genre as social action', *Quarterly Journal of Speech*, 70, 151–167. Reprinted in A. Freedman and P. Medway (eds) (1994), *Genre and the New Rhetoric*. London: Taylor and Francis, pp. 23–42.

Mills, S. (1997), *Discourse*. London: Routledge.

—(2003), *Gender and Politeness*. Cambridge: Cambridge University Press.

Mey, J. (2001), *Pragmatics: An Introduction* (2nd edn). Oxford: Blackwell.

O'Halloran, K. L. (2004), *Multimodal Discourse Analysis: Systemic-Functional Perspectives*. London: Continuum.

Rose, K. R. and Kasper, G. (2001), *Pragmatics in Language Teaching*. Cambridge: Cambridge University Press.

Sacks, H., Schegloff, E. A. and Jefferson, G. (1974), 'A simplest systematics for the organisation of turn taking for conversation', *Language*, 50, 4. 696–735.

Searle, J. R. (1969), *Speech Acts*. London: Cambridge University Press.

Seedhouse, P. (2005), 'Conversation analysis and language learning', *Language Teaching*, 38, 165–187.

Speer, S. A. (2005), *Gender Talk: Feminism, Discourse and Conversation Analysis*. London: Routledge.

Stokoe, E. and Edwards, D. (2007), '"Black this, black that": Racial insults and reported speech in neighbour complaints and police interrogations'. *Discourse & Society*, 18 (3), 337–372

Swales, J. M. (1990), *Genre Analysis: English in Academic and Research Settings*. Cambridge: Cambridge University Press.

—(2004), *Research Genres: Explorations and Applications*. Cambridge: Cambridge University Press.

Thomas, J. (1995), *Meaning in Interaction. An Introduction to Pragmatics*. London: Longman.

Thornbury, S. and Slade, D. (2006), *Conversation: From Description to Pedagogy*. Cambridge: Cambridge University Press.

van Dijk, T. (2001), 'Critical discourse analysis', in D. Schiffrin, D. Tannen and H. Hamilton (eds), *The Handbook of Discourse Analysis*. Oxford: Blackwell, pp. 352–371.

van Leeuwen, T. (2008), *Discourse and Practice: New Tools for Critical Discourse Analysis*. Oxford: Oxford University Press.

Wang, W. (2007), *Genre across Languages and Cultures: Newspaper Commentaries in China and Australia*. Saarbruecken, Germany: VDM Verlag Dr. Müller.

—(2008a), 'Intertextual aspects of Chinese newspaper commentaries on the events of 9/11', *Discourse Studies*, 10, 361–381.

—(2008b), 'Newspaper commentaries on terrorism in China and Australia: A contrastive genre study', in U. Connor, E. Nagelhout and W. Rozycki (eds), *Contrastive Rhetoric: Reaching to Intercultural Rhetoric*. Amsterdam: Benjamins, pp. 169–191.

Watts, R. (2003), *Politeness*. Cambridge: Cambridge University Press.

Weatherall, A. (2002), *Gender, Language and Discourse*. London: Routledge.

Wetherell, M. (2007), 'A step too far: Discursive psychology, linguistic ethnography and questions of identity', *Journal of Sociolinguistics*, 11, 661–681.

Wetherell, M. and Potter, J. (1992), *Mapping the Language of Racism: Discourse and the Legitimation of Exploitation*. Brighton: Harvester/Wheatsheaf.

Wetherell, M., Taylor, S. and Yates, S. J. (eds) (2001), *Discourse as Data: A Guide for Analysis*. London: Sage.

Wenger, E. (1998), *Communities of Practice: Learning, Meaning and Identity*. Cambridge: Cambridge University Press.

White, P. (2005), Appraisal Website. Retrieved 29/09/08, from http://www.grammatics.com/Appraisal/

Wodak, R. and Chilton, P. (eds), (2005), *A New Agenda in (Critical) Discourse Analysis*. Amsterdam: John Benjamins.

Wierzbicka, A. (2003), *Cross-Cultural Pragmatics: The Semantics of Human Interaction*. Second edition. Berlin: Mouton de Gruyter.
Yule, G. (1996), *Pragmatics*. Oxford: Oxford University Press.

Appendix 1: Newspaper Commentaries Examined in the Study

Chinese Newspapers		No of texts	Australian Newspapers		No of texts
Chinese national general newspapers	People Daily (Overseas edition)	2	Australian national general newspaper	The Australian	10
	People Daily	3			
	Guangmin Daily	1			
	Xinhua Daily Telegraph	2			
	China Youth Daily	1			
	Economic Daily	1			
Chinese national specialist newspapers	International Financial Daily	1	Australian national specialist newspapers	Australian Financial Review	5
	Security Times	2			
	China's Economic Times	1			
	China's Defence Post	1			
Chinese provincial newspapers	Hubei Daily	1	Australian state newspapers	Sydney Morning Herald	2
	Wenhui Daily	2		The Age	2
	Hebei Daily	1		The Courier Mail	2
	Jiefang Daily	2		Herald Sun	2
	Huaxia Times	3		Daily Telegraph	2
	Study Times	1			

Appendix 2: An Example of a Generic Structure and Rhetorical Structure Analysis

Generic structure		Rhetorical structure
Heading	*Base response on justice, not revenge*	Thesis
Subheading	*Terrorists are gangsters and should be treated as such*	
Name of author	Michael O'Connor	
Introduction	If the terrorist attack on the US constitutes a new form of warfare, it calls for new forms of resistance. In particular, any form of military retaliation must be precise and effective. A mere demonstration, especially one that kills innocents, will simply give birth to a new generation of terrorists who will exploit the unavoidable weaknesses of free and open societies.	Argument 1
Body	The decapitation of terrorist networks may not be sufficient. They have shown a hydra-like capacity to grow new organizations with plenty of sponsors. At the core of any campaign must be the ability and determination to deal with the sponsors, especially states whose sponsorship is based on a recognition of the West's conventional military power. Until the source of those attacks and their precise location at a particular time can be identified, any military action will not only be pointless but also counterproductive.	Argument 2
	Demonstrations of military readiness are designed primarily to boost community confidence but, beyond that, have little value. Ships at sea, fighter planes in the air and the mobilization of thousands of reservists cannot replace effective intelligence analysis or airport security.	Argument 3
	The most important work is being done by intelligence and law enforcement agencies. This will identify not only the perpetrators – mostly now dead – but also the guiding genius and his sponsors. The objective must be to gather sufficient evidence to place them before a US criminal court. In effect, terrorism is nothing more than a form of organized crime and its defeat depends upon it being treated as such.	Conclusion 1

	Osama bin Laden has no legitimacy in international law. He has no ideology and no objective other than to commit mass murder. His targets – as with all terrorists – are defenceless and innocent individuals. Bin Laden's claim to some sort of religious justification is supported by no teaching of any legitimate religion, certainly not Islam. If anything, his objective may be to take political control of Saudi Arabia by detaching that country from its de facto alliance with the West.	Argument 1
	Any response that treats terrorist organizations as some sort of pseudo state entitled to make war simply grants them the international status they seek. In fighting this war, the targets of terrorism, which could easily include Australia, must make it plain there are only two sides – the terrorists and their protectors on one hand, and their targets on the other. Any response by the targets can be justified by an appeal to Article 51 of the UN Charter, which protects the right of national or collective self-defence.	Argument 2
	Once the organizers and their locations have been identified, the nation state in which they are located must be required to hand them over, preferably through a proper legal process of extradition. If that state refuses to do so in the face of ample prima facie evidence, it should be treated as a belligerent.	Argument 3
Conclusion	Ultimately, as with any other criminals, terrorists must be left with nowhere to hide from the justice systems of civilization.	Conclusion 2

19 Researching Language Classrooms

Lesley Harbon and Huizhong Shen

Research into what happens in language classrooms is an important area of applied linguistics research. Second language classroom research is in many ways the link between theory and practice (Lightbown 2000). Well-planned and well-designed language classroom research can help us examine our theoretical assumptions as well as what happens in actual practice. There is also a wide range of aspects of language learning and teaching that might be examined in this research. This might include a focus on speaking, listening, reading or writing. It might examine the teaching and learning of grammar and vocabulary, or it might focus on issues in the area of pragmatics, motivation or identity development, to name just a few. Students and/or aspects of the teaching context itself can also become the focus of the classroom research. This chapter outlines current trends in classroom research. It will then discuss classroom observation and narrative inquiry as ways in which what goes on in the classroom might be examined. Finally a sample study is described which employs classroom observation as its key research technique.

Much classroom research has come about because teachers are seeking to solve problems or answer pressing questions about their current teaching practices (Mackay 2006). The teachers themselves may undertake the research, as is the case with action research (see Burns this volume), or they can become the subject studied by a researcher who is not from the teaching context. Classroom research can aim to test a hypothesis, test a theory or even replicate an earlier study. Some researchers explore hunches they have about their own teaching or student learning. Other researchers conduct research where funding has been granted for a specific purpose, so the focus of the research has already been established. Both quantitative (Phakiti this volume) and qualitative (Holliday this volume) methodologies can be employed in second language classroom research.

Often classroom research requires the researcher to work closely with the language teacher. Arrangements need to be made about observation times and places. The researcher's presence should not impose on what is happening in the classroom and needs to be considered in any arrangements for data collection that will take place. Classroom teacher/researcher collaborations can be extremely fruitful (Lightbown 2000) and teachers will trust the researcher if all purposes and processes are made explicit to them through the period of the research.

Important Considerations in Second Language Classroom Research

A glance through the contents pages of any of the current general research textbooks would see that there are often common stages in undertaking classroom research. Important reference manuals for this type of research include Denzin and Lincoln's (2005) *Handbook of Qualitative Research*, Cohen et al.'s (2007) *Research Methods in Education* and Lodico et al.'s (2006) *Methods in Educational Research*. Books that focus on classroom-based research, in particular, include Allwright and Bailey's (1989) *Focus on the Language Classroom*, Nunan's (1989) *Understanding Language Classrooms* and Wallace's (1998) *Action Research for Language Teachers*.

In the early stages of the project researchers need to consider their own beliefs and understandings of the topic. Researchers need to review the literature (primary sources especially) not only about the research problem itself, but also the research available on the method chosen for the project. The researcher then decides on the design, method, sampling and population, examines data collection instrumentation (and adapts or devises new versions), conducts the research and then analyses the data, reducing the data to smaller chunks of information, in order to link, compare and make meaningful findings from their study.

Researchers are obliged to conduct classroom research in an ethical manner. Much research is conducted under the auspices of higher education institutions and such institutions have committees especially set up for examining ethical procedures of the research undertaken in its name. Researchers need to follow research approval guidelines for ethical purposes. Research conducted with permissions and checks on ethical processes should guarantee anonymity and safety to participants.

From the time the research project is first conceived, right through to the point where the results are published, the researcher needs to aim for a positive, professional relationship with their participants. The researcher should never forget the human side of conducting classroom research. In the midst of all of classroom language learning and teaching, people are involved. The researcher, thus, must seek to develop good working relationships with the people involved in their project.

Research Techniques and Methods

Researchers can utilize a range of research techniques to gather data for language classroom research. For instance, introspective techniques such as think-aloud protocols and retrospective techniques such as interviews carried out after a classroom event has taken place have made an important contribution to classroom-based research. These techniques can be used to ask teachers and students to explain their thinking, beliefs, and perceptions of what goes on in the language-learning classroom (Mackay 2006). Researchers can also use diaries as a source of data. Studies of this kind, in which teachers or students write what they think about their teaching and learning, are another useful way of carrying out classroom-based research. Also through the analysis of interactional patterns, researchers can examine teacher-student discourse in order to uncover patterns that may, in some way, impact on language teaching and learning (Duff 2007). Two further research strategies, classroom observation and narrative inquiry, are discussed below as ways of conducting language classroom research.

Classroom Observation

Classroom observation is defined by Gebhard and Oprandy (1999, p. 35) as 'non-judgmental description of classroom events that can be analyzed and given interpretation'. The researcher will choose to take observations of either the whole language classroom or aspects of it, or activities within it. Observations may be taken of the teacher, a student or students. With a teacher focus, these aspects may range from the amount of teacher use of the target language, teacher use of materials, their handling of critical incidents, through to the type of praise given by teachers to student responses. With a student focus, the exploration can be anything from student questioning, to student eye contact with the teacher, to student participation in group work and more. As well, there are a multitude of aspects of the classroom context which can be examined, for example, gender and its impact on classroom processes, or issues of race. The number of research questions possible for language classrooms, thus, is considerable.

Researchers are also able to include *participant observation* or *non-participant observation* in their research design. In participant observation, researchers take part in the classroom processes they are investigating, taking notes on what they observe. In non-participant observation the researchers are present, but do not participate in the classroom processes. Researchers are therefore free to take notes and work with any devices they need to help them record what is happening in the classroom.

The terms *emic* and *etic* are very often mentioned in relation to classroom research due to an adopted role of the researcher in classroom observations. Researchers who try to get an inside view of what is happening in the classroom take an emic perspective in their research, whereas researchers who take more of an outside view on the event take an etic view of this (see Starfield this volume).

The researcher can carry out observations of the language classrooms very simply. By that we mean that all a researcher needs is a pen and paper to be able to take field notes about what they observe at a certain point in time. Field notes can provide detailed descriptions of people, places, activities and events, and are taken in conventional notation (as fast as the researcher can write or type). Sometimes, however, there are more complex and structured approaches to observing language classrooms that might be used. Over the years various observation schedules and schemes have been devised to take data from language classrooms.

Observational work came to the fore with the first well-documented scheme, known as the Flanders Interaction Analysis Category observation system (Flanders 1970) that allowed researchers to examine and interpret observable classroom verbal behaviours such as teacher praise, questioning, lecturing, giving directions and student talk or silence. The language teacher's classroom talk was divided into discrete categories which allowed the observing researcher to note down occurrences of the different categories of talk measured at fixed intervals and to assign numerical values to each of these. There was also describing, tracking of students' verbal behaviours in set of observational categories. Flanders' work led to many classroom studies applying using this system, or adaptations of it, to their own classroom research (see e.g., Harbon and Horton-Stephens 1997; Harbon 2001).

Critics of such structured systems claim, among other things, that the communicative language classroom is far too complex for all notions to be labelled and captured in this manner, and that the essential communicative nature of the language classroom is lost. In response to those criticisms, more sophisticated observation schedules such as the COLT (Communicative Orientation of Language Teaching) scheme have been designed (Allen et al. 1984) and implemented according to a detailed coding manual (Spada and Fröhlich 1995). The Spada and Fröhlich manual (1995) has allowed users to capture more of the communicative aspects of the classroom than did the earlier Flanders' (1970) scheme. The COLT scheme is one, however, that requires the user to be trained in its methods to be true to the scheme's intentions.

Whichever strategies and techniques are chosen for classroom observation research, it is important that the researcher has a tightly structured and systematic data gathering instrumentation. It is important that the instrument could be used by another researcher in a replication study, and the same types of findings emerge.

Narrative Inquiry

Early observational classroom studies quantified teacher-student interaction (Duff 2007). In the past 20 years, however, scholars have recognized that classrooms can be more fully understood from the views of participants. Narrative inquiry has come to the fore as one of the ways that second language classroom practices and processes can be explored and understood in this way. As teachers' personal and professional narratives embody their knowledge, values and understandings of the classroom, narrative inquiry is increasingly common in second language classroom research. Narrative inquiry allows researchers to investigate educational practices and explore different phenomena through the teachers' or their students' personal life stories (Zhao and Poulson 2006).

There are no specific steps for conducting narrative inquiry, however the end point must be the formulation of narratives. Zhao and Poulson (2006) describe biographical narrative inquiry and their suggested strategy to elicit teacher narratives. First they suggest undertaking an initial interview, then require their informants to narrate their personal and professional timelines and career paths, such as might be found in an oral history. After recording and transcribing this material, the accuracy of transcription is established by presenting informants with hard copies of the data to read and check.

A narrative analysis then follows. The researcher places together the larger narrative accounts which have been gathered during the initial interview phase. These may be accounts of classroom phenomena, actions, moments, metaphors and people. The accounts are then synthesized or condensed to create focused episodes or stories. They are matched with, and give further insight into the biographical data gathered earlier. What is key with narrative inquiry is that metaphors are identified and stories are constructed to produce narrative episodes.

The stories of three teachers in Golombek and Johnson's (2004) narrative inquiry study are an example of this. The reader of the research report meets the three teachers, Jenn, Michael and Lynne and their teacher-authored narratives as they make links between their teaching and their students' learning. Jenn's narrative of her practice is told through her story depicted as one of 'forgiveness and power in the classroom'. Michael's teacher narrative is told through the story of 'giving children quiet space'. Lynne's teacher narrative is told through the story of her 'letting . . . students read'. According to Golombek and Johnson (2004), the strength in such a narrative inquiry is how they are able to show, through teachers' own voices, how teachers come to know about their work, as well as what they come to know.

This type of research, then, allows 'fuller, more textured, humanized, and grounded accounts of the experiences of teachers and learners in contemporary classrooms' (Duff 2007, p. 983) than might be obtained with other research methods which take a more distanced view of what is happening in the language learning classroom.

Validity and Reliability in Classroom-Based Research

It is important for researchers in language classrooms to consider the validity and reliability of any data collection instruments they employ. A simple set of questions can provide useful assistance to guide the researcher from the conceptualization stage right through to the final reporting. Such questions may be about whether the instruments:

- provide the data which the researcher intended to gather
- capture all that is required about the people, classroom context, interactions and activities that are being examined, and
- were familiar enough to participants to cause as little disruption to the regular processes of the classroom as possible.

With observation instruments, the researcher must ensure that all those who will use the instruments are thoroughly trained and given sufficient opportunity to gain experience in its use in a number of situations, or pilot studies, prior to the main study. The same goes for the interpretation of observations. It is useful to work with other researchers in this so as to avoid the misinterpretation of events.

Problems Associated with Researching Language Classrooms

Researchers need to consider the problems they might encounter in undertaking classroom research. Both in observational research and in narrative inquiry there are a number of limitations that need to be acknowledged. With classroom observation, the data collected really just portrays snapshots of limited periods of time. The conclusions drawn are thus tentative and at best can be taken as indicative rather than conclusive. Other problems with gathering classroom observation data are concerned with issues of consistency in the data gathering. The researcher must ensure the research questions are tightly linked to the data collection and analysis so that the research can truly be considered to be a reflection of what it aims to research. The researcher's tight control of the relatedness of research questions, method, analysis and interpretation underpin the strength of the validity and reliability of the research findings.

The phenomenon of a researcher observing classrooms brings in the issue of having an outside observer, or possibly a participant observer taking part in classroom activities. Cameras pointing at the teacher or students, audio-recording devices placed near classroom members, all add to creating the impression that the classroom is 'on display'. The fear is that data collected if participants are 'playing to the camera' may not be as real a picture as possible. The researcher thus needs to ensure that the participants do not act or behave in a way that will impact on the researcher's attempt to obtain a 'real' or 'natural' view of the classroom processes under interrogation.

A Sample Study

The sample study chosen here as an example of second language classroom research is the paper, 'Where is the technology-induced pedagogy? Snapshots from two multimedia EFL classrooms' reported in the *British Journal of Educational Technology* (Zhong and Shen 2002). The research primarily employed classroom observation focusing on three aspects of the teachers' language pedagogy: the approach of the teacher towards teaching, the design of the course taught and procedures chosen for language teaching and learning in two multimedia English as a Foreign Language (EFL) classrooms.

The paper reports on a study set in a school in China where the language curriculum was becoming increasingly oriented towards and linked to Information Communication Technologies (ICT). The study was conducted in two ICT-supported EFL classrooms. With a school ICT integration orientation, there was an assumption that there would be technology-induced pedagogical changes in the EFL classroom. The researchers set out to test the hypothesis that 'there is no technology-induced pedagogy', which is implied in the title of the research paper: 'Where is the technology pedagogy?' The subtitle: 'Snapshots from two multimedia EFL classrooms' defines the nature and scope of the study. The study was a classroom-based project that used observation as its key research strategy.

After defining the study, three research questions were framed which were closely related to the research purpose and issues under examination. The research questions were: (1) What pedagogical models do teachers use in the multimedia classroom? (2) How does the multimedia classroom differ from the pre-multimedia classroom in classroom interaction? (3) What is the role of the teacher and the student in the technology-enhanced learning environment?

In the early sections of the paper, the researchers provide a simple outline of the key notions they found in the literature review which informed their decisions to undertake the project as they did. They note other studies which examined similar issues and the conclusions that had been reached in those studies.

Classroom observation was used as a key research strategy. The collection of the data, however, went beyond one single method. Based on the understanding that qualitative language classroom research is holistic in nature, the researchers saw no reason why research into the language classroom could not include elements of other research methods. The researchers examined teachers' detailed lesson plans as well as the courseware they had designed as an added way of collecting and validating the data gathered from in-class observation and video-taping. This allowed the researchers to cross-check the findings which contributed to establishing a validity within the research.

Video-recording of the classroom processes was effective in that it captured precisely what was happening in the multimedia language classrooms in teaching and learning, the context in which learning was taking place as well as many of the less-observable aspects of the classroom dynamics such as participants' general demeanours and other non-verbal actions in the process of classroom interaction.

Much of the data gathered from these instruments, however, was not used in this study. This is common practice, especially when researchers undertake a study with a very clear purpose in mind such as writing a paper for a specific academic journal. In this study the researchers examined and analysed only the most salient data which enabled them to provide an account or interpretations of what they believed to be the realities of instructional practices and processes in the two Chinese English language classrooms.

The qualitative exploration of the instructional procedures aimed to capture the classroom culture in an holistic way. However the researchers claimed to be aware that they may not have observed everything, as what they observed was only the tangible part of the classroom processes and interactions. As non-participant classroom researchers, they were only exposed to what was occurring around them in the classroom at one point in time. The researchers

did not claim to be inside the thinking of the teachers and students concerning the research focus.

The less-easily-observable elements of a second language classroom like this could, nevertheless, be reconstructed utilizing other research methods such as narrative inquiry, discussed earlier in this chapter. By interviewing the participants and inviting them to talk about their life histories, particularly critical incidents that happened in different points in time in their life, linking to images and metaphors of classroom incidents, the researchers may have been able to better understand the hidden factors such as traditional Chinese cultural and educational assumptions and practices, which may have contributed to who the participants are and what they believe and do in the classroom.

When designing a qualitative research into a language classroom, it is crucial to take into consideration the physical context in which the research is conducted. It often helps to establish a profile of the research site, including a brief description of the institution, its vision and expectations, the detail of the sample, specific techniques for ensuring a non-obtrusive approach to the classroom, research constraints and ethical considerations. These are included in detail on pages 40 to 43 in the published study (Zhong and Shen 2002).

The research questions were addressed by examination of the videotaped observations and examination of teachers' lesson plans. The focus of the observation was on the teacher and aspects of the context of teaching and learning in the two multimedia language classrooms. It was anticipated that this could be best addressed by observing how the teachers taught. A comparative study of the approaches the teachers employed, as well as the materials and tasks they designed for classroom interaction in the two multimedia EFL classrooms may provide empirical evidence to show how a multimedia English class differs (or not) from a traditional language class through a qualitative analysis of the learning events and instructional sequence recorded during classroom observation.

In the sample study, the researchers chose two schools, a government school and a private school in China. The government school was a selective school with good computer networks and an innovative language curriculum. The private school was well resourced and keen to integrate ICT into the teaching and learning at the school. This was followed up with a description of the classes to be observed as well as the teachers and the materials they would use for teaching in the two multimedia EFL classes. Pseudonyms were used for the two institutions and the teachers involved in the research project to protect their privacy.

Prior to the commencement of the actual research, permission was obtained in which the nature, scope and involvement of the school and participants were clearly outlined. The schools and the participants were also made aware of, and agreed to, the procedures of data collecting, validating and reporting.

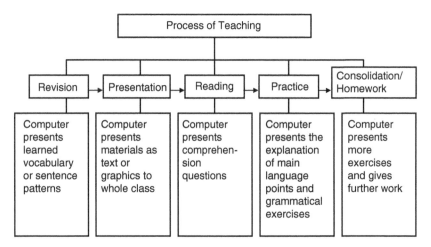

Figure 19.1 Structure of two lessons and the use of computers (Zhong and Shen 2002, p. 41)

As discussed above, data collection for this study involved classroom observation, video recording and examination of teachers' lesson plans. Once data were collected from the classes they were then analysed. The researchers also cross-checked the data from classroom observations against the teachers' lesson plans to identify the structure of the lessons. The researchers found that the two multimedia lessons were sequenced in a similar way, consisting of five phases: *revision, presentation, reading, practice* and *consolidation/homework*. The basic structure of the two lessons is shown in Figure 19.1.

Figure 19.1 is a graphic representation of the lesson construction showing the various phases and their relationships in the classroom instruction. The figure shows how the researchers reduced the whole gamut of classroom practices to meaningful data. The analysis of the events and tasks for different phases highlighted the role of the teacher and the students in the classroom as well as the function of the computer in each of the five phases. The computer was used in class not as a medium for interactive learning but an electronic tool for the teacher to present lesson materials in a teacher-led manner.

In the qualitative analysis, the researchers also examined in detail a range of lesson elements. It was found that new technologies were used as accessories and classroom procedures, and were predominantly teacher-driven. A linear sequence tended to be followed with a focus largely on language forms. The use of computers into the language class did not bring about any pedagogical changes. Teachers, rather used their traditional method of language teaching in the multimedia classroom, there was very little difference between the traditional English classroom and the multimedia classroom, and teachers retained a dominant role in knowledge transmission with students still on the receptive end of the continuum, something that neither of the researchers had anticipated.

Resources for Further Reading

Duff, P. A. (2007), Qualitative approaches to classroom research with English language learners, in J. Cummins and C. Davison (eds), *International Handbook of English Language Teaching*. New York, NY: Springer, pp. 973–986.

Duff's chapter in this handbook is an all-important read in any preparation to undertake language classroom research. As well as outlining the features of qualitative classroom research, she considers some properties of qualitative research, paradigm debates, the role of triangulation, emic perspectives, collection methods in qualitative research, combining macro-level and micro-level ethical issues, and criteria for evaluating qualitative research.

Gebhard, J. G. and Oprandy, R. (1999), *Language Teaching Awareness: A Guide to Exploring Beliefs and Practices*. Cambridge, UK: Cambridge University Press. Chapter 3 'Seeing teaching differently through observation'.

Chapter 3 in Gebhard's volume describes in detail the way teachers can collect and analyse descriptions of teaching, as non-participant observer and participant observer. There are tasks for the reader which allow fuller engagement with the subject of the text.

Holliday, A. R. (2007), *Doing and Writing Qualitative Research* (2nd edn). London: Sage.

Holliday's volume is an easy-to-read text that deals with various aspects of qualitative research, from the basics of starting out, deciding on the question and project, right through to data collection strategies, and writing up findings, much of which is relevant to classroom research.

References

Allen, J. P. B., Fröhlich, M. and Spada, N. (1984), 'The communicative orientation of second language teaching: An observation scheme', in J. Handscombe, R. A. Orem and B. P. Taylor (eds), *On TESOL '83: The Question of Control*. Washington, DC: TESOL, pp. 231–252.

Allwright, D. and Bailey, K. M. (1989), *Focus on the Language Classroom*. Cambridge: Cambridge University Press.

Cohen, L., Manion, L. and Morrison, K. (2007), *Research Methods in Education* (6th edn). New York: Routledge.

Denzin, N. and Lincoln, Y. (eds) (2005), *Handbook of Qualitative Research* (3rd edn). Thousand Oaks, CA: Sage.

Duff, P. A. (2007), 'Qualitative approaches to classroom research with English language learners', in J. Cummins and C. Davison (eds), *International Handbook of English Language Teaching*. New York, NY: Springer, pp. 973–986.

Flanders, N. A. (1970), *Analyzing Teacher Behaviour*. Reading, MA: Addison-Wesley.

Gebhard, J. G. and Oprandy, R. (1999), *Language Teaching Awareness: A Guide to Exploring Beliefs and Practices*. Cambridge, UK: Cambridge University Press.

Golombek, P. R. and Johnson, K. E. (2004), 'Narrative inquiry as a meditational space: Examining emotional and cognitive dissonance in second-language teachers' development.' *Teachers and Teaching: Theory and Practice*, 10(3), 307–327).

Harbon, L. (2001), 'Preparing for a future of increased global awareness: Teacher research tracking a "humanistic" implementation of curriculum policy.' *Australian Association for Research in Education (AARE) Annual Conference Proceedings*, University of Sydney, Sydney December. Paper har00202. Available online at http://www.aare.edu.au/index.htm

Harbon, L. and Horton-Stephens, P. (1997), 'It's what you do and the way you do it: The primary LOTE teacher in the classroom', in P. Voss (ed.), *Conference Proceedings of the AFMLTA 11th National Languages Conference*. Hobart: AFMLTA, pp 145–158.

Holliday, A. (2007), *Doing and Writing Qualitative Research* (2nd edn). London: Sage.

Lightbown, P. M. (2000), 'Anniversary article. Classroom SLA research and second language teaching.' *Applied Linguistics*, 21(4), 431–462.

Lodico, M. G., Spaulding, D. T. and Voegtle, K. H. (2006), *Methods in Educational Research: From Theory to Practice*. San Francisco, CA: John Wiley & Sons.

Mackay, S. L. (2006), *Researching Second Language Classrooms*. Mahwah, NJ: Lawrence Erlbaum Associates.

Nunan, D. (1989), *Understanding Language Classrooms*. New York: Prentice Hall.

Spada, N. and Fröhlich, M. (1995), *COLT Observation Scheme. Communicative Orientation of Language Teaching Observation Scheme: Coding Conventions and Applications*. Sydney, Australia: National Centre for English Language Teaching and Research, Macquarie University.

Wallace, M. J. (1998), *Action Research for Language Teachers*. Cambridge, UK: Cambridge University Press.

Zhao, H. Q. and Poulson, L. (2006), 'A biographical narrative inquiry into teachers' knowledge: An intergenerational approach'. *Asia Pacific Education Review*, 7(2), 123–132.

Zhong, Y. X. and Shen, H. (2002), 'Where is the technology-induced pedagogy? Snapshots from two multimedia EFL classrooms.' *British Journal of Educational Technology*, 33(1), 39–52.

20 Researching Language Testing and Assessment

John Read

Language testing, as a field of study in its own right, is conventionally considered to have been established around 1961, with the appearance of the first book on the subject (Lado 1961). Obviously tests and examinations were being administered to second language learners long before this seminal publication, as Spolsky (1995) has documented in his comprehensive history of the area. What Lado did was to provide a systematic account of language testing as a sub-discipline within applied linguistics, rather than merely part of the normal work of language teachers and educators. Although the book was published in the United Kingdom, it drew on two distinctively American influences of the time: structuralist linguistics and psychometrics. Lado's book did not lack insights gained from the author's extensive experience as a language teacher, but it introduced a 'scientific' approach to the design and evaluation of tests that came to dominate language testing research for the next thirty years or more. The focus on objectively scored test items, reliability of measurement and ever more complex statistical procedures has meant that language testing has been commonly perceived as an esoteric field with little appeal for most language teachers whose academic background is in the arts and humanities.

However, both the perception and the reality have been changing in recent years, in ways that are described below.

Testing and Assessment

The dominance of the psychometric paradigm has been increasingly challenged, particularly by those who are primarily concerned with the progress and achievement of learners in the classroom. Thus, the British educationalist Caroline Gipps (1994) delineates an alternative framework which she calls educational assessment. Rather than ranking students and schools by means of standardized tests and examinations, this alternative approach seeks to monitor how well learners are working towards their learning objectives and to provide useful feedback on the process, using methods such as project work and take-home assignments; the compiling of portfolios, journals and diaries by learners; self-assessment and peer assessment; conferencing between teacher and learners; and the systematic monitoring of regular learning activities. The contrast in the two paradigms has been explored in language education by authors such as Teasdale and Leung (2000) and Rea-Dickins and Gardner (2000).

Within the paradigm of educational assessment, there is a growing body of classroom-based research to investigate the beliefs and practices of teachers in the area of language assessment, using predominantly qualitative methods of enquiry: observation, recording, interviews and stimulated recall. A good starting point is to read the articles in a special issue of *Language Testing* (Rea-Dickins 2004).

Another recent trend has been, not to set up testing and assessment in opposition to each other, but to adopt 'assessment' as the general term for the process of designing and administering procedures to evaluate what language learners have achieved in terms of knowledge of, and ability in, the target language. Testing then becomes one very important form of assessment, particularly when large numbers of learners need to be assessed for high-stakes purposes such as university admission, employment or immigration. Brown and Hudson (1998) argue that we need to look broadly at 'alternatives in assessment', ranging from true-false and multiple-choice test items through to portfolios, selecting the most appropriate procedures according to the purpose of the assessment and the educational context. An example of this broader usage can be found in the title of the Cambridge Language Assessment Series, which is a comprehensive set of ten volumes published between 2000 and 2006. If the books had been published a decade or two earlier, it would almost certainly have been a language testing series. Similarly, a new journal first published in 2004 was named *Language Assessment Quarterly*, partly to differentiate it from the established journal *Language Testing*, but also to reflect the contemporary use of assessment as the cover term.

Nevertheless, neither of the distinctions outlined in the two preceding paragraphs is consistently maintained in the literature. There is a strong tendency for the two terms language testing and language assessment to be used interchangeably and, although the primary focus in this chapter is on formal tests and examinations, the general principles apply to other forms of assessment as well. Thus, both terms are used in the title of the chapter.

Test Validity

The central preoccupation of research in language testing (and assessment, for that matter) is with the concept of validity. From taking an introductory course or reading a textbook, many people are familiar with the conventional formulation that a test is valid to the extent that it tests what it is supposed to test, plus the idea that there are several so-called types of validity: face, content, concurrent, predictive, construct and maybe one or two others. This was always a somewhat simplistic account of what is involved in validation, but our understanding of test validity has been transformed over the past 20 years as language testers have become familiar with developments in validity theory in the general field of educational measurement, prompted by the work of two major scholars, Lee Cronbach (1989) and Samuel Messick (1989).

In the theoretical framework developed by Cronbach and Messick, construct validity has come to be the overarching concept. It is beyond the scope of this chapter to give a full account of the current theory of test validity (see Bachman 1990, Chapter 7; McNamara and Roever 2006, Chapter 2), but some key ideas can be summarized here:

- It is important to define carefully the construct underlying the test, that is, what specific language knowledge, skills or abilities are to be measured.
- Validity is not an inherent property of a test (as in the commonly seen statement 'This is a reliable and valid test'), but is a function of the way in which the results can be meaningfully interpreted when the test is administered to a specified population of test-takers.
- In order to justify their intended interpretations of the results, test developers need to build an argument for the validity of their test, drawing on both theoretical reasoning and various kinds of empirical evidence obtained from trying out the test with actual test-takers.

The need for construct validation of tests can be seen as generating research at two levels. The first, which represents perhaps the purest form of investigation in the field, involves the broad construct that is the basis for test performance, particularly in general language proficiency tests. This construct has been given various labels and conceptual representations over the years: pragmatic expectancy grammar (Oller 1979), communicative competence (Canale and Swain 1980; Canale 1983) and communicative language ability (Bachman 1990). Research at this level has been concerned with the question of whether language ability is divisible into components and, if so, what those components are. Is it meaningful to follow the common practice of assessing each of the four skills separately? To what extent should 'non-linguistic' aspects be taken into account in assessing speaking or writing ability? Recent developments have focused on the nature of performance in an oral interaction task such as an interview, role play or group discussion task (e.g., Chalhoub-Deville 2003; Bachman 2007). If the language that the test-takers produce is co-constructed through interacting with each other, what is the conceptual basis for rating each person's individual contribution?

The other level of construct validity relates to particular tests from a more practical perspective. The developers of a test need to gather various kinds of evidence to support their claims as to the meaningfulness of the results – and this can be seen as a major area of research activity in the field. Messick (1996) proposed that there are six main aspects of construct validation:

- Evidence that the test tasks are relevant to, and representative of, the domain of content to be assessed. For example, does a grammar test for high school students contain a good sample of the grammatical structures and skills specified in the school curriculum?
- Evidence that, when they respond to the test tasks, the test-takers engage in cognitive processes that are predicted by a theory of task performance. For example, in a reading comprehension test, do learners actually apply higher-order reading skills in order to answer test items that target global understanding of the text?
- Evidence that the scoring criteria for a test are consistent with the way that the test construct is defined. For example, in an academic writing task, should the quality of the content be a scoring criterion, and what weight (if any) should be given to features such as spelling, punctuation and formatting?
- Evidence that the test results can be generalized, both in the sense that they are reliable and that they apply beyond the specific tasks in the test. For example if an academic listening test includes a mini-lecture and a simulated tutorial discussion, can we infer from the results how well the test-takers can comprehend a seminar presentation or an individual consultation with a lecturer?
- Evidence that the test scores are consistent with external measures of the construct. For example, to what extent do the scores of health

professionals on an oral proficiency test relate to ratings of their ability to communicate effectively with patients in a clinical setting?

- Evidence that the test results are being used appropriately and fairly, and not to the detriment of the test-takers. For example, if applicants for citizenship are required to pass a language test, has a suitable test been adopted for the purpose and does it assess their proficiency without bias against migrants from particular countries or language backgrounds?

This last area, which Messick called the consequential aspect, has become a major focus of discussion in testing. Given that tests are often used to make significant decisions about those who take them, it is important that such decision-making should be soundly based and not tainted by factors such as political expediency. Of particular concern in the modern world is the potential and actual misuse of tests by governments in dealing with refugees, asylum seekers and migrants applying for residence in the host country, as well as the use of assessment procedures to promote standards and accountability in national education systems (see McNamara and Roever 2006, Chapters 6 and 7). Thus, Messick somewhat controversially extended the scope of validation beyond the technical quality of the test instrument to a consideration of the impact of the test in operational use. This raises ethical issues for language testers involved in developing tests which may serve dubious political or educational purposes. In response, the International Language Testing Association has adopted a Code of Ethics and Guidelines for Good Testing Practice (both accessible at www.iltaonline.com), and both major journals in the field have published special issues on ethical concerns (Davies 1997, 2004).

In terms of research on the consequential aspect, what has received most attention is the phenomenon of washback: the influence that major tests and exams exert on teaching and learning. Traditionally, washback has been seen in negative terms as encouraging students and their teachers to concentrate narrowly on intensive practice of test tasks at the cost of neglecting other important learning objectives. However, efforts have also been made to harness the washback effect in a positive way by introducing innovations into an exam, such as more communicative tasks, in order to modernize language teaching methods in schools. Inspired by a seminal article by Alderson and Wall (1993), numerous researchers have set out to investigate washback in a variety of national contexts, using classroom observation, teacher and student interviews, textbook analysis and other means. A definitive collection of articles on the topic can be found in Cheng et al. (2004).

Typical Stages in Language Testing Research

Research in language testing has become so diverse that it is difficult to identify any common set of steps that are taken in individual projects. However, what underlies research studies in the field is the process of developing a test, which is conventionally seen as comprising a series of stages following a broad linear sequence but also involving some cyclical processes.

The stages of test development are outlined in most introductory textbooks (see e.g., Alderson et al. 1995; Hughes 2003). A more formal account, which has been influential in the field, is presented by Bachman and Palmer (1996). They divide the development process into three broad stages:

Design. At this first stage it is necessary to clarify the purpose of the test and to define what it is supposed to be measuring in the form of at least one theoretical construct, which might be conversational proficiency in Spanish or academic writing ability in English. The developer should also describe the characteristics of the intended test-takers and the relevant domain of content for the test. The domain is mostly commonly specified in terms of typical language use tasks but it can also be delineated as aspects of language knowledge (grammar, vocabulary, phonology, discourse features). At this initial stage, especially when a large-scale testing project is being undertaken, the design statement should spell out the resources required, in the form of personnel, funding, materials, equipment and so on.

Operationalization. The second stage requires a detailed specification of the structure of the test and the various components within it. Tests are typically made up of more than one part, each consisting of a number of items or tasks. All of these components should be described in terms of their key features: what kind of input material the test-takers are presented with, how they record their responses and how those responses are scored. The specifications should include information about how the test is to be administered, the timing of the various parts and the instructions to be given to the test-takers. Explicit description of all these characteristics is desirable for any kind of test, but it is essential in the case of larger-scale projects when multiple forms of the test need to be produced by a whole team of item writers and when the test is to be administered at multiple sites.

Administration. The first two stages should logically precede the third one, which involves giving the test to a group of learners and analysing the results. Except in the case of relatively informal classroom assessments, the first step is to conduct at least one tryout (also known as a trial, a pre-test or a pilot) to see how the test works in practice. Even experienced test developers cannot predict how particular tasks or items will perform when learners respond to them. Inevitably a tryout leads to revisions of the test material, changes in procedures and also amendments to the test specifications. Further tryouts usually follow before the test is ready to be used operationally for its intended purpose. At this third stage, too, the technical quality of the test – and especially its reliability – needs to be evaluated, and various kinds of validity evidence should be obtained. Even after the test has been put to operational use, there should be ongoing monitoring of its performance, with further revisions as necessary. This monitoring has gained new significance under the influence of Messick's (1989) emphasis on the consequential aspect as a criterion for judging the validity of a test.

The process of test development serves as a backdrop to research on language tests. The process does not really count as a research activity in itself; it is unlikely that a detailed account of how a particular test was developed according to the steps outlined above would be accepted as a research article in a journal or as a thesis or dissertation in language testing. Rather, research questions are generated as part of the development process when the test developers address problem areas or explore innovations in test design, the nature of the input material, the medium of delivery, rating procedures and so on. Here are some recent examples related to the assessment of writing:

- Lee and Anderson (2007) studied the writing section of a university ESL placement test which used three different topics in rotation and found a significant topic effect in the test-takers' performance.
- East (2007) concluded that giving secondary school students access to a bilingual dictionary had no measurable effect on their performance in a foreign language writing exam.
- Knoch et al. (2007) found that a web-based program to train raters for an academic writing assessment could very usefully complement the standard face-to-face method of training.

A related point is that, particularly for postgraduate students, it is generally not feasible within a single study to develop a new test properly and tackle a research issue as well. Thus, most graduate researchers work with existing tests or test formats rather than creating their own, especially at the Masters level. Their university may have a testing programme to place international students into language learning courses, or to assess the oral proficiency of international teaching assistants, and these programmes offer opportunities for research. Another option is to be a member of a large-scale test development project directed by a professor at the student's university. A further possibility is that major testing organizations sometimes make test data available to approved outside researchers to conduct their own studies complementing those undertaken by in-house staff.

Whether researchers use an existing test or develop their own, it is an indispensable requirement that they should evaluate the technical quality of the instrument as a prelude to addressing their research questions. This means minimally reporting the reliability of the test when administered to the research participants. In this regard, language testers provide a model of good practice that should be emulated by those other frequent users of language tests, researchers in second language acquisition (SLA). As Norris and Ortega (2003) have pointed out, it is by no means a routine practice in published SLA studies to report on the reliability of the instruments used. This creates difficulties in determining to what extent measurement error has affected the results of individual SLA studies and also in building sound theory on the basis of a synthesis of research findings.

Research Strategies and Techniques

The most obvious tools to use in research on language tests are statistical procedures – the very thing that can deter mathematically challenged students of applied linguistics from considering language testing research in the first place. Before proceeding, then, I should make the point that not all research in the field involves the application of statistics, as we shall see below. The following section gives just a brief overview of test statistics; for a more comprehensive yet accessible account, see Bachman (2004).

Statistical Methods

Introductory textbooks on testing usually present the basic statistics belonging to the classical model of psychometrics, allowing the user to summarize score distributions (mean and standard deviation), estimate the reliability of the test (KR-20, Cronbach's alpha), analyse the functioning of individual test items (item difficulty and discrimination) and calculate correlations for various purposes. When the number of test-takers is reasonably small (in the tens rather than hundreds or thousands), the statistics can be worked out manually on a scientific calculator. They are more usually computed these days by means of standard statistical software such as Microsoft Excel and SPSS (www.spss.com), or by specialized programs like ITEMAN (www.assess.com).

However, the classical statistics have significant limitations and since the 1980s they have been supplanted to a large extent in language testing by Item Response Theory (IRT) and especially the version of IRT known as the Rasch Model. A full discussion of the technical merits of the theory is beyond the scope of this chapter, but briefly IRT has a number of advantages over the classical theory by, for instance, providing estimates of the reliability of individual test items rather than just the whole test, and making it easier to equate different forms of a test. In practical terms, IRT makes it possible to build a large bank of test items of known difficulty from which multiple forms of a test can be generated. This is the basis for computer-adaptive testing, with its promise of tests tailored to the ability level of individual test-takers – though for various reasons its potential remains only partly fulfilled.

The original Rasch Model, which applied just to test items scored right or wrong, has been extended to deal with items or questions worth more than one mark (the partial-credit model) and with rating scales. A further development is many-facet Rasch measurement, which provides a comprehensive evaluation of speaking or writing tasks, including on a single measurement scale estimates of the ability level of the test-takers, the difficulty of each task, the severity or leniency of the raters and the test-takers' relative performance on each of the rating criteria.

Another approach to the evaluation of tests, and in particular their reliability, is provided by Generalizability Theory (G-theory). Based on analysis of variance, a generalizability study (G-study) involves estimating the relative effects of the test-takers, the input texts, the items, the raters and other aspects of a test on the distribution of the scores. The primary purpose is to identify those facets of the measurement process that may be reducing the overall reliability of the test. The G-study can then be followed by a decision study (D-study), in which the test developer or researcher looks at how the reliability of the test might be improved by, say, adding 20 more items to the test or using three raters for each candidate's writing script rather than just two.

Perhaps the most sophisticated quantitative procedure in current use by language testing researchers is Structural Equation Modeling (SEM), which is used primarily in high-level research on the construct validation of tests. It involves calculating a complex set of correlations among numerous measures administered to the same group of learners in order to test a theoretical model of language ability. For instance, Shiotsu and Weir (2007) used SEM to demonstrate that syntactic knowledge was a better predictor than vocabulary knowledge of the reading comprehension ability of Japanese university students.

Although specialized software is available for IRT, G-Theory and SEM analyses, a great deal more is required to apply the procedures correctly than just entering test scores into the program and reporting the resulting statistics. Bachman quotes the authors of an introductory textbook on IRT as stating 'none of the currently available programs can be used with authority by researchers who are not well versed in the IRT literature' (Embretson and Reise 2000, cited in Bachman 2004, p. 151). Thus, a researcher who plans to use one of these analyses should have an understanding of the mathematical basis of the statistical procedures as well as the underlying assumptions, the minimum amount of input data required and the accepted guidelines for interpreting the output – much of which, to complicate matters, may be the subject of ongoing debate among the experts. This means that a graduate student embarking on a study of this kind needs not only to read the relevant texts and take appropriate courses on quantitative methods and educational measurement but also to seek expert advice, which may be available only outside their own applied linguistics programme.

Qualitative Methods

However, although the statistical analyses have a central place in language testing research, there is an increasing trend towards the use of qualitative methods of inquiry to complement, if not replace, the traditional quantitative approaches. This reflects the general trend in applied linguistics and the social sciences generally towards a mixed-methods approach to research methodology. Some types of non-statistical research have already been mentioned in the earlier discussion, such as the procedures for investigating educational assessment in the classroom and the methods involved in conducting washback studies.

It has become quite routine in testing research to obtain the perspective and insights of the test-takers themselves after they have completed the pilot version of a new test under development. By means of a questionnaire or interview, the test-takers can report on the level of difficulty of the test, any problems they had with the test instructions or with responding to novel test formats and also their perceptions of the fairness of the test as a measure of their ability. At a deeper level, researchers can probe the cognitive processes underlying test performance by eliciting verbal reports from individual test-takers either while they are responding to the test (think-aloud protocols) or immediately after they complete it. Such studies may seek to reveal the test-takers' reasons for choosing a particular response to multiple-choice or gap-filling items, or they may involve a more general investigation of test-taker strategies. For instance, the leading researcher in this area, Andrew Cohen, recently co-authored a study (Cohen and Upton 2007) of the reading and test-taking strategies adopted by learners responding to the reading formats of the new internet-based TOEFL (iBT).

With the emphasis today on tests of communicative performance, the cognitive processes of raters are also of great interest to researchers. The quality of the assessment in speaking and writing tests depends on the raters having a shared understanding of the rating criteria as well as an ability to apply them consistently to particular performances. By means of interviews and verbal reports, researchers can evaluate the effectiveness of rater training, explore the extent to which raters have difficulty in following the prescribed guidelines and reveal cases where raters choose to ignore the official criteria in making their judgement. These qualitative procedures complement the more objective evidence provided by statistical analyses such as many-facet Rasch measurement and G-studies.

Another area of research opened by the assessment of productive skills is the investigation of spoken performance by means of discourse analysis. The most common template for a speaking test is the oral interview, in which an examiner (or interlocutor) presents a series of questions and perhaps other tasks to each test-taker in turn. Discourse analyses have shown, first, that a test interview is quite different from a normal conversation, and that the role of the interlocutor in the assessment is by no means a neutral one. For instance, Brown (2003) demonstrated that the style of interaction adopted by an examiner in the IELTS speaking test could have a significant impact on the rating the candidate received. This kind of research can lead to fairer assessment procedures as well as the development of alternatives to the standard interview, such as the paired format, in which two test-takers have opportunities to interact with each other rather than just with the examiner.

A Sample Study

As an example of research in language testing, let us look at a study I published several years ago (Read 2002). Although I was the sole author of the article, it reported a project conducted jointly with Kathryn Hill and Elisabeth Grove of the University of Melbourne. The work grew out of a desire to explore a new approach to the assessment of listening comprehension ability within the context of English for academic purposes. There were a number of facets of listening test design that could potentially have been investigated, such as what type of source to use for the input material, how to present the input to the test-takers and what type of test items to use. The focus in this case was on the form of the input.

At both universities involved (one in Australia and the other in New Zealand), there were existing listening tests based on scripted talks that were either pre-recorded on audiotape or presented live to the students. Such mono- logues can be seen at best as representing only part of the construct of academic listening ability, namely comprehension of formal lectures. We were interested in whether students could also understand more interactive forms of talk, such as the discussions that occur in seminars and tutorials.

There had been one previous study (Shohamy and Inbar 1991), conducted with high school students in Israel, which was relevant to our emerging research question. These researchers prepared three versions of the input material with the same content, but one was a monologue designed to be like a news broadcast, whereas the other two involve varying degrees of interaction between the speaker and an interlocutor. Shohamy and Inbar found that monologue was significantly more difficult for the students to understand than the other two versions. They argued that a typical monologue has key features of written language, like relatively dense content, limited redundancy and greater gram- matical complexity, making the text more difficult for listeners to process than one which involves interaction between two or more speakers.

We decided to explore for ourselves the comparison between a scripted talk and a more interactive version of the same content. The first step was to prepare a talk on the topic of medical ethics, based on two cases that involved issues of informed consent and the acceptability of performing medical research on vulnerable patients. Once the script was written and edited, a set of 36 test items of the short-answer type were developed. Then we set out to produce the interactive version. A first attempt, which was simply an unscripted discussion of the two cases by three people, did not produce a recording that could be meaningfully compared with the scripted talk. Instead, we adopted a 'semi-scripted' approach that was designed to shadow more closely the discourse structure of the monologue version. One of the speakers performed the role of a tutor, allocating turns and ensuring that all the content required to answer the test items was covered. The other two speakers acted as students, who took turns to review the facts of each case and comment on the ethical issues.

The study was conducted with six classes in an intensive English programme at a New Zealand university. Most of the 96 students were from East or Southeast Asia and their main goal was to develop their proficiency in English for academic or professional purposes. In the eighth week of the course, the students took a pre-test in which they listened to a scripted talk about dreams. On the basis of the pre-test scores, they were divided into two groups that were matched in terms of listening ability. In Week 9 of the course, Group A took the monologue version of the experimental test, whereas Group B took the interactive version. For both groups it was quite a difficult test, with an overall mean score of just 16 out of a possible 36. When the two groups were compared, though, Group A obtained a mean score of 18.0, which was significantly higher than the Group B mean of 14.16. In other words, the monologue version was easier to understand.

This result contrasted with the findings of Shohamy and Inbar (1991), whose participants found the interactive test versions more comprehensible. In considering why our results were different, we identified a number of reasons. One may simply have been a practice effect, in that Group A had taken a similar test based on a scripted talk as the pre-test the week before, whereas Group B had to cope with a new kind of input which they might not have experienced previously in a listening test. A second factor is that the test items had originally been written on the basis of the scripted talk and thus they fitted better with the monologue than with the interactive version of the test.

Another source of evidence was a questionnaire administered to all the participating students after they completed the test. With regard to the speed of the speech, the students in Group B reported significantly more often that the speakers in the discussion spoke too fast for them, and overall more of them rated the test as being very difficult. Thus, in the students' judgement, it was the interactive version of the test that was more challenging to comprehend.

The other main difference between the two studies was in the nature of the input texts. Shohamy and Inbar's (1991) monologue was deliberately designed to have the features of a formal written text in terms of its vocabulary, grammar and density of content, whereas ours was written more as a text to be read aloud, with simpler sentence structures, repetition of key vocabulary items and explicit discourse markers. In the case of the interactive versions of the tests, Shohamy and Inbar's dialogues were carefully scripted in order to incorporate the features of two distinct genres. By contrast, as described above, our discussion involved three speakers rather than two and it was at the most semi-scripted, which meant that it was probably a more authentic sample of natural speech.

Thus, there are various ways in which the different outcomes of the two studies can be accounted for. At one level, they were both quite simple experiments but they serve to highlight the complexity of the factors that can influence the difficulty level – and ultimately the validity – of a listening test. This in turn reinforces the point that, no matter how much thought and care go into the design and writing of a new test, it must be tried out with a suitable group of learners, analysed and revised before being used for operational purposes. The design of listening tests is an under-researched area and there is certainly scope for studies of other variables besides the nature of the input texts. A lack of knowledge of statistics may seem like a deterrent but it should not discourage anyone from conducting worthwhile research on this and a whole range of other topics in the field of language testing and assessment.

Resources for Further Reading

Bachman, L. F. (2000), 'Modern language testing at the turn of the century: Assuring that what we count counts'. *Language Testing,* 17, 1–42.
   This is a comprehensive overview of developments in language testing in the 1980s and 1990s, together with a consideration of new directions in the field.
Cambridge ESOL Research Notes: www.cambridgeesol.org/rs_notes/
Cambridge Language Assessment series. Series editors: J. Charles Alderson and Lyle Bachman. Cambridge University Press.
   An authoritative series of ten books written by specialist authors and published between 2000 and 2006. Each volume includes a comprehensive survey of relevant research and deals with a particular area: listening, reading, speaking, writing, vocabulary, grammar, language for specific purposes, young language learners, the use of computer technology and statistical analysis.
IELTS Research Reports: www.ielts.org/researchers/research.aspx
Language Assessment Quarterly: www.tandf.co.uk/journals/titles/15434303.asp
Language Testing: http://ltj.sagepub.com
   These two specialist journals publish research articles as well as reviews of books and tests
McNamara, T. and Roever, C. (2006), *Language Testing: The Social Dimension*. Malden, MA: Blackwell.

This book gives an excellent overview of current concerns in language testing. The 'social dimension' in the title is interpreted broadly enough to encompass most of the major issues that researchers are addressing at the present time.

Resources in Language Testing: www.languagetesting.info

This is the single most useful website in the area of language testing. It is maintained by Glenn Fulcher at the University of Leicester in the UK, with multiple links to the websites of particular language tests and language testing organizations, as well as a range of other resources.

TOEFL Research Reports: www.ets.org/toefl Click on *TOEFL Research*.

The publishers of the Cambridge ESOL examinations, IELTS and TOEFL all disseminate the results of research by their staff and by outside researchers. Although the focus is on their own tests, the issues investigated are often of much wider interest.

References

Alderson, J. C. and Wall, D. (1993), 'Does washback exist?' *Applied Linguistics*, 14, 115–129.

Alderson, J. C., Clapham, C. and Wall, D. (1995), *Language Test Construction and Evaluation*. Cambridge: Cambridge University Press.

Bachman, L. F. (1990), *Fundamental Considerations in Language Testing*. Oxford: Oxford University Press.

—(2004), *Statistical Analyses for Language Assessment*. Cambridge: Cambridge University Press.

—(2007), 'What is the construct? The dialectic of abilities and contexts in defining constructs in language assessment', in J. Fox, M. Wesche, D. Bayliss, L. Cheng, C. E. Turner and C. Doe (eds), *Language Testing Reconsidered*. Ottawa: University of Ottawa Press, pp. 41–71.

Bachman, L. F. and Palmer, A. S. (1996), *Language Testing in Practice*. Oxford: Oxford University Press.

Brown, A. (2003), 'Interviewer variation and the co-construction of speaking proficiency'. *Language Testing*, 20, 1–25.

Brown, J. D. and Hudson, T. (1998), 'The alternatives in language assessment'. *TESOL Quarterly*, 32, 653–675.

Canale, M. (1983), 'On some dimensions of language proficiency', in J. W. Oller, Jr. (ed), *Issues in Language Testing Research*. Rowley, MA: Newbury House, pp. 333–342.

Canale, M. and Swain, M. (1980), 'Theoretical bases of communicative approaches to second language teaching and testing'. *Applied Linguistics*, 1, 1–47.

Chalhoub-Deville, M. (2003), 'Second language interaction: Current perspectives and future trends'. *Language Testing*, 20, 369–383.

Cheng, L., Watanabe, Y. and Curtis, A. (eds) (2004), *Washback in Language Testing: Research Contexts and Methods*. Mahwah, NJ: Lawrence Erlbaum.

Cohen, A. D. and Upton, T. A. (2007), '"I want to go back to the text": response strategies on the reading subtest of the new TOEFL'. *Language Testing*, 24, 209–250.

Cronbach, L. J. (1989), 'Construct validity after thirty years', in R. L. Linn (ed.), *Intelligence: Measurement, Theory and Public Policy*. Urbana: University of Illinois Press, pp. 147–171.

Davies, A. (ed.) (1997), Ethics in Language Testing (special issue). *Language Testing*, 14 (3).

—(2004), The Ethics of Language Assessment (special issue). *Language Assessment Quarterly*, 1 (2 and 3).

East, M. (2007), 'Bilingual dictionaries in tests of L2 writing proficiency: Do they make a difference?' *Language Testing*, 24, 331–353.

Gipps, C. (1994), *Beyond Testing: Towards a Theory of Educational Assessment*. London: Falmer.

Hughes, A. (2003), *Testing for Language Teachers* (2nd edn). Cambridge: Cambridge University Press.

Knoch, U., Read, J. and von Randow, J. (2007), 'Re-training writing raters online: how does it compare with face-to-face training?' *Assessing Writing*, 12, 26–43.

Lado, R. (1961), *Language Testing*. London: Longman.

Lee, H-K. and Anderson, C. (2007), 'Validity and topic generality in a writing performance test'. *Language Testing*, 24, 307–330.

McNamara, T. and Roever, C. (2006), *Language Testing: The Social Dimension*. Malden, MA: Blackwell.

Messick, S. (1989), 'Validity', in R. L. Linn (ed.), *Educational Measurement* (3rd edn). New York: American Council on Education and Macmillan, pp. 13–103.

—(1996), 'Validity and washback in language testing'. *Language Testing*, 13, 241–256.

Oller, J. W., Jr. (1979), *Language Tests at School*. London: Longman.

Read, J. (2002), 'The use of interactive input in EAP listening assessment'. *Journal of English for Academic Purposes*, 1, 105–119.

Rea-Dickins, P. (ed.) (2004), Exploring Diversity in Teacher Assessment (special issue). *Language Testing*, 21(3).

Rea-Dickins, P. and Gardner, S. (2000), 'Snares or silver bullets: Disentangling the construct of formative assessment'. *Language Testing*, 17, 215–243.

Shiotsu, T. and Weir, C. J. (2007), 'The relative significance of syntactic knowledge and vocabulary breadth in the prediction of reading comprehension test performance'. *Language Testing*, 24, 99–128.

Shohamy, E. and Inbar, O. (1991), 'Validation of listening comprehension tests: The effect of text and question type'. *Language Testing*, 8, 23–40.

Spolsky, B. (1995), *Measured Words: The Development of Objective Language Testing*. Oxford: Oxford University Press.

Teasdale, A. and Leung, C. (2000), 'Teacher assessment and psychometric theory: A case of paradigm crossing?' *Language Testing*, 17, 163–184.

21 Researching Motivation

Lindy Woodrow

Research into language learning motivation is relatively recent, with studies dating back to the mid-twentieth century. This chapter will provide an overview of the major thinking and research in motivation. Early research focused on the work of Robert Gardner and colleagues (e.g., Gardner and Lambert 1972; Gardner 1985). Their research was located within a *social-psychological paradigm* which dominated research into language learning motivation until the 1990s. In the 1990s, major academic journals called for a diversification of theorizing in motivation informed by other disciplines, notably education. This resulted in a number of new studies into language learning motivation that did not use the Gardnerian paradigm. In this chapter four areas of motivational research will be discussed. First, the Gardnerian socio-educational model of language learning will be briefly presented. Research since the 1990s will then be considered: self-determination theory (Deci and Ryan 1980, 1985), a process model of motivation (Dörnyei and Otto 1998) and goal orientation theory (Ames and Archer 1988). The section on goal orientation theory uses Woodrow's (2006) study to highlight confirmatory factor analysis as a technique that may be used to investigate latent constructs.

Gardner's Socio-Educational Model of Language Learning

The work of Gardner and colleagues into language learning motivation was the most significant contribution to research in the area in the twentieth century. Gardner's research into second language motivation was developed in bilingual Canada and resulted in the socio-educational model of second language learning. The model is based on the belief that the social and cultural setting can influence motivation which influences the formal and informal contexts of language learning which, in turn, results in linguistic and non-linguistic outcomes (Gardner 1985, 2006). The model has four distinct areas: *antecedent factors, individual difference variables, language acquisition contexts* and *outcomes*. In the model, goal orientations are viewed as antecedents of motivation. Motivation comprises the desire to learn the second language, motivational intensity and attitudes towards learning a language. It is the notion of goal orientations that captured the attention of the research world when the model was introduced. This was a very influential view of second language motivation for many years. Gardner referred to two orientations: *instrumental* and *integrative motivation*. An instrumental orientation refers to a situation whereby the learner is motivated to learn the language for extrinsic reasons, such as for financial gain or job promotion. An integrative orientation refers to the situation whereby the learner is motivated to learn the language because they identify with the target culture. In Gardner's theory these orientations do not appear in the core construct of motivation. However, in many research projects in the twentieth century, these orientations replace the motivation construct itself, thus, according to Gardner, over-simplifying the theory (Gardner 1988).

In the 1990s there was considerable debate through a series of journal articles that questioned the relevance of the Gardnerian model of motivation to contexts other than bilingual Canada where the research had originated (Dörnyei 1990, 1994; Crookes and Schmidt 1991; Oxford 1994; Oxford and Shearin 1994; Tremblay and Gardner 1995). For example, how relevant is an integrative orientation that focuses on the extent to which a learner wishes to identify with the target culture to Chinese students studying English as a subject in Chinese schools? As a result of this discussion, a number of studies emerged that focused on conceptualizations of motivation from research in areas other than language learning, notably, workplace and education motivation. Some of these research studies are presented in papers on language learning motivation published in the 1990s. Oxford's (1996) volume, for example, includes articles on a range of motivational issues, for example, goals and expectancy (Schmidt et al. 1996), and linguistic self-confidence and contextual influences (Dörnyei 1996). A further volume of research into motivation was published in 2001 (Dörnyei and Schmidt 2001) as a result of a state-of-the-art colloquium on second language motivation at the annual meeting of the American Association of Applied Linguistics held in Vancouver.

Self-Determination Theory

Self-determination theory (Deci and Ryan 1980, 1985; Ryan and Deci 2000) focuses on the extent to which individuals can exert control over their environment. This has been applied to language learning (Noels 2001). Central to this theory is the conceptualization of motivation as *intrinsic* and *extrinsic*. Intrinsic motivation reflects a willingness to engage in a given task for the inherent interest or pleasure gained from the task. Three types of intrinsic orientations have been suggested: intrinsic knowledge, where an individual is motivated by a quest for knowledge; intrinsic accomplishment, which refers to the satisfaction experienced by accomplishing a challenging task and, intrinsic stimulation, which refers to the enjoyment of the given task (Vallerand 1997; Noels 2001). Extrinsic motivation reflects a willingness to engage with tasks to achieve a specific outcome. Deci and Ryan classify extrinsic motivation according to level of internalization. Thus an external regulation could refer to passing an examination or to getting a good job while internal or integrated regulation could refer to improving an individual's opinion of their capability (Ryan and Deci 2000).

Noels and colleagues investigated extrinsic and intrinsic motivation in relation to the Gardnerian model of motivation. Their research indicated that the intrinsic and extrinsic conceptualization was applicable to language learners and suggested a model of motivation that integrated self-determination theory and the Gardnerian model of motivation. In particular they examined social contact, needs, orientations, second language use and linguistic and non-linguistic outcomes (Noels et al. 1999; Noels 2001; Noels, Pelletier et al. 2001; Noels et al. 2003).

A Process Model of Motivation

Dörnyei and Otto (Dörnyei and Otto 1998; Dörnyei 2000) proposed a *process model* of motivation which reflects dynamic and contextual aspects of second and foreign language motivation. This model includes a temporal dimension of motivation designed to account for changes in motivation over time. This, Dörnyei argues, is logical since language learning is a lengthy process and success is based on sustained learning over a period of years (Dörnyei 2001). The process model of motivation is complex. It is based on Heckhausen and Kuhl's action control theory (Heckhausen and Kuhl 1985; Heckhausen 1991). This model considers the stages of motivation from before engaging in a given task to after task completion. Three stages are hypothesized: the preactional stage that reflects desire and goal setting, the actional stage that reflects engagement and appraisal and the postactional stage that reflects causal attributions and further planning. The focus on the temporal element of motivation is relatively new in motivational research and promises an interesting avenue for further research.

Research Strategies and Techniques

The strategies used in second language motivation research are governed by the nature of motivation. Since motivation is a latent construct it cannot be observed directly and so depends upon self-report measures such as questionnaires and interviews. Usually motivation is not considered in isolation and often models are hypothesized as comprising a number of motivational variables. These variables are usually examined in relationship to a language variable such as achievement as measured by a language test.

The most common design in motivational research is a cross-sectional study which typically aims to provide a snapshot of a given aspect on a single occasion, for example, Dörnyei et al. (2006) large-scale study into language learning motivation in Hungary. Cross-sectional studies involve collecting data on one occasion and often involve questionnaires. For example, a researcher can collect data about the motivational profile at the time of data collection. Cross-sectional studies enable the researcher to examine relationships between variables. For example, such a design might measure motivation and compare this to language proficiency. The advantage in using a cross-sectional design is that it is easy to collect data from a large number of participants. Cross-sectional research can be contrasted with longitudinal research, which involves collecting data on a number of occasions over a period of time, such as Ushoida's (2001) study that collected qualitative data about motivation of language learners at university over a two-year period.

Second language research typically uses quantitative measures where the latent variable of motivation is operationalized by *observed variables*. To operationalize a variable means to make the variable measurable. In research into latent constructs this is usually done by asking questions of individuals, most frequently by constructing questionnaire items. Questionnaire items typically use some form of rating scale, such as a *Likert scale* or a *semantic differential* scale. These are closed questions that can be assigned a numerical value. A Likert scale item requires the respondent to indicate the extent to which they agree or disagree according to a numerical scale. For example, a five-point Likert scale ranges from 1 (strongly disagree) to 5 (strongly agree). In a similar manner, semantic differential scales ask for a rating on a line based on a statement.

```
┌─────────────────────────────────────────────────────────────────────────┐
│ Example of a Likert scale item                                            │
│                                                                           │
│ Fill in the circle that best expresses your view                         │
│                                                                           │
│ My teacher is efficient                                                   │
│                                                                           │
│ Strongly agree     Agree      Neutral      Disagree     Strongly disagree │
│        ○              ○           ○            ○                ○          │
│ Semantic differential scale                                               │
│                                                                           │
│ Rate the efficiency of your English teacher by marking an X on the scale. │
│                                                                           │
│                                                                           │
│ My English teacher is efficient :___: __: __: __: __: inefficient.        │
└─────────────────────────────────────────────────────────────────────────┘
```

Figure 21.1 Examples of questionnaire items

These are then assigned a numerical value in a similar way to a Likert scale. Figure 21.1 shows examples of a Likert type scale item and a semantic differential type item.

Questionnaires rely upon self-report, that is, the data come from the respondent's own account of their experiences or views. One issue concerning this is that participants may provide responses that reflect how they would like to be viewed (Oller 1982). For this reason, it is important that questionnaires are worded very carefully avoiding obvious desirable answers. It is also important that confidentiality is ensured.

The resulting data from questionnaires is typically analysed using inferential statistics (see Phakiti this volume). Inferential statistics refer to statistical techniques that can be used to make inferences from data from a small group of respondents to a larger population thus enabling findings to be generalized. Motivational research typically uses inferential statistical analysis on data provided by questionnaires. The relationship between variables, often presented in the form of a motivational model, is frequently the main concern of motivation research. Typical analyses are often based on correlations between variables.

Instrumentation and Data Analysis

The most widely used questionnaire or instrumentation to measure motivation and related variables is Gardner's (1985) *Attitudes/Motivation Test Battery*. This instrument operationalizes the variables proposed in his socio-educational model of language learning. These variables include attitudes toward target language speakers, teachers and learning situations; motivational orientations, desire and intensity, anxiety and parental encouragement. The scale uses three types of questionnaire items: Likert scale, multiple choice and semantic differential scale. The *Attitudes/Motivation Test Battery* instrument is a published standardized test of language learning motivation. It has sound psychometric properties (Gardner and MacIntyre 1993) and has been widely used and adapted. The instrumentation and instructions on how to use this are available from Gardner (1985).

Noels and colleagues devised the *Language Learning Orientations Scale* to measure motivation which comprised amotivation (lack of or passive engagement), external regulation, interjected regulation, indentified regulation, intrinsic motivation knowledge, intrinsic motivation, accomplishment and intrinsic motivation stimulation (Noels, Clement et al. 2001, 2003). It uses 7-point Likert scales to assess these motivational variables. The scale asks respondents to rate the extent to which they agree or disagree with a series of statements from 1 (disagree completely) to 7 (agree completely).

Dörnyei's process model (2000) is at present a theoretical rather than an empirical model. This means the model is based on theory rather than data. According to Dörnyei 'few of its tenets have been explicitly tested in second language contexts' (Dörnyei 2005, p. 87). Because the model includes a temporal dimension, empirical evidence must emerge from longitudinal studies rather than the more common cross-sectional research designs. This means that there is room for more qualitative research in the field. Qualitative methods are more capable of capturing in-depth data over a period of time. This can focus on the fluctuation of motivation during the lengthy process of learning a foreign language (for an example of recent qualitative research into the temporal dimension of motivation see Ushioda 2001).

Data Analysis

In motivation research, data are frequently analysed using statistical procedures using correlations. These include basic techniques such as *bivariate correlations* (see Phakiti this volume) that examine the linear relationship between two variables. More complicated procedures include *exploratory factor analysis*. This technique is used to investigate the extent to which observed variables are indicative of underlying latent variables or factors. More complex analyses include *structural equation modeling* which involves testing hypotheses about relationships between variables. Studies using structural equation modeling have increased in recent years. This is probably due to the development of powerful statistical analysis software that reduces the burden on the researcher who wishes to employ this kind of analysis.

There are two types of factor analysis: *exploratory factor analysis* and *confirmatory factor analysis*. Exploratory factor analysis is used in early stages of researching motivation. A large number of observed variables (questionnaire items) are analysed to examine the extent to which these correlate, which may provide evidence for the composition of a latent variable. The analysis produces a more manageable set of factors. Exploratory factor analysis is calculated using computer software such as the Statistical Package for the Social Sciences (SPSS Inc. 2007). This software generates output in the form of a table that includes *factor loadings*. A factor loading is a correlation coefficient. This is a number less than 1.00 that reflects the magnitude of the relationship between the variable and the factor. For example, a factor loading of 0.90 indicates a strong relationship while a loading of 0.2 indicates little relationship. Exploratory factor analysis is used a great deal in the preparatory stages of research where evidence is required of the make-up of a given variable. A great deal of Gardner's research used this technique (Gardner and Lambert 1959; Gardner and Lambert 1972; Gardner 1985).

There are a number of issues researchers need to be aware of when using exploratory factor analysis. The most important is deciding how many factors to extract and how the factors should be labelled. Two main methods are used for deciding how many factors should be extracted. First Catrell's (1996) *scree test* may be used to provide a visual representation of the data. This is a visual representation of the variables in the data set. The scree plot should indicate a line that sharply increases at a given point on a graph. Where this happens will indicate whether, for example, three or four factors be selected. The second method, known as *Kaiser's criterion* (Kaiser 1960), uses *eigenvalues* to determine factors. An eigenvalue represents the total variance explained by the factor. Only factors with eigenvalues higher than 1.00 are then considered for inclusion in the factor.

Once the number of factors is decided they need to be labelled. The choice of label should be evident from the *indicator variables*; that is, those variables within the factor that have the highest loadings. Consideration is also given to the common features of variables loading on that factor. Of course, this is can be quite controversial because it is based on the researcher's personal judgement.

Confirmatory factor analysis is conceptually similar to exploratory factor analysis but uses structural equation modeling to confirm rather than explore a latent model. Structural equation modeling is discussed below.

Structural Equation Modeling

Structural equation modeling is a relatively new development in data analysis. This technique has gained in popularity in recent second language motivation studies (Gardner et al. 1997; Dörnyei et al. 2006). This is because structural equation modeling is very useful when considering the nature of latent variables and for testing hypothesized models. Structural equation modeling can be used to identify relationships between variables. It is sometimes referred to as causal modeling, although this is not strictly true. Causality cannot be claimed based on statistical evidence alone, but needs substantial theoretical evidence. When using structural equation modeling, a model is proposed and then tested to examine how the data fit the model. Thus, a clear conceptual model is hypothesized based on theorizing and/or previous empirical evidence. The variables in the hypothesized model then need to be operationlized or measured by some form of research instrument. The data collected are then examined to determine to what extent the data fit the model. The following steps are usually followed in a research project using structural equation modeling (adapted from Blunch 2008, pp. 75–78):

1. Statement of research questions
2. Design of a hypothetical model including directional paths
3. Decide how concepts will be measured
4. Collect data
5. Test model fit using computer software
6. Examine computer output for model fit
7. If necessary, modify model
8. Accept or reject model

When specifying a structural model, rectangles are used to indicate an observed variable, an oval is used to indicate a latent variable, a small circle indicates the error associated with the variable and an arc is used to indicate a correlation. Figure 21.2 illustrates this.

Structural equation modeling requires the researcher to hypothesize a model with directional relationships between several variables – latent and observed. This model is then confirmed or rejected by using *goodness-of-fit-indices* that compare the hypothesized model with the data. There are a large number of fit indices that can be used to help researchers evaluate the extent to which the model is likely to be supported by the data. Because the indices reflect different views of model building, researchers usually use several fit indices to provide evidence to accept or reject the proposed model. Most structural equation modeling studies use the Chi square (χ^2) statistic. In structural equation modeling this statistic reflects the null hypothesis that is known to be false *a priori*, thus the null hypothesis states that the model is 100 per cent correct. So, a non-significant value indicates a good fit to the data. However, since structural equation modeling is very sensitive to sample size chi squared normed (χ^2/df), (chi square divided by the degrees of freedom) is often used as well.

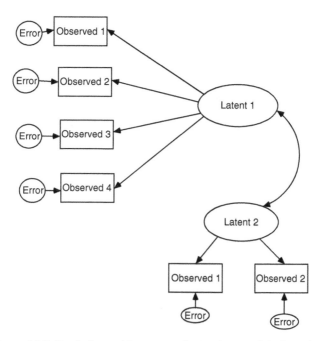

Figure 21.2 Symbols used in structural equation models (based on Holmes-Smith 2000)

Table 21.1 Fit indices for structural equation models (based on Holmes-Smith 2000)

Index	Symbol	Acceptable level
Chi-square	χ^2	Non-significant
Normed Chi-square (Chi-square divided by degrees of freedom)	$\chi^{2/df}$	1.00 – 3.00
Goodness-of-fit Index	GFI	0.90 or higher
Adjusted Goodness-of-fit Index	AGFI	0.90 or higher
Root Mean Square Residual	RMR	Region of 0.05
Root Mean Square Error of Approximation	RMSEA	Region of 0.05
Normed Fit Index	NFI	0.90 or higher
Nonnormed Fit Index	NNFI	0.90 or higher
Comparative Fit Index	CFI	0.90 or higher

In addition to this, other fit indices are also used. Table 21.1 presents some of these fit indices. Views on acceptable values associated with fit indices vary slightly in reported research. Table 21.1 shows those recommended by Holmes-Smith (2000) since these were used in the sample study.

There are a number of issues that a researcher needs to be aware of when using structural equation modeling. First, a proposed model may not be the best model to fit the data. The fit indices can only provide evidence on adequate versus inadequate models. Another issue is that it requires a large sample size which increases with the number of variables or model parameters. Usually samples under 200 are not appropriate for structural models (Holmes 2000). As mentioned, structural equation modeling is sometimes referred to as causal modeling; however, in models where causality is addressed this is inferred from the model rather than 'proved'. The model can only tell the researcher that a cause and effect relationship is feasible based on the data.

There are a number of data analysis techniques that can be facilitated using structural equation modeling. *Confirmatory factor analysis* is one such technique. Confirmatory factor analysis is similar to exploratory factor analysis described above except in that the model is first hypothesized and then tested rather than the data being explored first and then a model emerging. So, the researcher makes decisions before the analysis, based on theory and empirical research. The researcher follows the same steps for structural equation modeling outlined above. First the hypothesized model of relationships between variables is designed. These constructs need to be operationlized. This means items are designed that will measure the underlying construct. A questionnaire it often used for this. The data is then collected and put into a software program such as Analysis of Moment Structures (AMOS 2006) This can test the fit of the data to the model. This model is then accepted, adjusted or rejected.

In confirmatory factor analysis a model is proposed where one or more latent variables are hypothesized to be made up of particular observed variables. This model is then tested and may be modified. In confirmatory factor analysis, unlike exploratory factor analysis, observed variables can be removed from the model. As such, confirmatory factor analysis is very useful for the development of questionnaires focusing on latent variables. The researcher would start with a large bank of items (observed variables) and remove those that are not indicative of the latent variables.

A Sample Study

The study described in this section is Woodrow's (2006) examination of the notion of *adaptive language learning in a second language setting*. This study proposed and tested a model of adaptive learning that comprises several related variables: motivation, self-efficacy, anxiety and language learning strategies. Part of the study involved applying a goal orientation conceptualization of motivation as used in education (Ames 1992), to English language learners. This fitted in with the move in the 1990s to consider second language motivation from a broader perspective informed by theorizing outside of language learning. The research used a questionnaire to measure goal orientations of English for academic purposes (EAP) students. Based on theorizing and empirical evidence a three factor latent model was proposed and tested using confirmatory factor analysis. The study indicated that goal orientations were applicable to EAP learners. This has implications for classroom practice in terms of motivating EAP language learners.

Background to the study: The study used goal orientation theory from education research (Ames 1992; Ames and Archer 1988) as a conceptualization for second language motivation relevant to adult English for academic purposes students studying in an ESL environment. Gardner's proposed model of language learning included integrative and instrumental orientations. These are not central to the model and reflect a socio-cultural perspective whereby the learner has the assumed goal of integrating into the target culture. In contrast, goal orientation theory reflects a social-cognitive perspective with a focus on the learning process. In goal orientation theory, goals are typically classified as being task or performance (Ames and Archer 1988). A task goal (also known as a learning or mastery goal) is viewed as being desirable and most likely to result in positive learning outcomes. A learner adopting this goal would be motivated by learning tasks and achievement for its own sake; they would view competence as being related to effort and have a positive view of errors as contributing to the learning process. A performance goal (also known as an ego or ability goal) reflects a focus on ego or self rather than on achievement for its own sake. While a task goal is concerned with developing competence, a performance goal is concerned with displaying competence (Urdan et al. 2002). In recent years performance goals have been re-conceptualized as approach and avoid goals (Smith et al. 2002). A performance approach goal reflects a desire to demonstrate high ability while a performance avoid goal reflects the desire to avoid demonstrating low ability. (Elliot and Church 1997; Middleton and Midgely 1997; Midgley et al. 1998; Elliot et al. 1999).

The study: The study involved a sample of English for academic purposes (EAP) learners. The learners were given a questionnaire to measure their goal orientations. A model of goal orientations was proposed and tested using confirmatory factor analysis. The results indicated a good fit to the data. Based on these results it was evident that this conceptualization of motivation is relevant to EAP learners. The participants in this study were 275 students (male, $n = 139$; female, $n = 136$) taking EAP courses at intensive language centres in Australia prior to university entry. The students completed a 5-point Likert type questionnaire on goal orientations. The goal orientations were measured using sub-scales taken from the Patterns of Adaptive Learning Survey (PALS) (Midgley et al. 1997). The items were adapted for use with adult second language learners. The questionnaire comprised three sub-scales to measure task, performance approach, and performance avoid goal orientations. An example of a task goal item is: *I like English language learning tasks that I'll learn from even if I make a lot of mistakes*. An example of a performance approach goal item is: *Doing better than other students in this class is important to me*. An example of a performance avoid goal is: *It's very important to me that I don't look as though I can't speak English in my class*. The questionnaire used a 5-point Likert scale ranging from 1 *not at all true of me* to 5 *very true of me*. Each sub-scale comprised 5 items.

Confirmatory factor analysis was chosen as the most applicable method of data analysis because the research concerned a latent structure specified *a priori*. A model of motivation orientations comprising task, performance approach and performance avoid was specified using *Linear Structural Relations* (LISREL) computer software (Jöreskog and Sörbom 1996). While exploratory factor analysis can be computed using SPSS, confirmatory factor analysis needs structural equation modeling – specific software such as LISREL or the SPSS supported package *Analysis of Moment Structures* (AMOS 7, 2006). The confirmatory factor model was specified using a covariance matrix as data for the model. The model was then tested for fit using various fit indices (see Table 21.1).

The proposed *confirmatory factor* model of motivation indicated a moderate to good fit to the data according to the fit indices and the factor loadings. The factor loadings are interpreted as in exploratory factor analysis. High loadings indicate a strong relationship between the latent variable and the observed variable. The model confirmed three latent variables: task, performance approach and performance avoid goal orientations. The model includes error for each observed variable. Correlations between the latent variables are also illustrated. Thus, performance goals were highly correlated, probably because both are informed by self-referent perspectives. There was a small correlation between task and performance approach goals, which is in keeping with other researchers (Midgley et al. 1998). There was also a moderate correlation between a task goal and a performance avoid goal. This result indicates that for this sample participants could feasibly have both orientations. Figure 21.3 illustrates the model and Table 21.2 provides the fit indices.

Conclusions reached in the study: This study made a contribution to second language motivation research because it applied goal orientation theory to English language learning. It used this conceptualization of motivation for EAP learners. It seems reasonable to adopt an educational perspective with such a sample since the learners have both language and educational goals. The participants all intended to continue to study in a tertiary institution. The results from the confirmatory factor model indicated that goal orientation theory is applicable to EAP learners. The results also confirmed that a task goal is a variable of adaptive learning and that it was related to high achievement in language learning.

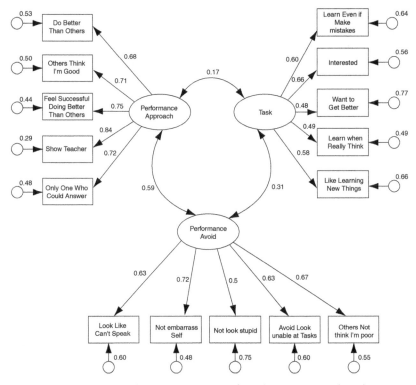

Figure 21.3 Confirmatory Factor Analysis for motivational goals
(Woodrow 2006, p. 301)

Table 21.2 Fit Indices for confirmatory factor analysis of second language motivation goal orientations

	χ^2	p	χ^2/df	RMR	RMSEA	GFI	AGFI	CFI	NFI	NNFI
Motivation Goals	194.96	0.000	2.22	0.06	0.07	0.91	0.87	0.90	0.84	0.88

This project examined a new way of thinking about motivation in language learning but like most research into motivation it used a cross-sectional design which provided a snapshot of the motivation of the sample. However, second language motivation may change over time as the second language develops and is influenced by many teaching and learning contexts. So, there is a need for more research that can reflect these contextual and temporal aspects of second language motivation. It would be valuable for such research to be qualitative, thus making it possible to examine motivation from various angles, reflecting the elements involved in the teaching and learning process. In order to capture developmental issues over time, a longitudinal research design would be most appropriate. The best approach is perhaps a mixed method approach that encompasses both generalizable and rich descriptions of motivated (and demotivated) learners and their environments.

Resources for Further Reading

Dörnyei, Z. (2001), *Teaching and Researching Motivation*. Harlow, UK: Longman.
This book is written in the author's usual highly accessible manner and provides an overview of research into second language motivation. There is a useful section on sources and resources for conducting research into motivation. These identify sources of information and databases in second language motivation as well as a collection of sample instruments used to measure second language motivation.

Dornyei, Z. and Schmidt, R. W. (eds) (2001), *Motivation and Second language Acquisition*. Manoa: University of Hawaii Press.
This collection of articles covers a range of different research projects in the field and contains a useful article by Tremblay that discusses the issues of good psychometric properties and research design in motivation.

Dörnyei, Z. and Ushioda, E. (eds) (2009), *Motivation, Language Identity and the L2 Self*. Clevedon, UK: Multilingual Matters.
Dörnyei is arguably the most prominent researcher and scholar in second language motivation today. This collection of research papers into second language motivation is a valuable contribution to the literature in the field. The collection includes qualitative studies into motivation.

Midgley, C. (2002) (ed.), *Goals, Goal Structures and Patterns of Adaptive Learning*. Mahwah, N.J.: Lawrence Erlbaum.
This is a selection of papers based on a long-term study using the Patterns of Adaptive Learning Survey (PALS) into motivation in a school setting. It includes a methodological focus and a chapter on methods to investigate motivation.

Oxford, R. (1996), *Language Learning Motivation: Pathways to the New Century*. Manoa: University of Hawai'i Press.
This is the first volume of research into language learning motivation. It emerged from the 1990s debate on the need for diversification of research into motivation.

Schunk, D. H., Pintrich, P. R. and Meece, J. (2008), *Motivation in Education: Theory, Research and Applications*. Upper Saddle River, NJ: Pearson.
This book provides an overview of the major theories of motivation in education research. It describes how these perspectives on motivation may be implemented in classrooms.

Woodrow, L. J. (2008), *Adaptive Second Language Learning*. Saarbruecken, Germany: VDM Verlag Dr. Muller.
This book presents the research that resulted in the motivation model of adaptive second language learning referred to in this chapter. The model comprises

self-efficacy, anxiety, motivation and language learning in relation to English language proficiency.

References

Ames, C. (1992), 'Classrooms: Goals and structures and student motivation'. *Journal of Educational Psychology*, 84(3), 261271.

Ames, C. and Archer, J. (1988), 'Achievement goals in the classroom: Students learning strategies and motivational processes'. *Journal of Educational Psychology*, 80, 260–267.

AMOS 7 (2006) SPSS Inc, Chicago, IL.

Blunch, N. J. (2008), *Introduction to Structural Equation Modeling using SPSS and AMOS*. London: Sage.

Crookes, G. and Schmidt, R. W. (1991), 'Motivation: Reopening the research agenda'. *Language Learning*, 41(4), 469–512.

Deci, E. L. and Ryan, R. M. (1980), 'The empirical exploration of intrinsic motivational processes'. *Advances in Experimental Social Psychology*, 13, 39–80.

—(1985), *Intrinsic Motivation and Self-determination in Human Behaviour*. New York: Plenum.

Dörnyei, Z. (1990), 'Conceptualizing motivation in foreign language learning'. *Language Learning*, 40(1), 45–78.

—(1994), 'Understanding L2 motivation: On with the challenge'. *Modern Language Journal*, 78(4), 515–523.

—(1996), 'Moving language learning motivation to a larger platform for theory and practice', in R. Oxford (ed.), *Language Learning Motivation: Pathways to the New Century* (Vol. Technical report 11). Manoa, Hawai'i: University of Hawai'i at Manoa, pp. 71–80.

—(2000), 'Motivation in action: Towards a process-oriented conceptualization of student motivation'. *British Journal of Educational Psychology*, 70, 519–538.

—(2001), 'New themes and approaches in second language motivation research'. *Annual Review of Applied Linguistics*, 21, 43–59.

—(2005), *The Psychology of the Language Learner: Individual Differences in Second Language Acquisition*. Mahwah: NJ: Lawrence Erlbaum.

Dörnyei, Z., Csizer, K. and Nemeth, N. (2006), *Motivation, Language Attitudes and Globalisation: A Hungarian Perspective*. Clevedon: Multilingual Matters.

Dörnyei, Z. and Otto, I. (1998), 'Motivation in action: A process model of L2 motivation'. *Working Papers in Applied Linguistics*, 4, 43–69.

Dörnyei, Z. and Schmidt, R. W. (eds) (2001), *Motivation and Second Language Acquisition*. Manoa, Hawai'i: University of Hawai'i at Manoa.

Elliot, A. and Church, M. (1997), 'A hierarchical model of approach and avoidance'. *Journal of Personality and Social Psychology*, 72, 218–232.

Elliot, A., McGregor, H. A. and Gable, S. (1999), 'Achievements goals, study strategies and exam performance: A mediational analysis'. *Journal of Educational Psychology*, 91(3), 549–563.

Gardner, R. C. (1985), *Social Psychology and Language Learning*. London: Edward Arnold.

—(1988), 'The socio-educational model of second language learning: Assumptions, findings and issues'. *Language Learning*, 38(1), 101–126.

—(2006), 'The socio-educational model of second language acquisition'. *EUROSLA Yearbook*, 6, 237–260.

Gardner, R. C. and Lambert, W. (1959), 'Motivational variables in second language acquisition'. *Canadian Journal of Psychology*, 13, 266–272.

—(1972), *Attitude and Motivation*. Rowley, M.A.: Newbury House.

Gardner, R. C. and MacIntyre, P. D. (1993), 'On the measurement of affective variables'. *Language Learning*, 43, 157–194.

Gardner, R. C., Tremblay, P. and Masgoret, A. (1997), 'Towards a full model of second language learning: An empirical investigation'. *The Modern Language Journal,* 81(3), 344–362.

Heckhausen, H. (1991), *Motivation and Action*. New York: Springer.

Heckhausen, H. and Kuhl, J. (1985), 'From wishes to action: The dead ends and short cuts on the long way to action', in M. Frese and J. Sabini (eds), *Goal Directed Behaviour: The Concept of Action in Psychology*. Hillsdale, NJ: Lawrence Erlbaum, pp. 134–160.

Holmes-Smith, P. (2000), *Introduction to Structural Equation Modeling using LISREL*. School Research, Evaluation and Measurement Services, Australia.

Jöreskog, K. G. and Sörbom, D. (1996), *LISREL 8: User's Reference Guide*. Chicago, Scientific Software International.

Kaiser, H. F. (1960), 'The application of electronic computers to factor analysis'. *Educational and Psychological Measurement*, 20,141–151.

Middleton, M. and Midgley, C. (1997), 'Avoiding the demonstration of lack of ability: An underexplored aspect of goal theory'. *Journal of Educational Psychology*, 89, 710–718.

Midgley, C., Maehr, M., Hicks, L., Roeser, R., Urdan, T., Anderman, E., Kaplan, A., Arunkumar, R. and Middleton, M. (1997), *Patterns of Adaptive learning Survey*. Michigan: University of Michigan.

Midgley, C., Kaplan, A., Middleton, M., Maehr, M., Urdan, T., Anderman, L., Anderman, E. and Roeser, R. (1998), 'The development and validation of scales assessing students' achievement goal orientations'. *Contemporary Educational Psychology*, 23(2), 113–131.

Noels, K. A. (2001), 'New orientations in language learning motivation: Towards a model of intrinsic, extrinsic and integrative orientations and motivation', in Z. Dörnyei and R. W. Schmidt (eds), *Motivation and Second Language Learning*. Honolulu: University of Hawai' i Press, pp. 43–68.

Noels, K. A., Clement, R. and Pelletier, L. C. (1999), 'Perceptions of teachers' communicative style and students' intrinsic and extrinsic motivation'. *The Modern Language Journal*, 83, 23–34.

—(2001), 'Intrinsic, extrinsic and integrative orientations of French Canadian learners of English'. *Canadian Modern Language Review*, 57(3), 424–442.

Noels, K. A., Pelletier, L. C., Clement, R. and Vallerand, R. J. (2001), 'Why are you learning a second language? Motivational orientations and self-determination theory'. *Language Learning*, 50(1), 57–85.

—(2003), 'Why are you learning a second language? Motivational orientations and self-determination theory'. *Language Learning*, 53(1), 33–64.

Oller, J. W. (1982), 'Gardner on affect: A reply to Gardner'. *Language Learning*, 32, 183–189.

Oxford, R. (1994), 'Where are we regarding language learning motivation?' *The Modern Language Journal*, 78(4), 512–514.

Oxford, R. L. (ed.), (1996), *Language Learning Motivation: Pathways to the New Century* (Vol. Technical report 11). Manoa, Hawai'i : University of Hawai'i at Manoa.

Oxford, R. and Shearin, J. (1994), 'Language learning motivation: Expanding the theoretical framework'. *The Modern Language Journal*, 78(1), 12–28.

Ryan, R. M. and Deci, E. L. (2000), 'Intrinsic and extrinsic motivations: Classic definitions and new directions'. *Contemporary Educational Psychology*, 25, 54–67.

Schmidt, R. W., Boraie, D. and Kassabgy, O. (1996), 'Foreign language motivation: Internal structure and external connections', in R. Oxford (ed.), *Language Learning Motivation: Pathways to the New Century* (Technical report vol. 11). Manoa, University of Hawai'i at Manoa, pp. 9–70.

SPSS Inc (2007), *SPSS Base 15*. SPSS Inc, Chicago IL.

Smith, M., Duda, J., Allen, J. and Hall, H. (2002), 'Contemporary measures of approach and avoidance goal orientations: Similarities and differences'. *British Journal of Educational Psychology*, 72, 155–190.

Tremblay, P. and Gardner, R. (1995), 'Expanding the motivation construct in language learning'. *The Modern Language Journal*, 79(4), 505–520.

Urdan, T., Ryan, R. M., Anderman, E. and Gheen, M. H. (2002), 'Goals, goal structures and avoidance behaviors', in C. Midgley (ed.), *Goals, Goal Structures and Patterns of Adaptive Learning*. Mahwah, NJ: Lawrence Erlbaum, pp. 55–84.

Ushioda, E. (2001), 'Language learning at university: Exploring the role of motivational thinking', in Z. Dörnyei and Schmidt (eds), *Motivation and Second Language Acquisition* (Technical Report Vol. 23) Manoa, Hawai'i: University of Hawai'i, pp. 93–125.

Vallerand, R. J. (1997), 'Toward a hierarchical model of intrinsic and extrinsic motivation', in M. P. Zanna (ed.), *Advances in Experimental Social Psychology*. New York: Academic Press, pp 271–360.

Woodrow, L. J. (2006), 'A model of adaptive language learning'. *The Modern Language Journal*, 90(3), 297–319.

22 Researching Language and Gender

Jane Sunderland

Chapter Overview

Language and gender is a wide-ranging field, encompassing gender and language use (talk and writing, production and reception), and language as 'code' (e.g., English, Gujarati, particular dialects). Modern, feminist-inspired language and gender studies first blossomed in the early 1970s, prompted by what can be called the 'second wave' of the western women's movement.[1] Since then, 'use' and 'code' have increasingly converged, with a shared movement towards and emphasis on *discourse* and *diversity* (among women, among men). Accordingly, the thrust of much empirical research now is not on *speakers*, embodied as female or male, but on *what is said or written*, about women, men, boys, girls and gender relations – what we might term 'gendered discourse'. This is to conceptualize gender as including, but going far beyond, 'differences' between women and men. It is also to see gender as not a matter of biology (though biology may have a role to play), or of socialization of children according to dominant gender stereotypes (though these may play a role too). Gender is now largely seen as a question of social construction *of and by* social, embodied individuals, in language and social (including institutional) practices, throughout those individuals' lifetimes, in ways which entail individual agency and resistance.

Approaches to Researching Language and Gender

Gone are the days when a researcher, perhaps inspired by Noam Chomsky, could introspect and use themself as a source of data – as Robin Lakoff did in her pioneer work *Language and Woman's Place* (1975), providing a spirited defence of her methodology (pp. 4–5). *Language and Woman's Place* was the first monograph in the field. A child of its time, the book focused on differences between women's talk and men's talk. There has been debate about whether Lakoff was following the 'deficit' (retrospectively named) approach, or the 'male dominance' approach (see e.g., Litosseliti 2006) to women's language.[2] But she was clearly conceptualizing gender as a male–female *binary*, something current research has moved on from.

Because the field is wide-ranging, so, accordingly, is the set of theoretical and empirical approaches which can be and are used to research it. Indeed, it is hard to imagine an approach which is not suitable for some form of language and gender investigation. Below I identify six different approaches, drawing on the recent *Gender and Language Research Methodologies* (Harrington et al. 2008), which readers are advised to consult for further detail and exemplification. (The first part of this chapter is based on the introductory chapter of this book by Jane Sunderland and Lia Litosseliti.) These (non-comprehensive, non-mutually-exclusive) approaches are broadly theoretical, with associated methodologies. They are:

- sociolinguistics
- corpus linguistics
- conversation analysis
- discursive psychology
- critical discourse analysis
- feminist post-structuralist discourse analysis

Sociolinguistics

Of these approaches, *Sociolinguistics* has the longest history, pre-dating the 1970s birth of (feminist-inspired) language and gender study. The original sociolinguistic paradigm was variationist (i.e., looking at differences in language use in, say, people of a different age, social class, geographical region or biological sex) and quantitative. The typical methodology for sociolinguistics-inspired gender and language studies was large-scale surveys in which men's and women's language use – for example, their pronunciation and grammar (e.g., William Labov 1966; Peter Trudgill 1972) – was compared in terms of standard and vernacular usage. The notion of gender was largely unproblematized (rather, 'sex' was the key independent variable).

Some pre-feminist 'gender differences' sociolinguistic work, in addition to that of Labov and Trudgill, though not carried out for feminist ends, produced findings of relevance to the later feminist project, in particular, the importance of context. Susan Gal (1978) revealed a striking tendency in Oberwart (on the Austrian-Hungarian border), i.e., that men were more likely to retain their Hungarian than were women – for the highly situated reason that, unlike the women, who tended to want to marry out of the community, the men were more likely to remain within it, doing traditional farming work. Lesley Milroy (1980) found that a group of women in one Belfast community (the Clonard) produced more of some vernacular forms than did their husbands (this in contrast to the findings of Labov and Trudgill), concluding that social network could be more relevant than gender. (Here she was anticipating the notion of 'relevance': that gender is sometimes, but sometimes is not, relevant to a given situation.) The notion of context is key to sociolinguistic work, and has been considerably refined with the emergence of 'Communities of practice' approaches (e.g., Eckert and McConnell-Ginet 1992), which emphasize the *local*. Eckert and McConnell-Ginet define a community of practice (CofP) as 'an aggregate of people who come together around mutual engagement in some common endeavour' (1992, p. 64): three examples might be a book club, a family breakfast and a school assembly. Gender will be enacted in different ways in each CofP, and may be more relevant in some CofPs than others.

Many modern gender and language studies (the numerous local, contextual-ized, qualitative explorations of intersections of gender with other social identities, including race, class and sexuality) can be described as *sociolinguistic*. An example of a recent study is Christine Mallinson and Becky Childs' (2007) investigation of language variation among rural Appalachian black women (two 'communities of practice' – the 'porch sitters' and the 'church ladies'). The two groups differed, *inter alia*, in their (non-) omission of the third person singular 's' (e.g., 'She like to eat'), omission being much more characteristic of the 'porch sitters' than the 'church ladies'. Mallinson and Child see this variation as contributing to the identity construction of members of the two groups (for the benefit of themselves, and of others). This study is concerned with diversity *among* women, and does not involve comparison between women and men.

Corpus Linguistics

Corpus linguistics quantitatively analyses corpora of up to several million words, which results in frequencies and probabilities of certain words or phrases, together with demographic characteristics of their users. In interpreta-tion, the 'co-text' (words on either side of the word/phrase in question) can be as wide as the analyst wishes to make it. Corpus linguistics is ideally placed to investigate such 'traditional' questions as whether a particular word or phrase is used more by men or women (with, if the analyst wishes, inflections of age, ethnicity and/or social class). However, it can also be used to investigate how women and men are differentially *constructed* in the way they refer to themselves or are referenced by others. For example, Sally Johnson and Astrid Ensslin (2007) explore how gendered language use is represented in newspaper texts, basing their analysis on 96 instances of the terms <his language> and <her language>. As an example of a finding, in an analysis of *bachelor* and *spinster* in the British National Corpus, Paul Baker (2008) shows that while the former collocates with positive words such as *eligible* and the latter is constructed as unattractive and lonely, the corpus also reveals a conflicting *feminist* discourse surrounding spinsters.

Corpus linguistics has the potential to make robust claims which other approaches cannot. Despite this, it faces a particular challenge in the current *qualitative* gender and language (indeed, social science) climate. However, frequencies and probabilities do not determine *interpretations,* and good corpus studies are by no means 'mechanical'. Depth does not have to be sacrificed for breadth, and indeed corpus linguistic studies can support and complement small-scale qualitative studies.

Conversation Analysis

Conversation analysis (CA) is concerned particularly with the sequential organization of naturally occurring, interactive talk (everyday conversations or institutional talk) and 'accomplishments' in that talk. Using micro-analysis, CA identifies recurrent, structural characteristics – namely organizational patterns such as turn-taking, interruptions and repairs. For example, Celia Kitzinger (2008), who examines 'interruption', shows how focusing on the details of how interruptions are achieved may point to positive outcomes for women (rather than 'male dominance') in particular interactional contexts.

The classic 'warrant' (see Swann 2002) for the relevance of gender in CA is *speakers' own orientation to gender,* for example, if a speaker starts an utterance with something like 'As a mother, . . .", or refers explicitly to women, men, boys or girls. Relatedly, Stokoe (2008) demonstrates how 'gender' can be studied in CA by looking *inter alia* at 'members' categories' (such as *girls/women, fellas/ men, secretary*). (CA is accordingly 'well-positioned to consider the constructed nature of gender in talk, and indeed speaker *agency*' (Kroløkke and Sørensen 2006, p. 49).) The *analyst* is thus not the judge of whether gender is relevant or not.

In rejecting 'prior variables' or analyst agendas, such as gender, CA however can be seen as problematic for gender study, and there has been a long-running debate about claims for gender in a localized stretch of talk, together with the role of the analyst and insights she can bring (e.g., Schegloff 1997, 1998; Wetherell 1998).[3]

Discursive Psychology

Discursive Psychology, a branch of social psychology, arguably shares more with linguistics than with psychology. Whereas traditional work on sex differences in psychology treated gender as a more-or-less fixed and monolithic entity, early work on discourse and gender in social psychology focused on the ways in which gender identity positions 'emerged' from discourses and were 'accomplished' locally, in spoken texts (Edwards and Potter, 1992). Key concepts are 'interpretive repertoires' and 'ideological dilemmas' (Billig et al. 1998; Edley 2001; see also below).[4]

Rather than being interested in cognitive processes, and indeed the 'inner self', discursive psychologists look at the different sorts of things that are *said, how*, to what *purpose* and to what *effect* in interaction. Discursive psychology has in fact taken two different directions (see McIlvenny 2002): one branch focusing on detailed fine-grained analysis and participants' concerns in talk, following the tradition of conversation analysis; the other branch being more closely related to post-structuralism and critical discourse analysis, drawing on the Foucauldian notion of *discourses*. Similar but not identical to 'interpretative repertoires', these are ways of seeing or representing the world which 'systematically form the objects of which they speak' (Foucault 1972, p. 49), that is, are constitutive. A challenge for discursive psychology is (whether) to combine analytical principles from both branches. Nigel Edley and Margaret Wetherell (2008), who argue precisely for such an integrative trajectory, claim that an expanded and integrative discursive psychology that aims to work across both the micro and the macro could combine a focus on how speakers *do* gender in their talk and 'how they are simultaneously *done* (constructed) as gendered beings in that talk: how speakers construct (and use) gender categories and how they are constructed – as gendered beings – by those very categories" (2008, p. 166).

Critical Discourse Analysis

Discourse analysis is largely concerned with naturally occurring language beyond the sentence (though not always – consider interjections such as 'No!'), and with what 'work' certain discursive features do (e.g., close a conversation).

Critical discourse analysis (CDA) also identifies and analyses the workings of discourses (many of which are gendered). CDA has very particular epistemological roots – including Critical linguistics, with its Marxist underpinnings (see Fairclough 1992, 2003).

There are several forms of CDA (see Wodak and Meyer 2009), which can be seen as constituting a 'programme' (Weiss and Wodak 2007). For example, Ruth Wodak (2008) has developed a 'discourse-historical' approach to CDA, and in a study of (female) migrant identities deploys an analysis that is both macro- and micro-, addressing different levels of spatial, historical and linguistic context. Konstantia Kosetzi (2008) in turn applies Faircloughian CDA to Greek TV fictional texts, and considers the special challenges of fiction for CDA. However, all CDA focuses on power (and contestation), works towards progressive social change, challenges assumptions and opens up new possibilities through different readings of texts. It considers both discursive and non-discursive practices, and assumes a dialectical relationship between discourse and the material, that is, that discourse shapes but is also shaped by some form of material reality (a position rejected by post-structuralist writers).

A question frequently raised is whether CDA's conventional focus on social class and on the 'dominant' and 'dominated' enables it to deal fully with gender (in which, for example, power and powerlessness may fluctuate – with context, within individuals and among gender groups; see Baxter 2003). Some gender and language analysts self-identify as Critical discourse analysts; others do not, though their work may well be feminist (hence 'critical') (see also Wodak 1997). One researcher who has explicitly used CDA effectively in her work on gender is Michelle Lazar (2005), who shows how the representation of the modern father in pro-natalist ads in Singapore 'continue[s] to maintain, through subtle and seemingly innocuous ways, gender difference and inequality' (p. 140).

Feminist Post-Structuralist Discourse Analysis

Developed by Judith Baxter, *Feminist post-structuralist discourse analysis* (FPDA) (Baxter 2002, 2003) has roots in post-structuralism and feminism. Its concern is 'to release the words of marginalised or minority speakers' (2002, p. 9). FPDA also 'responds' to CDA and CA (it is informed by broad social issues *and* includes very detailed analysis of talk). It is intended in part to *supplement* CDA by focusing on instances of power (or powerlessness) which may be too fleeting or unconventionally manifested for conventional CDA to deal with.

For FPDA, individuals not only have *agency*, manifested in different linguistic forms, but also the potential to recognize how and through which discourses they are being 'positioned', to *take up* particular subject positions, and to *resist* others. FPDA thus rejects the notion of individuals being 'at the mercy of competing discourses' (Baxter 2003, p. 31). Agency does not entail, however, what Baxter characterizes as a 'liberal-humanist conception of the free individual in control of their destiny' (2003, p. 31), as the range of possible subject positions for women remains limited.

It is not possible to identify the 'best' approach for gender and language study – or even for feminist study. We already have 'Feminist post-structural discourse analysis', 'Feminist CDA', 'Feminist conversation analysis' and indeed 'Feminist stylistics' (Mills 1995) and there is no reason why we should not have 'Feminist sociolinguistics/corpus linguistics/discursive psychology'.[5] However, discourse analysis (say) can be used in the interests of misogyny as well as feminism (see Gill 1995). A given researcher will choose her approach(es) in relation to her own epistemological stance, and of course her research question(s). However, while some approaches may be theoretically compatible, and hence 'combinable', and indeed some such can then be used to 'serve' others (corpus linguistics could serve CDA, for example), this may not be possible for all potential 'pairings' (CDA is unlikely to be used to 'serve' CA, say, because of the 'agenda-free' underpinning of CA). More than two compatible approaches can be combined, of course, as I show in the study below.

Data, Research Strategies and Techniques

In the early days of language and gender study, data was characteristically transcripts of naturally occurring talk in private contexts between white middle-class heterosexual couples. As the 'spoken' field has widened and developed, including into institutional talk, written texts (including electronic ones) of many genres have also come into their own. Of course, data for language and gender work does not have to be naturally occurring texts or talk, but can also be elicited through questionnaires, interviews or focus groups (e.g., in Discursive Psychology projects), then being, for example, *reported* beliefs or practices.

Both qualitative and quantitative approaches to data analysis are of value (alone or in combination) – as, indeed, are qualitative and quantitative *data*. As with approaches, it is not possible to exclude any research strategy or technique from the gender and language field. As regards data collection, methods frequently used include questionnaires, diary studies, interviews, focus groups, observation (including field-notes, audio- and video-recording),[6] researcher participation (e.g., in a particular Community of practice), compilation of corpora, as well as methods often associated with research in language education (in which there is huge scope for language and gender work (see Sunderland 2000), such as stimulated recall and think-aloud protocols). Needless to say, this is not a comprehensive list, neither are the methods mutually exclusive.

A Sample Study

The following example of current language and gender research is an investigation of a written text: a set of electronically circulated jokes about women, and how such jokes can be 'dealt with' by (feminist) readers. As such, it contributes to the growing field of gender and humour (e.g., Holmes 2000; Kotthof 2000). Although data-driven, the study is a largely theoretical one – but *empirical* work on readings of these jokes would constitute an important subsequent project. The theoretical insights, I hope, have implications for texts beyond this particular illustrative dataset – for both language and gender study, and reading theory (for a fuller version, see Sunderland, 2007). In terms of methodology, this study does not employ either Corpus Linguistics (the data consists of a single, small text) or Conversation Analysis (the text is written). It does, however, in ways which I shall show, draw substantially on Critical Discourse Analysis in terms of close textual analysis and text 'consumption' and on Discursive psychology and post-structuralism in its conceptualization. (These are of course shared by Feminist post-structuralist discourse analysis; however, FPDA is more usually applied to spoken texts). Lastly, it can also be seen as falling within a sociolinguistic paradigm, given its concern with language as a social and societal phenomenon.

As indicated above, Discursive psychology has conceptualized the notion of *ideological dilemmas*. Billig et al. (1998) cite examples of contradictory proverbs (e.g., 'look before you leap'/'he who hesitates is lost'). But we also *knowingly* use expressions such as 'On the one hand, . . . on the other . . .', and 'One part of me thinks . . . while the other part of me thinks . . .' And we draw on different discourses at different times and in different situations: 'Academically selective schools are socially divisive' on the one hand, and 'Parents should do the best for their children (and my child would do best at an academically selective school)' on the other. We may be able to discursively reconcile these two positions ('Academically selective schools are socially divisive *but* I can live with that as I have to do the best for my child'), but we may still experience the ideological dilemma as uncomfortable.

The Jokes

The data/jokes in question were circulated by email – I received them from an ex-student who shared my interest in gender, who would have received them from someone else, and so on – and they may thus have been changed, more than once, since their original launching. The set of jokes (Figure 22.1) is entitled:

NEW COURSES AVAILABLE FOR WOMEN: Training courses are now available for women on the following subjects.

- Silence, the Final Frontier: Where No Woman Has Gone Before.
- The Undiscovered Side of Banking: Making Deposits.
- Parties: Going Without New Outfits.
- Man Management: Minor Household Chores Can Wait until After The Game.
- Bathroom Etiquette I: Men Need Space in the Bathroom Cabinet Too.
- Bathroom Etiquette II: His Razor is His.
- Communication Skills I: Tears? The Last Resort, not the First.
- Communication Skills II: Thinking Before Speaking.
- Communication Skills III: Getting what you want without nagging.
- Driving a Car Safely: A Skill You CAN Acquire.
- Telephone Skills: How to Hang Up.
- Introduction to Parking.
- Advanced Parking: Backing Into a Space.
- Water Retention: Fact or Fat.
- Cooking I: Bringing Back Bacon, Eggs and Butter.
- Cooking II: Bran and Tofu are Not for Human Consumption.
- Cooking III: How Not to Inflict Your Diets on Other People.
- Compliments: Accepting Them Gracefully.
- PMS: Your Problem . . . Not His.
- Dancing: Why Men Don't Like To.
- Classic Clothing: Wearing Outfits You Already Have.
- Household Dust: A Harmless Natural Occurrence Only Women Notice.
- Integrating Your Laundry: Washing It All Together.
- Oil and Petrol: Your Car Needs Both.
- TV Remotes: For Men Only.
- Getting ready to go out: Start the day before.

Figure 22.1 'Training courses for women'

The list concluded: 'Please register immediately as courses are expected to be in great demand.'

The above is clearly a 'spoof' list of Adult Education courses, workshop sessions or even academic conference sessions. As spoofs, they may be found amusing because of the recognizable structural features of the genre: the initial short, snappy phrase (a rather general noun, noun phrase or gerund), followed by a colon anticipating the specific focus of the 'course'.

But the jokes are also clear expressions of familiar gender stereotypes, with the first, seventh, eighth, ninth and eleventh being folklinguistic stereotypes of women's talk. The jokes self-evidently, if jocularly, draw on a dominant 'gender differences' discourse (see Sunderland 2004) – 'a discourse' being an important notion for both CDA and post-structuralism – which allows neither for differences *among* women (and among men), nor similarities *between* women and men. So, assuming obvious contradictions between the premises of these jokes, and our own largely feminist convictions, why did I (and my 'Gender and Language Research Group' members) simultaneously recognize the sexism *and* find the jokes, or at least the experience of reading them, mildly amusing? Did we experience an 'ideological dilemma'? What, precisely, were we laughing *at*?

What/Who the Text is About

CDA extends beyond texts to their production and 'consumption' (see Fairclough 1992). Similarly, as regards consumption, but from a more Stylistics perspective:

> A dissatisfaction with formalist accounts [of written texts] and with attempts to trace author intentions have led to concerns with the reader. Once the author is considered 'dead' [Barthes 1986], then it seems to be a logical move to try to institute the reader in that position of stability (Mills 1994, p. 8).

Reader response may be particularly apposite when looking at electronically circulated texts, whose original author is not traceable. A reader is normally capable of saying what they see a text they are reading as being 'about'. They achieve this partly through the guidance of the text itself. This includes its *interpellation* (Althusser 1998), that is, who is being addressed, and as what? Althusser's own example is of a policeman addressing a guilty person by 'hailing' him or her with 'Hey, you there!', and the person turning round, that is, accepting that she/he is being addressed. That person is, however, also being addressed by *ideology*, that is, she/he turns through acknowledgment of guilt *within a particular ideological framework*. Similarly, readers will recognize particular ideological workings of gender in these jokes.

On the surface, bolstered by the title, the pronouns *you* and *your* suggest that it is *women* who are being 'hailed' in these jokes: 'Getting what you want without nagging', and so on. Deeper consideration of who the jokes are *actually (if indirectly)* interpellating and aimed at however suggests that the 'ideal readers' (see Talbot 1995) are primarily *men*, who are being invited to laugh at women's behaviours which apparently merit correction, that is, talking without thinking, nagging and being:

- excessively talkative
- spendthrift
- vain

- preoccupied with appearance
- manipulative
- bad drivers
- irrational
- non-technical
- disorganized

Conceptually related to *interpellation* is *focalization*, the 'presentation of a scene through the subjective perception of a character' (Benwell 2002; Felluga 2002).[7] This is often achieved through direct speech attributed to a particular speaker or through first-person narration. Here, however, where the focalization is arguably that of those men who apparently find these alleged behaviours of women incomprehensible, in need of correction and/or simply amusing, it is achieved through what has been called 'free indirect discourse' (e.g., Short 1996).

This masculine focalization builds on the principle of 'for *you*, read *women*'. However, it is achieved more broadly because these behaviours of women are all described in critical, prescriptive or proscriptive ways, which draw on existing stereotypes (e.g., talking too much, being serial clothes shoppers). Accordingly, it is *men's* interests that are being jocularly defended ('His razor is his'). Note the constructed opposition of interests (implicit or explicit) between the female (reader) and the implied male reader (see Sunderland 2004 on the 'Battle of the sexes' discourse). Even the 'gender-neutral' cases, like 'The Undiscovered Side of Banking: Making Deposits', can be read as being *about (not addressed to)* women, given the stereotype of women as spendthrift, and the co-text (this joke follows 'Silence, the Final Frontier: Where No Woman Has Gone Before').

Exploring Feminist Readings of the Jokes

Women sympathetic to feminism (as well as those who are not) may find these jokes amusing if, like it or not, they recognize themselves in them. Pleasure, Freud notes, can come from recognition (1905/1976, p. 170). But given the post-structuralist insight that the meaning of a text is never fixed, and that any text affords more than one reading (e.g., about women, about men), we can also acknowledge not only that two readers can respond differently to a particular joke – with different conceptualizations (what or who the joke is 'about') and evaluation (whether it is amusing, sexist, ironic, or whatever) – but also that a *single* reader can also simultaneously entertain more than one reading of a text. This takes us some way to looking at simultaneously critical and pleasurable responses to the same joke.

Reader response(s) is an overly straightforward and individual 'explanation'. CDA takes as given that certain ways of seeing, representing, conceptualizing and evaluating the world are more hegemonic than others. And here we return to discourses – value-laden and constitutive (within and potentially beyond texts themselves; manifested in and recognized through particular linguistic *cues* and *traces* (e.g., Talbot 1998). In these jokes, we can recognize an overall 'traditional', dominant gendered discourse: entailing that women are, *inter alia*, spendthrift and bad at reverse parking. Women readers are thus positioned by traditional discourses of gender as the very people who are the butt of the jokes. And, to make sense of such texts, women readers must *recognize* the indirect interpellation of women. If they do this they must – however indirectly – have been interpellated as such (Mills 1992).

However, importantly, feminist (and other) readers of the jokes are likely to be aware of other, intertextually related, oppositional, discourses – which as active readers they can 'invoke'. These, I suggest, include:

- a *critical anti-sexist discourse* (entailing awareness of sexism)
- a *feminist discourse of agency/non-victimhood/self-value* (entailing an awareness of women as strong, independent and worthy)
- a *post-feminist discourse* (see below)

Feminist readers can thus be seen as 'multiply positioned', given the inter-discursive links of these sexist jokes with *competing* as well as supporting discourses. A feminist reader, while acknowledging the jokes' sexism, might at the same time find them amusing given the awareness and self-confidence that can *simultaneously* come from also having access to the first two of these discourses (but see also Mills 2008).

But why *amusing*? The above argument can be made more convincing, I suggest, if the feminist reader is seen as also able to access a 'Post-feminist discourse'. I propose four possible meanings of *post-feminism* – none of which is 'The need for feminism is over' or 'Feminism is dead'. ('We', here, refers to feminist readers of these jokes.)

- although there is no longer a clear feminist platform for grievances, there has been in the past;
- we do and see things knowing about feminism and with the benefit of having experienced feminism;
- we can adopt a feminist perspective not just a 'sexism awareness' perspective;
- we see sexism *and beyond* (e.g., its causes, but also its spin-offs).

In other words, the relationship between such jokes and their readers can be seen broadly as: 'we know about feminism, others know, we know they know, and they know we know they know,' where 'we' can be the reader *or* producer.

This relationship holds true too for the producers and consumers of men's 'lifestyle' magazines such as *Loaded* (by-line: 'for men who should know better'). Acknowledging this 'knowingness', Bethan Benwell writes: 'it seems that the reader is required to tread a subtle and practised course though a minefield of irony, ambiguity and double-voicing' (2002, p. 166).

The concept of *double-voicing* (Bakhtin 1984) can be used to refer to the possibility of two or more readings of a text being made available simultaneously, something Benwell (2002) also claims of *Loaded*: ('Yes, it's sexist, but we know that, and (so) we're being ironic'). Here, I am suggesting that our experience of double-voiced texts, together with the accessibility of a range of discourses, allows us to actively 'double-voice' a text *for ourselves*, as a productive form of 'reading against the grain' (see Cosslett 1996). As *active* readers, we can deliberately read these jokes in more than one way, simultaneously; together with the text, we can *co-construct* irony.

Feminist Reading Positions

What, then, are some alternative *reading positions* for the feminist who encounters these jokes?

Sara Mills (1992) looks at alternative positions in relation to the individual reading of a male-focalized poem, 'Valentine', and I have adapted these here. I suggest that there are four possible positions, which shade into each other, *vis á vis* the jokes: critical rejection, resistant reading, critical enjoyment and feminist reclamation.

A feminist reader may *critically reject* these jokes materially, by deleting them, or discursively, by adding a critical rejoinder and/or asking the person who forwarded them not to do so again. If she engages in *resistant reading*, she may recognize and negatively evaluate the sexist discourse, positioning herself as an 'overhearer' of jokes addressed to men (though, as indicated, understanding means that she has been successfully interpellated (Mills 1992)).

Thirdly, she may *critically enjoy* the text. For example, as suggested above, she may co-construct the text's ironic potential, 'double-discourse' the text, and take intellectual pleasure in that. This also allows her to see different possibilities for what or who the joke is about. In the fourth (related) reading, *feminist reclamation*, she can also co-construct the jokes as being *not as much* about women as about men, the (presumed) writers and (ideal) consumers of the jokes. Cognitively more complex, but perhaps ultimately more satisfying, this is to 'refocalize' (ironize?) the jokes and take the woman's perspective (far beyond the 'your laundry' reading), actively moving the 'object' of the joke (women) to subject position and make the original focalizers, men, the object. She can then see humour in the fact that these tired old stereotypes are *still* in circulation and that some people *still* enjoy them: 'Nice spoofs – but how silly these jokes and their producers and the consumers who find their presuppositions funny are!'[8]

The four reading positions may provide psychological survival strategies, allowing readings which constitute critique, enjoyment and/or an achieved refusal to be subject positioned as manipulative, a bad driver or irrational. The fourth position additionally helps us identify what exactly is amusing when we find ourselves laughing at these jokes: rather than their sexism, it is the foolish assumptions behind them, and the fact that this foolishness retains some currency, that is entertaining. The 'real joke' is thus at the expense of these particular social norms and those who adhere to or enjoy them. (Note that the men in these jokes are also interpellated as not minding, or even as enjoying, being constructed as somewhat 'unreconstructed'.)

All this raises the wider question of how feminists handle sexism (explicit, subtle or ironic) in a 'post-feminist' age. Saying to a man who is audibly enjoying such jokes, 'Your reaction does you no favours, you know' sounds unproductively pompous. More effective may be a humorous, playful riposte – in the spirit of 'fun feminism' (Kamada 2008). 'Double-voicing' facilitates sexism in *Loaded*, because of the potential for irony. Can it also be deployed to allow for the *contestation* of sexism? Can societal familiarity with double-voicing ever work in favour of feminism?

A second question is whether – contradictions aside – such jokes point (in some sense) to a failure of feminism. Of *Loaded*, Benwell claims:

> [the] 'knowing' tone, the ambiguity, the double-voicing are all strategies employed to preserve [traditional, heterosexual] masculine values in the face of a disapproving world (2002, p. 170; see also Benwell 2004).

Johnson (1997) has similarly observed that, to survive, traditional institutions and practices simply need to *adapt* – and many do, despite the contradictions. The ironic potential of these jokes can be seen as just such a form of adaptation.

Notes

1. The 'first wave' being the campaign for women's suffrage in the early twentieth century; the 'third wave' being associated with postmodernist understandings and ways of being, and 'post-feminism' (see Mills 2003).
2. A third 'gender differences' approach is '(cultural) difference' (see Litosseliti 2006).
3. Interestingly, CA has also recently been *reclaimed* by and for gender and language study (e.g., Kitzinger 2000, 2008; Stokoe and Smithson 2001).

4. Another key concept of Discursive Psychology is 'subject positioning' (Billig et al. 1988).
5. See 'Further reading' for works on feminist methodologies.
6. Transcription is of course often associated with naturally occurring or elicited spoken data, making the transcript the 'object' of analysis.
7. Focalization is a notion largely employed by Stylistics. Stylistics is regrettably absent from the above non-comprehensive account of approaches to gender and language research. One relevant text here is Sara Mills' *Feminist Stylistics* (1995, Routledge).
8. She can even reject the premises on which the jokes are based, and consider, for example, the *value* of talk, getting rid of dust, etc. This also enables her to be *critical* of the specific masculine focalization. Actively making men the object of the jokes ('men simply do not appreciate the value of talk, etc.') allows her to see humour in this represented lack of appreciation.

Resources for Further Reading

Cameron, D., Frazer, E., Harvey, P., Rampton, B. and Richardson, K. (eds) (1992), *Researching Language: Issues of Power and Method*. London: Routledge.
Cameron et al. provide a penetrating examination of the ethics of research on language use. Gender is one of several foci here.

Gender and Genre Bibliography (3rd edn) (Centre for Language and Social Life, Lancaster University), http://www.ling.lancs.ac.uk/groups/gal/projects/index.html
This includes references to studies of gender and language in relation to wide range of written (and spoken) genres, including dictionaries, posters and classroom talk. Last updated 2005.

Hesse-Biber, S., Gilmartin, C. and Lyndenberg, R. (eds) (1999), *Feminist Approaches to Theory and Methodology: An interdisciplinary reader*. Oxford: Oxford University Press.
This is a collection of interdisciplinary work, focusing *inter alia* on feminist critique, identity and experience, and the social construction of difference. There is no explicit focus on language.

International Gender and Language Association (IGALA) http://www.lancs.ac.uk/fass/organisations/igala/index.html
This website includes resources for teaching language and gender.

Miller, C. with Treitel, C. (1991), *Feminist Research Methods: An Annotated Bibliography*. Connecticut: Greenwood Press.
This book is divided into disciplines. One is 'Communication', of which 'language and speech' is a sub-section.

Nielsen, J. M. (1990), *Feminist Research Methods: Exemplary Readings in the Social Sciences*. San Francisco: Westview Press.
The first half of this collection looks explicitly at feminist research methods, with a focus on science, sociology and oral history.

Sunderland, J. (2006), *Language and Gender: An Advanced Resource Book*. London: Routledge.

This includes extracts from important publications, as well as tasks which can be the basis of assignments or MA dissertations.

Sunderland, J. (2000), 'Review article: Issues of gender and language in second and foreign language education'. *Language Teaching*, 33(4), 203–223.

This includes a substantial Bibliography, including references to work on achievement, 'ability', the 'four skills', motivation/investment, teacher perceptions, learning styles and strategies, classroom interaction, English as a sexist/non-sexist language, teaching materials, language testing, teachers and professional organizations, teacher education and identities (including masculinities).

References

Althusser, L. (1998), 'Ideology and ideological state apparatuses', in J. Rivkin and M. Ryan (eds), *Literary Theory: An Anthology*. Malden: Blackwell Publishers, pp. 294–304.

Baker, P. (2008), '"Eligible" bachelors and "frustrated" spinsters: corpus linguistics, gender and language', in K. Harrington, L. Litosseliti, H. Sauntson and J. Sunderland (eds), *Language and Gender Research Methodologies*. London: Palgrave Macmillan, pp. 73–84.

Bakhtin, M. (1984), *Problems of Dostoevsky's Poetics* (ed. and trans. C. Emerson) Minneapolis: University of Minnesota Press.

Barthes, R. (1986), 'The death of the author', in R. Barthes (ed.), *The Rustle of Language*. Oxford: Blackwell.

Baxter, J. (2002), 'A juggling act: A feminist post-structuralist analysis of girls' and boys' talk in the secondary classroom'. *Gender and Education*, 14(1), 5–19.

—(2003), *Positioning Gender in Discourse: A Feminist Methodology*. London: Palgrave Macmillan.

Benwell, B. (2002), 'Is there anything "new" about these lads?: The textual and visual construction of masculinity in men's magazines', in L. Litosseliti and J. Sunderland (eds), *Gender Identity and Discourse Analysis*. Amsterdam: John Benjamins, pp. 149–176.

Benwell, B. (2004), 'Ironic discourse: Evasive masculinity in men's lifestyle magazines'. *Men and Masculinities*, 7(1), 3–21.

Billig, M., Condor, S., Edwards, D., Gane, M., Middleton, D. and Radley, A. (1988), *Ideological Dilemmas: A Social Psychology of Everyday Thinking*. London: Sage.

Cosslett, Tess (1996), 'Fairytales: revising the tradition', in T. Cosslett, A. Easton and P. Summerfield (eds), *Women, Power and Resistance*. Milton Keynes: Open University Press, pp. 81–90.

Eckert, P. and McConnell-Ginet, S. (1992), 'Communities of practice: Where language, gender and power all live', in K. Hall, M. Bucholtz and B. Moonwomon (eds), *Locating power: Proceedings of the Second Berkeley Women and Language Conference*. Berkeley, CA: Women and Language Group, pp. 89–99.

Edley, N. (2001), 'Analysing masculinity: Interpretive repertoires, ideological dilemmas and subject positions', in Wetherell, M., Taylor, S. and Yates, S. (eds), *Discourse as Data: A Guide for Analysis*. Milton Keynes: Open University Press, pp. 189–228.

Edley, N. and Wetherell, M. (2008), 'Discursive psychology and the study of gender: A contested space', in K. Harrington, L. Litosseliti, H. Sauntson and J. Sunderland (eds), *Language and Gender Research Methodologies*. London: Palgrave Macmillan, pp. 161–173.

Edwards, N. and Potter, J. (1992), *Discursive Psychology*. London: Sage.

Fairclough, N. (1992), *Discourse and Social Change*. Cambridge: Polity Press.

—(2003), *Analysing Discourse: Textual Analysis for Social Research*. London: Routledge.

Felluga, D. 2002. http://www.sla.purdue.edu/academic/engl/theory/narratology/terms/focalize.html.

Foucault, M. (1972), *The Archaeology of Knowledge*. London: Tavistock Publications.

Freud, S. (1905/1976), *Jokes and their Relation to the Unconscious*. London: Pelican.

Gal, S. (1978), 'Peasant men can't get wives: Language change and sex roles in a bilingual community'. *Language in Society* 7, 1–17.

Gill, R. (1995), 'Relativism, reflexivity and politics: Interrogating discourse analysis from a feminist perspective', in S. Wilkinson and C. Kitzinger, (eds), *Feminism and Discourse: Psychological Perspectives*. London: Sage, pp. 165–86.

Harrington, K. (2008), 'Perpetuating difference? Corpus linguistics and the gendering of reported dialogue', in K. Harrington, L. Litosseliti, H. Sauntson and J. Sunderland (eds), *Gender and Language Research Methodologies*. London: Palgrave Macmillan, pp. 85–102.

Harrington, K., Litosseliti, L., Sauntson, H. and Sunderland, J. (eds) (2008), *Gender and Language Research Methodologies*. London: Palgrave Macmillan.

Holmes, J. (2000), 'Politeness, power and provocation: how humour functions in the workplace'. *Discourse Studies*, 2(2), 159–185.

Johnson, S. (1997), 'Theorising language and masculinity: a feminist perspective', in S. Johnson. and U. H. Meinhof (eds), *Language and Masculinity*. Oxford: Blackwell, pp. 8–26.

Johnson, S. and Ensslin, A. (2007), '"But her language skills shifted the family dynamics dramatically": Language, gender and the construction of publics in two British newspapers'. *Gender and Language*, 1(2), 229–253.

Kamada, L. (2008), 'Discursive "embodied" identities of "half" girls in Japan: A multi-perspective approach', in K. Harrington, L. Litosseliti, H. Sauntson and J. Sunderland (eds), *Language and Gender Research Methodologies*. Palgrave Macmillan, pp. 174–192.

Kitzinger, C. (2008), 'Conversation analysis: Technical matters for gender research', in K. Harrington, L. Litosseliti, H. Sauntson and J. Sunderland (eds), *Language and Gender Research Methodologies*. London: Palgrave Macmillan, pp. 119–138.

Kotthof, H. (2000), 'Gender and joking: on the complexities of women's image politics in humorous narratives'. *Journal of Pragmatics*, 32, 55–80.

Kosetzi, Konstantia (2008), 'Harnessing a critical discourse analysis of gender in television fiction', in Harrington, K., Litosseliti, L., Sauntson, H. and Sunderland, J. (eds), *Gender and Language Research Methodologies*. Houndmills, UK: Palgrave Macmillan, pp. 227–239.

Kr---- Kroløkke, C. and Sørensen, A. S. (2006), *Gender Communication – Theories and Analyses*. London: Sage.

Labov, W. (1966), *The Social Stratification of English in New York City*. Washington, DC: Center for Applied Linguistics.

Lakoff, R. (1975), *Language and Woman's Place*. New York: Colophon Books.

Lazar, M. (2005), *Feminist Critical Discourse Analysis: Gender, Power and Ideology in Discourse*. London: Palgrave Macmillan.

Litosseliti, L. (2006), *Gender and Language: Theory and Practice*. London: Hodder Arnold.

Mallinson, C. and Childs, B. (2007), 'Communities of practice in sociolinguistic description: Analysing language and identity practices among black women in Appalachia'. *Gender and Language*, 1(2), 173–206.

McIlvenny, P. (2002), 'Introduction: Researching talk, gender and sexuality', in McIlvenny, P. (ed.), *Talking Gender and Sexuality*. Amsterdam, John Benjamins, pp. 1–48.

Mills, S. (1992), 'Knowing your place: A Marxist feminist stylistic analysis', in M. Toolan (ed.), *Language, Text and Context: Essays in Stylistics*. London: Routledge, pp. 241–59.

Mills, S. (1994), *Gendering the Reader*. Hemel Hempstead: Harvester Wheatsheaf.

Mills, S. (2003), 'Caught between sexism, anti-sexism and "political correctness": Feminist women's negotiations with naming practices'. *Discourse and Society*, 14(1), 87–110.

Mills, S. (2008), *Language and Sexism*. Cambridge: Cambridge University Press.

Milroy, L. (1980), *Language and Social Networks*. Oxford: Basil Blackwell.

Schegloff, E. (1997), 'Whose text? Whose context?' *Discourse and Society* 8(2), 165–87.

—(1998), 'Reply to Wetherell.' *Discourse and Society* 9(3), 413–416.

Short, M. (1996), *Exploring the Language of Poems, Plays and Prose*. London: Longman.

Stokoe, E. (2008), 'Categories, actions and sequences: Formulating gender in talk-in-interaction', in K. Harrington, L. Litosseliti, H. Sauntson and J. Sunderland (eds), *Language and Gender Research Methodologies*. London: Palgrave Macmillan, pp. 139–160.

Stokoe, E. and Smithson, J. (2001), 'Making gender relevant: Conversation analysis and gender categories in interaction'. *Discourse and Society*, 12, 217–244.

Sunderland, J. (2004), *Gendered Discourses*. London: Palgrave Macmillan.

Sunderland, J. (2007), 'Contradictions in gendered discourses: Feminist readings of sexist jokes?' *Gender and Language*, 1(2), 207–228.

Swann, J. (2002), '"Yes, but is it gender?"', in L. Litosseliti and J. Sunderland (eds), *Gender Identity and Discourse Analysis*. Amsterdam: John Benjamins, pp. 43–67.

Talbot, M. (1995), *Fictions at Work*. London: Longman.

—(1998), *Language and Gender*. London: Polity.

Trudgill, P. (1972), 'Sex, covert prestige and linguistic change in the urban British English of Norwich'. *Language in Society*, 1, 179–95.

Weiss, G. and Wodak, R. (eds) (2007), *Critical Discourse Analysis: Theory and Interdisciplinarity*. Houndmills: Palgrave Macmillan.

Wetherell, M. (1998), 'Positioning and interpretative repertoires: Conversation analysis and post-structuralism in dialogue'. *Discourse and Society* 9(3), 387–412.

Wodak, R. (1997), 'Introduction', in R. Wodak (ed.), *Gender and Discourse*. London: Sage.

Wodak, R. (2008), 'Controversial issues in feminist critical discourse analysis', in K. Harrington, L. Litosseliti, H. Sauntson, and J. Sunderland (eds), *Gender and Language Research Methodologies*. Houndmills: Palgrave Macmillan, pp. 193–209.

Wodak, R. and Meyer, M. (2009), 'Critical discourse analysis: history, agenda, theory and methodology', in Wodak, R. and Meyer, M. (eds), *Methods of Critical Discourse Analysis* (2nd edn.) London: Sage, pp. 1–33.

23 Researching Language and Identity

David Block

Identity has become a key construct in the social sciences in general, and applied linguistics in particular, in recent years. Following current post-structuralist and social constructivist thinking on the topic (e.g., Giddens 1991; Weedon 1997), many applied linguists today understand identities to be socio-culturally constructed ongoing narratives, which develop and evolve across different spatio-temporal scales, ranging from the micro, local and immediate to the macro, global and long-term (Lemke 2008). As regards the former spatio-temporal scale, these socio-culturally constructed narratives are seen to emerge during individuals' engagements in activities with others, with whom to varying degrees they share beliefs, motives and values, in communities of practice, where a community of practice is defined as 'an aggregate of people who come together around mutual engagement in an endeavour' (Eckert and McConnell-Ginet 1992, p. 464). Such activity-based communication can take place either face-to-face or in an electronically mediated mode, with the latter becoming increasingly more prevalent (see publications in journals such as *Language Learning and Technology* and *E-Learning*). In addition, and consistent with the macro, global and long-term scale cited above, identity construction is seen as the negotiating of subject positions at the crossroads of the past, present and future.

Following Giddens's (1984) structuration theory, many researchers also take as axiomatic that individuals are shaped by ever-emergent and evolving social, cultural and historical structures, but at the same time – and indeed, in recursive fashion – they shape these same emergent and ever-evolving social, cultural and historical structures as their lives unfold. Among other things, negotiation means that such processes involve both self-ascription or self-positioning by individuals who in turn – and simultaneously – are ascribed identities and are positioned in particular ways by others with whom they come in contact. In this process issues around perceived and invoked sameness and differences, and authenticity and inauthenticity, come into play.

All of this means that the process of identity construction is potentially and indeed often conflictive as opposed to harmonious, especially in situations involving movement across borders which are simultaneously geographical historical, cultural and psychological. In such circumstances, identity work is often characterized by the ambivalence that individuals feel about exactly who they are and where they belong (Block 2006). In addition, following Bourdieu (1984), individuals are seen to be embedded in multiple social milieus, or fields, in which they constantly encounter unequal power relationships related to their access to and their legitimate control over and use of different capitals in these fields – economic, cultural and social. Finally, identities are related to different traditionally demographic categories such as ethnicity, race, nationality, migration, gender, sexuality, religion, social class and language (Block 2006, 2007).

This view of identity to varying degrees underlies a good deal of applied linguistics research that has been carried out over the past two decades, particularly work on multilingualism, language education and second language learning. On the one hand, there are publications in journals such as *International Journal of Bilingual Education and Bilingualism* and *Journal of Language, Identity and Education*. On the other hand, there is a long list of recent books on identity and language practices which include more general overviews (e.g., Joseph 2004; Benwell and Stokoe 2006; Block 2007; Riley 2007), research monographs (e.g., Norton 2000; Kanno 2003; Miller 2003; Block 2006) and collections of chapters (Pavlenko et al. 2001; Pavlenko and Blackledge 2004; Benson and Nunan 2005; De Fina et al. 2006; Omoniyi and White 2006; Caldas-Coulthard and Iedema 2008). In these and other publications, researchers have focused on migration, literacies, language policy, language learning and language use in a wide variety of contexts, emphasizing particular dimensions of identity – age, ethnicity, race, nationality, migration, gender, sexuality, religion, social class and so on.

Typical Stages in Carrying out the Research

Applied linguists have tended to explore identity from two separate but often interlinked perspectives. On the one hand, many researchers have taken seriously the notion that all utterances constitute 'acts of identity in which people reveal both their personal identity and their search for social roles' (Le Page and Tabouret-Keller 1985, p. 14). As a first stage, these researchers typically collect samples of their informant's speech, either in the latter's day-to-day activities or in face-to-face interviews. The general view is that speakers' identities are indexed in how they draw on repertories of linguistic resources, which include language choice, accent, lexical choice and morpho-syntax. However, in recent years the interest has moved beyond language, to a multimodal approach which examines semiotic resources, including body movements, gaze, clothing and space (Blommaert 2005). The upshot of this interest, is that identity is seen as discursively constructed, where discourse, with a capital 'D', is understood in a broad sense as

> ways of being in the world, or forms of life which integrate words, acts,
> values, beliefs, attitudes and social identities, as well as gestures, glances,
> body positions, and clothes. A Discourse is a sort of identity kit which
> comes complete with the appropriate costume and instructions on how to
> act, talk and often write so as to take on a particular social role that others
> will recognize (Gee 1996, p. 127).

In addition, the process of indexing is not framed as two-dimensional, as was the case for early sociolinguistic work which focused on dyadic associations such as accent-social class and lexical choice-gender; rather, in keeping with the post-structuralist take on identity outlined above, it is reflexive and multidimensional. It is reflexive in that researchers generally do not posit a one-way deterministic flow from category to linguistic phenomenon (e.g., social class determines accent); rather, they see speech acts as constitutive of categories. Meanwhile, it is multidimensional in that few researchers suggest that just one dimension of identity can be enacted at a time; rather, it is difficult to focus on just one dimension (e.g., gender) without considering others (e.g., social class and ethnicity).

Many researchers have followed what has been termed by some a 'narrative turn' in the social sciences (Clandinin 2007), whereby there is progressively more and more interest in how individuals present their life stories when communicating with others. While life stories may be elicited by a variety of means, such as diaries or electronic logs, it is by far the face-to-face interview which has been the elicitation mode of choice in recent years. In such research, interviews are generally lengthy and relatively open-ended in nature, and they are often organized around particular stages in life, such as early childhood, early primary school, early adolescence and so on. The researcher may conduct just one life-story interview with an informant or he/she may conduct a set of two or three interrelated ones, fairly close together in time (Wengraf 2001). Alternatively, the researcher may adopt a longitudinal approach, which involves multiple interviews, carried out at intervals over a long period of time. Whatever the number of interviews per informants, in the end the interest is generally the same: 'the story a person chooses to tell about the life he or she has lived, told as completely and honestly as possible, what is remembered of it, and what the teller wants others to know of it ...' (Atkinson 1998, p. 3).

Research Strategies and Techniques: Doing Narrative Identity Research

In her detailed discussion of narrative methods, Catherine Kohler Riessman (2008) suggests that there are four distinct ways of dealing with narratives, three of which I will present here: *thematic analysis, structural analysis and dialogic/performative analysis. Thematic* analysis is primarily a focus on the content of what is said, leaving to the side other aspects of narrative such as how it is produced. Although some see this approach as intuitive and overly simplistic, Riessman makes clear that it requires a great deal of rigour. First, once spoken data have been transcribed, the researcher has to identify key themes and strands in the narrative. Second, the researcher needs to have a solid background in other social sciences such as history, sociology, anthropology in order to be able to connect narrative content to bigger and broader issues and constructs.

A second approach, *structural analysis*, addresses first and foremost how narratives are produced. On the one hand, such an approach may focus on the micro-level linguistic phenomena, such as grammar, lexis and accent; on the other hand, it may examine how different clauses are assembled to produce a storyline or the strategies adopted by the story teller as the story is told. Thus while some researchers may focus on phenomena such as pronoun use and what it might mean, others may follow a variation on Labov and Waletzky's (1967) classic and oft-cited model, whereby narratives are seen to involve a series of steps, beginning with a brief synopsis of the story to be told and the provision of key background information, before moving to the crux of the story, its ending and its meaning to narrator.

A third approach described by Riessman is what she calls *dialogic/performative*. In this case the analyst draws on elements of the previous two approaches, but in doing so creates a distinct third way beyond them. As Riessman notes, 'if thematic and structural approaches interrogate 'what' is spoken and 'how', the dialogic/performative approach asks 'who' an utterance may be directed to, 'when,' and 'why,' that is, for what purposes?' (Riessman 2008, p. 105). Thus, the analyst works from the immediate context, in terms of the minutiae of interaction, discourse patterns, the background of interlocutors, the general sociohistorical backdrop and so on, eventually working up to border social categories, related to institutions and cultures and the identity inscriptions outlined earlier in this chapter (e.g., social class, gender, ethnicity).

A good example of a dialogic approach in action is Donald Freeman's research on teacher knowledge and cognition. Freeman (1996) self-consciously combines a thematic approach (what he calls a 'representational approach') with a structural approach (what he calls a 'presentational approach'). In doing so, he examines his interviews with teachers in terms of three types of relationship:

- *expression* (what is said and how it is said)
- *voice* (what is said to whom and therefore how it may be heard and understood)
- *source* (what is said and where it comes from)

Being attentive to expression means a focus on the language that is used to say what is said. For example, Freeman examines the use of subject pronouns (I, you and they) and how speakers shift among them as they talk about different topics and personal and professional experiences. For Freeman, these pronoun shifts construct concomitant shifts in voice, which are related to – and indeed arise in the changing affiliations of teachers across the accounts of their experiences and their lives. Thus an informant might show shifts in affiliation to communicate her personal and singular experiences (using 'I'), her affiliation to fellow teachers (using 'we') or her lack of affiliation to fellow teachers whom she does not agree with (using 'they').

The idea that voices shift as an interaction unfolds is an essential characteristic of the dialogic/performative approach to narrative. Drawing on the work of Bakhtin (1981), Lemke makes the point that '[w]e speak with the voices of our communities, and to the extent that we have individual voices, we fashion these out of the social voices already available to us, appropriating the words of others to speak a word of our own' (Lemke 1995, pp. 24–25). Elsewhere, Stanton Wortham argues that '[s]peaking with a certain voice . . . means using words that index social positions because these words are characteristically used by members of a certain group' (Wortham 2001, p. 38). What both authors are saying is that in the process of telling their stories, informants do not just produce unique individualized accounts; rather, their voices are saturated with the voices of others who have preceded them and who are their contemporaries.

In her research focusing on young Greek women talking about their social lives in informal conversations, Alexandra Georgakopoulou (2006) adopts an approach which sees her first of all examining how talk-in-interaction unfolds in terms of linguistic features such as code, register and style. These features are seen as foundational to an examination of different local 'small, here-and-now identities', specifically participants' 'telling identities', which are related to aspects of group interactions such as amount of participation, floor holding, how much one's talk is ratified (validated) by others and so on. The latter inform the researcher about how participants position themselves and are positioned during the course of their interactions. These positionings include expert/novice, and advice giver/advice receiver, which in turn can be connected to extra-interactional roles played by individuals in the communities of practice of which they are members, such as good student/bad student. And with reference to the latter, there is a link to broader society-level identities related to gender, social class and so on. Thus, Georgakopoulou shows how her informants talk may be analysed, working from micro-level linguistic features, all the way up to macro-level social categories.

In the work of Freeman, Wortham, Georgakopoulou and many others, I see something akin to a consensus emerging among researchers interested in narrative, both those who focus on narratives elicited in interviews and those who focus on narratives arising in informal conversations. In both cases, researchers negotiate an appropriation of Reismann's thematic and structural approaches as they move towards a dialogic/performative approach. Some researchers offer a great deal of detail as they navigate their way through their concern with micro-level language practices and how they connect with larger social constructs such as voice and broader identity inscriptions. Meanwhile, others work more elliptically, moving to the macro-level fairly quickly, although once there, they may go into great detail as regards what they think their data are saying. However, in both cases, there is a common willingness and desire to engage with the complexity of identity in narrative. There is, therefore, a position that what is needed is dialectic analysis which slides back and forth, between and among three general interacting levels:

- *micro*: at the basic level of utterances, examining how what is said is said
- *meso*: at the intermediate level of positioning in the narrative, via the adoption of voices
- *macro*: at the broader, more macro-level, whereby what is said is related to identities and social groups in society

And in this sliding back and forth, there will inevitably be more emphasis on one level or another, a point to which I return in the next section.

Associated Problems with Narrative Analysis

The approach to identity in narrative outlined in the previous section is not without problems, which in turn are directly related to the complex task that researchers set themselves. On the one hand, there are foundational and conceptual issues, which are beyond the scope of this chapter (but see Block 2007). More relevant to this book are problems related to data analysis in applied linguistics research on identity and language. Aneta Pavlenko (2007) identifies what she sees as five major problems common in much narrative research based heavily or exclusively on thematic analysis:

> The first is the lack of theoretical premise, which makes it unclear where conceptual categories come from and how they relate to each other. The second is the lack of established procedure for matching instances to categories. The third is the overreliance on repeated instances which may lead analysts to overlook important events or themes that do not occur repeatedly or do not fit into preestablished schemes. The fourth is an exclusive focus on what is in the text, whereas what is excluded may potentially be as or even more informative. The fifth and perhaps most problematic for applied linguists is the lack of attention to the ways in which storytellers use language to interpret experiences and position themselves as particular kinds of people. (Pavlenko 2007, pp. 166–167)

The overriding and unifying issue here would appear to be transparency and rigour in analysis. These problems are addressed to a large extent in the work cited in the previous section, where researchers adopt a dialogic approach which allows them to better articulate a multitude of analyses across scales, ranging from the micro-local to the macro-global. However, as Wortham (2008) notes, even in such dialectic research, problems remain, mainly concerning the lack of explanation of how big constructs, such as identities and social structures come into existence and how they are maintained, strengthened and weakened over time. He proposes greater attention to the level of practice which means a close examination of the critical points in activities engaged in across space and time scales, where and when identities are, in a sense, made locally. This level of analysis then allows the researcher a clear path to making connections at higher levels (as regards structure) and longer scales (as regards time).

A Sample Study

As a way of concluding this chapter, I will now revisit a publication of mine (Block 2001) based on a study that I carried out several years ago, discussing it

343

more as a way not to proceed in this type of research than as a way to proceed. I will reproduce a section of the publication to show the reader how I presented and analysed interview data and then based on what has hitherto been discussed in this chapter, elaborate a brief critique of it. First, however, I provide some background.

The backdrop of the study which produced the publication was my reading about a shortfall in foreign language teachers in English secondary schools, which was being alleviated to a great extent by a flow of young adult French, German and Spanish nationals from their home countries to England. Interested in issues such as national identity and educational cultures in conflict, I conducted periodic interviews with nine such teachers between September 1999 and December 2002. The study began as the teachers began a Postgraduate Certificate of Education (PGCE) course in foreign language teaching and it then carried on subsequently as they settled into jobs in secondary schools in Greater London. Here I present a section of a discussion of how study participants dealt with being positioned as different or foreign by the students with whom they came in contact as they did their teaching practice during their PGCE course. The interviewees are two German nationals, whom I here call AA and HA. The interviews were carried out in English, and a language in which the two interviewees were extremely proficient.

The need for a reasoned response to national stereotyping was especially pronounced for German nationals, for if there is one nation which has inspired emotional responses in Britain over the past half decade, it is Germany. From the anodyne humour of Fawltey Towers and classic line, 'Don't mention the war', to the recent spectacle of football fans ecstatic because England managed to beat Germany in the 2000 European Cup (thus making up for the fact that England had not been able to beat the Germans since their famous 1966 World Cup victory), there is little ambivalence about the Germans: they are the enemy both in the trenches and on the football pitch. The two German teachers commented about this phenomenon of Germans as the nemesis in the following way:

> AA: You also feel sometimes that you are some kind of an ambassador or something for German culture, Germany, German politics, German history especially . . .

> HA: Oh, yeah. German history.

> DB: Did that come up very much? You know, the whole sort of 'German Thing'. . .

> HA: The German thing, yes . . .

> AA: So you always had to be quiet but I was always quite relaxed about that . . . Sometimes they would draw some swastikas just to see 'what are

you doing here?' (imitating dopey student voice) 'Ho-Ho-Ho' . . .
Of course they just waited for me to explode or really be upset but I never
was. So I really talked to them about it, although they were much too silly.
But then in the end, they even listened, so I said 'OK, that's the way it is.
We have to live with our past history. Imagine it is not always easy for
Germans as well . . .' And I hope, even though it was year 10 and they are
16 and really silly and thick at times . . . I think they understood it a little . . .
I mean it was just provoking me so they didn't expect that at all, that I
would take it seriously and say something. I'm relaxed with that . . . I know
that they all have some . . . Well, I have the feeling they have some
prejudice and it's really just stereotypes and you just try to . . . open their
mind up and say 'OK, . . . German people are exactly like you . . . What
comes to your mind when you think about Germany? And what do you
think is the media influence?' And they actually discuss things with you . . .

HA: It's society, it's on TV, and it's every night.

DB: And it'll all come out now with the football again . . .

HA: Exactly. I'm so glad I'm not at school at that time . . . And hopefully in
two years' time when the World Championship is on . . .

AA: And no matter if Germany or England wins, I will not be there the next
day . . .

HA: No, no way.

AA: Especially if England wins. (6 June 2000)

(Block 2001, pp. 297–298)

As regards the interview data discussed here, it is first of all noteworthy that
they are transcribed orthographically (that is, in cleaned up form), as opposed
to sociolinguistically (that is, with a view to capturing the detailed subtleties of
spoken language). Suspension points (. . .) are used variably to convey either
pauses or deleted words, which does little to recreate the interview as event.
For example, the inclusion of pause times would perhaps have been useful to
show any number of affective relationships with what was being said, such as
hesitance or an inability to articulate thoughts. Also missing in the transcriptions are other features of conversations, such as overlapping speech or inflections on what is said (e.g., rising intonation). On the other hand, there is an
attempt to mark with double quotation marks ('') what Bakhtin (1981) called
'double voicing', that is, instances where AA is speaking as the protagonists
in the story he is telling in his second turn. On the one hand, he double voices
his students, putting on what I refer to here as a 'dopey voice', and on the
other hand, he double voices the teacher (himself) with a more normal voice.

Neither the telling of the story by AA nor the way it is told is commented on in my article, and thus there is no consideration of AA's positioning himself as the more active interlocutor in this exchange (he has a story; HA does not) or how the double voicing draws lines between the sensible teacher and his students, described here as 'really silly and thick at times'. In sum, there is little that addresses what Pavlenko identities as key problems in narrative research.

Instead, the content of the exchange is somewhat superficially linked to what is said in the paragraph that opens this excerpt from my article, in which I very briefly gloss English stereotypes of Germans revolving around the Second World War and football. There is, therefore no overtly dialectic approach involving the moving back and forth across levels. There is no in-depth exploration, either sociologically or historically, of how Germany and Germans are discursively constructed in England today, and thus no attempt at an explanation of how the stereotypes mentioned came into existence and more importantly how they are maintained and strengthened in day-to-day life in England and in the school setting described by AA. There is HA's comment – 'It's society, it's on TV, and it's every night' – but this is not explored further.

Space does not allow further dismantling and critiquing of my analysis and discussion from several years ago. However, I think I have done enough here to make my point. This, I should emphasize, has not been to position myself as a poor researcher; rather, I have used my work as a foil in my attempt to discuss very briefly what a researcher might do with life-story interview data, when working dialectically across levels and scales. Indeed, it should be noted this is just a page-length section of a 20-page article and that in other parts of it there is in-depth discussion of issues around national identity and educational culture, which in turn is filtered into my analysis of a fair number of interview excerpts.

Still, there is one inescapable problem with all research which attempts to link what people say about their lives to identity issues. Any such example of analysis – no matter how meticulously carried out, detailed and articulated across spatio-temporal scales – will always be partial in that there will always be more that could be said. The researcher can always dig more at the micro-level, relating findings to the meso-level, and he/she can always say a great deal more about social identities that serve as a backdrop to recounted experiences and indeed the interviews themselves as social events. In addition, there is the notion, introduced above, that identity is not only language mediated, but more generally multimodally/semiotically mediated. If this notion is taken seriously, it means that any analysis which is exclusively language-based will be partial in that it misses many other aspects of communication, effectively ignoring the roles of other semiotic resources (gaze, posture, hand movements, dress and so on) as integral to identity construction. As Sigrid Norris (2004) argues, these other resources might even be more important than language at a given moment. From this point of view, researchers perhaps need to consider how phenomena such as gaze, posture and hand movements are part of interviews and how they might contribute to attempts to link the interview to meso- and macro-level constructs.

Resources for Further Reading

Benwell, B. and Stokoe, E. (2006), *Discourse and Identity*. Edinburgh: Edinburgh University Press.

This book offers extremely thorough coverage of different perspectives on identity in different discursive environments. In it, the authors examine a range of identities classified as approaches (conversational, institutional and narrative identities) and contexts (commodified, spatial and virtual).

Block, D. (2006), *Second Language Identities*. London: Continuum.

This book is a selective but in-depth overview of how identity is an issue in different language learning environments. It begins with an overview of the post-structuralist approach to identity that has become dominant in applied linguistics, before moving to consider how identity is an issue in naturalistic, foreign and study abroad language learning contexts.

Caldas-Coulthard, C. and Iedema, R. (eds) (2008), *Identity Trouble: Critical Discourse and Contested Identities*. London: Palgrave.

This is a timely, state of the art collection of chapters which also examines the interrelationships between language, discourse and identity. In 13 chapters, contributors discuss conceptual issues related to the analysis of narrative from different perspectives, such as conversational analysis and social semiotics, focusing especially on contexts and events in which the emergence of identity is problematic in some way.

De Fina, A., Schiffrin, D. and Bamberg, M. (eds) (2006), *Discourse and Identity*. Cambridge: Cambridge University Press.

This is an excellent collection of recent work in sociolinguistics and linguistic anthropology, which explores the interrelationships between language, discourse and identity. In 15 chapters, contributors explore conceptual issues and the specifics of research on public and private identities, masculinities and the inter-actions between person and place.

Riessman, C. K. (2008), *Narrative Methods for the Human Sciences*. London: Sage.

This book is a highly readable review of narrative methods in identity research. The author provides an excellent synthesis of her personal perspective and the work of other scholars, focusing on research processes and issues around data analysis.

References

Atkinson, R. (1998), *The Life-Story Interview*. London: Sage.

Bakhtin, M. (1981), *The Dialogic Imagination: Four Essays*. Austin: University of Texas Press.

Benwell, B. and Stokoe, E. (2006), *Discourse and Identity*. Edinburgh: Edinburgh University Press.

Block, D. (2001), 'Foreign Nationals on PGCE in Modern Languages Course: Issues in National Identity Construction'. *European Journal of Teacher Education*, 24(3), 291–312.

—(2006), *Multilingual Identities in a Global City: London Stories*. London: Palgrave.

—(2007), *Second Language Identities*. London: Continuum.

Blommaert, J. (2005), *Discourse*. Cambridge: Cambridge University Press.

Bourdieu, P. (1984), *Distinction: A Social Critique of the Judgement of Taste*. London: Routledge.

Caldas-Coulthard, C. and Iedema, R. (eds) (2008), *Identity Trouble: Critical Discourse and Contested Identities*. London: Palgrave.

Clandinin, J. (ed.) (2007), *Handbook of Narrative Inquiry: Mapping a Methodology*. London: Sage.

De Fina, A., Schiffrin, D. and Bamberg, M. (eds) (2006), *Discourse and Identity*. Cambridge: Cambridge University Press.

Eckert. P. and McConnell-Ginet, S. (1992), 'Think practically and act locally: Language and gender as community-based practice'. *Annual Review of Anthropology*, 21, 461–490.

Freeman, D. (1996), '"To Take Them at Their Word": Language Data in the Study of Teachers' Knowledge'. *Harvard Educational Review*, 66(4), 732–761.

Gee, J. P. (1996), *Social Linguistics and Literacies: Ideology in Discourses (2nd edn)*. London: Falmer.

Georgakopoulou, A. (2006), 'Small and large identities in Narrative (inter)action', in A. De Fina, D. Schiffrin and M. Bamberg (eds), *Discourse and Identity*. Cambridge: Cambridge University Press, pp. 83–102.

Giddens, A. (1984), *The Constitution of Society: Outline of the Theory of Structuration*. Berkeley, CA: University of California Press.

—(1991), *Modernity and Self-Identity: Self and Society in the Late Modern Age*. Cambridge: Polity.

Joseph, J. (2004), *Language and Identity*. London: Palgrave.

Kanno, Y. (2003), *Negotiating Bilingual and Bicultural Identities: Japanese Returnees Betwixt Two Worlds*. Mahwah, NJ: Lawrence Erlbaum Associates.

Labov, W. and Waletzky, J. (1967), 'Narrative Analysis: Oral Versions of Personal Experience', in W. Labov (ed.), *Language in the Inner City: Studies in the Black English Vernacular*. Philadelphia, PA: University of Pennsylvania Press, pp. 354–396.

Le Page, R. B. and Tabouret-Keller, A. (1985), *Acts of Identity: Creole-based Approaches to Language and Ethnicity*. Cambridge: Cambridge University Press.

Lemke, J. (1995), *Textual Politics: Discourse and Social Dynamics*. London: Taylor and Francis.

—(2008), 'Identity, development, and desire: Critical questions', in C. Caldas-Coulthard and R. Iedema (eds), *Identity Trouble: Critical Discourse and Contested Identities*. London: Palgrave, pp. 17–42.

Norris, S. (2004), *Analyzing Multimodal Interaction: A Methodological Framework*. London: Routledge.

Norton, B. (2000), *Identity and Language Learning: Gender, Ethnicity and Educational Change*. Harlow, UK: Longman.

Omoniyi, T. and White, G. (eds) (2006), *The Sociolinguistics of Identity*. London: Continuum.

Pavlenko, A. (2007), 'Autobiographic narratives as data in applied linguistics'. *Applied Linguistics*, 28(2), 163–188.

Pavlenko, A. and Blackledge, A. (eds) (2004), *Negotiation of Identities in Multilingual Settings*. Clevedon, UK: Multilingual Matters.

Pavlenko, A., Blackledge, A., Piller, I. and Teutsch-Dwyer, M. (eds) (2001), *Multilingualism, Second Language Learning, and Gender*. New York: Mouton De Gruyter.

Riessman, C. K. (2008), *Narrative Methods for the Human Sciences*. London: Sage.

Riley, P. (2007), *Language, Culture and Identity*. London: Continuum.

Weedon, C. (1997), *Feminist Practice and Poststructuralist Theory* (2nd edn). Oxford, UK: Blackwell.

Wengraf, T. (2001), *Qualitative Research Interviewing: Biographic Narrative and Semi-Structured Methods: Biographic Narrative and Semi-structured Methods*. London: Sage.

Wortham, S. (2001), *Narratives in Action: A Strategy for Research and Analysis*. New York: Teachers College Press.

—(2008), 'Shifting identities in the classroom', in C. Caldas-Coulthard and R. Iedem (eds), *Identity Trouble: Critical Discourse and Contested Identities*. London: Palgrave, pp. 205–228.

Glossary of Key Research Terms

Action research: Action research employs an approach that is cyclical in nature, alternating between action and reflection, continuously refining methods and interpretations based on understandings developed in earlier cycles of the research.

Case study: An approach which examines a single case, whether it be a single person, group, institution or community, either at one point in time or over a period of time. This allows for a project which produces in-depth descriptions of contexts, themes and issues.

Confirmability: A trustworthiness criterion in qualitative research which requires that researchers reveal the data they are basing their interpretation on, or at least make such data available. Other researchers should be able to examine the data to confirm or reject the claim that is made. Confirmability is analogous to the concept of replicability in quantitative research.

Construct: A construct is an abstract concept such as intelligence, motivation, or English proficiency that cannot be observed directly and needs to be measured empirically.

Construct validity: The construct validity of an instrument or measure is the extent to which it measures or captures what it is intended to measure, rather than measuring something else.

Control group: In experimental research, a control group is a group of participants who are treated or taught in the traditional or typical way, rather than undergoing the experimental treatment.

Correlation coefficient: A statistical measure ranging from -1 to $+1$ that indicates the strength of the relationship between variables. A correlation of 0 indicates no relationship at all, whereas a correlation of 0.9 indicates a strong positive relationship.

Correlational research: A type of non-experimental research that investigates whether there is a true association between two variables. Correlational research differs from experimental research in that there is no manipulation of the variables under examination.

Credibility: A trustworthiness criterion in qualitative research which requires researchers to accurately describe their definitions and the characterizations of the people or things under investigation. Credibility is more or less analogous to the concept of internal validity in quantitative research.

Cross-sectional research: Often associated with a quantitative research design, cross-sectional research involves collecting data on more than one case at a single point in time, often with a relatively large number of participants.

Data: Information gained through research that is used to respond to the research question or hypothesis.

Data coding: A process of assigning codes to the data. This process generally involves grouping instances in the data that share similarities together in categories. Data coding is related to data reduction as irrelevant data are not considered.

Deductive (Top-down) reasoning: The process of drawing a specific conclusion from a set of premises or theories (i.e., from general to particular).

Dependability: A trustworthiness criterion in qualitative research which requires that researchers account for any shifting conditions directly related to the people and things they are studying and any modifications they have made in their study as it has progressed. Dependability is analogous to reliability in quantitative research.

Dependent variable: The variable upon which the independent variable is acting. For example, improvement in writing proficiency (the dependent variable) as a result of a particular approach to teaching (the independent variable).

Descriptive statistics: Descriptive statistics describe measures of frequency (percentages), central tendency (mean, median, mode) and dispersion (such as standard deviation).

Effect size: Associated with statistical analysis, this term is a measure of the strength of the relationship between two variables. Effect size differs from a statistically significant effect in that it considers whether the size of the observed effects is robust enough or realistic.

Emic: Emic refers to an insider's perspective on events; that is, as the events are experienced by the participants in the particular social setting.

Ethics: Ensuring that research is conducted in an ethical manner. Ethical treatment of human participants in research is a fundamental concern in research practice, such as not abusing the participants in a study in any way, including abuses of time and effort.

Ethnography: A research method that focuses on cultural and societal behaviour. Ethnographic research investigates the naturally occurring behaviours of a group of people in their community; describes the beliefs, values, and attitudes of a group; and provides a holistic description of contexts and cultural themes.

Etic: Etic refers to an outsider's perspective on events.

Experimental group: In experimental research, this is the group of learners which receives a particular treatment or condition which is hypothesized to change the target behaviour (i.e., the dependent variable).

Experimental research: An experiment is a situation in which a researcher manipulates one or more variables (such as an approach to teaching speaking) while the others are kept constant in order to see the effect of manipulating the variable(s) on a dependent variable (such as speaking proficiency).

External validity: In quantitative research, external validity concerns whether the results of the research can be generalized to another situation (i.e., for different subjects/participants, settings, times and so forth). That is, to what degree the inferred (causal) relationship or differences between groups can be generalized to other persons, settings, and times.

Field notes: Notes from researchers' observations that are taken during the data collection process. The researcher may make brief notes during the observation and later expand these into field notes. These notes supplement information from other sources such as documents and interviews. There are two components of field notes: (1) description (e.g., setting, people, reaction, interpersonal relationship) and (2) reflection or observer comment (e.g., observer's personal feelings, impression about the events, comments, speculations about data analysis).

Focus group: This technique is an interview strategy. A small group of participants sharing similar characteristics are interviewed together by the researcher.

Grounded theory: Grounded theory starts with data rather than theory. It employs a cyclical process of theory building and testing the developing theory against the data.

Hypothesis: A predictive statement that can be tested empirically. It is mostly used in quantitative research.

Hypothesis testing: This involves two types of hypotheses. A null hypothesis (H0) is the prediction that, for example, there is no relationship between variables. The alternative hypothesis (H1) is the opposite of the null hypothesis. That is, that there will be a relationship between the variables.

Independent variable: A variable that is hypothesized to be related to a change in something (such as language learning). For example, the type of writing feedback students receive could be an independent variable that affects subsequent writing performance, which is the dependent variable.

Inductive (Bottom-up) Reasoning: The process of drawing a specific conclusion from a set of observations or data. To be absolutely certain of an inductive conclusion, researchers must observe all examples. Imperfect induction is a system in which researchers observe a sample of a group and infer from the sample what the characteristics of the entire population are likely to be.

Inferential statistics: Statistics that are used to make inferences about population parameters, such as the relationship between two variables or between two groups on a variable of interest.

Informed consent: The process whereby a research participant is informed of all potential risks and benefits associated with participating in the research before giving their consent.

Internal validity: One of the fundamental types of validity in quantitative research (see external validity) which concerns the relationship between the independent and dependent variables. It relates to the degree to which observed relationships between variables can be inferred to be causal-like (e.g., how strongly we can infer that variable A resulted in the observed effects (increased performance) in variable B.

Introspection: A data elicitation technique that explores an individual's cognitive processes while they are doing an activity or carrying out a task. Introspection is often used in conjunction with think-aloud protocols.

Likert scale: Named after Rensis Likert (1932), a Likert scale is a widely used technique to measure a construct. A Likert scale is constructed by assembling a large number of statements about a construct, and using continuous response categories to allow participants to respond to these statements (e.g., strongly agree, agree, undecided/neutral, disagree, and strongly disagree). It is widely used in questionnaires.

Longitudinal research: A study in which data is collected from the same participants at more than one point in time. It is carried out over a relatively long period of time, often with a small number of participants

Meta-analysis: An approach to analysis that systematically combines the results of previous studies that examined related research questions. It is a type of research synthesis. A meta-analysis is usually carried out by identification of a common measure of effect size. Meta-analysis yields a more robust estimate of the true effect size than that derived from a single study (see Effect size).

Mixed-methods research: A mixed methods design involves the collection or analysis of both quantitative and qualitative data in a single study. The purpose of mixed methods research is to achieve a fuller understanding of a complex issue and to verify one set of findings against the other.

Narrative study: Based on first-person accounts of experiences such as biographies, life stories, life narratives, and oral histories.

Naturalistic data: Data that is collected in a natural context without a researcher's attempt to control or manipulate the environment.

Normal distribution: A statistical term related to the spread of the data around the mean. Normal distribution is bell-shaped. In a perfect normal distribution, the mean, median and mode have equal values.

Observation: A basic method for obtaining data in qualitative research that involves the observation of a particular phenomenon, such as a particular set of lessons. The kind of observation carried out in qualitative research is more global and holistic than the systematic, structured observation used in quantitative research.

Outliers: Extreme cases or values which are not typical of the group of participants in a study. Outliers can distort statistical results.

Participant(s): Participants are people (e.g., learners, teachers) who take part in research by providing information about themselves that is used as research data. The term 'participants' is preferred to the term 'subjects'.

Participant observation: Three terms are commonly associated with participant observation. *Complete observer* is when the observer does not take part in the activities but simply observes what is going on. *Participant as observer* is when the observer actively participates in the activities being examined. *Observer as participant* is when the observer interacts with the participants sufficiently to establish a rapport with them but does not become involved in the activities of the group.

Probability: The degree to which a statistical finding is likely to occur by chance (see statistical validity). The p-value (p = probability) is the likelihood that researchers will be wrong in the statistical inferences that they make from the data. $p < 0.05$ (i.e., there are 5 in 100 chances of being wrong) is commonly used in applied linguistics research. If the probability based on the result of the statistical analysis is less than the significance level, the null hypothesis can be rejected.

Purposive sampling: This method of sampling differs from random sampling. Researchers identify the characteristics of participants or samples prior to data collection and base the sampling on this. Purposive sampling is often associated with qualitative research.

Qualitative research: An approach that seeks to make sense of social phenomena as they occur in natural settings. Rather than setting up a controlled environment, qualitative researchers are more interested in understanding contexts as they actually are. Qualitative researchers do not aim for quantification or standardization in the data collection and analysis of the data.

Quantitative data: Numerical data derived from quantitative measures such as language tests and Likert-scale questionnaires.

Quantitative research: A research approach that draws on numeric data. Variables are clearly defined, measurement is standardized, and data are generally analysed using statistical methods.

Quasi-experimental research: The underlying principles of quasi-experimental research are the same as experimental research. The difference is that there has been no random assignment of participants to groups.

Random assignment: A process of randomization in assigning participants to the experimental treatments. With random assignment, each participant has an equal and independent chance of being assigned to any group. Thus, the assignment is independent of the researcher's personal judgement or the characteristics of the participants themselves.

Random selection: A technique that aims to generate a sample that represents a larger population. Random selection is related to external validity in experimental research.

Reliability: This term relates to the quality of instruments/measures and results of a study. The reliability of an instrument or measure is concerned with the degree to which a research instrument or measure produces consistent information (e.g., whether the data would be the same if the instrument were administered repeatedly). The reliability of a result of a study is concerned with whether the result would be likely to reappear if the study were replicated under the same conditions.

Replicability: A requirement that researchers provide enough information about a study to allow other researchers to replicate or repeat the study exactly as it was originally conducted. This includes information about the participants involved in the study, how they were selected, the instruments that were used and the data collection and analysis procedures.

Replication: The process of conducting a new study closely based on a pervious study. The aim is to find out whether the new study will yield the same finding as in the original study. However, exact replication is often impossible in applied linguistics research and hence *conceptual replication* may be achieved (i.e., the research concept is replicated, rather than the context and time).

Research synthesis: An analysis of research evidence relating to a specific research question based on an analysis of previous studies on the topic. This can involve an examination of either quantitative or qualitative research. Research synthesis is a powerful tool in that it provides an overview of the overall body of research evidence.

Retrospection: This technique aims to access the thoughts and cognitive processes of participants while they carry out an activity or task. Unlike introspection, retrospection occurs once a task has been completed. Participants are asked to report on what they were thinking while they carried out the task.

SPSS: Statistical Package for the Social Sciences. A statistical program to help with the analysis of quantitative data.

Statistical validity: This validity is similar to internal validity in quantitative research. Researchers ask whether the observed relationship between the independent and dependent variables was a true relationship, incidental or found by chance.

Thick description: Devised by Geertz, the term thick description is often associated with ethnographic or case study research. Thick description refers to a detailed description of a phenomenon or event that includes the researcher's interpretation of what they have observed.

Transferability: A qualitative trustworthiness criterion which requires researchers to describe the research design, context and conditions so that other researchers can decide for themselves if the interpretations apply to another context with which they are familiar. Transferability is analogous to the concept of generalizability in quantitative research.

Triangulation: A research strategy that involves analysing data from multiple sources (e.g., surveys and interviews), multiple groups of participants (e.g., students, teachers and parents) and multiple research techniques (e.g., observation and interviews) to thoroughly examine the matter under investigation. Triangulation aims to collect multiple perspectives on an event so that the researcher can gain a more complete understanding of the topic under examination.

Trustworthiness: The term for validity in qualitative research. Trustworthiness is often a preferred term in qualitative research because it takes account of the different nature of the research methods and epistemological assumptions made in qualitative research compared to those used in quantitative research.

Validation: Procedures or steps taken by the researcher to make sure that the measure or instrument to be used for the research is valid and that proper inferences can be made about the construct of interest based on the data.

Validity: Validity is the extent to which the research actually studies what it claims to study. The *validity of an instrument* concerns whether the instrument actually measures what it claims to measure. For instance, a questionnaire designed to explore language learners' motivation which actually examines learners' anxiety is not a valid instrument. The instrument may, however, be reliable because individuals may consistently provide the same responses on different occasions. The *validity of the research* refers to the accuracy of the inferences, interpretations or actions made on the basis of the data.

Variable: An operationalized construct that can have different values or scores. Variable derives from the word 'vary', suggesting that individuals can vary in terms of their scores of the aspect under examination.

Index

NOTE: Page references in **bold** contain sample study(ies);
page references in *italics* refer to figures and tables.